Handbook of Research on Deep Learning–Based Image Analysis Under Constrained and Unconstrained Environments

Alex Noel Joseph Raj
Shantou University, China

Vijayalakshmi G. V. Mahesh
BMS Institute of Technology and Management, India

Ruban Nersisson
Vellore Institute of Technology, India

A volume in the Advances in Computational Intelligence and Robotics (ACIR) Book Series

Published in the United States of America by
IGI Global
Engineering Science Reference (an imprint of IGI Global)
701 E. Chocolate Avenue
Hershey PA, USA 17033
Tel: 717-533-8845
Fax: 717-533-8661
E-mail: cust@igi-global.com
Web site: http://www.igi-global.com

Library of Congress Cataloging-in-Publication Data

Names: Raj, Alex Noel Joseph, 1979- editor. | Mahesh, Vijayalakshmi G. V.,
    1978- editor. | Ruban, Nersisson, 1980- editor.
Title: Handbook of research on deep learning-based image analysis under constrained and
    unconstrained environments / Alex Noel Joseph Raj, Vijayalakshmi G.V.
    Mahesh and Nersisson Ruban, editors.
Description: Hershey, PA : Engineering Science Reference, 2021. | Includes
    bibliographical references and index. | Summary: "This book attempts to
    provide an overview of image analysis based on deep learning methods and
    their applications, allowing readers to learn and explore the latest
    advancements, developments, methods, systems, futuristic approaches and
    algorithms towards image analysis"-- Provided by publisher.
Identifiers: LCCN 2020026765 (print) | LCCN 2020026766 (ebook) | ISBN
    9781799866909 (h/c) | ISBN 9781799866916 (s/c) | ISBN 9781799866923
    (eISBN)
Subjects: LCSH: Image analysis--Data processing. | Machine learning.
Classification: LCC TA1637 .D427 2021 (print) | LCC TA1637 (ebook) | DDC
    621.36/70285631--dc23
LC record available at https://lccn.loc.gov/2020026765
LC ebook record available at https://lccn.loc.gov/2020026766

This book is published in the IGI Global book series Advances in Computational Intelligence and Robotics (ACIR) (ISSN: 2327-0411; eISSN: 2327-042X)

British Cataloguing in Publication Data
A Cataloguing in Publication record for this book is available from the British Library.

All work contributed to this book is new, previously-unpublished material. The views expressed in this book are those of the authors, but not necessarily of the publisher.

For electronic access to this publication, please contact: eresources@igi-global.com.

Advances in Computational Intelligence and Robotics (ACIR) Book Series

Ivan Giannoccaro
University of Salento, Italy

ISSN:2327-0411
EISSN:2327-042X

MISSION

While intelligence is traditionally a term applied to humans and human cognition, technology has progressed in such a way to allow for the development of intelligent systems able to simulate many human traits. With this new era of simulated and artificial intelligence, much research is needed in order to continue to advance the field and also to evaluate the ethical and societal concerns of the existence of artificial life and machine learning.

The **Advances in Computational Intelligence and Robotics (ACIR) Book Series** encourages scholarly discourse on all topics pertaining to evolutionary computing, artificial life, computational intelligence, machine learning, and robotics. ACIR presents the latest research being conducted on diverse topics in intelligence technologies with the goal of advancing knowledge and applications in this rapidly evolving field.

COVERAGE

- Pattern Recognition
- Artificial Life
- Adaptive and Complex Systems
- Cyborgs
- Fuzzy Systems
- Evolutionary Computing
- Brain Simulation
- Intelligent control
- Agent technologies
- Machine Learning

IGI Global is currently accepting manuscripts for publication within this series. To submit a proposal for a volume in this series, please contact our Acquisition Editors at Acquisitions@igi-global.com or visit: http://www.igi-global.com/publish/.

Titles in this Series

For a list of additional titles in this series, please visit: www.igi-global.com/book-series

Applications of Artificial Intelligence for Smart Technology
P. Swarnalatha (Vellore Institute of Technology, Vellore, India) and S. Prabu (Vellore Institute of Technology, Vellore, India)
Engineering Science Reference • ©2021 • 330pp • H/C (ISBN: 9781799833352) • US $215.00

Resource Optimization Using Swarm Intelligence and the IoT
Vicente García Díaz (University of Oviedo, Spain) Pramod Singh Rathore (ACERC, Delhi, India) Abhishek Kumar (ACERC, Delhi, India) and Rashmi Agrawal (Manav Rachna University, India)
Engineering Science Reference • ©2021 • 300pp • H/C (ISBN: 9781799850953) • US $225.00

Deep Learning Applications and Intelligent Decision Making in Engineering
Karthikrajan Senthilnathan (Revoltaxe India Pvt Ltd, Chennai, India) Balamurugan Shanmugam (Quants IS & CS, India) Dinesh Goyal (Poornima Institute of Engineering and Technology, India) Iyswarya Annapoorani (VIT University, India) and Ravi Samikannu (Botswana International University of Science and Technology, Botswana)
Engineering Science Reference • ©2021 • 332pp • H/C (ISBN: 9781799821083) • US $245.00

Handbook of Research on Natural Language Processing and Smart Service Systems
Rodolfo Abraham Pazos-Rangel (Tecnológico Nacional de México, Mexico & Instituto Tecnológico de Ciudad Madero, Mexico) Rogelio Florencia-Juarez (Universidad Autónoma de Ciudad Juárez, Mexico) Mario Andrés Paredes-Valverde (Tecnológico Nacional de México, Mexico & Instituto Tecnológico de Orizaba, Mexico) and Gilberto Rivera (Universidad Autónoma de Ciudad Juárez, Mexico)
Engineering Science Reference • ©2021 • 554pp • H/C (ISBN: 9781799847304) • US $295.00

Applications of Artificial Neural Networks for Nonlinear Data
Hiral Ashil Patel (Ganpat University, India) and A.V. Senthil Kumar (Hindusthan College of Arts and Science, India)
Engineering Science Reference • ©2021 • 315pp • H/C (ISBN: 9781799840428) • US $245.00

Analyzing Future Applications of AI, Sensors, and Robotics in Society
Thomas Heinrich Musiolik (Berlin University of the Arts, Germany) and Adrian David Cheok (iUniversity, Tokyo, Japan)
Engineering Science Reference • ©2021 • 335pp • H/C (ISBN: 9781799834991) • US $225.00

701 East Chocolate Avenue, Hershey, PA 17033, USA
Tel: 717-533-8845 x100 • Fax: 717-533-8661
E-Mail: cust@igi-global.com • www.igi-global.com

List of Contributors

Table of Contents

Detailed Table of Contents

Chapter 1

    Chandra Prabha R., BMS Institute of Technology and Management, India
    Shilpa Hiremath, BMS Institute of Technology and Management, India

In this chapter, the authors have briefed about images, digital images, how the digital images can be processed. Image types like binary image, grayscale image, color image, and indexed image and various image formats are explained. It highlights the various fields where digital image processing can be used. This chapter introduces a variety of concepts related to digital image formation in a human eye. The mechanism of the human visual system is discussed. The authors illustrate the steps of image processing. Explanation on different elements of digital image processing systems like image acquisition, and others are also provided. The components required for capturing and processing the image are discussed. Concepts of image sampling, quantization, image representation are discussed. It portrays the operations of the image during sampling and quantization and the two operations of sampling which is oversampling and under-sampling. Readers can appreciate the key difference between oversampling and under-sampling applied to digital images.

Chapter 2

    Naralasetty Niharika, Vellore Institute of Technology, India
    Sakshi Patel, Vellore Institute of Technology, India
    Bharath K. P., Vellore Institute of Technology, India
    Balaji Subramanian, Vellore Institute of Technology, India
    Rajesh Kumar M., Vellore Institute of Technology, India

Brain tumor is a hazardous disease. It has to be treated rightly because the patient cannot survive for even a year. This research work is to design a mechanized system that discerns benign and malignant tumor images and improves the classification accuracy. In this system, histogram equalization is used to raise the intensity of tumor so that it can be detected more precisely. In the projected system, segmentation is performed by k-means clustering and Gaussian mixture model (GMM). Along with them, the authors are extracting the features from discrete wavelet transform (DWT) and feature reduction from principal component analysis (PCA). The classifiers support vector machine (SVM) and artificial neural networks (ANN) are used to classify benign and malignant tumor from brain images.

Chapter 3

Breast cancer is a serious disease among women, and its early detection is very crucial for the treatment of cancer. To assist radiologists who manually delineate the tumour from the ultrasound image an automatic computerized method of detection called CAD (computer-aided diagnosis) is developed to provide valuable inputs for radiologists. The CAD systems is divided into many branches like pre-processing, segmentation, feature extraction, and classification. This chapter solely focuses on the first two branches of the CAD system the pre-processing and segmentation. Ultrasound images acquired depends on the operator expertise and is found to be of low contrast and fuzzy in nature. For the pre-processing branch, a contrast enhancement algorithm based on fuzzy logic is implemented which could help in the efficient delineation of the tumour from ultrasound image.

Chapter 4

Early prediction of cancer type has become very crucial. Breast cancer is common to women and it leads to life threatening. Several imaging techniques have been suggested for timely detection and treatment of breast cancer. More research findings have been done to accurately detect the breast cancer. Automated whole breast ultrasound (AWBUS) is a new breast imaging technology that can render the entire breast anatomy in 3-D volume. The tissue layers in the breast are segmented and the type of lesion in the breast tissue can be identified which is essential for cancer detection. In this chapter, a u-net convolutional neural network architecture is used to implement the segmentation of breast tissues from AWBUS images into the different layers, that is, epidermis, subcutaneous, and muscular layer. The architecture was trained and tested with the AWBUS dataset images. The performance of the proposed scheme was based on accuracy, loss and the F1 score of the neural network that was calculated for each layer of the breast tissue.

Chapter 5

Breast cancer is the second most prevalent type of cancer among women. Breast ultrasound (BUS) imaging is one of the most frequently used diagnostic tools to detect and classify abnormalities in the breast. To improve the diagnostic accuracy, computer-aided diagnosis (CAD) system is helpful for breast cancer detection and classification. Normally, a CAD system consists of four stages: pre-processing, segmentation, feature extraction, and classification. In this chapter, the pre-processing step includes speckle noise removal using speckle reducing anisotropic diffusion (SRAD) filter. The goal of segmentation is to locate the region of interest (ROI) and active contour-based segmentation and fuzzy C means segmentation (FCM) are used in this work. The texture features are extracted and fed to a classifier to categorize the images as normal, benign, and malignant. In this work, three classifiers, namely k-nearest neighbors (KNN) algorithm, decision tree algorithm, and random forest classifier, are used and the performance is compared based on the accuracy of classification.

Chapter 6

    Rekha K. V., Vellore Institute of Technology, India
    Anirudh Itagi, Vellore Institute of Technology, India
    Bharath K. P., Vellore Institute of Technology, India
    Balaji Subramanian, Vellore Institute of Technology, India
    Rajesh Kumar M., Vellore Institute of Technology, India

The research work is to enhance the classification accuracy of the pulmonary nodules with the limited number of features extracted using Gray level co-occurrence matrix and linear binary pattern. The classification is done using the machine learning algorithm such as artificial neural network (ANN) and the random forest classifier (RF). In present, lung cancer seems to be the most deadly disease in the world which can be detected only after the computerized tomography (i.e., CT scan images of the person). Detecting the infected portion at the early period is the challenging task. Hence, the recent researchers where under the detection of pulmonary nodules to categorize it either as benign nodules which named as non-cancerous or as malignant nodules which are named as cancerous. When associated the results with the recent papers, the accuracy has been improved in classifying the lung nodules.

Chapter 7

    Jiamin Luo, Shantou University, China
    Alex Noel Joseph Raj, Shantou University, China
    Nersisson Ruban, Vellore Institute of Technology, India
    Vijayalakshmi G. V. Mahesh, BMS Institute of Technology and Management, India

Color fundus image is the most basic way to diagnose diabetic retinopathy, papillary edema, and glaucoma. In particular, since observing the morphological changes of the optic disc is conducive to the diagnosis of related diseases, accurate and effective positioning and segmentation of the optic disc is an important process. Optic disc segmentation algorithms are mainly based on template matching, deformable model and learning. According to the character that the shape of the optic disc is approximately circular, this proposed research work uses Kirsch operator to get the edge of the green channel fundus image through morphological operation, and then detects the optic disc by HOUGH circle transformation. In addition, supervised learning in machine learning is also applied in this chapter. First, the vascular mask is obtained by morphological operation for vascular erasure, and then the SVM classifier is segmented by HU moment invariant feature and gray level feature. The test results on the DRIONS fundus image database with expert-labeled optic disc contour show that the two methods have good results and high accuracy in optic disc segmentation. Even though seven different assessment parameters (sensitivity [Se], specificity [Sp], accuracy [Acc], positive predicted value [Ppv], and negative predicted value [Npv]) are used for performance assessment of the algorithm. Accuracy is considered as the criterion of judgment in this chapter. The average accuracy achieved for the nine random test set is 97.7%, which is better than any other classifiers used for segmenting Optical Disc from Fundus Images.

    Vijayarajan Rajangam, Vellore Institute of Technology, Chennai, India
    Sangeetha N., Jerusalem College of Engineering, Chennai, India
    Karthik R., Centre for Cyber Physical Systems, Vellore Institute of Technology, Chennai,
        India
    Kethepalli Mallikarjuna, RGM College of Engineering and Technology, Nandyal, India

Multimodal imaging systems assist medical practitioners in cost-effective diagnostic methods in clinical pathologies. Multimodal imaging of the same organ or the region of interest reveals complementing anatomical and functional details. Multimodal image fusion algorithms integrate complementary image details into a composite image that reduces clinician's time for effective diagnosis. Deep learning networks have their role in feature extraction for the fusion of multimodal images. This chapter analyzes the performance of a pre-trained VGG19 deep learning network that extracts features from the base and detail layers of the source images for constructing a weight map to fuse the source image details. Maximum and averaging fusion rules are adopted for base layer fusion. The performance of the fusion algorithm for multimodal medical image fusion is analyzed by peak signal to noise ratio, structural similarity index, fusion factor, and figure of merit. Performance analysis of the fusion algorithms is also carried out for the source images with the presence of impulse and Gaussian noise.

    Anitha Ruth J., SRM Institute of Science and Technology, India
    Uma R., Sri Sairam Engineering College, India
    Meenakshi A., SRM Institute of Science and Technology, India

Apples are the most productive fruits in the world with a lot of medicinal and nutritional value. Significant economic losses occur frequently due to various diseases that occur on a huge scale of apple production. Consequently, the effective and timely discovery of apple leaf infection becomes compulsory. The proposed work uses optimal deep neural network for effectively identifying the diseases of apple trees. This work utilizes a convolution neural network to capture the features of Apple leaves. Extracted features are optimized with the help of the optimization algorithm. The optimized features are utilized in the leaf disease identification process. Here the traditional DNN algorithm is modified by means of weight optimization using adaptive monarch butterfly optimization (AMBO) algorithm. The experimental results show that the proposed disease identification methodology based on the optimized deep neural network accomplishes an overall accuracy of 98.42%.

    Julius Fusic S., Thiagarajar College of Engineering, India
    Karthikeyan S., Thiagarajar College of Engineering, India
    Sheik Masthan S. A. R., Thiagarajar College of Engineering, India

In this chapter, 500 different images of Tamil vowels that are hand written interprets that the Tamil alphabets model has trained about 75% accuracy with proposed U-net model algorithm. The introduction of various segmentation proportions was discussed for English and Tamil language text identification was explained. In this work, the selection of image is split into four segments and read the data during training itself. Thus, the Tamil and English font prediction accuracy of the model was improved about 85% using U-net architecture was explained.

Chapter 11
  Chandrakala H. T., Government First Grade College, Madhugiri, India & Tumkur
   University, India
  Thippeswamy G., BMS Institute of Technology, India

Edge detection from handwritten text documents, particularly of Kannada language, is a challenging task. Kannada has a huge character set, amounting to 17,340 character combinations. Moreover, in handwritten Kannada, the character strokes are highly variable in size and shape due to varying handwriting styles. This chapter presents a solution for edge detection of Kannada handwritten documents. Sobel edge detection method, which efficiently enhances the image contrast and detects the character edges, is proposed. Experimentation of this edge detection approach yielded high F-measure and global contrast factor values.

Chapter 12
  Geraldine Amali, Vellore Institute of Technology, India
  Keerthana K. S. V., Oracle, India
  Jaiesh Sunil Pahlajani, Grofers, India

Facial images carry important demographic information such as ethnicity and gender. Ethnicity is an essential part of human identity and serves as a useful identifier for numerous applications ranging from biometric recognition, targeted advertising to social media profiling. Recent years have seen a huge spike in the use of convolutional neural networks (CNNs) for various visual, face recognition problems. The ability of the CNN to take advantage of the hierarchical pattern in data makes it a suitable model for facial ethnicity classification. As facial datasets lack ethnicity information it becomes extremely difficult to classify images. In this chapter a deep learning framework is proposed that classifies the individual into their respective ethnicities which are Asian, African, Latino, and White. The performances of various deep learning techniques are documented and compared for accuracy of classification. Also, a simple efficient face retrieval model is built which retrieves similar faces. The aim of this model is to reduce the search time by 1/3 of the original retrieval model.

Chapter 13
  Wencan Zhong, Shantou University, China
  Vijayalakshmi G. V. Mahesh, BMS Institute of Technology and Management, India
  Alex Noel Joseph Raj, Shantou University, China
  Nersisson Ruban, Vellore Institute of Technology, India

Finding faces in the clutter scenes is a challenging task in automatic face recognition systems as facial images are subjected to changes in the illumination, facial expression, orientation, and occlusions. Also, in the cluttered scenes, faces are not completely visible and detecting them is essential as it is significant in surveillance applications to study the mood of the crowd. This chapter utilizes the deep learning methods to understand the cluttered scenes to find the faces and discriminate them into partial and full faces. The work proves that MTCNN used for detecting the faces and Zernike moments-based kernels employed in CNN for classifying the faces into partial and full takes advantage in delivering a notable performance as compared to the other techniques. Considering the limitation of recognition on partial face emotions, only the full faces are preserved, and further, the KDEF dataset is modified by MTCNN to detect only faces and classify them into four emotions. PatternNet is utilized to train and test the modified dataset to improve the accuracy of the results.

Chapter 14

Elena Lyakso, St. Petersburg State University, Russia
Olga Frolova, St. Petersburg State University, Russia
Yuri Matveev, ITMO University, Russia

The description of the results of five psychophysiological studies using automatic coding facial expression in adults and children (from 4 to 16 years) in the FaceReader software version 8.0 is presented. The model situations of reading the emotional text and pronouncing emotional phrases and words, natural interaction in mother-child dyads, child and adult (experimenter), and interaction of children with each other were analyzed. The difficulties of applying the program to analyze the behavior of children in natural conditions, to analyze the emotional facial expressions of the children with autism spectrum disorders and children with Down syndrome are described. The ways to solve them are outlined.

Chapter 15

Karthik R., Centre for Cyber Physical Systems, Vellore Institute of Technology, Chennai, India
Nandana B., Vellore Institute of Technology, India
Mayuri Patil, Vellore Institute of Technology, India
Chandreyee Basu, Vellore Institute of Technology, India
Vijayarajan R., Centre for Cyber Physical Systems, Vellore Institute of Technology, Chennai, India

Facial expressions are an important means of communication among human beings, as they convey different meanings in a variety of contexts. All human facial expressions, whether voluntary or involuntary, are formed as a result of movement of different facial muscles. Despite their variety and complexity, certain expressions are universally recognized as representing specific emotions - for instance, raised eyebrows in combination with an open mouth are associated with surprise, whereas a smiling face is generally interpreted as happy. Deep learning-based implementations of expression synthesis have demonstrated their ability to preserve essential features of input images, which is desirable. However, one limitation of using deep learning networks is that their dependence on data distribution and the quality of images used for training purposes. The variation in performance can be studied by changing the optimizer and loss functions, and their effectiveness is analysed based on the quality of output images obtained.

Chapter 16

    Amira Ahmad Al-Sharkawy, Electronics Research Institute, Egypt
    Gehan A. Bahgat, Electronics Research Institute, Egypt
    Elsayed E. Hemayed, Zewail City of Science and Technology, Egypt
    Samia Abdel-Razik Mashali, Electronics Research Institute, Egypt

Object classification problem is essential in many applications nowadays. Human can easily classify objects in unconstrained environments easily. Classical classification techniques were far away from human performance. Thus, researchers try to mimic the human visual system till they reached the deep neural networks. This chapter gives a review and analysis in the field of the deep convolutional neural network usage in object classification under constrained and unconstrained environment. The chapter gives a brief review on the classical techniques of object classification and the development of bio-inspired computational models from neuroscience till the creation of deep neural networks. A review is given on the constrained environment issues: the hardware computing resources and memory, the object appearance and background, and the training and processing time. Datasets that are used to test the performance are analyzed according to the images environmental conditions, besides the dataset biasing is discussed.

Preface

There is an old saying "A picture is worth a thousand words" and the automatic extraction of information from the pictures play a greater role in the development of autonomous systems.

Ths book explains the novel contributions of the authors in two different environments viz constraint: Images that acquired through proper data acquisition systems with adequate control on the illumination conditions and unconstraint: Images acquired from simple sensors with no control on the illumination or brightness aspects. An example of the former would be the medical images and latter could be natural scene images.

Over the years, deep learning based image analysis has broadened its horizons in various applications and has become more influential technique in medical image analysis, optical character recognition, geology, defense, remote sensing, biometrics, surveillance, automotive industry, machine vision, material science, robotics and more. Traditionally deep learning involves both feature extraction and classification and can be applied for different scenarios, but fine tuning of the trainable parameters, the employed performance metrics, selection of suitable architecture vary for images acquired from both constraints and unconstrained environments and therefore a book with concise information targeting both environments is always a necessity.

There are total of sixteen chapters arranged in orderly manner. Few chapters concentrate on the deep learning methodologies applied for medical images such as the breast Ultrasound, Pulmonary CT, Retinal images etc. The remaining chapters introduce the deep learning concepts towards interesting application such as the Apple leaf identification, facial biometrics, facial expression, facial ethnicity, handwritten text detection etc. The abstracts of all the chapters are presented below.

In Chapter 1, authors have briefed about, what is an image? What do you meant by digital image and how digital image can be processed? Image types like binary image, gray scale image, color image and indexed image and various image formats are also explained and further the chapter highlights major fields where digital image processing can be used. The purpose of this chapter is to introduce a variety of concepts related to digital image formation in a human eye. Authors also summarized the mechanism of human visual system which includes image formation, brightness adaption and discrimination. Next, authors illustrated about the very primary step of image processing that is image acquisition.

In Chapter 2, brain tumors are a hazardous disease and this chapter is focused on the classification of benign and malignant tumor images there by improving the detection accuracy. Here histogram equalization is used to amplify the intensity of tumor so that it can be detected more precisely. In the projected system segmentation is performed by K-means clustering and Gaussian Mixture Model (GMM) along with them we are extracting the features from discrete wavelet Transform (DWT) and feature reduction from Principal component analysis (PCA). The classifiers Support Vector Machine (SVM) and Artificial Neural networks (ANN) are used to classify benign and malignant tumor from brain images.

In Chapter 3, importance of early detection breast cancer for the effective treatment of cancer is dealt. To assist radiologists who manually delineate the tumor from the ultrasound image an automatic computerized method of detection referred as CAD (Computer Aided Diagnosis) is presented to provide valuable inputs for radiologists. The CAD system is divided into many branches like pre-processing, segmentation, feature extraction and classification. This chapter solely focuses on the first two branches of the CAD system the pre-processing and segmentation. Ultrasound images acquired depends on the operator expertise and is found to be of low contrast and fuzzy in nature. For the pre-processing branch a contrast enhancement algorithm based on fuzzy logic is implemented which could help in the efficient delineation of the tumor from ultrasound image.

In Chapter 4, early prediction of cancer type has become very crucial. Breast cancer is common to women and it leads to life threatening. Several imaging techniques have been suggested for timely detection and treatment of breast cancer. Automated whole breast ultrasound (AWBUS) is a new breast imaging technology that can render the entire breast anatomy in 3-D volume. The tissue layers in the breast are segmented and the type of lesion in the breast tissue can be identified which is essential for cancer detection. Here a U-Net Convolutional Neural Network Architecture is used to implement the segmentation of breast tissues from AWBUS images into the different layers viz. epidermis, subcutaneous and muscular layer. The architecture was trained and tested with the AWBUS dataset images.

In Chapter 5, Breast cancer is the second most prevalent type of cancer among women. Breast Ultrasound (BUS) imaging is one of the most frequently used diagnostic tools to detect and classify abnormalities in the breast. To improve the diagnostic accuracy, Computer Aided Diagnosis (CAD) system is helpful for breast cancer detection and classification. In this chapter, the pre-processing step includes speckle noise removal using Speckle Reducing Anisotropic Diffusion (SRAD) filter. The goal of segmentation is to locate the Region of Interest (ROI) and Active contour-based segmentation and Fuzzy C Means segmentation (FCM) are used in this work. The texture features are extracted and fed to a classifier to categorize the images as Normal, Benign and Malignant. The work employs three classifiers namely K-Nearest Neighbors (KNN) algorithm, Decision tree algorithm and Random Forest classifier are used and the performance is compared based on the accuracy of classification.

The Chapter 6 presents ways to enhance the classification accuracy of the pulmonary nodules with the limited number of features extracted using Gray level co-occurrence matrix and linear binary pattern. The classification is done using the machine learning algorithm such as artificial neural network (ANN) and the random forest classifier (RF). In present, lung cancer seems to be the most deadly disease in the world which can be detected only after the computerized tomography i.e. CT scan images of the person. Detecting the infected portion at the early period is the challenging task. Hence, the recent researchers where under the detection of pulmonary nodules to categorize it either as benign nodules which named as non-cancerous or as malignant nodules which named as cancerous. When associated the results with the recent papers, the accuracy has been improved in classifying the lung nodules.

In Chapter 7, color fundus image is the most basic way to diagnose diabetic retinopathy and glaucoma. In particular, since observing the morphological changes of the optic disc is conducive to the diagnosis of related diseases, effective positioning and segmentation of the optic disc is an important process. Optic disc segmentation algorithms are mainly based on template matching. This chapter uses Kirsch operator to get the edge of the green channel fundus image through morphological operation, and then detects the optic disc by HOUGH circle transformation. In addition, supervised learning in machine learning is also applied in this chapter. First, the vascular mask is obtained by morphological operation for vascular erasure, and then the SVM classifier is segmented by Hu moment invariant feature and gray level feature.

In Chapter 8, Multimodal imaging systems assist medical practitioners in cost-effective diagnostic methods in clinical pathologies. Multimodal imaging of the same organ or the region of interest reveals complementing anatomical and functional details. Multimodal image fusion algorithms integrate complementary image details into a composite image that reduces clinician's time for effective diagnosis. Deep learning networks have their role in feature extraction for the fusion of multimodal images. This chapter analyzes the performance of a pre-trained VGG19 deep learning network that extracts features from the base and detail layers of the source images for constructing a weight map to fuse the source image details. Maximum and averaging fusion rules are adopted for base layer fusion. The performance of the fusion algorithm for multimodal medical image fusion is analyzed by peak signal to noise ratio, structural similarity index, fusion factor, and figure of merit.

In Chapter 9, apples are the most productive fruits in the world with a lot of medicinal and nutritional value. The effective and timely discovery of apple leaf infection becomes compulsory. The proposed work uses Optimal Deep Neural Network for effectively identifying the diseases of apple trees. This work utilizes a Convolution Neural Network to capture the features of Apple leaves. Extracted features are optimized with the help of the optimization algorithm. The optimized features are utilized in the leaf disease identification process. Here the traditional DNN algorithm is modified by means of weight optimization using Adaptive Monarch Butterfly Optimization (AMBO) algorithm.

In Chapter 10, detection of Tamil vowels from 500 different handwritten images (அ ஆ இ ஈ உ ஊ எ ஏ ஐ ஒ ஓ ஔ ஃ) using a U-net model is proposed. The introduction of various segmentation proportions was discussed for English and Tamil language text identification. The font prediction accuracy of the model was improved of about 85% using the proposed U-net architecture.

In Chapter 11, detection from handwritten text documents, particularly of Kannada language is proposed. Kannada has a huge character set, amounting to 17340 character combinations. Moreover in handwritten Kannada the character strokes are highly variable in size and shape due to varying handwriting styles. This paper presents a solution for Edge detection of Kannada handwritten documents. Sobel Edge Detection method which efficiently enhances the image contrast and detects the character edges is proposed. Experimentation of this Edge Detection approach yielded high F-measure and Global Contrast Factor values.

In Chapter 12, facial images carry important demographic information such as ethnicity and gender. Recent years have seen a huge spike in the use of Convolutional Neural Networks (CNNs) for various visual, face recognition problems. The ability of the CNN to take advantage of the hierarchical pattern in data makes it a suitable model for facial ethnicity classification. As facial datasets lack ethnicity information it becomes extremely difficult to classify images. In this chapter a deep learning framework is proposed that classifies the individual into their respective ethnicities which are Asian, African, Latino and White. The performance of various deep learning techniques are documented and compared for accuracy of classification. Also a simple efficient face retrieval model is built which retrieves similar faces. The aim of this model is to reduce the search time by 1/3 of the original retrieval model.

In Chapter 13, finding faces in the clutter scenes is a challenging task in automatic face recognition systems as facial images are subjected to changes in the illumination, facial expression, orientation, and occlusions. Also in the cluttered scenes faces are not completely visible and detecting them is essential as it is significant in surveillance applications to study the mood of the crowd. This chapter utilizes the deep learning methods to understand the cluttered scenes to find the faces and discriminate them into partial and full faces. The work proves that MTCNN used for detecting the faces and Zernike moments based kernels employed in CNN for classifying the faces into partial and full takes advantage in delivering a notable performance as compared to the other techniques. Considering the limitation of recognition on partial face emotions, only the full faces are preserved and further the KDEF dataset is modified by MTCNN to detect only faces and classify them into four emotions. PatternNet is utilized to train and test the modified dataset to improve the accuracy of the results.

In Chapter 14, the description of the results of five psychophysiological studies using automatic coding facial expression in adults and children (from 4 to 16 years) in the Face Reader software version 8.0 is presented. The model situations of reading the emotional text and pronouncing emotional phrases and words, natural interaction in mother - child dyads, child and adult (experimenter), and interaction of children with each other were analyzed. The difficulties of applying the program to analyze the behavior of children in natural conditions, to analyze the emotional facial expressions of the children with autism spectrum disorders and children with Down syndrome are described. The ways to solve them are outlined.

In Chapter 15, facial expressions are an important means of communication among human beings, as they convey different meanings in a variety of contexts. All human facial expressions, whether voluntary or involuntary, are formed as a result of movement of different facial muscles. Despite their variety and complexity, certain expressions are universally recognized as representing specific emotions - for instance, raised eyebrows in combination with an open mouth are associated with surprise, whereas a smiling face is generally interpreted as happy. Deep learning based implementations of expression synthesis have demonstrated their ability to preserve essential features of input images, which is desirable. However, one limitation of using deep learning networks is that their dependence on data distribution and the quality of images used for training purposes. The variation in performance can be studied by changing the optimizer and loss functions, and their effectiveness is analyzed based on the quality of output images obtained.

In Chapter 16, object classification problem is essential in many applications nowadays. Human can easily classify objects in unconstrained environments easily. Classical classification techniques were far away from human performance. Thus, researchers try to mimic the human visual system till they reached the deep neural networks. This chapter gives a review and analysis in the field of the deep convolutional neural network usage in object classification under constrained and unconstrained environment. The chapter gives a brief review on the classical techniques of object classification and the development of bio-inspired computational models from neuroscience till the creation of deep neural networks. A review is given on the constrained environment issues; the hardware computing resources and memory, the object appearance and background, and the training and processing time. Datasets that are used to test the performance are analyzed according to the images environmental conditions, besides the dataset biasing is discussed.

By all, the book presents a detailed illustration of different architectures such the VGG16, U-Net, GANs etc. and concentrates in-depth on the experimental analysis, performance measures and visualization of the outputs. Some chapters describe the limitations of the proposed model too. Furthermore, the book will be boom to the research scholars working in the transdisciplinary area which require engineering concepts to be applied in various transdisciplinary fields. Also due to simplicity in explaining the techniques, the graduate level students would prefer it as a reference material towards understanding deep learning algorithms.

Finally the book *Handbook of Research on Deep Learning-Based Image Analysis Under Constrained and Unconstrained Environments* would indeed add value to the existing literature.

Alex Noel Joseph Raj

Ruban Nersisson

Vijayalakshmi G. V. Mahesh

Acknowledgment

For the past 12 months we have been actively working on the pre-production of the book. Written proposals, invited authors, reviewers, waited for their comments, revisions and finally analyzed and accepted 16 full chapters out of the total 29 chapter proposals that we received. These would not have been possible without the support of many people.

We sincerely thank the IGI global team who were happy to accept our proposal and provided timely help in solving various administrative issues.

We thank the invited authors and reviewers for the continuous support and their efforts in making this book into this wonderful technical resource for Deep Learning Based Image Analysis under Constrained and Unconstrained Environments.

During these tough times, we understand the support provided by our institutions and we would like to sincerely thank Shantou University, China, Vellore Institute of Technology, Vellore, India and BMS Institute of Technology and Management, Bengaluru, India for their unrelenting confidence in our abilities.

Our families too need a special mention. Finally, we thank the Almighty for giving us this wonderful opportunity.

We end with the quotes of William Arthur Ward, where we equate our book to the teachers
"The Good **BOOK** Explains,
The Superior **BOOK** Demonstrates and
The Great **BOOK** Inspires"

Alex Noel Joseph Raj

Ruban Nersisson

Vijayalakshmi G. V. Mahesh

Chapter 1
Computer Processing
of an Image:
An Introduction

Chandra Prabha R.

BMS Institute of Technology and Management, India

Shilpa Hiremath

BMS Institute of Technology and Management, India

ABSTRACT

In this chapter, the authors have briefed about images, digital images, how the digital images can be processed. Image types like binary image, grayscale image, color image, and indexed image and various image formats are explained. It highlights the various fields where digital image processing can be used. This chapter introduces a variety of concepts related to digital image formation in a human eye. The mechanism of the human visual system is discussed. The authors illustrate the steps of image processing. Explanation on different elements of digital image processing systems like image acquisition, and others are also provided. The components required for capturing and processing the image are discussed. Concepts of image sampling, quantization, image representation are discussed. It portrays the operations of the image during sampling and quantization and the two operations of sampling which is oversampling and under-sampling. Readers can appreciate the key difference between oversampling and under-sampling applied to digital images.

1. INTRODUCTION

Images are all around us. Among the five sense organs, the human eye gives visual information about the things we look at, which can be in the form of a text or the drawing. This visual information is processed through the human brain and accordingly the person acts to it. Similarly, analog images are captured through the sensors which can be converted to digital images either through sensors or can be done before processing the image with the help of the computer system. The main advantage of image processing is

DOI: 10.4018/978-1-7998-6690-9.ch001

that according to the requirement of the person, the data can be altered and the same can be used further for any specific application. The field of digital image processing has grown enormously over the past few decades. The development of digital image processing has been inclined by technological advancement in digital image processing, advanced computer processors, and huge mass storage devices. Image processing is a technique where the acquired image is an input and the output can be in the form of an enhanced image or it can be an attribute. The main intension of this chapter is to present the outline of the course, digital image processing. Different elements of the image processing system are also covered in this chapter. The highpoint of this chapter is the discussion of the different image types and also various types of image formats in practice (Gonzalez, R. C., Woods, R. E., & Eddins, S. L.,2004).

2. DIGITAL IMAGE PROCESSING

Any three-dimensional scene represented in the form of a two-dimension is said to be an image this image can be represented in the form of f (x, y) where x, y are spatial coordinates and f is the intensity at that point. Images are of two types: analog image and digital image. The analog image has a continuous range of values representing position and intensity. For example, an image produced on the screen of a CRT monitor is an analog image. The storage requirement for such images is very high. In digital image x, y and f are all finite, and discrete quantities. Hence, the conversion of an analog image to a digital image is very necessary before processing it. This conversion is just done using two simple steps- sampling and quantization. In sampling, it discretizes in the coordinate values x, and y whereas in quantization, it discretizes in the amplitude value f. Each element in a digital image is said to be a pixel or pels or picture element or image elements. Manipulation of this digital image using a digital computer is said to be a digital image processing.(Shilpa Hiremath et al., 2018).

Digital image processing has many advantages when compared to analog image processing below mentioned are a few of them,

- Fast processing
- Cost-effective
- Effective storage
- Efficient transmission
- Scope for versatile image manipulation covering the entire Electromagnetic spectrum

Three major use of digital image processing are:

- Human perception that is to improve the pictorial information: Processing of the image is done to improve the image quality for better human interpretation and analysis.
  Example: filtering of the noise present in an image, enhancing the content of an image like contrast enhancement, deblurring, and also remote sensing.
- For autonomous machine application: Processing of an image is done to extract the image information which is suitable for computer processing.
  Example: Industry machine vision for product assembly and inspection, detect and track the target automatically, fingerprint and face recognition, machine processing of aerial and satellite imagery for weather prediction or crop assessment.

- Efficient storage and transmission: An image is processed to reduce the space required to store that image and if it's transmitted it should consume less bandwidth. An image usually contains two entities namely: information & redundancy. In image processing to achieve better storage or transmission of an image, image compression is applied where the redundancy part is removed and only the information content is present (Gonzalez, R. C., Woods, R. E., & Eddins, S. L.,2004). **Example:** image compression

2.1 Image Types

Images can be categorized into 4 types: Binary image, greyscale image, color image, and indexed image. (Shilpa Hiremath & Dr. A Shobha Rani,2020).

1) Binary image: In this type of image, the image can take only two-pixel levels either a zero which is indicated by black color, or one value which is indicated by white color. Hence, it is represented using only one binary digit. This type of image is simple to process and analyze. It is commonly used in Optical character recognition (Singh, D. V. 2013).

Figure 1. Binary image

2) Greyscale image: In the greyscale image, the image generally has values ranging from 0 to 255 i.e a total of 256 different grey colors which means 8 bits/pixels are used for the representation of the grey image, color information is not present in this type of image. It is commonly used in the medical and astronomy field.

Figure 2. Gray image

3) Color image: In this type of image, the image is generally composed of three bands namely red, green, and blue (RGB) hence it is sometimes called a three-band monochrome image. The information stored in the digital image is in the form of a grey level in each spectral band.

Figure 3. Color image

4) Indexed image: In this type of image, the image has pixel values and a colormap value. This indexed image maps the pixel values to the colormap values and identifies the color value of each pixel. The pixel values of an image which are stored in the form of an integer are the indices to color values stored in the colormap.

Figure 4. Indexed image

2.2 Image File Format

The image format is the standardized means of organizing and storing the digital image. The data stored in an image file format can be in any one of the forms namely: compressed, uncompressed, or vector format. Below are a few image files format (Sakshica, D., & Gupta, K), (Almutairi, A,2018).

1) Graphic Interchange Format (GIF): In this format, the image is compressed, and the compression technique is lossless. Since it has limited colors and requires very little memory it is used in web and animation but not in photography and printing.

2) Joint Photographic Experts Group (JPEG): In this format, images are compressed to store a lot of information in a small size file. JPEG usually uses a discrete cosine transform for performing a compression technique to reduce the size of an image. Since it drops some information while performing a compression technique it is said to be as lossy compression. Usually, it is used for photography on the web because of its small size and easy to load but not in the graphics, logos, and line drawings.

3) JPEG 2000: In this format, both lossless and lossy compression storage techniques are supported. The compression methods used in JPEG 2000 and JPEG are different from each other; it uses a discrete wavelet transform. These are the additional features that are missing in JPEG. No matter that JPEG 2000 improves quality and compression ratio but it also requires computational power to process. Example: JPEG 2000 is used is in movie editing (professional) and distribution.

4) Portable Network Graphics (PNG): This type of image file format is popularly used as it is an open-source format that is used to replace the Graphic Interchange Format (GIF). The main advantage of the PNG file format over the GIF is that it allows for a full range of color and better compression. It's used almost exclusively for web images. For photographs, PNG is not as good as JPEG, because it creates a larger file. But for images with some text or line art, it's better because the images look less bitmapped.

5) Tagged Image File Format (TIFF): Images are uncompressed and thus contain a lot of detailed image data, hence the images are very large in file size. TIFF is also extremely flexible in terms of color like it can be in terms of grayscale or CMYK for printing and RGB for the web. The contents can be in terms of layers or image tags. TIFF is commonly used in photo software like in photoshop, page layout software like in Quark and InDesign.

6) PhotoShop Document (PSD): In this image file format, the image is stored with the support for most imaging options available in Photoshop which includes layers with masks, transparency, text, alpha channels, and spot colors, clipping paths, and duotone settings. This is in contrast to many other file formats that restrict content to provide streamlined, predictable functionality. The main advantage of this type of file format is that it has a maximum height and width of 30,000 pixels, and a length limit of 2GB.

2.3 Image Processing Application

Image processing is used in every walk of our life which can be categorized based on the source of an image being obtained namely electromagnetic spectrum, acoustic, ultrasonic, and electronic. Synthetic images are also a source of an image, but these are generated by the computer. There are endless situations calling for image processing done by software. In general, it can be classified into a few groups (S. Muthuselvi and P. Prabhu, 2016).

- Checking for presence: If we need to locate the parts in an image then matching is done which means looking for regions that are similar to or same as a predefined template. This template can either be an image or a geometric pattern that contains information regarding edges and geometric features. These methods are called correlation patterns and geometric pattern matching respectively.
- Measurement: The main use of measurement with the help of image processing is in alignment or inspection application. Most measurement techniques use edge detection algorithms. An edge is an area in an image displaying significant change in the image intensity. The software analyzes the gray levels of the image and based on this, it identifies shapes, measures distances, and calculates the geometry which in turn will map with the real-world units.
- Identification and verification: Object detection and identification are very essential factors that use image processing. Few examples which use this are Barcodes and 2D matrix code reading, optical character recognition (OCR).

Example 1: Facial Recognition

This is the fastest and more accurate under all conditions. It's a real-time watchlist detection that identifies known individuals and can be used in flow and queue management, access control to provide authentication of the individual in the secure or controlled area.

Example 2: Weather Forecasting

The activities of obtaining information about an object by the sensor without being in direct contact with it are said to be remote sensing. The output of this remote sensing is an image representation that can be used in meteorology i.e. identification of clouds, rainfall prediction, etc.

3. HUMAN VISUAL SYSTEM

The human eye allows us to see the world around us. The human eye works with the brain to identify and recognize the object. The main work of the human eye is to detect the patterns of light and they work with the brain to identify these patterns as images. Light rays fall on the object which we are looking at and the reflected rays from the object fall on the human eye, then the light enters the outer part of our eye called the cornea. This cornea is clear like a window which helps the eye to focus the light and make things short and clear. Then, the light rays pass through an opening called a pupil which is a dark circle and colored part in the human eye. Iris is the colored part in the human eye which indicates how large the pupil is and how much light can pass into the human eye. The iris expands in dim light and narrows in bright light to adjust the amount of light entering the human eye. Behind the iris is the lens, it helps to focus the light entering the eye so that the object is clearly visible. When the cornea, pupil, and lens are all working correctly they focus light on the back of the eye called the retina. When light falls on the retina, it is converted into electrical signals and these signals are passed to the brain through the optic nerve which is the connectivity between the retina and the human brain. Since the image formed on the retina is up-side-down, the brain converts it right side up. Also, when we look at an object, each eye gives a slightly different view the brain combines those views and makes them into one picture.

Figure 5. Human Eye Structure

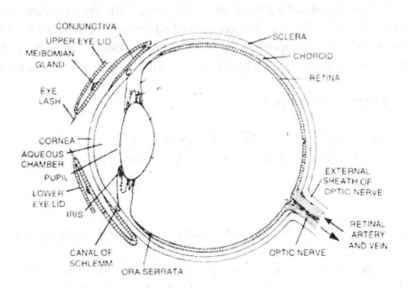

Figure 6. Image Formation In Human Eye

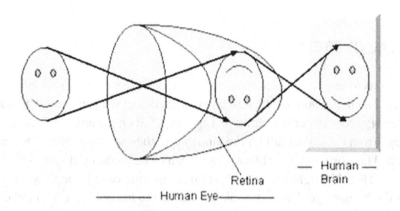

Retina

— Human —
Brain

——————— Human Eye———————

3.1 Brightness Adaption and Discrimination

The sensitivity of the eye to light depends on the illumination of an object. The ability of the eye to adapt to changes in the light intensity is called adaptation.

Dark adaptation: A person entering a dark room from the bright light is initially blinded; gradually the objects are seen in outline and then in detail. Here the pupils dilate to allow more light to enter the eye.

Light adaptation: A person is temporarily blinded, and the person is suddenly exposed to a bright light who is coming from a dark room, the eyes gradually adapt to the light. Here the pupils constrict so that less light enters the eye.

The brightness adaptation level is the current sensitivity level of the visual system for a given set of conditions. Digital images are displayed as a discrete set of intensities, the eye's ability to discriminate between different intensity levels is important. The total range of distinct intensity levels the eye can discriminate simultaneously is rather small when compared with the total adaptation range.

3.2 Basic Image Formation Model

The digital image is represented by two-dimensional functions f (x, y). The value of f at coordinates (x, y) is a positive scalar quantity. The function f (x, y) must be nonzero and finite value hence,

$$0 < f(x, y) < \infty$$

The function f (x, y) may be characterized by two components called illumination and reflectance:

- Illumination: It is the amount of source illumination incident on the scene being viewed i (x, y)
- Reflectance: It is the amount of illumination reflected by the objects in the scene r (x, y)

These two functions are used to represent the image f (x, y):

$$f(x, y) = i(x, y) r(x, y)$$

where $0 < i(x, y) < \infty$
and $0 < r(x, y) < 1$
which indicates reflectance is bounded by total absorption (0) and total reflectance (1).

4. IMAGE SENSOR

Image acquirement in image processing can be defined as the act of recovering an image from a source which is usually a hardware-based source. Image acquisition is always the first step while working with image processing because without an image no processing is possible. Images can be acquired using a sensor. (Reader, C.L.I.F.F.O.R.D.,& Hubble, L.A. R. R. Y,1981).

The digital sensors work artificially as the transduction process of a biological eye. Transduction is the action or a process of converting one energy form into another form. In the human eye, rod and cone receptors work in combination with ganglion cells to convert photons into an electrochemical signal which is the occipital lobe in our brain, and then this signal is processed in our brain. In the case of an image sensor, though photons are captured as charged electrons in silicon which is the sensing material and converted to a voltage value through the use of capacitors and amplifiers then later transferred into digital code which can be processed by a computer.

The image sensor appreciates features like amplitude, intensity, and other factors of the image which is later given to the hardware of the image processing system for further processing. Images can be captured in three ways using a single sensor, line sensor, or array sensor.

Figure 7. Working of sensor

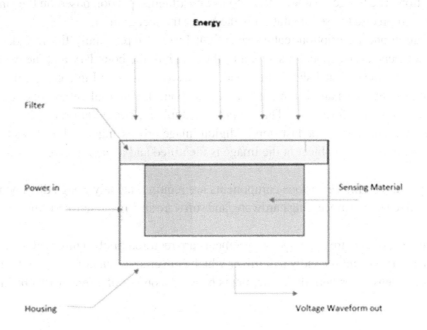

5. FUNDAMENTAL STEPS AND COMPONENTS OF DIP

Fundamental steps help to divide the material of digital image processing into two broad categories, in the first methods both input and output are images, and in the second type inputs may be images, but the outputs are attributes extracted from those images(Koli, M., & Balaji, S,2013)

- Knowledgebase: It is the database with all prior knowledge about the problem domain.
- Image acquisition: This is the very main phase in image processing which captures the image and the image is available in the digital form for further pre-processing.
- Image filtering and enhancement: In this step, the pictorial and information content of the image is improved based on the specific application (Hall, E. L,1974).
- Image restoration: The raw form of an image is improved using the probability and mathematical model of image degradation (Andrews, H. C., & Hunt, B. R,1977)
- Color image processing: If the image is a color image that has the three basic colors red, green, and blue then color image processing is done. Other colors can be derived from these three basic colors. Color image processing is broadly used in a variety of uses namely printing, internet, etc (Radewan, C. H,1975, March).
- Wavelets and multiresolution processing: wavelets are small waves that vary in frequency and have a limited duration. Here the images are subdivided into smaller regions. Each resolution has some information in it hence the images are considered at various resolutions and information is obtained from each resolution.
- Compression: Compression is a technique to decrease the image size to store the image or to reduce the bandwidth when transmitted. Various image file formats discussed in section 1 use this compression technique (A. K. Jain, 1981).
- Morphological processing: This step helps in fetching the image portions like image boundary, which further helps in representation and description.
- Segmentation: The image is subdivided into its constituents' portion based on the similarity in the image. Added precise the segmentation is the better the recognition.
- Representation and description/feature selection: In this step, usually the raw data is obtained from the segmentation step and it segregates the data into the boundary and the complete region. If the data gives the external shape information such as corners and inflections, then it is considered to be as boundaries and if the data mentions about the internal details like texture then it is considered as region information. This output is suitable for computer processing.
- Object recognition: This is the last step in digital image processing which follows the representation and description. The object in the image is identified and a label is given to it.

In order to process an image various components are required namely image display, mass storage, hardcopy, specialized image processing hardware, and software and image sensors(Andrews, H. C,1970).

- Image sensors: To capture an image two elements are required firstly a physical device that is used to capture an image and secondly a digitizer which converts this analog image into a digital form. Sometimes, a sensor has both the components hence the output of a sensor will be in digital form.

Figure 8. Sensor types

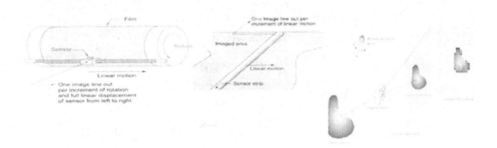

- Image processing hardware: the output of a sensor is given to the hardware for further processing. If a sensor doesn't have a digitizer then digitization of the signal is done here followed by further arithmetic and logic operations (ALU) on the entire image.
- Computer: Depending upon the application the computer can be a personal computer or a supercomputer.
- Image processing software: This includes software to do the image processing task. This software has various modules that do a specific task. Users can also write code in order to reduce the module size and also use a combination of these modules to perform a specific task (Andrews, H. C., Tescher, A. G., & Kruger, R. P,1972). (Azad, M. M., & Hasan, M. M,2017).
- Mass storage: Storage of an image is measured in bytes which is equal to 8 bits, it can be in kilobytes (KB), mega-bytes (MB), gigabytes (GB), terabytes (TB). Storage is a must for an image, which stores pixels of the images during the processing. The size of a single image without compression requires around a megabyte of storage hence a lot of space is required in the system. There are three types of mass storage.
  a. Short term storage: this is used during processing
  b. Online storage: this is used for fast recall
  c. Archival storage: this is characterized by infrequent access.
- Image displays: Images are usually displayed over a color TV monitor which is implemented using display cards. Few applications require a stereo display which is implemented using headgear.
- Hardcopy: This is used to record an image usually it is a paper and sometimes laser printer, digital units, inkjet units, film cameras, or heat-sensitive devices are also used.
- Network: this connects all the components of the digital image processing. There is a lot of data that has to be transmitted hence bandwidth is the most important factor that has to be considered in image processing application.

6. IMAGE SAMPLING AND QUANTIZATION

The domain and the range of an original signal y(t) are always assumed to be continuous. That is, both the time coordinate t and the value y(t) of the signal are allowed to take an arbitrary real value. These signals whose coordinates can take the arbitrary values, that is the one which has a specific value, are called as the analog signals. So it means that such signals are always continuous in nature. It is conve-

Figure 9. Fundamental Steps In DIP

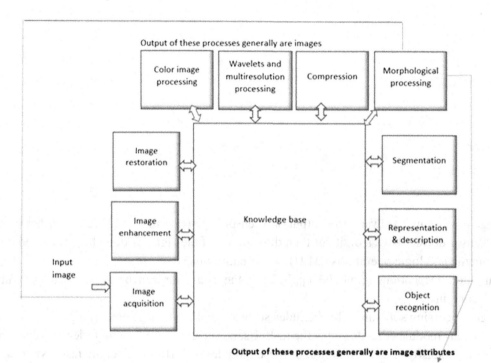

nient enough to work with such signals. But for some applications, digital signals are very essential. Digital signals are those which have a discrete domain and range (Jayaraman, S,S. Esakkirajan dan and T. Veerakumar,2009).

The process of digitizing the domain of a function y(t), that is, digitizing the set of all values for which a function y(t) is defined is called as sampling.

The process of digitizing the range of a function y(t), that is, digitizing all the set of values which the function y(t) can take is defined as quantization.

SAMPLING

As we know that, most of the devices provide output in the form of analog signals. But the digitization of signals is very much essential because many devices take only the digital input. So to facilitate this, we are supposed to convert a signal from analog to digital.One of the techniques to achieve this type of conversion is by sampling.

The sampling of the image is represented as in figure 12

The process of digitizing or discretizing the coordinates of the given image f(x.y) is called as sampling. The image f(x,y) which is assumed to be continuous in nature, that is, analog in nature (to be more precise), is approximated by the samples which are placed such that the distance between each and every sample is equal. And these equally spaced samples are arranged in the form of a matrix, usually taken as an NxM matrix where each and every element of a matrix is unique in nature. Thus an analog

Figure 10. Components of DIP

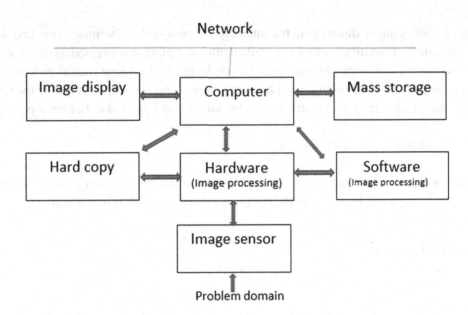

or the continuous form of an image can be represented in the form of digital values. (Jayaraman, S,S. Esakkirajan dan and T. Veerakumar,2009).

The rate at which the digitizer can sample the image determines the number of pixels utilized in the construction of that particular image. As the sampling rate increases, the amount of approximation of the analog signal to the digital signal is said to be increased. That is, the image is now called as a digital image, as it has moved from its continuous property to discrete property.

Figure 11. Basic Digital To Analog System

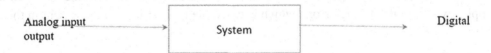

Figure 12. Sampling Of Signals

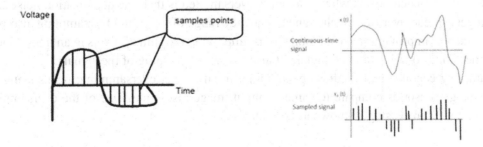

QUANTIZATION

The process of digitizing or discretizing the intensity of the signal or the image is called as quantization. The magnitude of the image which is obtained after sampling is expressed as the digital values in the image processing techniques. So, the quantization levels of the image should be high enough that is, as the intensity of the image increases, it becomes easier for us to read or visualize the given image.

If quantization is divided into n intervals, and the number of bits used in L, then n is given by-

$n = 2^L$. The number of bits per pixels used is 8.

Quantization is a compression technique that involves compressing a range of values into a single value. This can be achieved by reducing the number of discrete symbols in a stream.

Figure 13. Quantized signal

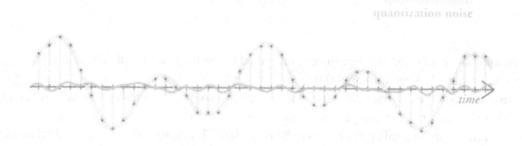

6.1 Over Sampling and Under Sampling

The condition for the sampling is given by Nyquist rate, that is, the minimum rate at which a signal can be sampled without introducing errors, which is twice the highest frequency present in the signal.

OVER SAMPLING

Oversampling of the signal occurs when we sample the signal more than the level which is set by Nyquist. The problem which occurs when a signal is oversampled is that, the quantization noise from the conversion gets spread over to a much higher frequency range of a signal. Oversampling also provides advantages such as improving the resolution that is, improving the sum of pixels in an image and it also improves the signal-to-noise ratio of signals. It also avoids overlapping of the signals.

Oversampling can also be called as up-sampling. In an image, oversampling means using a high-resolution image sensor as compare to camera output image resolution. One of the oversampling applications in image processing is known as zooming.

Figure 14. Over and under-sampled signals

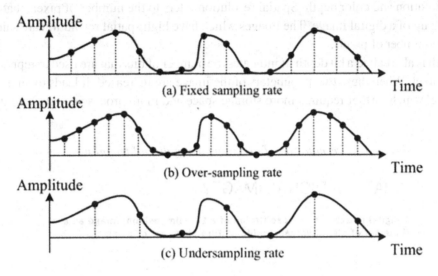

UNDER SAMPLING

Under-sampling is a method where one samples a band pass-filtered signal at a sample rate below its Nyquist rate. Under-sampling is also called as band-pass sampling.

Under-sampling has the effect of changing the image details such as exaggerating the image (which makes the image something different than it was before), which occurs when the under-sampled high spatial frequencies which is pretended to be as lower spatial frequencies.

6.2 Digital Image Representation

An image can be called as a two-dimensional function which is given by f(x,y), where x and y are the spatial coordinates, that is, which are used to represent the image with greater granularity than the pixel coordinates. The intensity of the image F at the point (x,y) is the amplitude of the image at that point. When a, b, and the amplitude values of F are finite, that is, which are limited in size, then F(x,y) is called as a digital image.

Figure 15. Representation of a digital image

$$f(x,y) = \begin{bmatrix} f(0,0) & f(0,1) & f(0,2) & \cdots & f(0,N\text{-}1) \\ f(1,0) & f(1,1) & f(1,2) & \cdots & f(1,N\text{-}1) \\ \cdot & \cdot & \cdot & & \cdot \\ \cdot & \cdot & \cdot & & \cdot \\ \cdot & \cdot & \cdot & & \cdot \\ f(M\text{-}1,0) & f(M\text{-}1,1) & f(M\text{-}1,2) & \cdots & f(M\text{-}1,N\text{-}1) \end{bmatrix}$$

There are a number of factors that can determine the image quality. The two most important factors are spatial resolution and color depth. Spatial resolution refers to the number of pixels that are required in the building up of a digital image. The images which have high spatial resolution are said to be composed of more number of pixels.

Color depth is also called a bit depth. It indicates the number of bits that are used to represent the color of the single pixel. When these two parameters of the image are increased, it leads to an increase of the image file size, which further requires more storage space and more processing time and display time.

Figure 16. Processing and representation of an image using digital techniques

WHAT IS A DIGITAL IMAGE?

A digital image is a representation of a two-dimensional image as a finite set of digital values, called picture elements or pixels

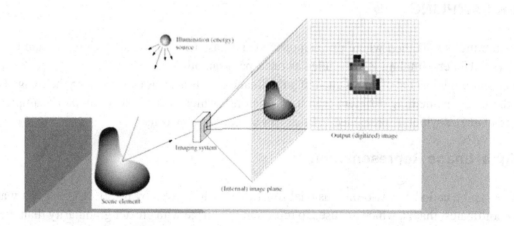

Digital images are comprised of information. This information is meaningful data that is used to represent the image digitally. The digital image can be represented by the unit of measurement called the pixel. A pixel refers to the picture element. It is the smallest unit of any image. One pixel represents a single color. Colors can be represented in any scheme. The most common scheme used is RGB, which stands for Red Green Blue. Pixels can be identified by the location in their respective coordinates.

The image which consists of a rectangular grid of pixels, has a finite set of digital values called as pixels. As mentioned above, the pixel is the smallest individual element in an image, which holds a specific value. It is used to represent the brightness of a given color at any specific point(Shilpa Hiremath, Sneha A, N Bhavya, Rachna Singh, and Meenakshi Biradar,2018).

Figure 17. Pixel representation

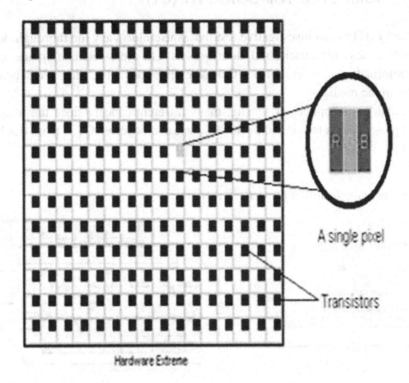

A single pixel

Transistors

Hardware Extreme

7 CASE STUDY ON MEDICAL IMAGE ANALYSIS MEDICAL IMAGE ANALYSIS: INTRODUCTION AND OVERVIEW

The fabric of the pattern analysis and machine intelligence (PAMI) community is a merged part medical images analysis. Medical image analysis contributes majority part to the market for machine vision systems. This majority section not only belongs to hospitals and health care, but also to many other modalities(Dougherty G, 2010)

The major area of Modality are X-ray, Ultrasound, Computed Tomography (CT), Magnetic Resonance (MRI), Nuclear Imaging (PET SPECT),Organ appearance. The Clinical Indications which uses medical imaging are Radiology, Cardiology, Oncology, Neurology, Obstetrics & gynaecology, Breast mammography. The benefit of medical images analysis also reaches end users who are Hospitals, Diagnostic (multispecialty hospitals), broiling Research centre's

Medical image analysis involves a holistic model

The various shares of medical imaging analysis are modality, physics, image processing, and graphics machine learning. In modality, the healthy organs and unhealthy organs appearance is viewed. The physics sectors deal with instruments in which image formation and its statistics is obtained. Image processing and graphics deals with de-noising, segmentation, feature extraction, edge detection and its visualization. The last section is artificial intelligence which deals with prediction and classification of the essential.

CASE STUDY 1: COMPUTED TOMOGRAPHY (CT)

Computed tomography (CT) is an investigative test that is useful to view the thorough descriptions of an internal body part, bones, soft muscle, and blood vessels. The cross-sectional images created due to a CT scan will be reformatted in several planes (both the directions). The images can be observed and printed through electronic media.

CT scanning technique is applied for sensing many different cancers since the images allow the doctor to ratify the presence of a tumor and decide its sizes and position. CT is firm, trouble-free, non-invasive and precise

Figure 18. Color image representation using RGB format

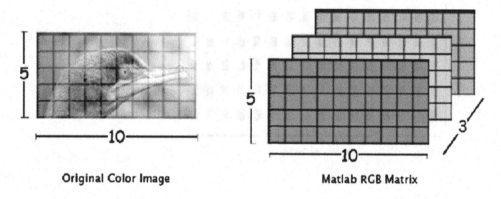

Original Color Image   **Matlab RGB Matrix**

Components of the system are represented by blocks and signals. The original object has some property, for example, X-ray absorption that varies within the x, y-plane. The detector collects X-ray intensity as a function of scan direction t and scan angle θ in the (x, y)- plane, and provides a proportional voltage. In the image formation stage, these data are transformed into a cross-sectional map of apparent X-ray opaqueness. The display outputs a light intensity which is proportional to opaqueness and approximates

The purpose of CT is to acquire a spatially determined map of absorption coefficients $\mu(x, y)$ in one portion of the patient's body.

A CT scan is applied for sensing both critical and prolonged changes in the lungs tissue. It is predominantly used because normal two-dimensional X-rays. Thin slices with high spatial frequency reconstructions is applied for the estimation of interstitial process.. This special technique is called high-resolution CT that produces a sampled version.

Figure 19. Overview of medical imaging analysis

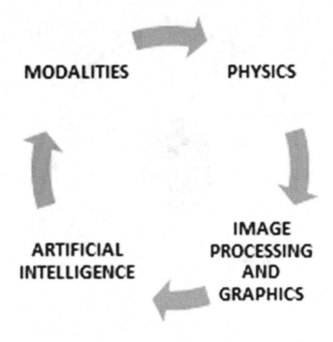

Figure 20. Systems interpretation of a computed tomography scanner.

CASE STUDY 2: DERMATOLOGY

Dermatology (skin disease) is also a major field where image processing can be used. A person suffering from skin disease can be diagnosed and treated from a far distance with the help of image processing. In humans, skin disease is the most familiar form present where a person needs to be treated in the early stages (Shilpa Hiremath, et al., 2017).

Fig 22 shows about its flow in analyzing the skin diseases. Initially, the skin diseased image portion on the human body is captured by the patient using the smartphone and then the patient needs to upload this image wherein the image is enhanced by applying the filtering technique to remove the noise present in the image. As the human body is covered by tiny hair, this has to be eliminated by proper selection of the imaging technique for further improvement in image clarity and analysis of the particular skin disease. For analysis for the identification of particular skin disease can be done with the help of artificial intelligence (Chandraprabha, R & Seema Singh,2016).

Figure 21. Sketch of the CT scanner

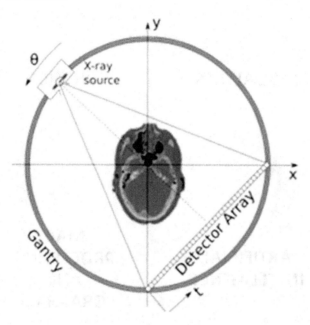

Figure 22. Analysis of skin disease

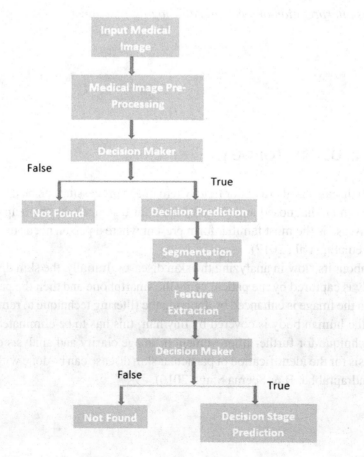

REFERENCES

Almutairi, A. (2018). A Comparative Study on Steganography Digital Images: A Case Study of Scalable Vector Graphics (SVG) and Portable Network Graphics (PNG). *Images Formats. Int. J. Adv. Comput. Sci. Appl, 9*, 170–175.

Andrews, H. C. (1970). *Computer techniques in image processing*. CTIP.

Andrews, H. C., Tescher, A. G., & Kruger, R. P. (1972). Image processing by digital computer. *IEEE Spectrum, 9*(7), 20–32. doi:10.1109/MSPEC.1972.5218964

Azad, M. M., & Hasan, M. M. (2017). Color image processing in digital image. *International Journal of New Technology and Research, 3*(3).

Chanda, B., & Dutta Majumder, D. (2002). *Digital Image Processing and Analysis* (1st ed.). Prentice-Hall of India.

Chandraprabha, R., & Singh, S. (2016). Artificial Intelligent System For Diagnosis Of Cervical Cancer: A Brief Review And Future Outline. *Journal of Latest Research in Engineering and Technology*, 38-41.

Chhabra, T., Dua, G., & Malhotra, T. (2013). Comparative analysis of denoising methods in CT images. *International Journal of Emerging Trends in Electrical and Electronics, 3*(2).

Dougherty, G. (2010). Digital Image Processing for Medical Applications. Cambridge University Press.

Gonzalez, R. C., Woods, R. E., & Eddins, S. L. (2004). *Digital image processing using MATLAB. Pearson Education India.*.

Hall, E. L. (1974). Almost uniform distributions for computer image enhancement. *IEEE Transactions on Computers, 100*(2), 207–208. doi:10.1109/T-C.1974.223892

Hiremath, Akshay, Aditya, Chetan Murthy, & Niranjan. (2017). *Skin Disease Detection using Image Processing*. Academic Press.

Hiremath, Bhavya, Singh, & Biradar. (2018). Digital Image Forgery Detection Using Zernike Moment and Discrete Cosine Transform: A Comparison. *International Research Journal of Engineering and Technology, 5*(5).

Hiremath & Rani. (2020). A Concise Report on Image Types, Image File Format and Noise Model for Image Preprocessing. International Research Journal of Engineering and Technology, 7(8).

Hosseini, H., & Marvasti, F. (2013). Fast restoration of natural images corrupted by high-density impulse noise. *EURASIP Journal on Image and Video Processing, 2013*(1), 15. doi:10.1186/1687-5281-2013-15

Jain, A. K. (1981). Image data compression: A review. *Proceedings of the IEEE, 69*(3), 349–389. doi:10.1109/PROC.1981.11971

Jayaraman, S. (2009). Digital Image Processing. New Delhi: Tata McGraw-Hill Education Private Limited.

Ketenci, S., & Gangal, A. (2017). Automatic reduction of periodic noise in images using adaptive Gaussian star filter. *Turkish Journal of Electrical Engineering and Computer Sciences, 25*(3).

Koli, M., & Balaji, S. (2013). Literature survey on impulse noise reduction. *Signal and Image Processing: an International Journal*, *4*(5), 75–95. doi:10.5121ipij.2013.4506

Muthuselvi, S., & Prabhu, P. (2016). Digital image processing technique-A survey. International Multidisciplinary Research Journal Golden Research Thoughts, 5(11).

Radewan, C. H. (1975, March). Digital image processing with pseudo-color. In *Acquisition and Analysis of Pictorial Data* (Vol. 48, pp. 50–56). International Society for Optics and Photonics. doi:10.1117/12.954071

Reader, C., & Hubble, L. (1981). Trends in image display systems. *Proceedings of the IEEE*, *69*(5), 606–614. doi:10.1109/PROC.1981.12028

Singh, D. V. (2013). *Digital Image Processing with MATLAB and Lab VIEW*. Reed Elsevier India Private Limited.

Chapter 2
Brain Tumor Detection and Classification Based on Histogram Equalization Using Machine Learning

Naralasetty Niharika
Vellore Institute of Technology, India

Sakshi Patel
Vellore Institute of Technology, India

Bharath K. P.
Vellore Institute of Technology, India

Balaji Subramanian
Vellore Institute of Technology, India

Rajesh Kumar M.
(iD) https://orcid.org/0000-0003-0350-4397
Vellore Institute of Technology, India

ABSTRACT

Brain tumor is a hazardous disease. It has to be treated rightly because the patient cannot survive for even a year. This research work is to design a mechanized system that discerns benign and malignant tumor images and improves the classification accuracy. In this system, histogram equalization is used to raise the intensity of tumor so that it can be detected more precisely. In the projected system, segmentation is performed by k-means clustering and Gaussian mixture model (GMM). Along with them, the authors are extracting the features from discrete wavelet transform (DWT) and feature reduction from principal component analysis (PCA). The classifiers support vector machine (SVM) and artificial neural networks (ANN) are used to classify benign and malignant tumor from brain images.

DOI: 10.4018/978-1-7998-6690-9.ch002

I. INTRODUCTION

Signal Processing is a vast area of research consisting of various fields, one among them are, the Digital Image Processing (DIP) (Gonzalez, R. C., et.al. 2002,) which allow us to play with components of images as required in desired application. DIP has vast area of research and is used in various fields such as medical imaging, satellite images of planets, and also many industrial applications. Among all these applications, medical field mostly depends on images such as MRI, X-rays, Ultrasound, CT scan and other bio-medical images to identify the exact problem in the patient's body. These images give the detail study of various diseases such as brain tumor, cancer, swelling, etc. So for the physicians to treat and diagnose the problem in a better way needs the images to be in good quality giving all the necessary information about the infected body part (Devasena, C. L., & Hemalatha, M. 2013). Using image enhancement techniques to improve the images visual quality help us to make better localization of pixels present in the input image which will then result in good contrast images. MRI images are low contrast images. Various methods of image enhancement help to improve the brightness and contrast of the image for practitioners to analyze and treat the infected area, (Amien, M. B., et.al., 2013).

After enhancement of images and identifying the tumor region, it is necessary to define the grade of the tumor. Brain tumor can be classified into two grades i.e. low grade and high grade and also four stages. In this paper we will first segment the tumor using K-means algorithm, this method will help us to extract the infected area from the body part (Ramaswamy Reddy, et.al., 2013).

The two grades of tumor can be expressed in a well defined manner. The low grade tumor is called "Benign" and the high grade tumor as "Malignant". The benign tumor is a low grade disease which does not spread over the body. Although they can be life threatening. In this the tumor cells do not grow and remain confined to a particular area but starts destroying the normal cells and tissues of that part of the brain. Therefore this grade is also a serious issue for the patient's health. On the other hand if we talk about the high grade tumors, they spread in the body part with time. These are very dangerous for patient's health and should be treated as early as possible. They spread in the brain exponentially replacing the normal cells with the infected ones by killing the tissues and veins of the brain, which eventually result in the brain to die slowly.

Cancer is an anomalous cell expansion that has the possibility of invading to remaining organs. It involves a group of diseases.Cancer is prominent factor of death worldwide. Brain tumor is a collection of anomalous cells in brain. Brain is very rigid and encircled with skull any growth inside this restricted place can lead to problems. When these tumors grow inside the brain it raises intra cranial pressure, which can cause brain damage and may also cause throttle of life.

The benign tumors are those which do not invade to other parts of the body. Benign brain tumors are normally characterized as a class of identical cells that grow patterns and do not result normal cell partition and grow into a group of cells that do not have the peculiar appearance of a cancer under the microscope. The brain tumors at the most benign are identified by MRI brain scans and CT scans. These kinds of tumors normally grow slowly and does not spread into nearby cells or invade to remaining parts of body. These tumors hardly evolve as metastatic i.e., cancerous tumors. Mostly the brain tumors which are benign can be removed and normally these benign tumors do not reoccur after removal. Malignant tumor is formed of tumor tissues, and can spread to neighboring tissues. The process in which the tumor tissues can invade into blood flow or lymph cells and spread to the corresponding cells present in the body is called metasis.

Figure 1. Benign tumorMalignant tumor

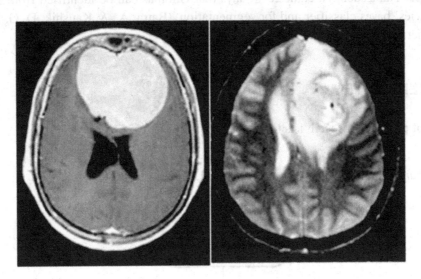

Based on level of hardness, different grades of tumor have been present. They are

- Grade-1 (Pilocytic astrocytoma): least dangerous tumor
- Grade-2 (Low grade astrocytoma): Grade 2 tumor grows normally but casts as anomalous when we view in a microscopic
- Grade-3 (Anaplastic astrocytoma): This type of tumor is malignant but there is no much difference between grade 2 and grade 3 types.
- Grade-4 (Glioblastoma): Grade 4 is complete malignant and dangerous tumor.

The paper script is traced out as follows: in section II, the previous researches related to this paper are discussed. In section III, the proposed system with detailed view of each block is explained. Section IV, shows the obtained results and comparison of accuracy with different techniques.

The system proposed in paper Amin, J. et.al. 2017, is for the detection of brain tumor at an early stage. Based on severity the system classifies image into four grades. The system proposed by Polly. F. P et al., differentiates normal and abnormal tumor. By using SVM techniques we are further classifies it to low grade and high grade (Polly, F. P et.al. 2018),. In paper Dandıl, E., et.al. 2014, they proposed a system that states the classification of normal and abnormal tumor can be done by SVM. Feature extraction is done by gray level occurrence matrix. Probabilistic neural networks can be used for classification (Dandıl, E., et.al. 2014),. A. Batra at.el., proposed a technique that is combination of FCM and SVM is used. Along with that Haar wavelet transform is used for feature extraction (Lavanyadevi, R, et.al. 2017,. N. Kaur et al)., August proposed a system that uses self-adaptive K-means clustering. In that system Sobel edge detection techniques are used to extract the edges.The final segmented image is applied to size estimation algorithm for tumor area and perimeter estimation.

Computer Aided Design for detection of tumor has developed (Chithambaram, T, et.al. 2017), .SVM and ANN are used for classification of tumor. The Glioblastomas in Brain MRI are clustered by K-means, (Kaur, N., et.al. 2017), and segmented Using Machine Learning Techniques Janani, V., et.al.

2013,. The paper Nabizadeh, N, et.al. 2014, says that Gliomas can be identified from MRI image of brain using navies' bayes classifier and for segmentation, (Batra, A., & Kaushik, D. G. 2017). we can use adaptive thersholding.

II. PROPOSED SYSTEM

The structure of proposed research is shown below.

Figure 2. Mechanized system for tumor detection

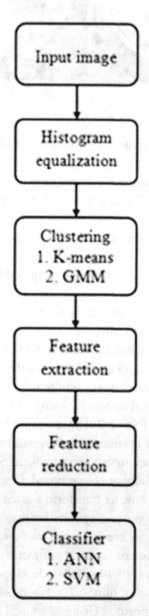

Detailed explanation of each block of the structure is given below

A. Input Image

The dataset was taken from BRATS2017. The size of the database is 16.16MB (benign is 9.03MB and malignant is 7.13MB).

Figure 3. Sample images from dataset

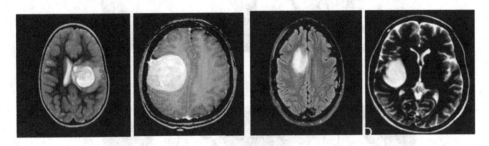

B. Histogram Equalization

Histogram equalization is method for modifying image intensities to improve contrast.
There are different kinds of histogram equalization techniques. They are

1. Local Histogram Equalization
2. Global Histogram Equalization
3. Brightness preserving Bi-Histogram Equalization
4. Dualistic Sub-Image Histogram Equalization
5. Recursive Sub-Image Histogram Equalization
6. Recursive Mean Separate Histogram Equalization

1. Local histogram equalization (LHE):

LHE implements block-overlapped technique, which is sub-block implementation to enhance the image. Then centre pixel value is calculated of sub-block, for CDF using typical HE. The sub-block is moved one by one pixel and repeated to get the desired output image. DHE algorithm mainly focuses on performing enhancement of the image without losing important details contained it. This method decomposes the input image histogram into many sub- sections until a new histogram is constructed that does not contain any dominating part in it. All the dynamic grey level in each of the sub-histogram is then mapped by typical HE method. All the available dynamic grey levels are divided between sub-sections on the basis of their dynamic range present in the original image and also with respect to the cumulative distributive frequency values of histograms. Separate transformation function is calculated for each sub divisions on the basis of traditional HE method having the grey levels of both original and resultant picture that are mapped.

Figure 4. Some of the histogram equalized images

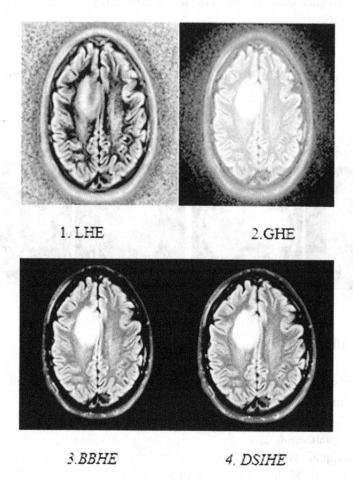

1. LHE   2.GHE

3.BBHE   4. DSIHE

LHE gives good contrast enhancement which can sometimes be considered over-enhancement which is the limitation of this method. LHE technique is complex than other algorithms as for every image pixel local histogram is build and processed.

2.   Global histogram equalization (GHE):

To enhance the contrast of image we use GHE. The basic idea is to yield an image that has evenly assigned grey levels. To generate better histogram the GHE levels out and expand the active extent of grey ranges.

3.   Brightness preserving Bi-Histogram Equalization (BBHE):

BBHE is the process where we partition histogram into sub histograms. In this method first we need to find the histogram of input image then we equalize both sub-histograms separately, then we combine them which is the output of BBHE. BBHE algorithm is basically the upgraded version of typical HE whose main goal is to preserve brigthness and avoid false coloring. This technique partition the input picture histogram into two sub parts. The division is carried out using the average intensity of all the pixels which is said to be the input mean brightness value of all pixels that is present in the input image. After the division process using mean, these two histograms are equalized independently using the typical histogram equalization method. After performing this step, it is observed that, in the resultant image, mean brightness is present exactly between the input mean and the middle gray level. Then the two equalized images are combined together to get the resultant image. This method increases the brightness as well as the contrast of each and every pixel in a well defined manner. Using this idea it is proved that the original brightness of the input image is not lost. The partitioning is done based on mean value of grey levels. Usually the grey level is 0 to 255. So we divide the sub-histograms as 0 to L and L-1 to 255. This process is done mainly to preserve brightness. By using BBHE we can change the intensity values by preserving brightness.

4.   Dualistic Sub-Image Histogram Equalization (DSIHE):

The DSIHE is also similar to BBHE, here also we partition the histogram of image into sub-histograms then we perform equalization. The main variation between BBHE and DSIHE is the way of partitioning. In DSIHE the histogram is divided into bright image and dark image, to avoid false coloring. The partitioning is based on parameters like median of grey scale level.

C. K-Means Clustering

The machine learning technique that can group similar objects based on their properties is known as K-means clustering. It groups the objects in K clusters, where K is non-negative integer. Clustering is made by calculating the minimum value for sum of squares of distances amongcluster centroid to equivalent data. The K-mean clustering is used to distinguish information into similar groups. K-means is a method to cluster the image into K segments such that points in each cluster tend to be near to each other. It is an unsupervised method because it does not uses external classification to segment the image. Here, as we are dealing with medical images like, brain tumor image, so the picture will be segmented according to the gray level values. Area is segmented according to the center of each cluster which is the mean of data points belonging to each cluster. It is basically a method to classify or group the pixels according to the features into K groups. This process is done to locate the Region of Interest (ROI) and its boundaries in the image. If the value of K=2 then the image will be divided into K gray levels, if K=3 then into K clusters, and so on. Liu, J. W., ., et.al. 2015,

The mathematical representation of Euclidean distance that is required to cluster is

$$D = \sqrt{(p_i - q_i)^2 + (p_j - q_j)^2} \tag{1}$$

Where (p_i, p_j) are the points of centroid of cluster and (q_i, q_j) are the data points. K-means is centroid based clustering technique since the main principle of trooping is depend on distance of sample to centroid.

The points tangled for K-means clustering are

1.   Consider the value of k which is equal to number of clusters.

Figure 5. K-means clustering

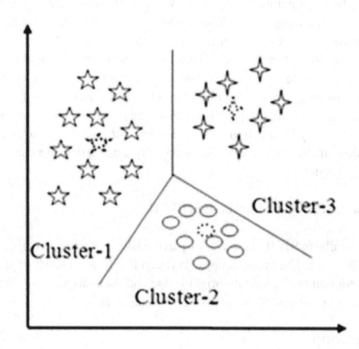

2. Classify the data into k clusters, by assigning the training samples randomly at any initial partition as the following:
    i. The single-element clusters are taken from the first k training samples.
    ii. The samples that are remained i.e., (N-k) training samples are assigned to each cluster which is present in nearest centroid. The centroid of the achieving cluster is recomputed after each assignment.

    By performing the mean of all the samples present in the cluster the new centroid is arrived.
    New centroid,

$$N_i = \frac{1}{n} \sum_{y_j \to N_i} y_j(p) \tag{2}$$

3. Consider each and every sample one by one and calculate its path from the each of the clusters to its centroid. If any sample is not closest to the centroid of the cluster which it is currently present then shift the point to its closest group and revise the centroid of the new group achieving the point and that of old group is discharging the point.
4. Continue the process till concurrence is reached i.e., till the process of updating achieving and discharging cluster has no new positions.

If the number of data samples present is fewer when compared to number of clusters then we consider the centroid as data itself. The cluster number was given to that centroid.

Similarly, if the number of data samples present are larger when compared to number of clusters. Then calculate the distance from data to centroid of each cluster. The data belongs to particular cluster which has minimum distance from the data to centroid.

D. Gaussian Mixture Model

The probabilistic model that resembles normally distributed subpopulations from the overall population is known as Gaussian mixture models. In general mixture models don't require any basic knowledge of which subpopulation the data point has to be placed with, enabling the model to become familiar with the subpopulations consequently. At the beginning we don't know the subpopulation arrangement hence we comprise it as a type of unsupervised learning.

Let the parameters of Gaussian component denoted as $\varphi_i = \{\phi_i, \mu i, \Sigma_i\}$, where ϕ_i is known as the blending coefficient, it depicts the general load of ith component of the whole model. The vector of mean is μ_i, Σ_i is known as the co-variance matrix and mean of vector is indicated by μ_i. The complete model can be written $\psi = \{k, \varphi i..., \varphi k\}$, the number of component in the data are represented by k.

The marginal distribution of each class y is

$$M(y) = \sum_{q=1}^{n} \pi_q N(x \mid \mu_q, \Sigma_q) \tag{3}$$

Where π_q is the probability of cluster, μ_z is the mean of the cluster and $\sum_z$ is co-variance matrix of cluster.

The likelihood function for probability model is represented as

$$L(\pi, \mu, \Sigma) = \prod_{j=1}^{m} \sum_{q=1}^{n} \pi_q N(x \mid \mu_q, \Sigma_q) \tag{4}$$

From the equation above, the log likelihood function is

$$L(\pi, \mu, \Sigma) = \log(\prod_{j=1}^{m} \sum_{q=1}^{n} \pi_q N(x \mid \mu_q, \Sigma_q)) \tag{5}$$

The Gaussian Mixture Model log likelihood function is

$$J(\pi, \mu, \Sigma) = \sum_{j=1}^{m} \log(\sum_{q=1}^{n} \frac{\pi_q}{\sqrt{\mid 2\pi\Sigma \mid}} \exp(\frac{1}{2}(y - \mu)^T \Sigma^{-1}(y - \mu)) \tag{6}$$

The parameters of each class mixture model can be estimated using standard expectation maximization algorithm in a maximum likelihood formulation.

To estimate a better first data, these new values are recursively used by filling up missing points until the values get fixed.

These are mainly two key points of the Exception Maximization algorithm.

- Estimation step: In this step we initialize Σ_q, μ_q and π_q by some random values.. The value of the latent variables is estimated for those given parameter values.
- Maximization Step: In this step update the value of the parameters calculated using ML method.

The parameters of a new cluster with new estimators are

$$\mu_c^{new} = \frac{1}{m_c} \sum_{j=1}^{m} \gamma_j^c x_i \tag{7}$$

$$\Sigma_c^{new} = \frac{1}{m_c} \sum_{j=1}^{m} \gamma_j^c x_i (y_j - \mu_c^{new})(y_j - \mu_c^{new})^T \tag{8}$$

$$\pi_c^{new} = \frac{n_c}{n} \tag{9}$$

Where, γ_j^c is the probability from desired value y_j that arrives by cluster is

$$\gamma_j^l = \frac{\pi_l N(y_j \mid \mu_l \Sigma_l)}{\sum_{c=1}^{n} \pi_c N(x_j \mid \mu_c, \Sigma_c)} \tag{10}$$

Steps of GMM:

i. First Load the dataset
ii. Then plot the dataset
iii. Now fit the data as a mixture of k Gaussians.
iv. Then assign a label to each observation and perform clustering. Also find the converged log-likelihood value by finding the number of iterations needed for the log-likelihood function to converge.
v. Print the no. of iterations needed for the model to converge and its log-likelihood value.

E. Feature Extraction

The optimal features are extracted by dwt. In this paper 2-level DWT is used for extraction of features. The procedure of dissipation of the image into required number of levels using DWT is called feature extraction. For proper approximation these N levels are filtered and terminated and the detailed coefficients are extracted. The optimal features are extracted out the DWT coefficients. The generated DWT

Figure 6. GMM trooping

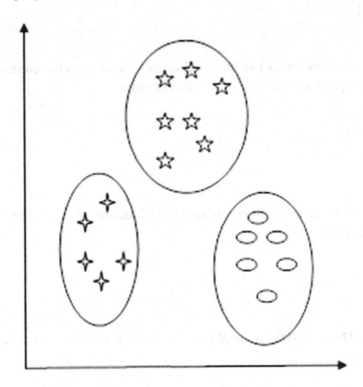

coefficients are treated as favourable features and are applied as input to the SVM classifiers. Because of quadratic and packed backing capacity, the family of daubechies wavelet is the most accepted amongst the family of wavelets that is utilized for analysis of texture features. To revert all the variations between pixel intensities the wavelet uses overlapping windows, the DWT performs the average over more number of pixels hence it is effortless when compared to remaining wavelets. In this projected paper DWT is used which can be disintegrated into two levels. The output of early level calculated component is utilized as an input to the second level and the approximated value from second level is given to third level and so on.

Some of the features are given below

Contrast: Contrast is the calculation of variation among maximum pixel intensity and minimum pixel intensity.

$$C_{on} = \sum_{i=0}^{p-1} \sum_{j=0}^{q-1} (i-j)^2 M(i,j) \tag{11}$$

Energy: Energy is the limited variation in picture. This estimates the consistency present in the picture.

$$\varepsilon = \sqrt{\sum_{i=0}^{p-1}\sum_{j=0}^{q-1} M^2\left(i,j\right)} \tag{12}$$

Correlation: Correlation estimates how the pixel depends linearly on the corresponding pixels. It measures how the corresponding pixels are similar to each other.

$$C = \frac{\sum_{i=0}^{p-1}\sum_{j=0}^{q-1}\left(i,j\right) M\left(i,j\right) - \mu_i \mu_j}{\sigma_i \sigma_j} \tag{13}$$

Entropy: Entropy estimates the destruction of signal in a broadcasted image, furthermore calculates the data present in the picture.

$$E = -\sum_{i=0}^{p-1}\sum_{j=0}^{q-1} M\left(i,j\right)\log_2 M\left(i,j\right) \tag{14}$$

Inverse Difference Moment: IDM is mainly used to check whether the structure belongs to same quality or of similar kind.

$$I = \sum_{i=0}^{p-1}\sum_{j=0}^{q-1}\frac{1}{1+\left(i-j\right)^2} M\left(i,j\right) \tag{15}$$

Kurtosis: It describes the frame of a random variables probability distribution.

$$k = \left(\frac{1}{p \times q}\right)\frac{\sum\left(M\left(i,j\right)-\mu_i\right)^4}{\sigma_i^4} \tag{16}$$

Skewness: Skewness is an estimate of similar pixels or the pixels that loss symmetry.

$$S = \left(\frac{1}{p \times q}\right)\frac{\sum\left(M\left(i,j\right)-\mu_i\right)^3}{\sigma_i^3} \tag{17}$$

Mean: The standard metrics are mainly computed by using mean. Mean of a signal calculates the donation of single picture element that esteems to whole picture.

$$\mu = \left(\frac{1}{p \times q}\right)\sum_{i=0}^{p-1}\sum_{j=0}^{q-1} M\left(i,j\right) \tag{18}$$

Variance: The variance of the image is the average squared difference of mean.

$$\sigma^2 = \sum_{i=1}^{p}\sum_{j=1}^{q}\left(M\left(i,j\right) - \mu_i\mu_j\right)^2 \tag{19}$$

RMS: RMS is nothing but the square root calculation of mean of each squared pixels present in an image.

$$MSE = \left(\frac{1}{p \times q}\right)\sum_{i=0}^{p-1}\sum_{j=0}^{q-1}M^2\left(i,j\right) \tag{20}$$

Standard deviation: It measures the variation of image with respect to mean. Mathematically, it is the square root of variance is measured as standard deviation.

$$SD = \sqrt{\sum_{i=1}^{p}\sum_{j=1}^{q}\left(M\left(i,j\right) - \mu_i\mu_j\right)^2} \tag{21}$$

Homogeneity: It measures the non-zero entries.

$$H = \sum_{i=0}^{p-1}\sum_{j=0}^{q-1}\frac{M\left(i,j\right)}{1+\|\,i-j\,\|} \tag{22}$$

Smoothness: It is performed to reduce noise in pixels. Smoothness is unit amount that symbolize the whole image.

$$S_m = 1 - \frac{1}{\sum_{i=0}^{p-1}\sum_{j=0}^{q-1}M\left(i,j\right)} \tag{23}$$

F. Feature Reduction

PCA calculation is fundamentally used to reduce features after performing DWT. PCA decimates the most of the unnecessary information by transforming the original dataset in terms of principal components. Now the features will be more minimum and accurate, the collection of larger dimensional data present in MRI data is done very easily. The most primary advantage of utilizing PCA is it reduces the computational load on classifier. By doing so the classifier classifies the data easily with less complexity and fast speed. The system with feature reduction and without has a lot of difference in compilation speed and complexity.

G. Classification

a) ANN: Artificial Neural Networks is a machine learning algorithm. It is a frame work of different techniques that work with complex data. The number of neurons used is 10. Inputs of the network are represented by the symbol X_n. Each of the input is multiplexed by its corresponding weight W_n. The resultant of this multiplexer is added and send over transfer function to produce output.

$$S = w_1x_1 + w_2x_2 + \ldots\ldots + w_nx_n \tag{24}$$

Figure 7. Structure of Artificial Neural Networks

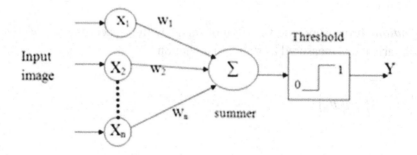

The steps involved in ANN are

- ANN first sets the initial values randomly
- It then takes the input data i.e., images
- Then it computes the output by using transfer function i.e., calculating equation(24) and threshold value
- Now it uses RMSE to compare the difference.
- After knowing the difference it changes the weights correspondingly.
- This loop continues until the threshold condition is satisfied.

b) SVM: Machine learning contains two different types of learning. They are supervised learning and unsupervised learning. SVM comes under supervised learning model used regression analysis and for classification. It is correlated with learning algorithms that analyze data. Here we are using SVM classifier.

- SVM is based on supervised learning. It is a binary classifier.
- SVM creates a hyper plane between two classes and classifies them.
- It learns from the past input data and makes predictions on future output.
- Depending upon the training data, it works and tries to find hyper plane which has the maximum distance from adjacent data point of any training class.

SVMs not only perform linear classification efficiently, they can also achieve a non-linear classification with the help of kernel trick. Kernel trick is essentially matching the inputs into their larger spatial

Figure 8. Block diagram of SVM classifier

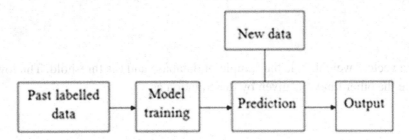

component spaces. Extreme points as regards to hyper plane are support vectors. If we were not having a perfect boundary value, we cannot correctly classify the data. D+ is smallest distance to the nearest positive point and D- is smallest distance to the nearest negative point. The margin is whole region of positive and negative points. The line that divides the positive and negative plane is hyper plane. Since it classifies the linear data, this is also known as linear support vector machine.

The above figure shows how SVM performs classification. It creates hyper plane with the help vectors. In the figure both dotted lines represents the support vectors. They help us to differentiate whether the tumor is benign or malignant. The place between these vectors is known as hyper plane. The samples above the hyper plane belong to one kind and below the plane correspond to other kind. This bifurcation is done based on the features i.e., the thirteen features which we extracted in subsection E.

Figure 9. SVM hyper plane

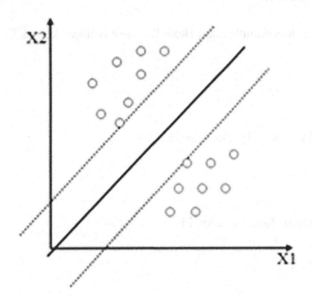

The upper dotted line is represented by the equation

P.Y-t=1 $\qquad$ (25)

Where P is the vectors weight, Y is the sample of database and t is threshold. The lower dotted line is used to separate the other kind it is given by the equation as

P.Y-t=-1 $\qquad$ (26)

The line between the vectors is

P.Y-t=0 $\qquad$ (27)

This arrangement of vectors is known as hyper plane. The maximum distance between the two support vectors is $\dfrac{2}{\|P\|}$ .If we need to increase the distance, the amount of ‖P‖ has to be decremented.

To classify non linear data we go for higher dimensions i.e., we convert 1d to 2d or other higher dimensions which is estimated to be more expensive. Hence we are going for a kernel trick. The kernel is a function that takes vectors in computational space as input and results the inner product of those points in future arena is kernel function or kernel trick.There are some popular kernel types

- Linear kernel
- Polynomial kernel
- Random basis function kernel.

The kernel function that is less complex and flexible to use is linear kernel.The equation for linear kernel is

$$G(y_p, y_q) = y_p.y_q$$ (28)

The equation that is used to find polynomial kernel is

$$G(y_p, y_q) = (y_p^T y_q)^n$$ (29)

The equation for random basis function kernel is

$$G(y_p, y_q) = \exp(-\lambda \mid y_p - y_q \mid)^2$$ (30)

III. RESULTS AND DISCUSSION

The database is of MRI images of brain. The results are computed using MATLAB.The outcomes are plotted by using confusion matrix. Confusion matrix gives the parameters like true positive, true negative and efficiency. Accuracy is the ratio of real positive and real negative.

Figure 10. Confusion matrix

True class

		Positive	Negative	
Predicted values	**Positive**	True positive TP	False positive FP	Positive predicted value $= \dfrac{TP}{FP+TP}$
	Negative	False negative FN	True negative TN	Negative predicted value $= \dfrac{TN}{FN+TN}$
		Sensitivity $\dfrac{TP}{FN+TP}$	Specificity $\dfrac{TN}{FP+TN}$	Accuracy $\dfrac{TP+TN}{TP+FP+FN+TN}$

The dataset is taken from BRATS2017. The whole number of images in data set is 451, they consists of both benign brain tumor images and malignant brain tumor images. Amongst the 451 images the benign tumor images are 247 and malignant tumor images are 203. Out of 247 benign images 172 are used for training and 75 for testing. Similarly, out of 203 malignant brain images 142 are used for training and 61 images are used as testing dataset.The Figure 11 gives the step by step pictorial representation of detection and classifier.

Step 1. Images (Fig a) from database which is given as input.

Step2. Equalized image (Fig b) here we can clearly see that the intensity of each pixel is increased after performing equalization.

Step3. The Fig c is the output image of k-means clustering. Here the number of clusters assumed as 3. Hence the K value is 3. The clustering segmented the image into three parts.

Step4, The Fig d is the output of GMM. The GMM segmented the image into five segments. The segmented parts of GMM are much clearer than K-means.

Step5. The Fig e segmented image. This gives the exact tumor portion from the given input image, the segmented image is given as input to classifier. The classifier displays a dialog box as shown in below figure and tells us whether the tumor is benign or malignant.

Figure 11. step by step pictorial representation of detection and classifier: a) Input image b) Histogram equalizer c) k-means clustered image d) GMM e) Segmented image

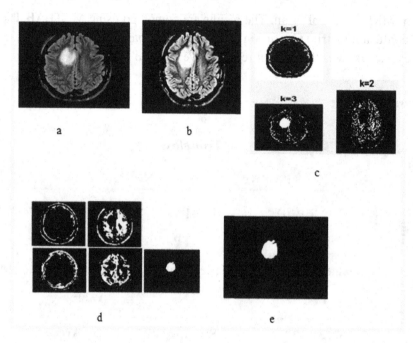

In this paper we are performing segmentation and classification by using different combinations like SVM, K-means and SVM, GMM and ANN, K-means and ANN, GMM with histogram equalization and also without histogram equalization. The accuracy of segmentation and classification with these different techniques were plotted in the table given below.

By using K-means for segmentation and SVM for classification the accuracy achieved is 97.1% in paper Amin, J. et.al. 2017,. In this proposed work we are using GMM for segmentation and SVM for classification with histogram equalization the accuracy achieved is 98.4%. The proposed system gives better accuracy than previous works. The high contrast of histogram equalization enhanced the tumor part and GMM segments the tumor part more precisely, due to these reasons there is an improvement in the accuracy of proposed system.

IV. CONCLUSION AND FUTURE WORK

In this paper, the automatic system is introduced to detect the tumor in the brain image. The aim of this work is to propose a system that can detect tumor with better accuracy. The tumor images are segmented using k-means clustering and GMM. These tumor images are classified into benign and malignant using ANN and SVM. This system is verified using different equalization techniques. By comparing all the results as tabulated in TABLE III, the blend of GMM and SVM with Brightness preserving Bi-Histogram Equalization (BBHE) gave better accuracy. The future work can be done to improve the performance of classifier by using different classifiers. We can also make changes in feature extraction i.e., by extracting optimized features we can improve the performance of classifier.

Table 1. shows the features extracted from multiple test images.

Parameters	Test Image1	Test Image2	Test Image3
No. of white pixels	1224	4747	1465
Area	426	1224	717
Perimeter	117.453	138.252	135.63
Contrast	0.0751	0.2237	0.2989
Correlation	0.9662	0.9584	0.9527
Energy	0.9617	0.8606	0.8591
Homogeneity	0.996	0.9987	0.9906
Mean	3.8808	16.7536	17.3523
Standard Deviation	28.2866	60.3934	62.907
Entropy	0.1339	0.3749	0.6839
RMS	10.465	33.5422	2.6602
Variance	0.016	0.0512	0.0576
Smoothness	1	1	1
Kurtosis	12.5456	53.7946	12.3476
Skewness	3.375	7.2286	3.3624
IDM	0.1172	1.7462	1.2871
Grade	Benign	Malignant	Malignant

Table 2. Comparison of different techniques

	Histogram Equalizer	Segmenatation	Classification	Accuracy
Proposed	DSIHE	GMM	SVM	98.4
	DSIHE	K-Means	SVM	96
	DSIHE	GMM	ANN	97.3
	DSIHE	K-Means	ANN	91.5
	BBHE	GMM	SVM	93.4
	BBHE	K-Means	SVM	89.4
	BBHE	GMM	ANN	90.2
	BBHE	K-Means	ANN	86.2
	GHE	GMM	SVM	85.9
	GHE	K-Means	SVM	82.5
	GHE	GMM	ANN	83.3
	GHE	K-Means	ANN	81.7
	LHE	GMM	SVM	79.8
	LHE	K-Means	SVM	72.9
	LHE	GMM	ANN	75.9
	LHE	K-Means	ANN	70
	Without HE	GMM	SVM	83.5
	Without HE	K-Means	SVM	90

REFERENCES

Amien, M. B., Abd-elrehman, A., & Ibrahim, W. (2013). An intelligent-model for automatic brain-tumor diagnosis based-on MRI images. *International Journal of Computers and Applications*, *72*(23).

Amin, J., Sharif, M., Yasmin, M., & Fernandes, S. L. (2017). A distinctive approach in brain tumor detection and classification using MRI. *Pattern Recognition Letters*. doi:10.1016/j.patrec.2017.10.036

Batra, A., & Kaushik, D. G. (2017). SECTUBIM: Automatic Segmentation And Classification of Tumeric Brain MRI Images using FHS (FCM HWT and SVM). *International Journal of Engineering Science and Computing*, *7*(6), 13190–13194.

Chithambaram, T., & Perumal, K. (2017, September). Brain tumor segmentation using genetic algorithm and ANN techniques. In *2017 IEEE International Conference on Power, Control, Signals and Instrumentation Engineering (ICPCSI)* (pp. 970-982). IEEE. 10.1109/ICPCSI.2017.8391855

Dandıl, E., Çakıroğlu, M., & Ekşi, Z. (2014, September). Computer-aided diagnosis of malign and benign brain tumors on MR images. In *International Conference on ICT Innovations* (pp. 157-166). Springer.

Devasena, C. L., & Hemalatha, M. (2013). Efficient computer aided diagnosis of abnormal parts detection in magnetic resonance images using hybrid abnormality detection algorithm. *Open Computer Science*, *3*(3), 117–128.

Gonzalez, R. C., & Woods, R. E. (2002). *Digital Image Processing* (2nd ed.). Prentice Hall.

Janani, V., & Meena, P. (2013). Image segmentation for tumor detection using fuzzy inference system. *Int J Comput Sci Mobile Comput*, *2*(5), 244–248.

Kaur, N., & Sharma, M. (2017, August). Brain tumor detection using self-adaptive K-means clustering. In *2017 International Conference on Energy, Communication, Data Analytics and Soft Computing (ICECDS)* (pp. 1861-1865). IEEE. 10.1109/ICECDS.2017.8389771

Lavanyadevi, R., Machakowsalya, M., Nivethitha, J., & Kumar, A. N. (2017, April). Brain tumor classification and segmentation in MRI images using PNN. In *2017 IEEE International Conference on Electrical, Instrumentation and Communication Engineering (ICEICE)* (pp. 1-6). IEEE. 10.1109/ICEICE.2017.8191888

Liu, J. W., & Guo, L. (2015, July). Selection of initial parameters of K-means clustering algorithm for MRI brain image segmentation. In *2015 International Conference on Machine Learning and Cybernetics (ICMLC)* (Vol. 1, pp. 123-127). IEEE. 10.1109/ICMLC.2015.7340909

Nabizadeh, N., John, N., & Wright, C. (2014). Histogram-based gravitational optimization algorithm on single MR modality for automatic brain lesion detection and segmentation. *Expert Systems with Applications*, *41*(17), 7820–7836. doi:10.1016/j.eswa.2014.06.043

Polly, F. P., Shil, S. K., Hossain, M. A., Ayman, A., & Jang, Y. M. (2018, January). Detection and classification of HGG and LGG brain tumor using machine learning. In *2018 International Conference on Information Networking (ICOIN)* (pp. 813-817). IEEE. 10.1109/ICOIN.2018.8343231

Ramaswamy Reddy, A., Prasad, E. V., & Reddy, L. S. S. (2013). Comparative analysis of brain tumor detection using different segmentation techniques. *International Journal of Computer Applications, 82*(14).

Chapter 3
Breast Ultrasound Image Processing

Strivathsav Ashwin Ramamoorthy
https://orcid.org/0000-0003-2195-3428
National Institute of Technology, Tiruchirappali, India

Varun P. Gopi
https://orcid.org/0000-0001-5593-3949
National Institute of Technology, Tiruchirappali, India

ABSTRACT

Breast cancer is a serious disease among women, and its early detection is very crucial for the treatment of cancer. To assist radiologists who manually delineate the tumour from the ultrasound image an automatic computerized method of detection called CAD (computer-aided diagnosis) is developed to provide valuable inputs for radiologists. The CAD systems is divided into many branches like pre-processing, segmentation, feature extraction, and classification. This chapter solely focuses on the first two branches of the CAD system the pre-processing and segmentation. Ultrasound images acquired depends on the operator expertise and is found to be of low contrast and fuzzy in nature. For the pre-processing branch, a contrast enhancement algorithm based on fuzzy logic is implemented which could help in the efficient delineation of the tumour from ultrasound image.

INTRODUCTION

Breast cancer is one of the most common cancers and it is still a serious disease among women in the world. It can be inferred that despite the advances made by healthcare technology in the last few decades, the diagnosis of breast cancer is still a prominent problem. Early detection of breast cancer is vital to start the treatment early for cancer patients. Commonly used methods for aiding in the detection of breast cancer are mammography and ultrasonography.

DOI: 10.4018/978-1-7998-6690-9.ch003

Mammography has been one of the most reliable methods for early diagnosis of breast cancer since it has reduced the mortality rates due to cancer by 30% – 70%. But, the sensitivity of mammography is affected due to image quality and the radiologist's level of expertise. Moreover, mammography wasn't found to be effective in the detection of tumours for young patients with dense breasts. The ultrasonic detection makes use of high-frequency sound waves to produce ultrasound images of internal organs within the human body. The breast ultrasound (BUS) imaging is non-invasive, does not involve radiation, and provides real-time detection because of which it is one of the most prevalently used methods for tumour detection. The ultrasound images acquired depends on the operator expertise and the majority of the images were of low contrast, the boundaries of the tumour region were not clear and fuzziness present in the images made the task of identification and manual delineation of tumours time consuming for the radiologists resulting in a delay and in cases not detecting the tumour in the image.

To help radiologists assist in the tumour detection, researchers and engineers working in the field of breast imaging came up with the idea of developing Computer-Aided Diagnosis (CAD) of tumour detection as it could help radiologists provide valuable inputs, in turn, speeding up the process of tumour detection as it is vital to start the treatment early. A CAD system is divided into branches like pre-processing, segmentation, feature extraction, classification. The crucial step in developing a CAD-based system for tumour detection is to choose a segmentation framework that extracts the tumour from the ultrasound image with higher accuracy. But this can be difficult in most of the ultrasound images due to the low contrast, speckle noise in the images, etc., In this chapter, we will focus on the image pre-processing and extraction of features based on texture to improve the process of segmentation of ultrasound images in a CAD system.

BACKGROUND

The ultrasound images acquired during ultrasonography were found to be of low contrast, fuzzy in nature, not having properly defined shapes, and in cases having tumours of different densities. The pre-processing branch of CAD does contrast enhancement to visually enhance the image without changing the features of the images and is subjected to further steps like segmentation and classification of tumours.

So, what is image enhancement? It is the process of applying transformations to obtain a visually enhanced image to reveal more details is referred to as image enhancement. Many algorithms have been specifically developed by researchers to enhance ultrasound images. According to (Gonzalez & Woods, 2001), the majority of the image enhancement algorithms developed can be grouped within categories like point operations, spatial operations, and transform operations.

Point operations consist of contrast stretching, window slicing, and histogram modelling. Algorithms like histogram equalization and linear contrast stretching are automatic. The limitation of the point operations is that these operations process the image pixel by pixel. Now let us see what spatial operations are. The term spatial refers to the image plane and spatial operations mean direct manipulation of pixels in an image. The limitations of these operations are there is excessive enhancing of noise and smoothening particular areas of the image which need sharpening.

(Munteanu & Rosa, 2004) proposed a novel objective criterion for enhancement with the employment of an evolutionary algorithm based on genetic algorithms as a global search strategy for obtaining the best enhancement. The limitation of this algorithm is that it requires high computational power as more iterations are required to arrive at a result. (Guo et al., 2006) use a contrast enhancement algorithm that incorporates fuzzy logic and takes into account the characteristics of the breast ultrasound images. They normalized the ultrasound image and mapped the image into a fuzzy domain with the application of the maximum Fuzzy Entropy Principle. Edge and texture information is extracted to evaluate the lesion features and the scattering phenomenon of the ultrasound image. Criteria for enhancement are defined by the local information of the ultrasound images.

Segmentation is one of the most crucial tasks in medical image analysis. The objective of segmentation here is to locate the suspicious areas in the breast ultrasound to assist radiologists for diagnosis. Some of the segmentation frameworks for breast cancer segmentation from various literature are graph-based approach, deformable models, deep learning-based approach, thresholding, region growing, watershed, etc., For a segmentation framework to yield results with higher accuracy it is important to have better pre-processing and more features extracted from the US image.

CONTRAST ENHANCEMENT

In this section, our focus will be on the contrast enhancement algorithm used by (Guo et al., 2006)
Steps involved in the pre-processing approach of (Guo et al., 2006):

1) Image normalization.
2) Image fuzzification
3) Edge information and textural information extraction
4) Contrast enhancement using local criteria.
5) Defuzzification.

Image Normalization

Normalization is a process through which we can change the range of pixel intensity values. The need for normalizing the image is because the distribution of grey levels of breast US images may vary largely and the range of intensities is quite narrow. Here, we normalize the ultrasound images by mapping the intensity levels within $[g_{min}, g_{max}]$.

Linear Normalization of the greyscale image is achieved using the following equation:

$$g(i,j) = g_{min} + \frac{(g_{max} - g_{min}) \times (g_o(i,j) - g_{omin})}{(g_{omax} - g_{omin})} \tag{1}$$

In equation (1):

$g_o(i,j)$ and $g(i,j)$ represent the grey levels of a pixel (i,j) before and after normalization
g_{omin} and g_{omax} denote the minimum and maximum intensity levels of the original image.
g_{min} and g_{max} denote the minimum and the maximum intensity levels of the normalized image.
Here, $g_{min}=0$ and $g_{max}=255$.

Image Fuzzification

The concept of fuzzy logic was introduced by Zadeh in 1965 in his proposal of the Fuzzy set theory. Fuzzy logic is based on degrees of truth which include 0 and 1 as extreme cases of truth but also include the various states of truth in between. The fuzzy logic can be applied in image processing to analyze the vague or uncertain properties of the images by considering the values between 0 and 1.

Fuzzy logic has been found useful for many commercial and practical purposes as it helps deal with uncertainty, gives some of the acceptable reasoning at places where there is no accurate reasoning, and helps us to process information by representing in the form of if-then rules.

A fuzzy set is one whose elements will be having degrees of membership with the application of a membership function which might be either a full member (100% membership) or a partial member (between 0% and 100% membership). The membership value is assigned to an element that is not restricted to two values 0 or 1 but it can also have a value in between 0 and 1. A mathematical function that is used to define the degree of an element's membership in a fuzzy set is the membership function.

Let X represent a space of points, with a generic element of X denoted by x. A fuzzy set A in x is characterized by a membership function $f_A(x)$ which associates with each point in X a real number in the interval $[0,1]$.with the value $f_A(x)$ at x representing the grade or degree of membership of x in A. Nearer the value of $f_A(x)$ to unity, higher is the grade or degree of membership of x in A. Commonly used membership functions include Gaussian, Sigmoid, Trapezoidal, etc.,

A collection of different fuzzy approaches of image processing providing a mathematical framework to represent, process the images and also playing an important role in representing uncertain data is referred to as Fuzzy Image Processing. Difficulties in image processing arise due to uncertain data or results. This uncertainty rises due to ambiguity, vagueness, and randomness problems. In Image Processing, the question can be whether a pixel should become darker or brighter than it already is or the question can be how the boundary between two image segments could be identified and so on. These kinds of similar questions can make use of a fuzzy approach because of the uncertainty associated with the questions.

Fuzzy image processing consists of three stages: Fuzzification, modification of membership values, image defuzzification. To deal with the fuzzy nature of the breast US images with the help of fuzzy logic a suitable membership function is found which maps all the elements of the set between 0 and 1.

The membership function used for fuzzification is the S function proposed by (Pal & Majumder, 1986):

$$\mu(i,j) = S\big(g(i,j);x,y,z\big).$$

$$S(g:x,y,z) = \begin{cases} 0 & g \leq x \\ \dfrac{(g-x)^2}{(y-x)(z-x)} & x < g \leq y \\ 1 - \dfrac{(g-z)^2}{(z-y)(z-x)} & y < g \leq z \\ 1 & g > z \end{cases} \tag{2}$$

The value of the *S* function as per equation (2) represents the degree of brightness of the pixel intensities and the function is controlled by parameters x, y, z. The upcoming sections discusses how to calculate the value of the parameters from the histogram of the image.

a) Calculation of parameter *y*. Parameter *y* is determined with the help of the maximum fuzzy entropy principle which states that the greater the value of the entropy more will be the information included.

p_i represents the original probability distribution of grey levels i. ($i=1,2,\ldots,N$) given by equation (5). The entropies of the distributions below and above the threshold t are denoted by $H_l(t)$, $H_g(t)$ respectively, and are defined by equation (3) and (4).

$$H_l(t) = -\sum_{i=1}^{l} \frac{p_i}{P_l} \ln \frac{p_i}{P_l}. \tag{3}$$

$$H_g(t) = -\sum_{i=l+1}^{N} \frac{p_i}{1-P_l} \ln \frac{p_i}{1-P_l}. \tag{4}$$

$$P_l = \sum_{i=1}^{l} p_i. \tag{5}$$

where t denotes the threshold and N is the maximum grey level of the image. The maximum entropy is obtained by the following equation (6):

$$y = Arg \max_{i=1\ to\ N} \left\{ H_l(t) + H_g(t) \right\}. \tag{6}$$

a) Calculation of parameter x, z.

$$h_g(m) = \sum_{m=0}^{\max_{0 \le i, j \le h-1}(g(i,j))} \delta\big(g(i,j)-m\big). \tag{7}$$

$$\delta(t) = \begin{cases} 1, & t=0 \\ 0, & otherwise \end{cases}. \tag{8}$$

where $h_g(m)$ from equation (7) represents the grey-level histogram of the image, m denotes the grey-level of the image, h and w denote the height and width of the image. The value of x, z are given by the grey levels corresponding to the first peak and the last peak of the histogram $h_g(m)$.

By using parameters x, y, z the ultrasound image is transformed from the intensity domain into a fuzzy domain using the S-shaped function by equation (2).

Edge Information Extraction

Among the early indicators of breast cancer, the mass shape, margin, membrane smoothness are the primary features. To obtain the edge features of the tumour, we use an edge operator called the Sobel operator which is applied to the fuzzified image, and then the value of the edge information is normalized.

The Sobel operator performs a 2-D spatial gradient measurement on an image considering both horizontal and vertical directions. It emphasizes regions of high spatial frequency that correspond to edges.

$$G_x = \begin{bmatrix} -1 & 0 & 1 \\ -2 & 0 & 2 \\ -1 & 0 & 1 \end{bmatrix}.$$

$$G_y = \begin{bmatrix} 1 & 2 & 1 \\ 0 & 0 & 0 \\ -1 & -2 & -1 \end{bmatrix}.$$

G_x and G_y denotes the horizontal and vertical Sobel convolution kernels. These kernels are designed to respond maximally to edges running vertically and horizontally relative to the pixel grid, one kernel for each of the two perpendicular orientations. The kernels are applied separately to the input image to produce separate measurements of the gradient component in each orientation which are combined to find the absolute magnitude of the gradient at each point.

The edge information is normalized using equation (9):

$$e_\mu(i,j) = \frac{\delta_\mu(i,j) - \delta_{\mu min}}{\delta_{\mu max} - \delta_{\mu min}}. \tag{9}$$

$\delta_\mu(i,j)$ represents the edge value computed by using the Sobel operator. $\delta_{\mu max}$ denote the maximum edge value of the Sobel operator and $\delta_{\mu min}$ is the minimum edge value of the Sobel Operator.

Texture Information Extraction

The scattering phenomenon in ultrasound images occurs when tissues are comparable to or smaller than the scale of the wavelength and this phenomenon provides information related to small lesions and tissue features. Texture information can give us the knowledge about the group of mutually related pixels in a selected region which is useful for the process of segmentation.

In the early 1980s, in the report titled *Textured image segmentation* Laws (1980) suggested a method on how to measure texture by making use a set of one-dimensional center-weighted vector masks which are row vectors. These row vectors can have three, five, or seven entries in them. Alphabets used in representing the vectors are mnemonics for Level(L), Edge(E), Spot(S), Wave(W), Ripple(R), Undulation(U) and Oscillation(O)

Row vectors of order three

$$L3 = \begin{bmatrix} 1 & 2 & 1 \end{bmatrix}$$

$$E3 = \begin{bmatrix} -1 & 0 & 1 \end{bmatrix}$$

$$S3 = \begin{bmatrix} -1 & 2 & -1 \end{bmatrix}.$$

The above three vectors (L3, E3, S3) serves as a basis for the vectors of order five and seven.

Row vectors of order five

$$L5 = \begin{bmatrix} 1 & 4 & 6 & 4 & 1 \end{bmatrix}$$

$$E5 = \begin{bmatrix} -1 & -2 & 0 & 2 & 1 \end{bmatrix}$$

$$S5 = \begin{bmatrix} -1 & 0 & 2 & 0 & 1 \end{bmatrix}$$

$$W5 = \begin{bmatrix} -1 & 2 & 0 & -2 & 1 \end{bmatrix}$$

$$R5 = \begin{bmatrix} 1 & -4 & 6 & -4 & 1 \end{bmatrix}.$$

The 1×5 vectors are generated by the convolution of any two 1×3 vectors.

Ex: Possible combinations of convolution to generate S5 vector can be $(L3)*(S3),(S3)*(L3),(E3)*(E3)$. Row vectors of order seven

$$L7 = \begin{bmatrix} 1 & 6 & 15 & 20 & 15 & 6 & 1 \end{bmatrix}$$

$$E7 = \begin{bmatrix} -1 & -4 & -5 & 0 & 5 & 4 & 1 \end{bmatrix}$$

$$S7 = \begin{bmatrix} -1 & -2 & 1 & 4 & 1 & -2 & -1 \end{bmatrix}$$

$$W7 = \begin{bmatrix} -1 & 0 & 3 & 0 & -3 & 0 & 1 \end{bmatrix}$$

$$R7 = \begin{bmatrix} 1 & -2 & -1 & 4 & 1 & -2 & -1 \end{bmatrix}$$

$$O7 = \begin{bmatrix} -1 & 6 & -15 & 20 & -15 & 6 & -1 \end{bmatrix}.$$

The 1×7 vectors are generated by the convolution of any 1×3 vector with a 1×5 vector. The properties of these vectors are:

- All the vectors are weighted toward the center.
- All of these are either symmetric or anti-symmetric.
- The vectors in each set are independent, but not orthogonal.

(Guo et al., 2006) use three vectors of order five which are texture descriptors useful in enhancing an image namely Level, Edge, Spot, and with the help of these vectors, four masks are obtained to gather information related to edge and spot features of scattering.

Vector 1: $L5 = \begin{bmatrix} 1 & 4 & 6 & 4 & 1 \end{bmatrix}.$
Vector 2: $E5 = \begin{bmatrix} -1 & -2 & 0 & 2 & 1 \end{bmatrix}.$
Vector 3: $S5 = \begin{bmatrix} -1 & 0 & 2 & 0 & 1 \end{bmatrix}.$

Each of the four masks are obtained from the combination of any two of the 1×3 vectors:

$$L5^T \times E5; L5^T \times S5; E5^T \times L5; S5^T \times L5$$

Mask -1:

$$L5^T \times E5 = \begin{bmatrix} -1 & -2 & 0 & 2 & 1 \\ -4 & -8 & 0 & 8 & 4 \\ -6 & -12 & 0 & 12 & 6 \\ -4 & -8 & 0 & 8 & 4 \\ -1 & -2 & 0 & 2 & 1 \end{bmatrix}$$

Mask -2:

$$
L5^T \times S5 = \begin{bmatrix} -1 & 0 & 2 & 0 & -1 \\ -4 & 0 & 8 & 0 & -4 \\ -6 & 0 & 12 & 0 & -6 \\ -4 & 0 & 8 & 0 & -4 \\ -1 & 0 & 2 & 0 & -1 \end{bmatrix}
$$

Mask-3:

$$
E5^T \times L5 = \begin{bmatrix} -1 & -4 & -6 & -4 & -1 \\ -2 & -8 & -12 & -8 & -2 \\ 0 & 0 & 0 & 0 & 0 \\ 2 & 8 & 12 & 8 & 2 \\ 1 & 4 & 6 & 4 & 1 \end{bmatrix}
$$

Mask-4:

$$
S5^T \times L5 = \begin{bmatrix} -1 & -4 & -6 & -4 & -1 \\ 0 & 0 & 0 & 0 & 0 \\ 2 & 8 & 12 & 8 & 2 \\ 0 & 0 & 0 & 0 & 0 \\ -1 & -4 & -6 & -4 & -1 \end{bmatrix}
$$

Computation of Texture Value

Convolution of the fuzzified image with all the four masks is done individually and with the convolution results the computation of the texture. The texture value at pixel (i,j). $f_\mu(i,j)$ is computed as per equation (10):

$$
f_\mu(i,j) = \frac{abs\left(f_{\mu L5^T \times E5}(i,j)\right)}{f_{\mu L5^T \times E5_{max}}} \times \frac{abs\left(f_{\mu L5^T \times S5}(i,j)\right)}{f_{\mu L5^T \times S5_{max}}} \times \frac{abs\left(f_{\mu E5^T \times L5}(i,j)\right)}{f_{\mu E5^T \times L5_{max}}} \times \frac{abs\left(f_{\mu S5^T \times L5}(i,j)\right)}{f_{\mu S5^T \times L5_{max}}}.
$$

$$
(10)
$$

$$
f_{\mu L5^T \times E5}(i,j), f_{\mu L5^T \times S5}(i,j), f_{\mu E5^T \times L5}(i,j), f_{\mu S5^T \times L5}(i,j)
$$

represents the convolution of $\mu(i,j)$.with four masks.

Here,

$$f_{\mu L5^T \times E5max} = max\left(abs\left(f_{\mu L5^T \times E5}(i,j)\right)\right)$$

$$f_{\mu L5^T \times S5max} = max\left(abs\left(f_{\mu L5^T \times S5}(i,j)\right)\right)$$

$$f_{\mu E5^T \times L5max} = max\left(abs\left(f_{\mu E5^T \times L5}(i,j)\right)\right)$$

$$f_{\mu S5^T \times L5max} = max\left(abs\left(f_{\mu S5^T \times L5}(i,j)\right)\right)$$

respectively where $\left(0 \le i \le h-1, 0 \le j \le w-1\right)$. The *abs*() operator gives the absolute value of an element and the *max*() operator gives the maximum value.

Contrast Enhancement Using Local Criteria

The contrast C is defined as $C = \dfrac{f-b}{f+b}$ .where f and b, denote the maximum and minimum intensity of the image. The above contrast equation is used to track the changes between the current pixel and the neighbouring pixels defined by a window.

The membership value $\mu(i,j)$ .is compared with local mean $\overline{\mu_w}(i,j)$ .ith the help of a window whose size is $w \times w$. To track changes in both the edge and texture information in the fuzzy domain, the local mean value $\overline{\mu_w}(i,j)$ .should be calculated not only by using the membership in a window but also by incorporating the values computed during texture and edge extraction denoted by $f_\mu(i,j)$ .and $e_\mu(i,j)$ .as per equation (10) and equation (9) respectively.. The contrast is given by equation (11):

$$C_\mu(i,j) = \frac{\left|\mu(i,j) - \overline{\mu_w}(i,j)\right|}{\left|\mu(i,j) + \overline{\mu_w}(i,j)\right|}. \tag{11}$$

where $\overline{\mu_w}(i,j)$ .denotes the local mean of a window whose size is $w \times w$ and centered at the location (i,j) computed using equation (12):

$$\overline{\mu_w}(i,j) = \frac{\sum_{m=i-\frac{(w-1)}{2}}^{i+\frac{(w-1)}{2}} \sum_{n=j-\frac{(w-1)}{2}}^{j+\frac{(w-1)}{2}} \left(\mu(m,n) \times f_\mu(m,n) \times e_\mu(m,n)\right)}{\sum_{m=i-\frac{(w-1)}{2}}^{i+\frac{(w-1)}{2}} \sum_{n=j-\frac{(w-1)}{2}}^{j+\frac{(w-1)}{2}} f_\mu(m,n) \times e_\mu(m,n)}. \tag{12}$$

The new contrast C' can be obtained either by using a nonlinear function of C or an empirically determined relationship between C and C'. Analytic functions like square root, exponential, and logarithmic have been predominantly used.

(Guo et al., 2006) use the exponential function $k(i,j)$ to transform C_μ into C'_μ in turn boosting the perceptibility of regions with low contrast without affecting high-contrast regions.

$$C'_\mu(i,j) = \left(C_\mu(i,j)\right)^{k(i,j)}.$$

(13)

In the equation (13) $k(i,j)$ denotes the local contrast amplification constant of a pixel (i,j) and reportedly affects the degree of the contrast enhancement. The amplification constant varies according to the nature of the image.

Local contrast amplification constant $k(i,j)$ is given by equation (14):

$$k(i,j) = k_{min} + \frac{\left(En(i,j) - En_{min}\right) \times \left(k_{max} - k_{min}\right)}{En_{max} - En_{min}}.$$

(14)

where $En(i,j)$ denotes the local fuzzy entropy, En_{max} and En_{min} represent the maximum and minimal local fuzzy entropies, k_{min} and k_{max} denote the minimal and the maximal amplification constants. The upcoming sections focus on how to calculate the amplification constants.

Local Fuzzy Entropy

The local fuzzy entropy, $En(i,j)$ is used to evaluate the uniformity degree of the local region. The amplification exponent constant $k(i,j)$ is determined by $En(i,j)$ using equation (14). If $En(i,j)$ is low then the fuzzy membership of the region varies sharply and the degree of enhancement will be high, which in turn implies that the amplification constant $k(i,j)$ is small. Whereas if $En(i,j)$ is high, the fuzzy membership varies slowly and $k(i,j)$ will be large.

To determine the local fuzzy entropy, the edge and texture features extracted from the image are taken into account and is given by equation (15):

$$E_n(i,j) = -\frac{1}{\log_{10}(w \times w)} \sum_{m=i-\frac{w}{2}}^{i+\frac{w}{2}} \sum_{n=j-\frac{w}{2}}^{j+\frac{w}{2}} \psi_w(m,n) \times \log_{10}\left(\psi_w(m,n)\right).$$

(15)

where, $\psi_w(i,j)$.is:

$$\psi_w(i,j) = \frac{E_\mu(i,j)}{\sum_{m=i-\frac{w}{2}}^{i+\frac{w}{2}} \sum_{n=j-\frac{w}{2}}^{j+\frac{w}{2}} E_\mu(m,n)}.$$

(16)

$$E_\mu(i,j) = \mu(i,j) \times f_\mu(i,j) \times e_\mu(i,j). \tag{17}$$

$$En_{min} = min\{En(i,j)\}; En_{max} = max\{En(i,j)\}. \tag{18}$$

En_{min} and En_{max} denote the minimal and maximal local fuzzy entropies.

$\mu(i,j)$ represent the values after the fuzzification of the original image,

$f_\mu(i,j)$ denote the texture value of pixel (i,j).

$e_\mu(i,j)$ represents the normalized edge information where the *Sobel* operator is used to extract the edge information. The determination of the maximal and minimal amplification constants k_{min} and k_{max} relates to the contrast of the original image. The local contrast of the image is also taken into account along with the global contrast while finding the amplification constants.

The local contrast of the original image $C(i,j)$ is given by equation (19):

$$C(i,j) = \frac{|g(i,j) - g_s(i,j)|}{|g(i,j) + g_s(i,j)|}. \tag{19}$$

$C(i,j)$ represents the local contrast of pixel (i,j) and $g_s(i,j)$ represents the local mean of the grey levels in the window with size $s \times s$ centred at pixel (i,j) given by equation (20):

$$g_s(i,j) = \frac{1}{s \times s} \sum_{m=i-\frac{(s-1)}{2}}^{i+\frac{(s-1)}{2}} \sum_{n=j-\frac{(s-1)}{2}}^{j+\frac{(s-1)}{2}} g(m,n). \tag{20}$$

The mean contrast value of a region R is represented by $\overline{C_R}$ .which is defined by equation (21):

$$\overline{C_R} = \frac{1}{M} \sum_{\substack{0 \le i \le h-1 \\ (i,j) \in G(R)C(i,j)<R}}^{0 \le j \le w-1} C(i,j). \tag{21}$$

In equation (21) h and w denote the height and width of the image. $G(R)$ is a region of the image in which the contrast values of the pixels are smaller than R where R is a very small value less than one. M represents the number of pixels in the region R and $\overline{C_R}$ is the mean contrast value of the region R.

The maximal and minimal amplification constants k_{min} and k_{max} are determined as follows:

$$k_{max} = \frac{\log R}{\log \overline{C_R}} . \text{and } k_{min} = \frac{\log R}{\log C_{min}} . \tag{22}$$

where C_{min} denotes the minimal value of the contrast.

After determining the amplification constants, the contrast is amplified as defined in the equation:

$$C'_\mu (i,j) = \left(C_\mu (i,j) \right)^{k(i,j)}.$$

(23)

After, the contrast is enhanced exponentially by equation (23), contrast values are further modified by equation (24):

$$\mu'(i,j) = \begin{cases} \dfrac{\overline{\mu_w}(i,j)\left(1 + C'_\mu(i,j)\right)}{\left(1 - C'_\mu(i,j)\right)} & \mu(i,j) \geq \overline{\mu_w}(i,j) \\[4mm] \dfrac{\overline{\mu_w}(i,j)\left(1 - C'_\mu(i,j)\right)}{\left(1 + C'_\mu(i,j)\right)} & \mu(i,j) < \overline{\mu_w}(i,j) \end{cases}.$$

(24)

where $\overline{\mu}_w (i,j)$ .epresents the local mean of a window with size $w \times w$ centred at location (i,j).

DEFUZZIFICATION

The enhanced intensity of a pixel is obtained by using the inverse function $S^{-1}\left(\mu'(i,j); x,y,z\right)$ defined in equation (25).

$$g'(i,j) = S^{-1}\left(\mu'(i,j); x,y,z\right)$$

$$= \begin{cases} g_{min} + \dfrac{g_{max} - g_{min}\sqrt{\mu'(i,j)\times(y-x)\times(z-x)}}{z-x} & 0 \leq \mu'(i,j) \leq \dfrac{(y-x)}{(z-x)} \\[4mm] g_{min} + \dfrac{g_{max} - g_{min}}{z-x}\left(z-x-\sqrt{(1-\mu'(i,j))\times(z-y)\times(z-x)}\right) & \dfrac{(y-x)}{(z-x)} < \mu'(i,j) \leq 1 \end{cases}$$

(25)

Here, g_{min} and g_{max} denotes the minimum and maximum grey level after the enhancement. This step brings the image back into intensity domain from fuzzy domain.

BUSIMAGES AFTER CONTRAST ENHANCEMENT

After the enhancement of the images, the next step is to segment the tumour from the ultrasound images.

Figure 1. The image on the left is the acquired image and the image on the right is the contrast-enhanced image.

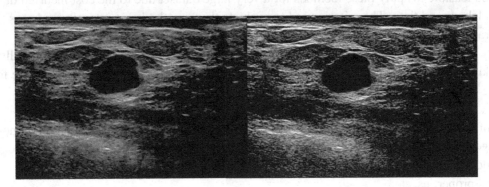

Figure 2. The image on the left is the acquired image and the image on the right is the contrast-enhanced image.

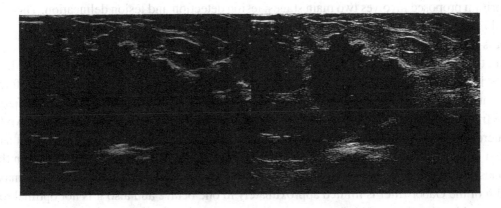

SEGMENTATION

The partitioning of a digital image I into multiple non-overlapping regions such that the union of any two adjacent regions is not homogenous is called Image Segmentation. If $P()$ is a homogeneity predicate which is defined on a group of connected pixels, then segmentation is the partition of the set F into connected subsets or regions $(S_1, S_2, \ldots, S_n)$ such that:

$$U_{i=1}^{n} S_i = F \text{ with } S_i \cap S_j = \Phi (i \neq j).$$

Segmentation frameworks can be classified into semi-automatic and fully automatic according to the degree of human intervention involved in the segmentation process.

i)   Semi-automatic segmentation: In the semi-automated models of segmentation radiologist needs to specify a Region of Interest (ROI) including the lesion, a seed in the lesion, or an initial boundary. Radiologist's interactions are used in cases when it is difficult to segment images due to the poor quality of images. These interactions make these methods more reliant on the operator. It might not be feasible to apply these methods for a very large dataset due to the cost incurred due to human labour and time. The criteria used to evaluate these methods are intensity and sensitivity of interaction.

ii) Fully automatic segmentation: These methods function operator-independent and usually model the knowledge of breast ultrasound as the prior constraints. These methods are suitable for large scale tasks.

Most of the image segmentation frameworks which has been successful in segmenting tumour from BUS images have prior knowledge modelled based on the ultrasound images. Prior knowledge modelled includes intensity distribution, texture, and local region statistics, edge or gradient, layer structure, topological properties, etc.,

(Gomez-Flores & Ruiz-Ortega, 2016) proposed an image segmentation framework that is automatic which makes use of texture for segmenting the tumour cell. The texture of the ultrasound image is one of the important characteristics which can be used to identify the lesion region in an ultrasound image. The algorithm proposed involves two main stages: lesion detection and lesion delineation. The contrast-enhanced image is transformed into a texture domain with the help of Log-Gabor filters.

What is the Log-Gabor filter?

Before the introduction of the Log-Gabor function, one of the most preferred filters to get localized frequency-information was the Gabor function. Gabor's theory suggests that we can represent information present in an image with an amplitude of functions that are localized in terms of both space and frequency.

In the frequency domain, the Gabor transfer functions are constructed as the sum of the two Gaussians centered around the origin of the spectrum. The Gabor function had some limitations as if the bandwidth of the Gaussian function is greater than the one-third of the center frequency then the tails of the Gaussian functions overlap at the origin resulting in a non-zero DC component. The maximum bandwidth of the Gabor filter is limited approximately to one octave and also it is not optimal to use if the user is seeking more spectral information with maximized special localization.

(Field, 1987) in his study of various coding schemes of representing the information present in natural images proposed the Log-Gabor function as a derivative of the Gabor function. The frequency response of the Log-Gabor function is described by equation (26):

$$G(\omega, \theta) = exp\left\{ -\frac{\log(\omega/\omega_o)^2}{2\sigma_\omega^2} \right\} exp\left\{ -\frac{(\theta - \theta_o)^2}{2\sigma_\theta^2} \right\}. \tag{26}$$

where (ω, θ) are the polar coordinates;

ω_o is the filter center frequency;

θ_o is the filter orientation angle;

σ_ω defines the frequency bandwidth;

σ_θ determines the angular bandwidth.

The ratio $k = \sigma_\theta / \sigma_\omega$ .determines the filter bandwidth. The value of k=0.74 will result in a filter bandwidth of approximately one octave, k=0.55 will result in two octaves and k=0.41 will produce three octaves.

Characteristics of Log-Gabor filters

- Log-Gabor functions have no DC component and this overcomes the limitations of the Gabor functions having a DC component.
- Log-Gabor filters are constructed in terms of both radial and angular components. Radial components control the frequency band and require the number of scales. Angular components deal with the orientation selectivity and it requires the number of orientations (θ).

Image filtered by a log-Gabor function in the frequency domain is $F'(u,v) = F(u,v).G(u,v)$ where $G(u,v)$ denotes the expression of the log-Gabor filter in cartesian coordinates, $F(u,v)$ and $F'(u,v)$ denotes the original and filtered spectra of the image respectively. After the filtering has been completed by the bank of log-Gabor filters the real part of the inverse Fourier transform of each filtered spectrum is obtained to recover the spatial domain data containing texture information.

The image is decomposed into a set of texture channels in the frequency domain by using Log-Gabor filters. (Gomez-Flores & Ruiz-ortega, 2016) in their study made use of two octaves, 24 orientations $(\theta = \{0°, 15°, \ldots, 345°\})$ six scales $(S_1, \ldots, S_6)$ to achieve complete coverage of the whole spectrum. To reduce the dimensionality of the feature space, the images of the same scales were averaged over all orientations to create 6 texture channels. Resulting channels are quantized to $Q = 64$ levels, a typical value that is used in ultrasound image texture analysis to reduce the computational cost while adequately preserving details.

TEXTURE FEATURES

To describe the local texture, the texture channels obtained during log-Gabor filtering is divided into overlapping lattices to correlate between adjacent neighbourhoods. A central window is created which overlaps with the four lattices so that the local texture description considers the texture information of the five regions. (Liu B et al., 2009) proposed using the size of lattice of 16×16.pixels and if the tumour region overlaps with the central window then we label it as a "breast lesion".

Texture features which are extracted from the lattices are namely autocorrelation, autocovariance coefficients, GLCM (Gray-Level Co-occurrence Matrix) features, and fractal features. These texture descriptors have been adopted successfully in lesion detection and segmentation of ultrasound images.

Autocorrelation

$\mathcal{L}$ is a single lattice region of size $M \times N$. The autocorrelation feature defined as per equation (27):

$$\tilde{R} = \sum_{n=0}^{N-1} \frac{\overline{R}_n}{\overline{R}_0}. \tag{27}$$

The autocorrelation in terms of depth and the sum in the lateral direction are defined in equation (28) and (29):

$$R_{m,n} = \sum_{k=0}^{N-1-n} \mathcal{L}(m, n+k)^2 \, \mathcal{L}(m,k)^2 . \tag{28}$$

and

$$\bar{R}_n = \sum_{m=0}^{M-1} R_{m,n} . \tag{29}$$

respectively, where $\mathcal{L}(.)$ denotes the intensity of the pixel.

Autocovariance

The normalized autocovariance coefficients describe the inner-intensity variance within the lattice region is defined in equation (30):

$$\bar{S}_{\Delta m, \Delta n} = \frac{S_{\Delta m, \Delta n}}{S_{0,0}} . \tag{30}$$

where the entries of the autocovariance matrix are computed as follows by equation (31):

$$S_{\Delta m, \Delta n} = \frac{\sum_{m,n} \left[\mathcal{L}(m,n) - \bar{\mathcal{L}} \right] \left[\mathcal{L}(m + \Delta m, n + \Delta n) - \bar{\mathcal{L}} \right]}{(M - \Delta m)(N - \Delta n)} . \tag{31}$$

$\bar{\mathcal{L}}$ denotes the mean value of $\mathcal{L}$ and the displacement Δm and Δn have its values in the range from [1,5] because of which a 5×5 autocovariance matrix is generated. The coefficient $S_{0,0}$ is discarded because of its value being always unity due to which the final feature vector contains 24 autocovariance coefficients.

Grey Level Co-Occurrence Matrix (GLCM)

GLCM represents the joint frequencies of all pairwise combinations of intensity i and j separated by a distance of d units along the direction θ and is defined by equation (32):

$$C(i,j) = \left[(m_1, n_1), (m_2, n_2) \right] \mid m_2 - m_1 = d\cos\theta, n_2 - n_1 = d\sin\theta, \mathcal{L}(m_1, n_1) = i, \mathcal{L}(m_2, n_2) = j . \tag{32}$$

where (m_1, n_1) and (m_2, n_2) represent the pixel locations and denotes the number of pixel pairs that satisfy the condition specified. For each lattice, 16 co-occurrence matrices with four directions $(\theta = 0°, 45°, 90°, 135°)$, and four distances ($d$=1,2,4,8) is obtained. Each GLCM is normalized by the sum of all its elements to calculate the co-occurrence probability, $P(i,j)$ such that $\sum_{i,j} P(i,j) = 1$. $p(i,j)$ refers to the $(i,j)^{th}$ entry from the normalized matrix.

$p_x(i)$ refers to the ith entry in the marginal-probability matrix obtained by summing the rows of $p(i,j)$. N_g is Number of distinct grey levels in the quantized image

Table 1. Equations for texture features extracted from GLCM

FEATURES	EQUATION
Contrast	$\sum_{i,j} (i-j)^2 p(i,j)$
Correlation	$\sum_{i,j} \dfrac{(i-\mu_x)(j-\mu_y) p(i,j)}{\sigma_x \sigma_y}$
Entropy	$-\sum_{i,j} p(i,j) log(p(i,j))$
Homogeneity	$\sum_{i,j} \dfrac{p(i,j)}{1+(i-j)^2}$
Sum average	$\sum_{i=2}^{2Q} i \cdot p_{x+y}(i)$
Sum entropy	$-\sum_{i=2}^{2Q} p_{x+y}(i) log(p_{x+y}(i))$

where

Mean: $\mu_x = \sum_i i \sum_j p(i,j), \mu_y = \sum_i j \sum_i p(i,j)$. $\qquad$ (33)

Variance: $\sigma_x^2 = \sum_i (i-\mu_x)^2 \sum_j p(i,j), \sigma_y^2 = \sum_j (j-\mu_y)^2 \sum_i p(i,j)$. $\qquad$ (34)

$P_{x+y}(k) = \sum_{i,j:i+j=k} p(i,j) \, where \, k = 2,3,\dots,2Q$

Six texture features obtained from each GLCM are contrast, entropy, sum average, sum entropy, correlation, and homogeneity. A total of 96 GLCM features are to be extracted. To reduce, the dimensionality of the feature space, texture descriptors with the same distance are averaged over all orientations. Hence, it will result in 24 GLCM features being computed in a single lattice.

Fractal Features

The term fractal refers to sets of pixels that display a degree of self-similarity at different scales. To compute the fractal features, the multiscale intensity difference vector D_k is computed by equation (35):

$$D_k = \frac{1}{4} \left[\begin{array}{l} \frac{1}{a} \sum_{m=0}^{M-1} \sum_{n=0}^{M-k-1} \left| \mathcal{L}(m,n) - \mathcal{L}(m,n+k) \right| + \\ \frac{1}{a} \sum_{n=0}^{M-1} \sum_{m=0}^{N-k-1} \left| \mathcal{L}(m,n) - \mathcal{L}(m+k,n) \right| + \\ \frac{1}{c} \sum_{m=0}^{Mb-1} \sum_{n=0}^{Mb-1} \left| \mathcal{L}(m,n) - \mathcal{L}(m+b,n+b) \right| + \\ \frac{1}{c} \sum_{m=0}^{Mb-1} \sum_{n=0}^{Mb-1} \left| \mathcal{L}(m,M-n) - \mathcal{L}(m+b,M-n+b) \right| \end{array} \right] . \tag{35}$$

where $a = M(M-k)$ $b = k / \sqrt{2}$. $c = (M-b)^2$ and the scaling constant take the values $k = 1, \ldots, 8$. The factional Brownian motion feature vector is calculated as $F_k = \log D_k - \log D_1$. The fractal dimension (FD) feature is slope of the graph F_k vs $\log k$ obtained using linear regression. FD is joined with the vector F_k to form eight fractal features. Feature F_1 is removed since its value is always zero.

After the texture features have been extracted from the lattice, they are concatenated into a single feature vector with 57 attributes. A local texture is described with the help of 5 lattices and is represented with the help of a central window. x_i^j represents the ith texture feature ($i = 1, \ldots, 57$) extracted from j^{th} lattice ($j = 1, \ldots, 5$) in the neighbourhood. Then, the local texture value is calculated as the average $\bar{x}_i = \frac{1}{5} \sum_{j=1}^{5} x_i^j$. Concatenation of the six texture channels from the same neighbourhood results in a feature vector having 342 attributes. For a single central lattice, the feature vector is denoted by $\mathbf{x} = \left[\bar{x}_1, \ldots, \bar{x}_{342} \right]^T$ and its associated class label is $\mathbf{y}$ ('0' for normal tissue and '1' for breast lesion).

ADJACENCY INFORMATION AND LOCATION PROBABILITY

Neighbouring central lattices are more likely to belong to the same texture class. The spatial adjacency information is included as an additional feature. $c = [x_c, y_c]^T$ represent the spatial coordinates of the centroid of the central lattice. To make c .independent of the image size, the coordinates are normalized within the range (0,1) by setting the spatial coordinates to $\hat{x}_c = x_c / W$ and $\hat{y}_c = y_c / H$ where W and H are the width and height of the input image. Hence, the spatial adjacency information is represented by the vector $\hat{c} = \left[\hat{x}_c, \hat{y}_c \right]^T$.

The majority of fully automatic segmentation algorithms employ empirical rules to determine the approximate location of tumour which in most cases is present near the center of the ultrasound image. The limitation is that this assumption isn't capable of generalizing a wide range of images and could result in an error. To overcome the above limitation the adjacency information of actual lesions is taken and used to model their location in the image using a Gaussian probability density function (PDF) p defined by equation (36):

$$p = \exp\left[-\frac{1}{2}\left(\hat{c} - \mu\right)^T \sum\nolimits^{-1} \left(\hat{c} - \mu\right) \right]. \tag{36}$$

where μ is the mean vector, Σ represents the diagonal covariance matrix from the training observations. The larger the value of p, the greater is the probability of it being a tumour region.

Combination of texture features, adjacency information, and location probability results in the final feature vector having 345 attributes. The complete feature set for a single central lattice is denoted as $\mathbf{z} = \left\{ x, \hat{c}, p \right\}$ which is further classified.

STATISTICAL CLASSIFICATION

Central Limit Theorem (CLT) states that the arithmetic mean of a large number of observations of independent random variables, each with a well-defined expected value and variance, is approximately normally distributed. The feature extraction procedure generates observations related to the central lattice for each ultrasound image and subsequently for the whole dataset. By CLT, the features associated with normal tissue and breast lesions are modelled using the mean vector and the corresponding covariance matrix.

Discriminant Analysis (DA) is a multivariate statistical technique commonly used to build a predictive model based on a set of measurable features. DA assumes that distinct classes generate data based on different normal distributions. If additionally, assuming that the classes are linearly separable which implies that they can be separated by a linear combination of their features, then linear discriminant analysis (LDA) can be used. LDA guarantees the maximum separability between classes because it maximizes the ratio of the between-class variance to the within-class variance.

For ultrasound images, the majority of the algorithms employ LDA to classify breast lesions as it is parameter-free and easy to learn. A classification rule is created by LDA to have the largest mean difference between normal tissue and breast lesion classes. μ_1 and μ_2 represent the mean vectors of class 1 (normal tissue) and class 2 (breast lesion), estimated from the learning set. $\sum_1$ and $\sum_2$ correspond to the estimated covariance matrices, n_1 and n_2 denote the number of cases from class 1 and class 2 respectively. LDA score $D(z)$ or some arbitrary pattern $\mathbf{z}$ is defined by equation (37):

$$D\left(z\right) = \left[z - \frac{1}{2}\left(\widehat{\mu_1} + \widehat{\mu_2}\right) \right]^T \hat{S}^{-1}\left(\widehat{\mu_2} - \widehat{\mu_1}\right). \tag{37}$$

where the pooled covariance matrix $\hat{S}$ is computed using the following equation (38):

$$\hat{S} = \frac{1}{n_1 + n_2 - 2}\left[\left(n_1 - 1\right)\widehat{\sum\nolimits_1} + \left(n_2 - 1\right)\widehat{\sum\nolimits_2}\right]. \tag{38}$$

Before tumour classification, rescaling of vector z is done by Softmax normalization to reduce the influence of extreme feature values.

METRICS FOR EVALUATING THE SEGMENTATION

(Boaz Shmulei, 2019b) explains to us that metrics are defined to evaluate and to quantify the degree to which extent the computerized method result (represented by S_c) agrees with the radiologist delineation (represented by S_r) or the ground truth used as a reference.

Segmentation of ultrasound images can be treated as a binary classification problem where the classification is the lesion and the background. The majority of the segmentation frameworks make use of the four basic ratios which are true positive (TP), true negative (TN), false positive (FP), false negative (FN). **False-positive (FP):** Denotes the area falsely identified by S_c when compared with S_r. **False-negative (FN):** Denotes the area in S_r that was missed by S_c. **True-positive (TP):** Indicates the total area of S_r that was covered by S_c. **True-negative (TN):** Denotes the total area in S_r which is not present in the lesion as well as excluded by S_c.

Using the above four ratios calculation of scalar metrics like precision, recall, Dice Coefficient (F1-score). and accuracy can be done. But there are some issues associated with the scalar metrics such as accuracy being sensitive to class imbalance and metrics like precision, recall, F1- score being asymmetric. Some of the metrics which can be used apart from precision, F1-score and accuracy can be Mathews correlation coefficient (MCC), Intersection-Over-Union (IoU) also known as Jaccard Index,

(Boaz Shmulei, 2019a) explains that MCC can be used to measure the quality of the segmentation as it makes a balanced measure when the classes are of different sizes and overcomes some of the limitations of the other metrics like F1-score, precision, recall, and accuracy. MCC is computed according to equation (39):

$$MCC = \frac{TP \times TN - FP \times FN}{\sqrt{\left(TP + FP\right)\left(TP + FN\right)\left(TN + FP\right)\left(TN + FN\right)}}. \tag{39}$$

The properties of MCC are:

- When the classification is perfect (FP = FN = 0) the value of MCC is 1 indicating perfect positive correlation.
- When the classification is not done properly (TP = TN = 0) the value of MCC is -1 representing negative correlation.
- MCC is perfectly symmetric which means that no class is more important than the other. Even if the positive and negative values are interchanged, the same value is obtained.

- MCC has values in the range [-1,+1] where +1 indicates perfect matching, 0 represents random segmentation, and -1 indicates total disagreement with the results obtained from segmentation.
- The similarity between S_r and S_c will make the value of MCC tending towards +1.

IoU or Jaccard Index is defined as the area of the overlap between the output obtained from segmentation and the ground truth. The range of IoU is from $0 - 1$ with 0 implying there is no overlap between the output and the ground truth and 1 representing the perfect overlap between the output and ground truth.

FUTURE RESEARCH DIRECTIONS - DEEP LEARNING BASED METHODS FOR LESION DETECTION AND SEGMENTATION

(Yap et al., 2017) gives insight by comparing the performance of the existing state of the art rule-based image processing algorithms with deep learning models. Image processing-based approaches are based on rules and assumptions which can result in lower accuracy in lesion detection, segmentation, and these algorithms are not quite robust. Deep learning models don't rely on any assumptions. Popular deep learning models used on image data sets are based on Convolutional Neural Networks (CNNs). Some of the important applications implemented with the help of CNN's are object detection in self-driving cars, face recognition tasks, and solving classification problems.

Some of the deep learning models proposed by (Yap et al., 2017) for lesion detection from ultrasound images are Patch-based LeNet, U-Net, and transfer learning. In the transfer learning approach, the deep learning models are already trained on an image dataset and the pre-existing weights are used in training the model on the breast ultrasound images. The transfer learning approach overcomes the limitation of deficiency in data. Making use of performance metrics like TPF (True Positive Fraction), FPs (False Positives)/image, and F-measure it was found that deep learning models like LeNet, U-Net, FCN-Alex Net performed better compared to the well-known state of the art algorithms used in lesion detection like Radial Gradient Index (RGI) filtering, multifractal filtering, Rule-based region ranking (RBRR) and Deformable Part Models (DPM).

(Byra et al., 2020) proposes an attention gated U-Net network for the segmentation of tumours from US images. The study conducted suggests that using statistical parametric maps like entropy maps generated from the ultrasound image results in a higher accuracy of segmentation of ultrasound images compared to segmentation on original ultrasound images.

Data deficiency can be addressed by data augmentation techniques through which the number of images available for training can be increased. Most of the current deep learning methods derive from a fully convolutional network architecture (FCN) where the fully connected layers are being replaced by convolutional layers. In cases where we have small region-of-interest (ROI) more discriminative models such as attention gated networks have been proposed. Apart from using deep learning models for segmentation, we can also use it for the classification of tumours as benign and malignant based on the features extracted from the tumour.

CONCLUSION

To aid radiologists in lesion detection a CAD system is developed to improve the decision-making process of the radiologists. The system has its functionality divided into many branches like pre-processing, segmentation, classification, and detection. The ultrasound images acquired depend on the expertise of the operator and are found to suffer from low contrast, unclear boundaries, etc., The pre-processing branch is the contrast enhancement which improves the low contrast ultrasound images based on fuzzy logic.

Ultrasound image segmentation is a crucial element in the CAD system. The segmentation can be both semi-automatics as well as automatically based on the degree of human interaction with the CAD system. Deep learning-based segmentation frameworks are found to perform better compared to rule-based image processing algorithms. Features based on texture extracted from the US image can improve the accuracy of the segmentation framework. Metrics like F1 score, Jaccard Index, etc. are used to evaluate the performance of segmentation frameworks. Thus, a selection of proper segmentation framework plays a crucial role in the diagnosis of tumour by a CAD system.

REFERENCES

Byra, M., Jarosik, P., Dobruch-Sobczak, K., Klimonda, Z., Piotrzkowska-Wroblewska, H., Litniewski, J., & Nowicki, A. (2020). *Breast mass segmentation based on ultrasonic entropy maps and attention gated U-Net.* arXiv preprint arXiv:2001.10061

Field, D. J. (1987). Relations between the statistics of natural images and the response properties of cortical cells. *Journal of the Optical Society of America. A, Optics and Image Science, 4*(12), 2379–2394. doi:10.1364/JOSAA.4.002379 PMID:3430225

Gomez Flores, W., & Ruiz Ortega, B. A. (2016). New Fully Automated Method for Segmentation of Breast Lesions on Ultrasound Based on Texture Analysis. *Ultrasound in Medicine & Biology, 42*(7), 1637–1650. doi:10.1016/j.ultrasmedbio.2016.02.016 PMID:27095150

Gonzalez, R. C., & Woods, R. E. (2001). *Digital Image Processing* (2nd ed.). Prentice-Hall.

Guo, Y., Cheng, H. D., Huang, J., Tian, J., Zhao, W., Sun, L., & Su, Y. (2006). Breast ultrasound image enhancement using fuzzy logic. *Ultrasound in Medicine & Biology, 32*(2), 237–247. doi:10.1016/j.ultrasmedbio.2005.10.007 PMID:16464669

Laws, K. I. (1980, Jan). *Textured image segmentation* (No. USCIPI-940). University of Southern California Los Angeles Image Processing INST.

Liu, B., Cheng, H. D., Huang, J., Tian, J., Liu, J., & Tang, X. (2009). Automated Segmentation of Ultrasonic Breast Lesions Using Statistical Texture Classification and Active Contour Based on Probability Distance. *Ultrasound in Medicine & Biology, 35*(8), 1309–1324. doi:10.1016/j.ultrasmedbio.2008.12.007 PMID:19481332

Munteanu, C., & Rosa, A. (2004). Gray-Scale Image Enhancement as an Automatic Process Driven by Evolution. *IEEE Transactions on Systems, Man, and Cybernetics. Part B, Cybernetics, 34*(2), 1292–1298. doi:10.1109/TSMCB.2003.818533 PMID:15376874

Pal, S. K., & Majumder, D. K. D. (1986). *Fuzzy mathematical approach to pattern recognition.* New York, NY: Wiley.

Shmueli, B. (2019b, Jul 2). *Multi-Class Metrics Made Simple, Part I: Precision and Recall.* Retrieved from https://towardsdatascience.com/the-best-classification-metric-youve-never-heard-of-the-matthews-correlation-coefficient-3bf50a2f3e9a

Shmulei, B. (2019a, Nov 22). *Matthews Correlation Coefficient Is the Best Classification Metric You've Never Heard Of.* Retrieved from https://towardsdatascience.com/the-best-classification-metric-youve-never-heard-of-the-matthews-correlation-coefficient-3bf50a2f3e9a

Yap, M. H., Pons, G., Martí, J., Ganau, S., Sentís, M., Zwiggelaar, R., ... Martí, R. (2017). Automated breast ultrasound lesions detection using convolutional neural networks. *IEEE Journal of Biomedical and Health Informatics, 22*(4), 1218–1226. doi:10.1109/JBHI.2017.2731873 PMID:28796627

ADDITIONAL READING

Chen, D. R., Chang, R. F., Chen, C. J., Ho, M. F., Kuo, S. J., Chen, S. T., & Moon, W. K. (2005). Classification of breast ultrasound images using fractal feature. *Clinical Imaging, 29*(4), 235–245. doi:10.1016/j.clinimag.2004.11.024 PMID:15967313

Cheng, H. D., Jiang, X. H., Sun, Y., & Wang, J. L. (2001). Color image segmentation: Advances and prospects. *Pattern Recognition, 34*(12), 2259–2281. doi:10.1016/S0031-3203(00)00149-7

Drukker, K., Giger, M. L., Horsch, K., Kupinski, M. A., Vyborny, C. J., & Mendelson, E. B. (2002). Computerized lesion detection on breast ultrasound. *Medical Physics, 29*(7), 1438–1446. doi:10.1118/1.1485995 PMID:12148724

Flores, W. G., de Albuquerque Pereira, W. C., & Infantosi, A. F. C. (2014). Breast ultrasound despeckling using anisotropic diffusion guided by texture descriptors. *Ultrasound in Medicine & Biology, 40*(11), 2609–2621. doi:10.1016/j.ultrasmedbio.2014.06.005 PMID:25218452

Fuzzy Image Processing. (n.d.). Retrieved from http://neuron.csie.ntust.edu.tw/homework/93/Fuzzy/%E6%97%A5%E9%96%93%E9%83%A8/homework_2/M9309001/FIP.htm

Haralick, R. M., Shanmugam, K., & Dinstein, I. (1973). Textural Features for Image Classification. *IEEE Transactions on Systems, Man, and Cybernetics, SMC-3*(6), 610–621. doi:10.1109/TSMC.1973.4309314

Jiang, L. (Ed.). (2012). *Proceedings of the 2011 International Conference on Informatics, Cybernetics and Computer Engineering (ICCE2011) November 19-20, 2011, Melbourne, Australia. Advances in Intelligent and Soft Computing.* (pp. 307-313)

Peter Kovesi. (n.d.). *What are Log-Gabor Filters and why are they good?* Retrieved from https://www.peterkovesi.com/matlabfns/PhaseCongruency/Docs/convexpl.html

KEY TERMS AND DEFINITIONS

Computer-Aided Diagnosis: Systems assisting doctors or radiologists in the interpretation of medical images like X-ray, MRI, and ultrasound.

Fuzzy Logic: A logic based on computing degrees of truth rather than the Boolean approach (true or false).

Membership Function: The membership function for a fuzzy set on the universe of discourse X is defined as $\mu_A : X \to [0,1]$ and every element of X is mapped to a value between 0 and 1. The value called membership value or degree of membership quantifies the grade of membership of the element in X to the fuzzy set A.

Segmentation: Partitioning of a digital image I into multiple non-overlapping regions such that the union of any two adjacent regions is not homogenous is called Image Segmentation.

Texture: An entity consisting of mutually related pixels and a group of pixels having similar properties.

Tumour: It is a mass of abnormal tissue. There are two types of tumours – benign and malignant. Benign is non-cancerous and malignant is cancerous

APPENDIX

Images in Figure 1, Figure 2, Figure 3, Figure 4, Figure 5, and Figure 6 were acquired using an ultrasound system. The images were obtained from Shantou First Affiliated Hospital Shantou China.

Chapter 4
Layer-Wise Tumor Segmentation of Breast Images Using Convolutional Neural Networks

Nishanth Krishnaraj

National Institute of Technology, Tiruchirappalli, India

Bhaskar M.

National Institute of Technology, Tiruchirappalli, India

A. Mary Mekala

Vellore Institute of Technology, Vellore, India

Ruban Nersisson

(iD) https://orcid.org/0000-0003-1695-3618

Vellore Institute of Technology, Vellore, India

Alex Noel Joseph Raj

Shantou University, China

ABSTRACT

Early prediction of cancer type has become very crucial. Breast cancer is common to women and it leads to life threatening. Several imaging techniques have been suggested for timely detection and treatment of breast cancer. More research findings have been done to accurately detect the breast cancer. Automated whole breast ultrasound (AWBUS) is a new breast imaging technology that can render the entire breast anatomy in 3-D volume. The tissue layers in the breast are segmented and the type of lesion in the breast tissue can be identified which is essential for cancer detection. In this chapter, a u-net convolutional neural network architecture is used to implement the segmentation of breast tissues from AWBUS images into the different layers, that is, epidermis, subcutaneous, and muscular layer. The architecture was trained and tested with the AWBUS dataset images. The performance of the proposed scheme was based on accuracy, loss and the F1 score of the neural network that was calculated for each layer of the breast tissue.

DOI: 10.4018/978-1-7998-6690-9.ch004

INTRODUCTION

The most common cancer in women is breast cancer, and it was the second leading cause of mortality for women in 2013. Early diagnosis and treatment of breast cancer are useful in reducing mortality rates. Two screening modalities, mammography and breast ultrasound are the popular modalities for the detection and diagnosis of breast tumor. Typically, mammography was the primary imaging tool on clinical examinations. An advantage of conventional ultrasound exams with hand-held probes is its real-time nature. During the diagnostic reviews after suspicious findings in screening, target regions can be thoroughly examined. However, in the screening setting, complete perusal takes time, and the results are operator dependent. Recently, screening exams using automated breast volume scanners are increasing. It is in general operator-independent and provides whole breast data, which facilitate double reading, and longitudinal comparison Automated whole breast ultrasound (AWBUS) is a relatively new imaging technique which was approved by the FDA in 2012 (Pellegretti et al., 2011). The AWBUS technique can depict the entire breast anatomy automatically in a 3D volume. Therefore, it may thus enable thorough offline image reading. The radiologists can check every detail of the AWBUS volume multiple times to find out potential breast lesions, and hence the hand-held scanning mistakes like missing of lesions can be possibly avoided.

Current automated breast scanners often acquire whole breast data in several separate volumes. Therefore, one patient exam can include 6 to 10 volumes with many slices, which require radiologists to spend a considerable amount of time for review. For radiologists' efficient diagnosis, the computer-aided detection system is studied. Despite the volumetric imaging advantage, the major problem that limits the popularization of AWBUS lies in the difficulty of understanding the AWBUS images. The interpretation of AWBUS images requires the knowledge of breast anatomy and ultrasonic physics, as well as enough clinical scanning experience. In such a case, the learning curve for AWBUS images can be extended. Figure1 shows the different types of layers in the breast. The epidermis layer, the subcutaneous layer, the muscle layer and the cavity layer are the four different types of layers. The decomposition of anatomic breast layers in the AWBUS images helps junior radiologists and residents for the image reading.

Meanwhile, the segmentation of anatomical breast layers can also support the computation of breast density, which is the volume ratio of breast parenchyma against all breast tissues above the chest wall. The breast density is an essential biomarker for breast cancer risk, which can be calculated by the layer segmentation of AWBUS images. In this paper, we have used a U-Net Convolutional Neural Network Architecture to implement the layer segmentation of AWBUS (Prabhakar & Poonguzhali, 2017). This network architecture has a contracting path and an expansive path, which gives it the U-Shaped architecture. The contracting path consists of repeated application of convolutions, which is then followed by a rectified linear unit and a max-pooling operation. There is a reduction in spatial information and an increase in feature information during contraction. The expansive pathway combines the feature and spatial data through a sequence of up-convolutions and concatenations with high-resolution features from the contracting path.

BACKGROUND

Detection of the early stage indications of breast cancer is difficult. Hence the initial screening and pursuing the treatment for the breast cancer is very essential. X-ray mammography, magnetic resonance

Figure 1. Different layers of breast

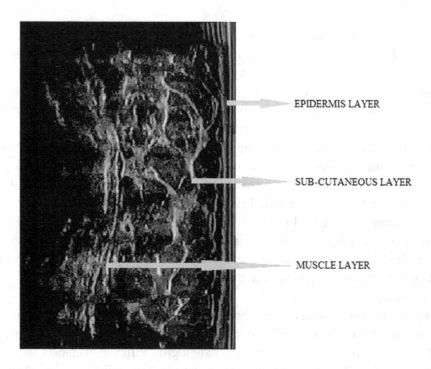

imaging (MRI) and breast ultrasounds are the different ways to perform breast cancer medical imaging. The women in Asian countries have complex breast thickness. Therefore X-ray mammography is commonly used but it can produce false positive results (Del et al., 2007). Compared to other ultrasound testing, the X-ray mammography has the benefits of low cost and no radiation. During the mammography, to reduce the breast thickness, a compression is applied to the patient's breast. As a result, the quality of the image is improved (Chen et al., 2012). The compression force may vary depends upon the different radiographers, countries and the screening centers. With a help of X-ray mammography devices, the compression force applied at the time of imaging procedure can be measured. But no instructions or guidelines are mentioned for the radiographers about how much compression force should be applied to the patient's breast for the acquirement of a suitable mammogram (Mercer et al., 2015). The usual discomfort of this type of screening is that most of the patients complain about the pain they undergo during the compression force (Waade et al., 2017). The hand held ultrasound (HHUS) images are proved as the efficient tool and it is mainly used for diagnosing the breast tumors. In case of two dimensional probe, the breast tumor scanning may ignore the small tumors. Using two dimensional images proper decisions cannot be taken, because some important features are unnoticed like whether the lesion is present or not. Also for some irregular patchy tumor features cannot be visibly obtained from the two dimensional breast ultra sound images (Watermann et al., 2005).

SuperSonic Imagine is a French company that is involved in the development of three dimensional ultrasound medical imaging system for breast tumor examination. Automated whole breast ultrasound system (AWBUS) is a 3D ultra sound imaging system which is used to overwhelm the disadvantages of the two dimensional breast ultrasound images. This automated whole breast ultrasound system is a trouble-free, non-invasive and non-radiative equipment. This technology is mainly established for the entire breast imaging. The AWBUS is a 3D ultrasound equipment produces images with very high resolution (Lin et al., 2012). The 3D AWBUS imaging system scans the whole breast in a direction and it is combines to an AWBUS image. This ultra sound imaging system scans even small tumors. In such a way this technique overcomes the limits of the conventional hand held ultra sound images. This 3D imaging equipment is one of the advance technology used for the whole breast tumor detection and it is otherwise known as automated whole breast scan and automated breast volume scanner.

Even though automated whole breast ultra sound outperforms well it faces some of the diagnosis complications as well. The three dimensional AWBUS images contains more number of two dimensional ultrasound images. At the time of manual analysis of these ultrasound images, some smaller tumors images may be missed carelessly (Hsu et al., 2014). In addition to that, though the AWBUS images have enough essential information, the medical practitioner should see the 3D ultrasound images from various different aspects. Finally still there is a lacking to measure the significant parameters like how the lesions are distributed and their shapes. Hence the identification and the lesion segmentation in AWBUS images are necessary. Hyperechoic lesions and hypoechoic lesions are the two different types of breast lesions. Each lesion possesses various characteristics. Hence segmenting these lesions is a challenging task. Various computer aided mass detection (CADe) systems for automated whole breast ultra sound images were surveyed and analysed (Kozegar et al., 2019). The author Ikedo et al. (2007) suggested a method for segmenting breast lesions automatically. A Canny edge detection algorithm is used here to detect the edges of the breast tumors. Both Ikedo et al. (2007) and Lo et al. (2014) have used the watershed technique to extract the possible inconsistent regions in AWBUS images. This watershed technique collects similar intensity blocks hat is very close to the local minimum and then converts them into a similar region. Then the image is divided into multiple blocks. Otsu's algorithm and morphology is applied to extract the tumors in AWBUS images and then the features are extracted. Finally the support vector machine (SVM) classifier is used to check whether the region is a tumor (Kim et al., 2014). Moon et al. (2014) used a 3D mean shift algorithm. Using this algorithm the tumors are segmented very fast compared to other methods. In this method, the specked noises are removed and then the tissues with same characteristics are separated. A Generative Adversarial Network (GAN) algorithm was suggested by Negi et al. (2020) for segmenting the lesion in Breast Ultrasound images.

Chang et al. (2010) proposed an algorithm where the screening is done automatically. Firstly to improve the quality of the image, pre-processing is performed. Secondly according to the grayscale distribution values, the regions are divided. Lastly seven different characteristics such as area size, darkness, width and height ratio, uniformity, continuity of the region, non-determination, and size of the coronal area are defined to check the presence of tumor. An improved U-Net model so-called GRA U-Net was suggested to determine a tumor in an Automated Whole Breast Ultrasound (AWBUS) ultrasound image. The GRA U-Net algorithm is a mixture of few existing methods. The nipple in the breast is segmented from the images and it helps in finding the tumor exactly with respect to its position (Zhuang et al., 2019).

Lei et al. (2018) proposed a Convolutional encoder-decoder network technique in which the convolutional encoder-decoder network is used for breast anatomy segmentation which may potentially assist the exclusion of false positives and improve the efficiency of clinical image reading. This technique can achieve relatively better segmentation performance by comparing to the baseline deep learning implementation schemes for segmentation. Moon et al. (2013) suggested a Blob detection technique. This method is based on level set. A computer-aided detection system based on multi-scale blob detection for analyzing AWBUS images. After speckle noise reduction, Hessian analysis with multi-scale blob detection was adopted to detect the lesions by using blobness measurements of AWBUS images. Tumor candidate selection was then applied to remove the redundant non-tumors from the tumor candidates. The tumor likelihoods of the remaining tumor candidates were estimated using a logistic regression model with blobness, internal echo, and morphology features. Finally, the tumor candidates with tumor likelihoods higher than a specific threshold were tumors.

Muramatsu et al. (2018) proposed a convolutional neural network technique to detect an automated breast ultrasound. The Convolutional Neural Network (CNN) architecture employed in this study was DetectNet, which is fully convolutional network based on GoogLeNet. The network detects the candidate boxes based on the predictions of box coverage and box corners. The network was trained with the axial and reconstructed sagittal slices that depict at least one mass. In order to include clearly visible slices, only the slices at the central third portion of the masses were employed.

Chiang et al. (2019) suggested a 3-D convolutional neural network technique for tumor detection in automated whole breast ultrasound. A computer-aided detection system based on 3-D CNN for lesion detection of AWBUS images was proposed in this study. An application independent sliding window detector is adopted for volume of interest (VOI) extraction. Then, a 3-D CNN is used for tumor probability estimation of each VOI, and VOIs of probability higher than a threshold are considered as tumor candidates. The overlapped candidates are combined with a novel aggregation scheme. Finally, the same process is executed multiple times with different target sizes for multi scale lesion detection. The performance of the system was evaluated with a database containing 171 lesions and 37 normal cases, and the system achieved sensitivities of 95%, 90%, 85%, and 80% with 14.03, 6.92, 4.91, and 3.62 false positives, respectively.

Vakanski et al. (2020) proposed a deep learning architecture which incorporated visual attention for breast. This used a U-Net architecture with blocks combined along the tightening path in the layers of the encoder tumor separation. A channel attention component with multiscale grid average pooling (MSGRAP) was proposed for the specific separation of breast cancer sections in ultrasound images (Lee et al., 2020).

METHODOLOGY

Deep learning is a subsection of the broader topic of machine learning methods based on the layers used in artificial neural networks. The learning in deep learning can be either supervised, semi-supervised or unsupervised. Deep learning architectures such as convolutional neural networks, recurrent neural networks and deep neural networks are being used in fields like computer vision, speech recognition, natural language processing and audio recognition, and the produced results are comparable to human experts.

Deep learning architecture uses a series of nonlinear processing representational layers for feature extraction and transformation, where each successive layer uses the previous layers' output as its input. In the learning phase, where the architecture extracts the features, each level of layer learns to transform its input data into a more abstract and complex representation.

A convolutional neural network (CNN) is a subsection of deep neural networks. It is most commonly used for analyzing visual imagery as CNN's use relatively little pre-processing compared to other image analyzing algorithms. CNN's are regularized versions of multiple layers of supervised binary classifiers known as perceptrons. In a multilayer perceptrons, each neuron in a layer is connected to all other neurons in the next layer and is therefore referred to as fully connected networks. The "fully-connectedness" of such networks makes them susceptible to overfitting data, which is usually solved by adding a magnitude of weights to the loss function. However, CNN's solves the problem of overfitting by making use of the hierarchical pattern in data and using smaller patterns to construct intricate patterns.

Fully convolutional network means that the neural network is composed of convolutional layers without any fully connected layers, which is usually found at the end of the network. A fully convolutional network tries to learn representations and make decisions based on local spatial input.

U-Net is a Convolutional Neural Network based on Fully Convolutional Network. It was developed for biomedical image segmentation and its modified architecture yields more accurate segmentation with fewer training images. The network architecture consists of a contraction path and an expansive path. This is what gives it a shape, thereby getting the name U-Net (Ronneberger et al., 2015). The contracting path consists of the repeated operations of two 3x3 convolutions, each followed by a rectified linear unit and a 2X2 max pooling operation with stride 2 for down sampling.

At each down sampling step, the number of feature channels is doubled. In the expansive path, every level consists of an up sampling of the feature map followed by a 2x2 up-convolution operation which reduces the number of feature channels by half, a concatenation with the correspondingly cropped feature map from the contracting path, and two 3x3 convolution operations, each followed by a Rectified Linear Unit.

Due to the loss of border pixels, cropping becomes necessary after every convolution. At the final layer, a 1x1 convolution operation maps each of the 64-component feature vectors to the desired number of classes. The network has a total of 27 convolutional layers.

The architecture of U-Net is shown in Figure 2. It is identical to the architecture of encoder-decoder. Essentially, it is a deep-learning framework based on Fully Convolutional Networks. It comprises of two

Figure 2. U-Net architecture

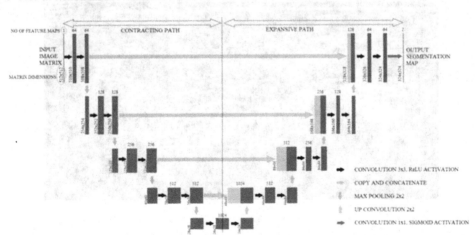

parts. The contracting path captures context via a compact feature map, which is like an encoder. The expanding path allows precise localization, which is like a decoder. This step is done to retain boundary and spatial information despite down sampling and max-pooling performed in the encoder stage. In total, the network has 27 convolutional layers which accept input images of size 512 x 512.

The input images and their corresponding segmentation mask are used to train the network. The output image is smaller than the input image with a constant border width as the convolution operation is carried out with unpadded kernel.

Algorithm:

1. The image is reduced from 512 x 1023 to 512 x 512. It is done mainly to decrease the training time, reduce the memory requirement and reduce the number of computation operations per layer.
2. Get the AWBUS dataset images and split it into two categories: Training data set and testing data set.
3. For the training data set, mark the labels for the epidermis, subcutaneous and muscle layer and save it along with the training data set.
4. Train the model with the test images and its corresponding labels and save the training weights as a Hierarchical Data Format (.h5) file.
5. Test the model using the saved weights and find the predicted result.

Data augmentation is a technique to increase the size of training set artificially without actually collecting new data in order to improve the performance, accuracy and the ability of the model. It can be a horizontal flip, vertical flip, rotation, rightward or leftward shift etc. It is essential to teach the network the desired invariance and robustness properties when only few training samples are available. We primarily need shift and rotation invariance as well as robustness to deformations and grey value variations.

Figure 3. Test AWBUS image

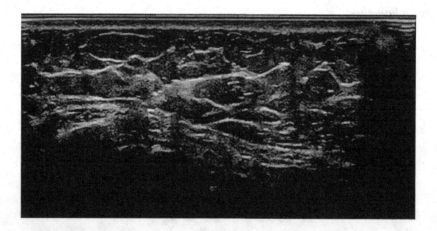

Figure 4. Predicted epidermis layer for test AWBUS image

Figure 5. Predicted sub-cutaneous layer for test AWBUS image

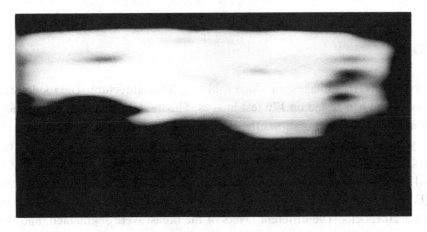

Figure 6. Predicted muscle layer for test AWBUS image

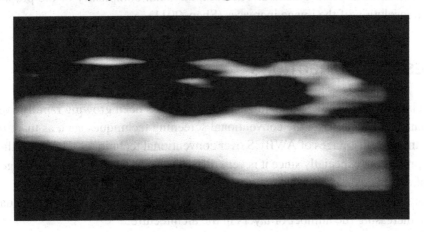

Figure 7. Training and validation loss for epidermis layer

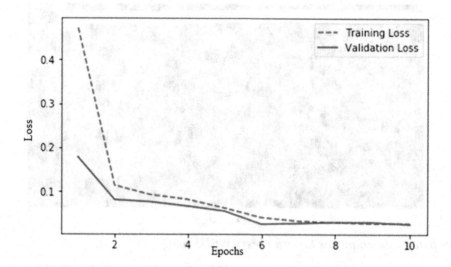

CONCLUSION

The segmentation of AWBUS images was done using U-Net architecture. The model was trained with 250 training images and was tested on 176 test images. The model showed high accuracy and low loss which is given in table 1. Figures 7 shows the loss of the model which is 0.0284 and Figure 8 shows that the accuracy of the model was found to be 98.85% for the epidermis layer after 10 epochs. Figures 9 shows the loss of the model which is 0.1490 and Figure 10 shows that the accuracy of the model was found to be 94.17% for the subcutaneous layer after 20 epochs. Figures 11 shows the loss of the model which is 0.1593 and Figure 12 shows that the accuracy of the model was found to be 93.23% for the muscle layer after 20 epochs. The different layers of the breast were segmented, and the edges of the segmented regions were marked for ease of identification and determining the density of the breast layers. Figure 13 shows the edges segmented. The computational complexity of the proposed algorithm increases as the resolution of the image increases (Shan, 2011).

FUTURE RESEARCH DIRECTIONS

AWBUS is a relatively new medical imaging technique and has been growing rapidly over the past few years. It has many advantages over the conventional screening techniques such as mammogram. There are several volumetric advantages of AWBUS over conventional techniques. However, there is still a lot of room for improvement especially since it is very difficult to understand AWBUS images and requires the guidance of experts.

The accuracy of the U-Net architecture can further be improved by increasing the dataset used for training and by increasing the number of layers in the architecture.

Figure 8. Training and validation accuracy for epidermis layer

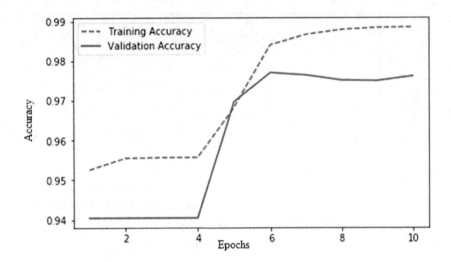

Figure 9. Training and validation loss for sub-cutaneous layer

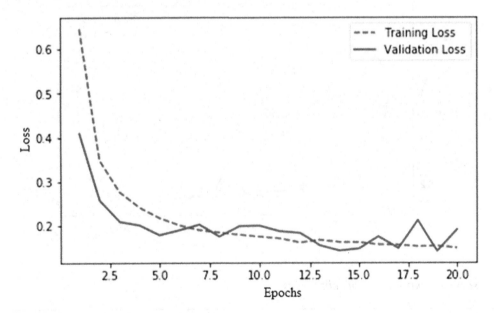

Figure 10. Training and validation accuracy for sub-cutaneous layer

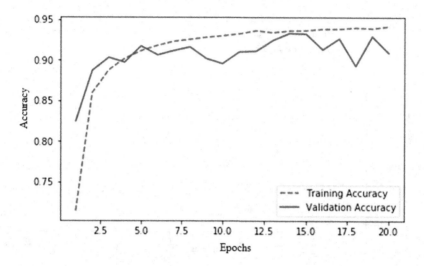

Figure 11. Training and validation loss for muscle layer

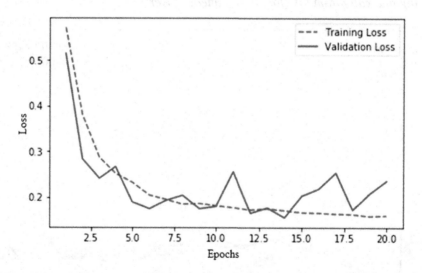

Table 1. Assessment parameters of skin layers

Layer	Loss	Accuracy	Precision	Recall	F1 Score	Epochs
Epidermis	0.0284	0.9885	0.8815	0.8568	0.8690	10
Sub-cutaneous	0.1490	0.9417	0.9244	0.9427	0.9335	20
Muscle	0.1593	0.9323	0.8075	0.7419	0.7733	20

Figure 12. Training and validation accuracy for muscle layer

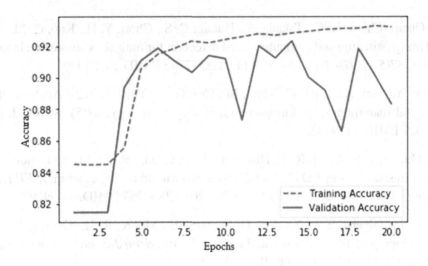

Figure 13. Edge segmented AWBUS Image

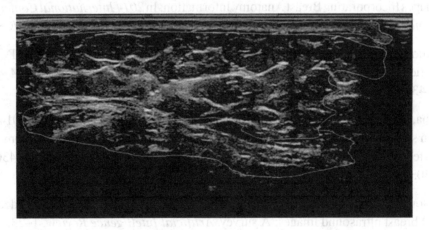

FUNDING

This research was financially supported by the Scientific Research Grant of Shantou University, China, Grant No: NTF17016.

ACKNOWLEDGMENT

We would like to acknowledge the funding and the support given by Shantou University China. Also we would thank Vellore Institute of Technology for providing this opportunity and supporting us.

REFERENCES

Chang, R. F., Chang-Chien, K. C., Takada, E., Huang, C. S., Chou, Y. H., Kuo, C. M., & Chen, J. H. (2010). Rapid image stitching and computer-aided detection for multipass automated breast ultrasound. *Medical Physics*, *37*(5), 2063–2073. doi:10.1118/1.3377775 PMID:20527539

Chen, B., Wang, Y., Sun, X., Guo, W., Zhao, M., Cui, G., ... Yu, J. (2012). Analysis of patient dose in full field digital mammography. *European Journal of Radiology*, *81*(5), 868–872. doi:10.1016/j.ejrad.2011.02.027 PMID:21397423

Chiang, T. C., Huang, Y. S., Chen, R. T., Huang, C. S., & Chang, R. F. (2019). Tumor detection in automated breast ultrasound using 3-D CNN and prioritized candidate aggregation. *IEEE Transactions on Medical Imaging*, *38*(1), 240–249. doi:10.1109/TMI.2018.2860257 PMID:30059297

del Carmen, M. G., Halpern, E. F., Kopans, D. B., Moy, B., Moore, R. H., Goss, P. E., & Hughes, K. S. (2007). Mammographic breast density and race. *AJR. American Journal of Roentgenology*, *188*(4), 1147–1150. doi:10.2214/AJR.06.0619 PMID:17377060

Hsu, C. Y., Chou, Y. H., & Chen, C. M. (2014, March). A Tumor Detection Algorithm for Whole Breast Ultrasound Images Incorporating Breast Anatomy Information. In *2014 International Conference on Computational Science and Computational Intelligence* (Vol. 2, pp. 241-244). IEEE. 10.1109/CSCI.2014.128

Ikedo, Y., Fukuoka, D., Hara, T., Fujita, H., Takada, E., Endo, T., & Morita, T. (2007). Development of a fully automatic scheme for detection of masses in whole breast ultrasound images. *Medical Physics*, *34*(11), 4378–4388. doi:10.1118/1.2795825 PMID:18072503

Kim, J. H., Cha, J. H., Kim, N., Chang, Y., Ko, M. S., Choi, Y. W., & Kim, H. H. (2014). Computer-aided detection system for masses in automated whole breast ultrasonography: Development and evaluation of the effectiveness. *Ultrasonography (Seoul, Korea)*, *33*(2), 105–115. doi:10.14366/usg.13023 PMID:24936503

Kozegar, E., Soryani, M., Behnam, H., Salamati, M., & Tan, T. (2019). Computer aided detection in automated 3-D breast ultrasound images: A survey. *Artificial Intelligence Review*, 1–23.

Lee, H., Park, J., & Hwang, J. Y. (2020). Channel Attention Module with Multi-scale Grid Average Pooling for Breast Cancer Segmentation in an Ultrasound Image. *IEEE Transactions on Ultrasonics, Ferroelectrics, and Frequency Control*, 1. doi:10.1109/TUFFC.2020.2972573

Lei, B., Huang, S., Li, R., Bian, C., Li, H., Chou, Y. H., & Cheng, J. Z. (2018). Segmentation of breast anatomy for automated whole breast ultrasound images with boundary regularized convolutional encoder–decoder network. *Neurocomputing*, *321*, 178–186. doi:10.1016/j.neucom.2018.09.043

Lin, X., Wang, J., Han, F., Fu, J., & Li, A. (2012). Analysis of eighty-one cases with breast lesions using automated breast volume scanner and comparison with handheld ultrasound. *European Journal of Radiology*, *81*(5), 873–878. doi:10.1016/j.ejrad.2011.02.038 PMID:21420814

Lo, C. M., Chen, R. T., Chang, Y. C., Yang, Y. W., Hung, M. J., Huang, C. S., & Chang, R. F. (2014). Multidimensional tumor detection in automated whole breast ultrasound using topographic watershed. *IEEE Transactions on Medical Imaging*, *33*(7), 1503–1511. doi:10.1109/TMI.2014.2315206 PMID:24718570

Mercer, C. E., Szczepura, K., Kelly, J., Millington, S. R., Denton, E. R., Borgen, R., ... Hogg, P. (2015). A 6-year study of mammographic compression force: Practitioner variability within and between screening sites. *Radiography, 21*(1), 68–73. doi:10.1016/j.radi.2014.07.004

Moon, W. K., Lo, C. M., Chen, R. T., Shen, Y. W., Chang, J. M., Huang, C. S., ... Chang, R. F. (2014). Tumor detection in automated breast ultrasound images using quantitative tissue clustering. *Medical Physics, 41*(4), 042901. doi:10.1118/1.4869264 PMID:24694157

Moon, W. K., Shen, Y. W., Bae, M. S., Huang, C. S., Chen, J. H., & Chang, R. F. (2013). Computer-aided tumor detection based on multi-scale blob detection algorithm in automated breast ultrasound images. *IEEE Transactions on Medical Imaging, 32*(7), 1191–1200. doi:10.1109/TMI.2012.2230403 PMID:23232413

Muramatsu, C., Hiramatsu, Y., Fujita, H., & Kobayashi, H. (2018, January). Mass detection on automated breast ultrasound volume scans using convolutional neural network. In *2018 International Workshop on Advanced Image Technology (IWAIT)* (pp. 1-2). IEEE. 10.1109/IWAIT.2018.8369795

Negi, A., Raj, A. N. J., Nersisson, R., Zhuang, Z., & Murugappan, M. (2020). RDA-UNET-WGAN: An Accurate Breast Ultrasound Lesion Segmentation Using Wasserstein Generative Adversarial Networks. *Arabian Journal for Science and Engineering, 45*(8), 6399–6410. doi:10.100713369-020-04480-z

Pellegretti, P., Vicari, M., Zani, M., Weigel, M., Borup, D., Wiskin, J., ... Langer, M. (2011, October). A clinical experience of a prototype automated breast ultrasound system combining transmission and reflection 3D imaging. In *2011 IEEE International Ultrasonics Symposium* (pp. 1407-1410). IEEE. 10.1109/ULTSYM.2011.0348

Prabhakar, T., & Poonguzhali, S. (2017, August). Automatic detection and classification of benign and malignant lesions in breast ultrasound images using texture morphological and fractal features. In *2017 10th Biomedical Engineering International Conference (BMEiCON)* (pp. 1-5). IEEE. 10.1109/BMEiCON.2017.8229114

Ronneberger, O., Fischer, P., & Brox, T. (2015, October). U-net: Convolutional networks for biomedical image segmentation. In *International Conference on Medical image computing and computer-assisted intervention* (pp. 234-241). Springer. 10.1007/978-3-319-24574-4_28

Shan, J., (2011). *A fully automatic segmentation method for breast ultrasound images*. Academic Press.

Vakanski, A., Xian, M., & Freer, P. E. (2020). Attention-Enriched Deep Learning Model for Breast Tumor Segmentation in Ultrasound Images. *Ultrasound in Medicine & Biology, 46*(10), 2819–2833. doi:10.1016/j.ultrasmedbio.2020.06.015 PMID:32709519

Waade, G. G., Moshina, N., Sebuødegård, S., Hogg, P., & Hofvind, S. (2017). Compression forces used in the Norwegian breast cancer screening program. *The British Journal of Radiology, 90*(1071), 20160770. doi:10.1259/bjr.20160770 PMID:28102696

Watermann, D. O., Földi, M., Hanjalic-Beck, A., Hasenburg, A., Lüghausen, A., Prömpeler, H., ... Stickeler, E. (2005). Three-dimensional ultrasound for the assessment of breast lesions. *Ultrasound in Obstetrics and Gynecology: The Official Journal of the International Society of Ultrasound in Obstetrics and Gynecology, 25*(6), 592–598. doi:10.1002/uog.1909 PMID:15912473

Zhuang, Z., Raj, A. N. J., Jain, A., Ruban, N., Chaurasia, S., Li, N., ... Murugappan, M. (2019). Nipple Segmentation and Localization Using Modified U-Net on Breast Ultrasound Images. *Journal of Medical Imaging and Health Informatics, 9*(9), 1827–1837. doi:10.1166/jmihi.2019.2828

Chapter 5
Breast Cancer Detection Using Random Forest Classifier

Pavithra Suchindran
Avinashilingam University, India

Vanithamani R.
Avinashilingam University, India

Judith Justin
Avinashilingam Institute for Home Science and Higher Education for Women, India

ABSTRACT

Breast cancer is the second most prevalent type of cancer among women. Breast ultrasound (BUS) imaging is one of the most frequently used diagnostic tools to detect and classify abnormalities in the breast. To improve the diagnostic accuracy, computer-aided diagnosis (CAD) system is helpful for breast cancer detection and classification. Normally, a CAD system consists of four stages: pre-processing, segmentation, feature extraction, and classification. In this chapter, the pre-processing step includes speckle noise removal using speckle reducing anisotropic diffusion (SRAD) filter. The goal of segmentation is to locate the region of interest (ROI) and active contour-based segmentation and fuzzy C means segmentation (FCM) are used in this work. The texture features are extracted and fed to a classifier to categorize the images as normal, benign, and malignant. In this work, three classifiers, namely k-nearest neighbors (KNN) algorithm, decision tree algorithm, and random forest classifier, are used and the performance is compared based on the accuracy of classification.

INTRODUCTION

Breast cancer is one of the leading causes of death worldwide. The key factor in reducing the mortality is to find signs and symptoms of breast cancer in its early stage by clinical examination. The earlier the cancers are detected, the better the treatment provided. However, early detection requires an accurate and reliable diagnosis which should also be able to differentiate benign and malignant tumors. Previously, the

DOI: 10.4018/978-1-7998-6690-9.ch005

most effective modality for detecting and diagnosing breast cancer is mammography (Cheng HD et al., 2006). However, there are some limitations of mammography in breast cancer detection. Mammography can hardly detect breast cancer in young women with dense breasts. Besides, the ionizing radiation of mammography can increase the health risk for the patients and radiologists. An important alternative to mammography is Breast Ultrasound (BUS) imaging. BUS imaging is preferred because of its noninvasive, nonradioactive and cost-effective nature (Cheng HD et al., 2006) and it is more suitable for large-scale breast cancer screening and diagnosis. Also, the Ultrasound is more sensitive than mammography for detecting abnormalities in dense breasts; hence, it is more valuable for women younger than 35 years of age. Computer-Aided Diagnosis (CAD) methods have been developed to improve the performance of the breast cancer diagnosis. In this work a CAD system is developed incorporating preprocessing by Speckle Reducing Anisotropic Diffusion (SRAD) (Yu & Acton, 2015), and segmentation using the active contour model. The texture features are extracted using Gray Level Co-occurrence Matrix (GLCM) and are input to the classifier. K-Nearest Neighbors (KNN) algorithm, Decision tree algorithm and Random Forest classifier are used and the accuracy of the classifiers is computed to identify the most effective one for breast cancer detection using BUS images.

RELATED WORK

The major limitations of BUS imaging are low contrast and interference with speckle. The main aim of the pre-processing step is to improve the contrast of the image and reduce the speckle noise. Speckle noise is a random multiplicative noise and it occurs in all coherent imaging such as LASER, SAR and ultrasound imaging. Speckle noise makes the visual observation and analysis challenging. Therefore, removing speckle without destroying the important features for diagnosis is difficult. In this section, some speckle reduction techniques are reviewed.

Many speckle reduction techniques have been proposed and are classified as spatial domain filters, wavelet domain techniques, compounding approaches and non-linear diffusion. Certain speckle reduction techniques enhance the image and remove speckle at the same time. Nonlinear diffusion is such an example. It not only preserves edges but also enhances edges by inhibiting diffusion across edges and allowing diffusion on either side of the edges (Cheng HD et al., 2006). Speckle Reducing Anisotropic Diffusion (SRAD) is proposed particularly for Ultrasound images (Yu & Acton S.T. 2002). Zhenyu Zhou et al. (2015) developed a nonlinear diffusion filter denoising framework for multiplicative noise removal. The authors have presented a doubly degenerate diffusion model and demonstrated that their model outperformed its competitors both visually and quantitatively.

The most important step after preprocessing in CAD is segmentation. Segmentation helps to partition the image into non-overlapping regions. (Horsh et al., 2009) Proposed a method for automatic segmentation of breast lesions from Ultrasound images includes thresholding enhanced mass structures. The active contour model, generally known as snake, is a framework for outlining an object from a 2D image, and has been extensively used for US images. (Abdul Kadir Jumaat et al., 2010) Used active contour to identify the boundaries and adopted mathematical concepts for energy minimization. Balloon Snake algorithm was used for segmenting the masses from BUS images. The accuracy of the Balloon Snake algorithm was calculated by comparing the masses between the radiologist's observation and it was found to be 95.53%. Neural Network (NN) based methods (Chen. D. R. et al., 2002) are widespread in image segmentation, which convert the segmentation problem into classification decision based on a set of input features.

The preprocessing stage includes median and morphological filtering. The initial contour of the model is obtained using Fuzzy C Means (FCM) clustering. Through multiple sets of iteration the target is found. By this algorithm the time required for segmentation is greatly reduced (Sen Qian et al., 2016). Hong Huang et al., (2018) proposed a new model combining the FCM algorithm and the set theory. The brain image is segmented using the FCM clustering algorithm. In this algorithm, first the C centers are selected randomly, and then each data points are mapped to the nearest central cluster. Finally, the average value of each of the data point is calculated. Tanimoto coefficients are used to evaluate the accuracy of different segmentation algorithms.

For the traditional Ultrasound CAD system, the feature selection and extraction are necessary steps (Ravindraiah. R. & Tejaswini, K., (2013). The effective features can increase the accuracy and decrease the computational complexity of the system. The texture is one of the most important features in the Ultrasound CAD system. The texture features reflect the characteristics of the lesion region. Gray-Level Co-occurrence Matrices (GLCM) measure is one of the most important measures that can be used to describe the texture. Gomez et al., (2012) performed an analysis of co-occurrence texture statistics as a function of gray-level quantization for classifying breast ultrasound and confirmed that GLCM features are useful when considering automatic classification. Local Binary Pattern (LBP) method describes local structure of the Ultrasound image (Qinghua Huang et al., 2018). LBP is an operator for texture description. In a 3x3 neighborhood, the center is taken as the threshold and the other 8 gray values are compared with the threshold. If the value of the pixel greater than the threshold, that pixel will be replaced by 1; otherwise, it will be marked as 0. In this approach, every 3×3 neighborhood will be converted into an 8-bit binary number. (Yali Huang et al., 2008) Utilized the wavelet transform for texture analysis of ultrasonic liver image and the classification of liver abnormalities.

Most of the CAD systems for breast cancer detection using BUS images classify the images as normal, benign or malignant. The Bayesian classifier is one of the most frequently used methods and the mostly used Bayesian classifier is the Naïve Bayesian Classifier. Min-Chun Huang et al. (2012) used Naïve Bayes for the lesion detection and the pixels of the BUS image are classified into lesions or normal tissues.

In the field of breast cancer detection and classification, Artificial Neural Networks (ANN) is frequently used. BPN is a feed-forward ANN with supervised learning process. A BPN was used to classify the breast lesions on sonograms (Chen et al., 2003). The Support Vector Machine (SVM) is a supervised learning method which can be applied for classification and the target of SVM is to build a hyper plane to divide the sample into different classes. It used the kernel functions to map the original data into the higher dimensional space to find the decision hyper plane. SVM is widely useful for the analysis of ultrasound images (Prabusankarlal. K. M et al., 2015).

Decision tree approach is much simpler and faster compared to neural networks (4) However, it is highly dependent on the design of classification rules on each non-terminal node. The terminal node contains the final result of classification. K- Nearest Neighbor (KNN) algorithm is used for classification and regression. Prabhakar. T & Poonguzhali. S., (2016) used KNN algorithm for detection of breast tumor in Ultrasound images. Random forest is a supervised machine learning algorithm which is mainly used for classification problems.

The Random Forest algorithm proposed by Mr. Ho (1995), analyzed the data from a different perspective (randomness) to achieve higher accuracy. The Eigen values and the output from the decision trees are combined for a better accuracy in the Random Forest classification (Bin Dai et al., 2018).

Wisconsin Breast dataset is used for the analysis of the breast cancer by using Random forest classifier along with feature extraction technique. The redundant information is removed by weighting technique and an average accuracy of 99.8% was achieved (Cuong Nguyen et al., 2013).

METHODOLOGY

The proposed method is illustrated in Fig. 1. It classifies the BUS images into Normal, Benign and Malignant.

Figure 1. Block Diagram of proposed method

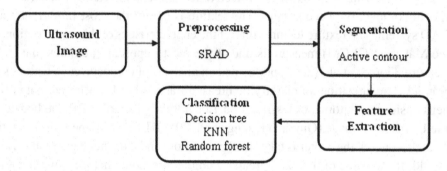

Ultrasound Image Database

The Ultrasound image dataset used in this study is taken from the publicly available database (Al-Dhabyani et al., 2020). The database contains a total of 780 Breast Ultrasound images classified as Normal (133), Benign (439) and Malignant (210). In this study, 780 images are utilized, out of which 655 images are used for training (Benign - 380, Malignant- 175 and Normal-100) and the remaining 115 images are used for testing (Benign- 50, Malignant -35 and Normal-30). The samples of BUS image for the three classes normal, benign and malignant are given in Fig.2.

Pre-processing

The most challenging task in pre-processing is the noise removal, since Ultrasound images are corrupted by speckle noise. Doubly degenerate diffusion model proposed by Zhenyu Zhou et al. (2015) considers not only the information of the gradient of the image, but also the information of gray levels of the image. They have utilized a scheme called Fast Explicit Diffusion (FED) to accelerate the whole numerical implementation of their nonlinear diffusion equation models. The performance of this method is compared with a standard speckle reduction filter SRAD (Yu & Acton S.T., 2002) in terms of the image quality evaluation metrics such as Signal to Noise Ratio (SNR), Peak Signal to Noise Ratio (PSNR), Mean Square Error (MSE) and Structural Similarity Index Measure (SSIM). SNR is defined as the ratio of the signal power and the noise power and is computed as in equation (1). SNR is expressed in decibel.

Figure 2. Samples of BUS images from Dataset (Al-Dhabyani et al., 2020)

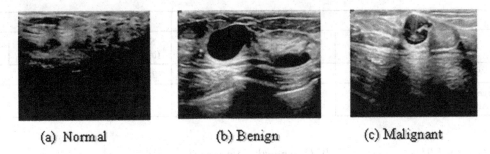

$$\text{SNR} = 10.\log_{10}\left[\frac{\sum_{0}^{M-1}\sum_{0}^{N-1}\left[r\left(x,y\right)\right]^{2}}{\sum_{0}^{M-1}\sum_{0}^{N-1}\left[r\left(x,y\right)-t\left(x,y\right)\right]^{2}}\right]. \tag{1}$$

Peak Signal to Noise Ratio (PSNR) (R.C. Gonzalez & R.E. Woods, 2008) is used to measure the difference between the original and denoised images of size M x N. It is estimated using equation (2) and is expressed in decibel (dB). The original image and despeckled images are represented as $r\left(x,y\right)$ .and $t\left(x,y\right)$ .respectively.

$$PSNR = 10log_{10}\frac{255^{2}}{MSE}. \tag{2}$$

where 255 is the maximum intensity in the gray scale image and MSE is the Mean Squared Error and is given in equation (2).

$$MSE = \frac{\sum_{M,N}\left[r\left(x,y\right)-t\left(x,y\right)\right]^{2}}{M*N}. \tag{3}$$

The Structural Similarity (SSIM) index (Zhou Wang et al., 2004) is a method for measuring the similarity between two images and is calculated as in equation (4).

$$\text{SSIM} = \frac{\left(2\mu\mu_{w}+C_{1}\right)\left(2\sigma\left(I,I_{w}\right)+C_{2}\right)}{\left(\mu^{2}+\mu_{w}^{2}+C_{1}\right)\left(\sigma\left(I\right)^{2}+\sigma\left(I_{w}^{2}\right)+C_{2}\right)}. \tag{4}$$

The SNR, PSNR, MSE and SSIM values are listed in Table 2.

From the table it is observed that the SNR and PSNR values are higher in case of SRAD filter when compared to Double Degenerative Diffusion Algorithm. The SSIM values ranges between 0 to 1 and from the SSIM values of both the filters in Table 2, it is inferred that the performance of SRAD is better. The value of MSE is also less in case of SRAD compared to Double Degenerative Diffusion Algorithm. The

Table 2. Quality Evaluation Metrics

Filter	Test Image 1				Test Image 2			
	SNR (in dB)	PSNR (in dB)	SSIM	MSE	SNR (in dB)	PSNR (in dB)	SSIM	MSE
SRAD	23.31	29.03	0.93	1.91	22.42	29.35	0.92	1.72
Double Degenerative Diffusion Algorithm	21.86	27.59	0.81	2.54	22.07	29.00	0.83	3.74

Figure 3. Original BUS images (a & d), De-speckled images (b, c, e & f)

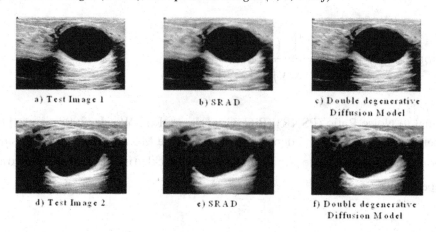

a) Test Image 1   b) SRAD   c) Double degenerative Diffusion Model

d) Test Image 2   e) SRAD   f) Double degenerative Diffusion Model

quality evaluation metrics show that the speckle suppression capability of SRAD (Yu & Acton S.T. 2002) is good, it is utilized in this work for de-speckling of BUS images. The de-speckled images are shown in Fig.3.

Segmentation

Image segmentation is an important and one of the toughest tasks in image processing and pattern recognition. The goal of the image segmentation is to locate the suspicious areas for better diagnosis.

Active Contour-based Segmentation

Active contour is one of the frequently used methods for segmentation, which makes use of the energy constraints and forces in the image for separation of region of interest. Active contour outlines a separate boundary for the regions of target object for segmentation. The active contour models are used in numerous medical applications. The extended version of active contour model known as Balloon model is used for segmentation of lesion from dermal images for early detection of skin cancer (Hemalatha.R.J et al., 2018). This work makes use of Balloon model to segment the lesion region from BUS images.

Figure 4. Mapping of FCM from input space to characteristic space (Hong Huang et al., 2018).

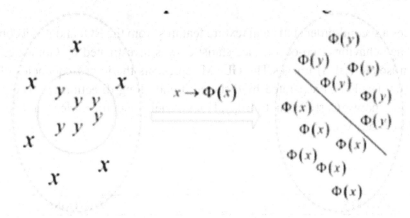

Fuzzy C Means Segmentation

Clustering is a process in which the samples of similar elements in the group are categorized together leaving behind the samples from a different group. The main purpose of FCM segmentation algorithm is that the C subspaces are obtained by dividing the sample points of the vector spaces (Hong Huang et al., 2018). Figure 4 illustrates the mapping of FCM from the input space to the characteristic space.

Fig. 5 shows the original BUS image and the segmented image using Active contour and FCM based segmentation. From the results it is observed that active contour based Balloon snake model yielded a better result compared to FCM segmentation.

Figure 5. Lesion segmentation from BUS images

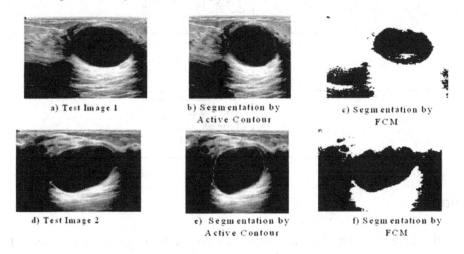

Feature Extraction

The GLCM provides a second-order statistical texture features from the ROI and it is a common feature in CAD system. The behavior of co-occurrence statistics was investigated by Gomez et al. (2012) to classify Breast Ultrasound (BUS) images.The GLCM represents the joint frequencies of all pairwise combinations of gray levels and separated by distance d and along direction θ . The seven textural features extracted are Energy, Correlation, Entropy, Homogeneity, Contrast, Mean and Standard Deviation and are listed in Table 3.

Table 3. GLCM Features

FEATURES	EQUATIONS
Energy	$\sum_{x=0}^{N-1}\sum_{y=0}^{N-1} p(x,y)^2$
Correlation	$\sum_{x=0}^{N-1}\sum_{y=0}^{N-1} \dfrac{(1-\mu_x)(1-\mu_y)p(x,y)}{\sigma_x \sigma_y}$
Entropy	$\sum_{x=0}^{N-1}\sum_{y=0}^{N-1} p(x,y)\log(p(x,y))$
Homogeneity	$\sum_{x=0}^{N-1}\sum_{y=0}^{N-1} \dfrac{p(x,y)}{1+|x-y|}$
Contrast	$\sum_{x=0}^{N-1}\sum_{y=0}^{N-1} |x-y|^2\, p(x,y)$
Mean	$\dfrac{1}{n}\sum_{i=0}^{L-1} r_i p(r_i)$
Standard deviation	$\sqrt{\dfrac{\sum_{i=1}^{N}(x-\overline{x})^2}{N-1}}$

Classification

In this chapter, the three different classifiers used for CAD of breast cancer are K-Nearest Neighbor algorithm, Decision Tree Algorithm and Random Forest Classifier. The three classifiers are described in this section.

K-Nearest Neighbor Algorithm

KNN is one of the simplest algorithms and supervised learning methods used to classify the features into different classes. It stores the entire training data set and makes predictions by calculating the similarity between an input sample and each training instance. Euclidean distance is used to decide which of the K instances in the training dataset are utmost similar to a new input. The prediction gives the output as a class with the majority in the 'K' nearest neighbors. It is used for the classification of breast cancer (Tahmooresi et al., 2018). Figure 6 depicts the flowchart of the KNN. The Euclidean Distance D(x, y) is calculated using equation (5).

$$D(x,y) = \sqrt{\Sigma(x_i - y_i)^2} \tag{5}$$

Figure 6. Flowchart of KNN Classifier

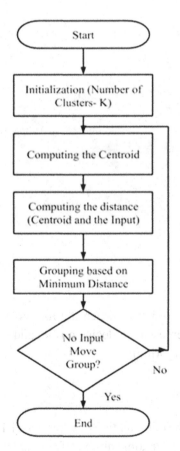

Decision Tree Algorithm

The Decision tree is a tree-based classification, commonly used in data mining (Tahmooresi et al., 2018), which classifies the input data set into predefined classes.

Figure 7. Architecture of Decision Tree

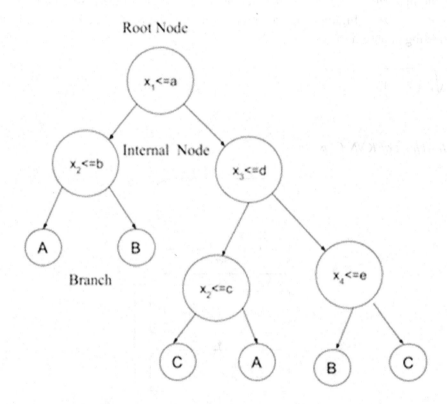

A decision tree is drawn upside down in which the root is at the top, an internal node represents feature (or attribute), the branch represents a decision rule, and each leaf node represents the classes. Fig.7. illustrates the decision tree algorithm.

Random Forest Classifier

Random forest algorithms rely on the combination of several decision trees as shown in Fig.8. A random forest creates n random trees from a random subset of features from the data. After the creation of the forest, a new object which is to be classified is presented for classification by each of the trees in the forest. A vote is cast by each of the trees to specify the tree's decision about the class of the object. The class with the majority of the votes is selected by the forest.

Figure 8. Architecture of Random forest classifier

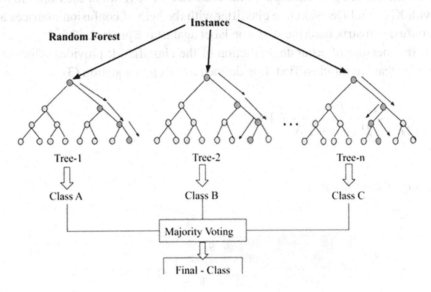

Table 4. Confusion matrix of Decision Tree

	Predicted Label		
Categories	Benign	Malignant	Normal
Benign	44	3	3
Malignant	3	31	1
Normal	3	2	25

Table 5. Confusion matrix of KNN

	Prediction Label		
Categories	Benign	Malignant	Normal
Benign	50	0	0
Malignant	1	33	1
Normal	2	1	27

Table 6. Confusion matrix of Random Forest

	Prediction Label		
Categories	Benign	Malignant	Normal
Benign	49	1	0
Malignant	0	34	1
Normal	0	0	30

The features extracted are given as input to the classifiers. The result of the Random forest classifier is compared with KNN and Decision tree classifier with the help of confusion matrices as in Tables 4, 5 and 6. The confusion matrix describes the true label against the predicted label.

Accuracy is the measure of accurate prediction of the classifier. It provides information about the number of samples that are misclassified. It is defined as given in equation (3)

$$Accuracy\% = \frac{TP + TN}{TP + FP + TN + FN} X100 \tag{3}$$

Figure 9. Accuracy of the Classifiers

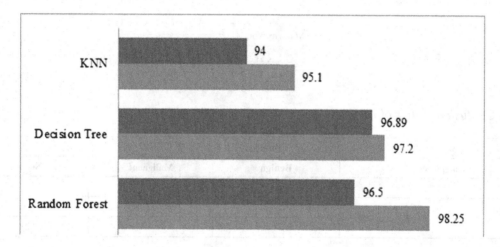

From the Fig. 9, it is inferred that the Random forest classifier outperformed the other two classifiers KNN and Decision tree classifier and achieved an accuracy of 98%. The above figure clearly states about the performance of SRAD with Active Contour based Segmentation and FCM in CAD system.

CONCLUSION

According to World Health Organization (WHO), Breast cancer is considered as a serious issue and can be cured if it is diagnosed at an early stage. Hence, a computer aided method is proposed. In the pre-processing stage, SRAD filter is utilized for effective speckle reduction and enhancement. As the Active contour-based segmentation is mostly used for breast ultrasound lesion detection, it is preferred for effectively identifying the ROI. The texture features are extracted by applying GLCM. The comparison of the performance of the three classifiers validates the accuracy of the Random Forest classifier and is higher compared to the Decision tree classifier and KNN. The proposed CAD procedure helps to identify the cancer at an early stage and also characterizes the cells as Normal, Benign or Malignant.

REFERENCES

Al-Dhabyani, M., Gomaa, M., Khaled, H., & Fahmy, A. (2020). Dataset of Breast Ultrasound Images. *Data in Brief, 28*, 1–5. doi:10.1016/j.dib.2019.104863 PMID:31867417

Chen, C. M., Chou, Y. H., Han, K. C., Hung, G. S., Tiu, C. M., Chiou, H. J., & Chiou, S. Y. (2003). Breast lesions on sonograms: Computer-aided diagnosis with nearly setting- independent features and artificial neural networks. *Radiology, 226*(2), 504–514. doi:10.1148/radiol.2262011843 PMID:12563146

Chen, D. R., Chang, R. F., Kuo, W. J., Chen, M. C., & Huang, Y. L. (2002). Diagnosis of breast tumors with sonographic texture analysis using wavelet transform and neural networks. *Ultrasound in Medicine & Biology, 28*(10), 1301–1310. doi:10.1016/S0301-5629(02)00620-8 PMID:12467857

Cheng, H., Shi, X., Min, R., Hu, L., Cai, X., & Du, H. (2006). Approaches for automated detection and classification of masses in mammograms. *Pattern Recognition, 39*(4), 646–668. doi:10.1016/j.patcog.2005.07.006

Cheng, Shana, Ju, Guo, & Zhang. (2010). Automated breast cancer detection and classification using ultrasound images: A survey. *Pattern Recognition, 43*, 299 – 317.

Dai, B., Chen, R., Zhu, S., & Zhang, W. (2018). Using Random Forest Algorithm for Breast Cancer Diagnosis. *International Symposium on Computer, Consumer and Control (IS3C)*, 449-452. 10.1109/IS3C.2018.00119

Dubey, Y. K., & Mushrif, M. M. (2016). FCM Clustering Algorithms for Segmentation of Brain MR Images. *Advances in Fuzzy Systems, 2016*, 1–14. doi:10.1155/2016/3406406

Gomez, W., Pereira, W. C. A., & Infantosi, A. F. C. (2012). Analysis of co-occurrence texture statistics as a function of gray-level quantization for classifying breast ultrasound. *IEEE Transactions on Medical Imaging, 31*(10), 1889–1899. doi:10.1109/TMI.2012.2206398 PMID:22759441

Gonzalez, R. C., & Woods, R. E. (2008). Digital image processing (3rd ed.). Academic Press.

Hemalatha, Thamizhvani, Dhivya, Joseph, Babu, & Chandrasekaran. (2018). Active Contour Based Segmentation Techniques for Medical Image Analysis. *Medical and Biological Image Analysis,* 17-34.

Horsch, Giger, Venta, & Vyborny. (2001). Automatic segmentation of breast lesions on ultrasound. *Medical Physics, 28*(8), 1652–1659.

Huang, Chen, & Chang. (2012). *Whole Breast Lesion Detection Using Naive Bayes Classifier for Portable Ultrasound*. Academic Press.

Huang, H., Meng, F., Zhou, S., Jiang, F., & Manogaran, G. (2019). Brain Image Segmentation Based on FCM Clustering Algorithm and Rough Set. *IEEE Access : Practical Innovations, Open Solutions, 7*, 12386–12396. doi:10.1109/ACCESS.2019.2893063

Huang, Q., Zhang, F., & Li, X. (2018). Machine Learning in Ultrasound Computer-Aided Diagnostic Systems: A Survey. *BioMed Research International, 2018*, 1–10. PMID:29687000

Huang, Y., Wang, L., & Li, C. (2008). Texture Analysis of Ultrasonic Liver Image Based on Wavelet Transform and Probabilistic Neural Network, *IEEE International Conference on Biomedical Engineering and Informatics*, 248-252. 10.1109/BMEI.2008.156

Jumaat, A. K., Wan, E. Z. W. A. R., Ibrahim, A., & Mahmud, R. (2010). Segmentation of Masses from Breast Ultrasound Images using Parametric Active Contour Algorithm. *Procedia: Social and Behavioral Sciences*, *8*, 640–647. doi:10.1016/j.sbspro.2010.12.089

Nguyen, C., Wang, Y., & Nguyen, H. (2013). Random forest classifier combined with feature selection for breast cancer diagnosis and prognostic. *Journal of Biomedical Science and Engineering*, *6*(05), 551–560. doi:10.4236/jbise.2013.65070

Prabhakar, T., & Poonguzhali, S. (2016). Denoising and automatic detection of breast tumor in ultrasound images. *Asian Journal Information Technology*, *15*(18), 3506–3512.

Prabusankarlal, K. M., Thirumoorthy, P., & Manavalan, R. (2015). Assessment of combined textural and morphological features for diagnosis of breast masses in ultrasound. *Human-centric Computing and Information Sciences*, *5*(1), 1–17. doi:10.118613673-015-0029-y

Prochazka, A., Gulati, S., Holinka, S., & Smutek, D. (2019). Classification of Thyroid Nodules in Ultrasound Images Using Direction-Independent Features Extracted by Two-Threshold Binary Decomposition. *Technology in Cancer Research & Treatment*, *18*, 1–8. doi:10.1177/1533033819830748 PMID:30774015

Qian & Weng. (2016). Medical image segmentation based on FCM and Level Set algorithm. *7th IEEE International Conference on Software Engineering and Service Science (ICSESS)*, 225-228.

Ravindraiah, R., & Tejaswini, K. (2013). A survey of image segmentation algorithms Based on fuzzy clustering. *International Journal of Computer Science and Mobile Computing*, *2*(7), 200–206.

Tahmooresi, M., Afshar, A., Bashari, R., Babak, B. N., & Bamiah, K. M. (2018). Early Detection of Breast Cancer Using Machine Learning Techniques. Journal of Telecommunication. *Electronic and Computer Engineering.*, *10*, 21–27.

Wang, Z., Bovik, A. C., Sheikh, H. R., & Simoncelli, E. P. (2004). Image quality assessment: From error visibility to structural similarity. *IEEE Transactions on Image Processing*, *13*(4), 600–612. doi:10.1109/TIP.2003.819861 PMID:15376593

Chapter 6
Pulomonary Nodule Classification From CT Scan Images Using Machine Learning Method

Rekha K. V.
Vellore Institute of Technology, India

Anirudh Itagi
Vellore Institute of Technology, India

Bharath K. P.
Vellore Institute of Technology, India

Balaji Subramanian
Vellore Institute of Technology, India

Rajesh Kumar M.
iD https://orcid.org/0000-0003-0350-4397
Vellore Institute of Technology, India

ABSTRACT

The research work is to enhance the classification accuracy of the pulmonary nodules with the limited number of features extracted using Gray level co-occurrence matrix and linear binary pattern. The classification is done using the machine learning algorithm such as artificial neural network (ANN) and the random forest classifier (RF). In present, lung cancer seems to be the most deadly disease in the world which can be detected only after the computerized tomography (i.e., CT scan images of the person). Detecting the infected portion at the early period is the challenging task. Hence, the recent researchers where under the detection of pulmonary nodules to categorize it either as benign nodules which named as non-cancerous or as malignant nodules which are named as cancerous. When associated the results with the recent papers, the accuracy has been improved in classifying the lung nodules.

DOI: 10.4018/978-1-7998-6690-9.ch006

I. INTRODUCTION

Human Body consists of thousands and thousands of cells, which multiplies and dies conventionally. Due to uncontrolled growth of the cells, which goes wrong from the regular conventional manner causes cancer. Cancer is known as a deadly disease all over the world. Cells causing cancer are combined together in the form of mass tissue defined as a tumor. Tumor is of two types which is known as benign and malignant, where sometimes these tumors do not spread fully inside the body but it starts to grow out of control known as Benign. And the tumor which slowly starts to spread completely inside the body known as Malignant. Normally the cells inside the body have the control on their growth and when it becomes unhealthy, it destroys itself. Most of the people are affected by the cancer which occurs at different organs of the body such as brain, lung, breast, liver and throat and even it occurs in the bloodstream.

This research work is done on lung cancer. Biologically, here pulomonary refers to the lungs. Nodules are the ones which occur in the oval shape or any irregular pattern. Detection of lung cancer at the early stage is still a crucial role. The clinical treatment has been improved a lot when compared to those days. Research says that there are many risk factors which cause cancer due to the consumption of tobacco, alcohol, exposure of UV radiation, obesity. All over the world merely 7.6 million people are affected by the cancer in the different organs of their body and leads to death.

The aim of this chapter is to reduce the features in use from the paper Li, X. X., et.al., (2018) for training the classification algorithm and improve the accuracy by detecting it either as benign or malignant lung nodules. The research is carried over by the images taken from the Lung Image Dataset Consortium (LIDC) which is easily accessible. This dataset consists of 1012 patients computed tomography images. The CT scan images are used to identify the clear vision of the affected lungs in the axial view, coronal view and Sagittal view. From the above declared views, the axial view is chosen to clearly view the lungs as such it helps to inspect and diagnose the lungs affected by cancer. Every lung image chosen from the dataset has been preprocessed with the appropriate isotropic filter which gives better results for the medical images.

In recent times, the Random walk segmentation process gained major attention due to the effective results obtained through it. For the interactive segmentation of an image Random walk has been introduced by Grady Grady, L. (2006). . Whereas, the weighted graph indicates the issue in labelling the seeds. The operator should foremost mark the seeds which in turn indicates the regions belonging to the K object. The tuple vector K is assigned by the user to every node. It indicates that the random walk reaches the labelled contiguous nodes first from the starting point of the unlabeled nodes. Final results are obtained from the k tuples which selects the most prominent seed destination. And moreover this segmentation technique Eslami, et.al., (2013) is executed in the medical field effectively Ju, W., Xiang, et.al., (2015).

With the help of neighbors, the spatial info is captured in the random walk hence, the limitation in the noise can be eased. Feature extraction is carried over by the Gray level Co-occurrence matrix (GLCM) where the set of features are tracked from the segmentation results and then those features are said to be used for training the machine learning algorithms. The major contribution of the research is done in the feature extraction by reducing the amount of features chosen for the training purpose and also helps to improve the accuracy in the classification part.

The machine learning algorithms used in this research process are artificial neural networks and the random forest algorithm. ANN is the collection of neurons as it is compared with the brain functioning neuron. Such that each and every node is connected so if the particular node fails to give the data the neural network tries to recover the data with the help of other nodes. Every information has been trained so there is no need for re-programming the algorithm. It works effectively for the linear as well as non-linear data. Random forest Li, X. X., et.al., (2018) algorithm is known for the tree structured classifier where it can be used either for regression purpose or for the classification purpose which consists of the collaborative results of binary decision trees and the combined function of entire decision trees. In the stage of training, the tree is said to be constructed with the help of bootstrap sampling which is selected from the given input. This makes the algorithm to remove the overfitting issues. This technique executes the embedded set of features to be selected so it is insensitive to the large data of features which is not relevant. Decision tree helps out to split the node and RF has the capability to choose the correctly predicted one in random. Finally the results are calculated based on the average score of the decision tree or the majority of the predicted result . This algorithm has the ability to deal with the non-linear high dimensional data. Thus, when the decision tree is said to be in large account the error may occur. Addressing this issue, the mathematical model of probability density function is taken at every feature vector to each tree.

This chapter is outlined as follows: in Section 2, the related research works to this chapter have been discussed. In section 3, an in depth explanation for the proposed model is described. Section 4, shows the results accomplished through the proposed model and the comparison with the recent research papers were done.

II. RELATED WORKS

This section precisely describes the research works done agreeing to the pulmonary nodule classification is as follows: On comparing the performance between the machine learning algorithms of artificial neural network and the logistic regression Chen, H, et.al., (2012) in differentiating the pulmonary nodules it is said that the artificial NNs gives the better classification results with the accuracy 90%. Another paper describes a multi-crop model Shen, W, et.al., (2017), He, Z,, et.al., (2020) for the classification of lung nodules based on its malignancy level done with the help of convolutional neural networks, Kumar et.al., (2020) . In this, the nodules are ranked based on the size which comes under less than 3mm has the benign and other one has the malignant nodules and the classification process is done with the help of convolutional NNs which tends to give almost 87% of accuracy. De Pheno, et.al., (2020), Automatically detecting the nodules either as benign or as malignant Li, X. X., et.al., (2018) with random forest machine learning classifier Monakam et.al., (2020) . This chapter explains that the image has been preprocessed with the help of the anisotropic filter and then the segmentation step is carried out by the random walk method in which it focuses only on the nodules. Moreover it separates the nodules, and from that separation the features are said to be extracted. The features extracted are of intensity, texture and the geometric features. In which merely three techniques were involved to extract the texture features they are of gray level co-occurrence matrix, linear binary pattern and the Gabor filtering. The values obtained from these features are said to be trained for the random forest classifier to calculate the accuracy, sensitivity and the specificity. This method gives 90% of accuracy.

In turn, to improve the performance in classifying the lung (pulmonary) nodules and to optimize the features used in the paper Li, X. X., et.al., (2018) the proposed systematic model is used in the way to resolve the upcoming issues and it is programmed in such a way that it tends to gives the better performance in the accuracy when compared with the recent research works.

III. SYSTEM MODEL

This chapter helps to improve the features extracted for training the classification of nodules in terms of benign and malignant. Thus, this method contains the steps of: pre-processing, nodule segmentation, extracting the features of the nodules and then the classifiers are described briefly below.

A. Pre-Processing

The non-linear diffusion anisotropic filter is processed more than other filtering techniques because this filtering method has the ability to suppress the noise present in the image and is also good in preserving the boundaries of the nodules.

B. Segmentation of Nodules

The segmentation is the major contribution step for the upcoming features extracted from the nodules. When compared with the nodule segmentation techniques Dong, X, et.al., (2015) discussed in the recent research works it is said that random walk gives better results.

- The filtered image has been taken has the input
- The distance is calculated between the neighboring node pairs on each feature space.
- To identify the desired vector probabilities the energy based function is used.
- In this function, it holds the seed information and then the cost for allocating the neighboring node pairs to the different probability and then the nodules are segmented.

This technique separates the foreground from the background intensity by labelling the pixels. And nowadays it is made automatic with help of acquisition of seeds. The nodules present in the lungs are cropped and then the nodule center is calculated by the geodesic distance Diciotti, S, et.al., (2011). The nodule seeds are marked with the radius R from the circle. The background seeds are said to be sampled with the 4R radius distance from the center. From the input data, the foreground and the respective background are adaptively sampled. This segmentation technique is said to be useful in segmenting the different kinds of nodules and it gives out the better segmentation quality.

Figure 1. systematic flow of proposed model

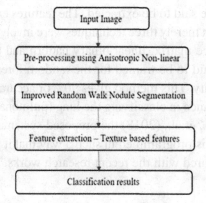

C. Feature Extraction of Pulmonary Nodules

The major contribution of this research work is to optimize the features that are used in the paper Li, X. X., et.al., (2018) . This chapter presents an optimized work by calculating only the texture features from the segmented nodules. Thus the texture based features are obtained by the two well-known methods such as Gray-level co-occurrence matrix and the linear binary pattern. Such that the omission of intensity and geometric features are done to analyze the result with the help of textures based features.

The gray level co-occurrence matrix Shen, W, et.al., (2017) is known as the second order in the statistical technique for extracting the features based on texture. Foremost, the segmented nodules are converted into the l- gray level form and then the co-occurrence matrix is calculated by the present and the neighboring pixels intensity pairs are noted for every scale orientation. These orientations are set up with an interval of 45 degree, such as 0, 45, 90, and 135 degrees. The vector is constructed by taking the average of all matrices. The normalized value for the GLCM is obtained by the equation mentioned below.

$$G(i,j) = \frac{N(i,j)}{\sum_{m=0}^{l-1} \sum_{n=0}^{l-1} N(m,n)} \tag{1}$$

Here, i and j represents the gray values in the l- gray level of an image and $N(i,j)$ $N(i,j)$Said to be relative co-occurrence frequency matrix obtained as

$$N(i,j)num(\{[x_i, y_i), (x_j, y_j)]\}, x_2 - x_1 = d\cos\theta,$$
$$y_2 - y_1 = d\sin\theta, I(x_1, y_1) = i, I(x_2, y_2)j) \tag{2}$$

Where, $x(x_1, y_1)$, $(x_2, y_2) - (x_1, y_1), (x_2, y_2)$-represents the positions of the pixels. I (.) Indicates the image gray level and num (.) denotes the pairs of pixels satisfying the conditions.

In this work, nearly 6 texture based features are considered from the GLCM technique: contrast, energy, correlation, dissimilarity, homogeneity and the angular secondary moment. Only based on this features the segmentation of the nodules features are extracted Li, X, et.al., (2017).

a)   a) Contrast: It is used for calculating the grayness difference present in the nodule images. When the grayness difference seems to be higher, then the contrast is high. It is proportionally related to each other. The value is 0 for the constant image.

$$Contrast = \sum_{i,j}^{l-1} |i - j|^2 N(i,j) \tag{3}$$

b)   b) Energy:Energy describes the distribution of grayness in the lung nodule images. Energy remains 1 for the constant image.

$$Energy = \sum_{i,j}^{l-1} N(i,j)^2 \tag{4}$$

c)   c) Dissimilarity:The dissimilarity is measured by taking the image color intensity variations into account.

$$Dissimilarity = \sum_{i,j}^{l-1} |i - j| N(i,j) \tag{5}$$

d)   d) Homogeneity:The homogeneity measures the nearest element distribution present in the Gray level co-occurrence matrix to its diagonal element and returns the value 1 for the diagonal element.

$$Homogeneity = \sum_{i,j} \frac{N(i,j)}{1 + |i - j|} \tag{6}$$

e)   e) Correlation:Correlation defined as the measure of interconnecting a pixel to its neighbor pixel on the whole image.

$$Correlation = \sum_{i,j} \frac{(i - u_i)(j - u_j)p(i,j)}{\sigma_i \sigma_j} \tag{7}$$

f)   f) Angular Secondary Moment: It is used for measuring the acceleration rotation.

$$Angular \, Sec \, ondary \, moment = \sum_{i,j}^{l-1} N(i,j)^2$$
$$Angular \, Sec \, ondary \, moment = \sum_{i,j}^{l-1} N(i,j)^2 \tag{8}$$

Linear binary pattern is one of the texture based features which is already applied in the application of breast cancer Rastghalam, R, et.al., (2016), sub-solidity of the lung nodules and also in renal lesion Liu, J, et.al., (2015). These type of features are said to be extracted with the help of the neighborhood pixels at the distance of R to center, which is indicated as

$$LBP_{P,R}(c) = \sum_{i=0}^{N-1} s(g_i - g_c)2^i \, s(x) = \{1 \, x \geq 0 \, 0 \, x < 0 \tag{9}$$

Where, g_i and g_c g_i and g_c - are the neighbor pixel intensity i, center pixel intensity c on the radius of circle R.

The s (.) indicates that the binary pattern code is basically invariant to any monotonic transformation of the intensity of an image. P denotes the pixel sampled values at radius R. When the neighbor pixel intensity is greater than the center pixel intensity then the s(x) is 1 or it is set to 0. Here, 2^N 2^N binary pattern is used and N=8. Then from the obtained pattern the six texture features are calculated.

D. Classification Of Pulmonary Nodules

The machine learning algorithm named as Artificial Neural network and the Random Forest Classifier is used in this chapter for classifying the lung nodules either as benign or as malignant. Artificial Neural Network (ANN) based back propagation method Adi, K.,, et.al., (2018) is designed in such a way that it works like the human brain.

Back propagation is used for calculating the gradient error with reference to modifiable weights of the network. Error seems to propagate from backwards (i.e., from output to input). This algorithm is framed in four steps. They are

1.   Weight Initialization
2.   Feed forwarding
3.   Errors occur in back propagation
4.   Weight and bias updating

Figure 2. Network model of artificial neural network

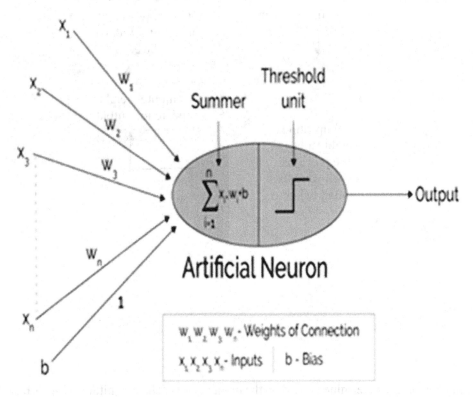

Figure 3. Flowchart of back propagation neural network

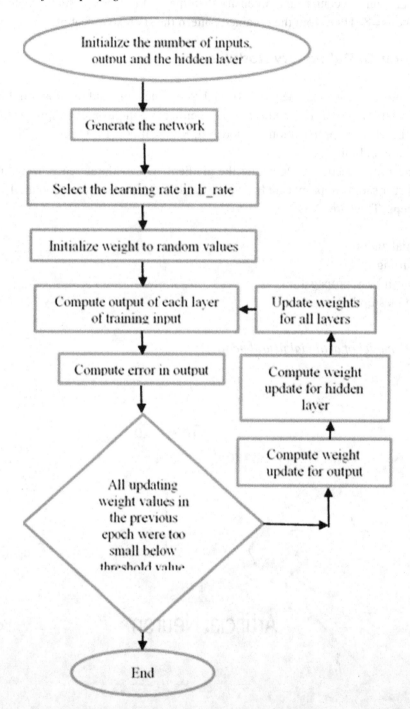

The weighting factors are determined based on the input vectors. The magnitude offset is based on the internal threshold value of the nodes. The sigmoid activation function is used in the hidden layer where the decision making is made by this function whether to activate the layer or need not to be activated and the decision is taken only after the calculated of the weighted sum. This type of function is used to turn out the linearity inputs into the nonlinearity outputs, so that it is capable for the execution of difficult tasks. In this network Han, F, et.al., (2015), the synapse of the human brain is compared with the weights and the neurons are compared with the nodes, where the synapse in the brain permits to transfer the information to axons and dendrites. Axons transmit the activation to other neurons and dendrites receive the function activation from further neurons. This network consists of 25 hidden layers in the process and the learning rate seems to be 0.001. Such that, the features are trained through the ANN algorithm and the nodules are tested to analyze the classification performance of this neural network.

Random forest classifier Li, X. X., et.al., (2018) is also trained in such a way to predict the class labels. Here, the bootstrap method is used to find the apt split from the feature subset which is selected at every node from the tree. Each node split is related to the split function to decide where to place the node either to the left or right of the tree as the child node. The six features extracted are considered as the vector form as follows:

$$f(v,\theta_j) : R^d \times x \rightarrow \{0,1\}$$
$$f(v,\theta_j) : R^d \times x \rightarrow \{0,1\}$$
(10)

Where,
The v denotes the vector form of input features,

θ_j - Indicates parameter of the features,

x- Denotes the spilt parameter spaces and

$_R d$ - Represents the dimension of the feature spaces.

Here, the threshold value τ_j, is carefully chosen to fix the split of the node, only after that the trained nodule images are divided either into left or into right. When the input feature vector v and the parameter θ_j is lesser than the decided threshold value then the node is moved to the left and when it is greater than the threshold then it is moved to the right. The multivariate probability density function (pdf) at every feature vector of the tree is

$$p_\tau(L) = \frac{1}{(2\pi)^{\frac{d}{2}}} e^{-\frac{1}{(2)(v-v)}\wedge^{-1}(v-\underline{v})}$$
(11)

Where,

$_{Pc(L)pc(L)}$ - Multivariate probability density function,

d- Dimension of the feature vector,

v– mean value and

$_\wedge$-1 – Covariance matrix.

The weight function is calculated as

$$w_i^{'} = \sum_j p_t(v_i | L) \ln \ln \frac{p_t(v_i | L)}{p_t(v_j | L)} \qquad (12)$$

Here,

$_{L.}$ Is the binary label of classes when $L=0$ then it is noted as benign and when it is 1 it is noted as malignant. i and j- The pixels and

$_{vi,vj}$ - The feature vectors

Figure 4. Flowchart of Random forest classifier

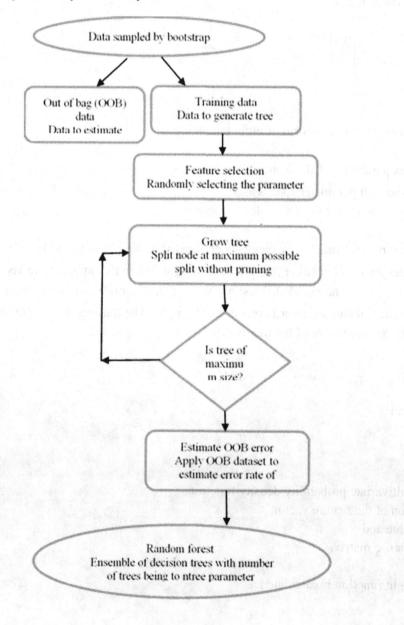

The depth of the tree has been increased when the new node is added to the tree. When the threshold value is greater than the number of nodes then the growth of the tree stops. The final result of this classifier is predicted by the weight of all tree predicted values, such as

$$p(v) = \frac{1}{T} \sum_{t=1}^{T} \sum_{i=1}^{NP} w_i' p_t(v_i) \tag{13}$$

Where,

$P_{(v)}$ – Multivariate probability density function (pdf)

Thus, the features are trained through this process and the nodule is tested by pushing into each tree and the related tests are taken to identify the malignancy level of the nodules to declare whether it falls under the benign or the malignant category.

IV. EXPERIMENTAL RESULTS

The data acquired for experimenting and analyzing the results of this chapter were taken from the Lung Image dataset Consortium. The number of images and the characteristics of the images are as described in Table 1. A machine learning algorithm requires a dataset to be characterised in two halves, a training data for optimizing and tuning the algorithms and its associated parameters; and a testing data for evaluating the merits of the algorithms. It is preferred that the locus of these data are not dissimilar and such is the case for the data relevant to this chapter.

Table 1. Dataset Specification

Name	Lung Image dataset Consortium (LIDC)
Access	Free online access
Link	http://www.cancerorg.com
No. of lung images used	150
No. of image nodules trained	120
No. of image nodules tested	30

The input images are taken from the LIDC datasets Diciotti, S, et.al., (2011), Armato et.al., (2011), as mentioned in the above table. The results of the process are discussed in detail as given below:

Step 1: Input Image is acquired. The nature of this image is that it is unprocessed and raw. It may be in Raw or JPEG or PNG formats. Raw formats such as ".nef" formats usually have the highest data integrity with minimal image compression. Consequently the image size is more and so is the time taken for processing it.

Figure 5. Input lung image

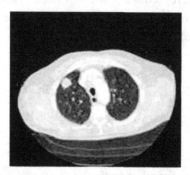

Step 2: Pre-processing using Anisotropic Non-Linear filter: This step is a sort of colloquial "clean-up" of the image. It smoothes out the jitter and aberrations present in the image, if any.

Figure 6. Anisotropic Non-linear filter pre-processed Image

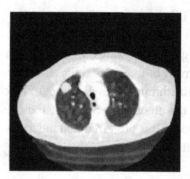

Step 3a: Nodules marking: This step performs the identification of the nodules. It is coherent to follow that identification is easier after the filtering as the nature of the filter is to target not just the edges and curves of polygon-like shapes but to soften and trim them where noise may be antithetical enough to stand out.

Figure 7. foreground and background seeds

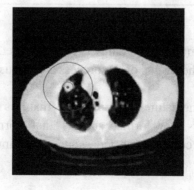

Step 3b: Improved random walk segmentation: identifying the nodules aids only to identify the locus or rather the possible locus of the nodule. It does not identify the boundary, size or nature of the nodule. Random walk segmentation is used to circumscribe this identified locus and taper its boundary. Thus, this step yields a more understandable and operable nodule for further processing.

Figure 8. Improved random walk segmentation

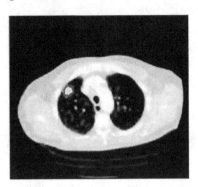

Step 4: Feature extraction: This steps extracts the features of the nodule by deploying two feature extraction techniques. The observations of which have been described in Table 2.

Table 2. Average of 120 nodule feature extraction values

Technique	GLCM	LBP
Contrast	3019.23	193.382
Dissimilarity	25.936	8.985
Energy	0.3708	0.3883
Homogeneity	0.4336	0.4395
Correlation	0.7139	0.2734
ASM	0.1775	0.1880

Step 5: Classification Results

$$Accuracy = \frac{TP + TN}{TP + TN + FP + FN} \tag{14}$$

Where,

TP- true positive indicates the malignant nodules that are correctly predicted by the classifiers.
TN- true negatives indicate the benign nodules that are predicted correctly by the classifiers.
FP- false positive indicates that the benign is wrongly decided as the malignant.
FN- false negative indicates that the malignant nodules predicted wrongly as the benign.

Figure 9. Confusion matrix

	Predicted Benign	Predicted Malignant	
Actual Benign	TN	FP	TN+FP
Actual Malignant	FN	TP	FN+TP
	TN+FN	FP+TP	

From the above process, the nodule obtained in figure 8 is found to be a malignant nodule.

For justifying the proposed research work performance the results has been compared with other previous research papers and their results are tabulated as follows:

Table 3. Comparison of Classification performance

	Classifiers used	Accuracy (percentage)
Chen, H, et.al., (2012)	Artificial neural network and logistic regression	90
Shen, W, et.al., (2017)	Convolutional neural network	87
Li, X. X., et.al., (2018)	Random forest classifier	90
Proposed research work	Back propagation based artificial neural network	100
	Random forest Classifier	91.5

V. DISCUSSION

This chapter has thus far elucidated in detail the concept and the process that drives it. Figure 5 shows that the lung images input is of axial view of CT scan images to clearly view the nodules .Figure 6 shows that the lung image has been pre-processed using the anisotropic filter only to suppress the noise present in the image without damaging the nodule boundaries. In the figure 7, center of the nodules are obtained by the geodesic distance and the background seeds are marked such as where the red color point denotes the nodule and the blue color point denotes the background seeds. In the figure 8, the red color boundary indicates the nodule has been segmented from the lung region.

Further the process continues by extracting the features from the segmented lung nodule and those values are trained for the machine learning algorithm indicating the benign and the malignant nodules. Then the classification performance of the optimized proposed model is tested from the confusion matrix with the accuracy parameter calculated from the matrix.

In the paper Chen, H, et.al., (2012), the comparison between the artificial neural network and the regression algorithm takes place to achieve the classification performance. From this chapter it is concluded that the neural network algorithm has the higher accuracy rate when compared with the regression. In Shen, W, et.al., (2017) convolutional neural network algorithms are used for classification purposes and achieved almost 87% accuracy. The random forest classifier Li, X. X., et.al., (2018) the hybrid feature extraction is used along with the random walk segmentation achieved the accuracy of 90%. The proposed model achieves more accuracy compared to previous papers. Thus, the features are completely reduced in the sense to give more classification accuracy and it is tested using the neural network and the random forest classifier. Where, the proposed model gives much satisfying results after the testing process. The accuracy is increased when compared with the recent research works.

VI. CONCLUSION AND FUTURE WORK

The features calculated from the segmented nodules has been reduced, such that to show that the above mentioned features are more than sufficient to classify the nodules present in lung cancer. By following the process almost 91.5% accuracy has been detected by the random forest classifier and 100% in the artificial neural network algorithm. Due to less features obtained from the nodule segmentation it becomes more accurate to find out the results. Neural networks work well for small datasets and for large datasets the complexity of the network increases. In the future work, the number of lung nodules used can be increased in number, for training the classifiers and in turn to improve the classification performance in identifying the nodules present in the lung. And added to that feature extraction technique can be revised to bring out the more accurate texture based features to improve the performance.

REFERENCES

Adi, K., Widodo, C. E., Widodo, A. P., Gernowo, R., Pamungkas, A., & Syifa, R. A. (2018). Detection Lung Cancer Using Gray Level Co-Occurrence Matrix (GLCM) and Back Propagation Neural Network Classification. *Journal of Engineering Science & Technology Review, 11*(2).

Armato, S. G. III, McLennan, G., Bidaut, L., McNitt-Gray, M. F., Meyer, C. R., Reeves, A. P., ... Kazerooni, E. A. (2011). The lung image database consortium (LIDC) and image database resource initiative (IDRI): A completed reference database of lung nodules on CT scans. *Medical Physics, 38*(2), 915–931. doi:10.1118/1.3528204 PMID:21452728

Chen, H., Zhang, J., Xu, Y., Chen, B., & Zhang, K. (2012). Performance comparison of artificial neural network and logistic regression model for differentiating lung nodules on CT scans. *Expert Systems with Applications, 39*(13), 11503–11509. doi:10.1016/j.eswa.2012.04.001

de Pinho Pinheiro, C. A., Nedjah, N., & de Macedo Mourelle, L. (2020). Detection and classification of pulmonary nodules using deep learning and swarm intelligence. *Multimedia Tools and Applications*, *79*(21), 15437–15465. doi:10.100711042-019-7473-z

Diciotti, S., Lombardo, S., Falchini, M., Picozzi, G., & Mascalchi, M. (2011). Automated segmentation refinement of small lung nodules in CT scans by local shape analysis. *IEEE Transactions on Biomedical Engineering*, *58*(12), 3418–3428. doi:10.1109/TBME.2011.2167621 PMID:21914567

Dong, X., Shen, J., Shao, L., & Van Gool, L. (2015). Sub-Markov random walk for image segmentation. *IEEE Transactions on Image Processing*, *25*(2), 516–527. doi:10.1109/TIP.2015.2505184 PMID:26661298

Eslami, A., Karamalis, A., Katouzian, A., & Navab, N. (2013). Segmentation by retrieval with guided random walks: Application to left ventricle segmentation in MRI. *Medical Image Analysis*, *17*(2), 236–253. doi:10.1016/j.media.2012.10.005 PMID:23313331

Grady, L. (2006). Random walks for image segmentation. *IEEE Transactions on Pattern Analysis and Machine Intelligence*, *28*(11), 1768–1783. doi:10.1109/TPAMI.2006.233 PMID:17063682

Han, F., Wang, H., Zhang, G., Han, H., Song, B., Li, L., ... Liang, Z. (2015). Texture feature analysis for computer-aided diagnosis on pulmonary nodules. *Journal of Digital Imaging*, *28*(1), 99–115. doi:10.100710278-014-9718-8 PMID:25117512

He, Z., Lv, W., & Hu, J. (2020). A Simple Method to Train the AI Diagnosis Model of Pulmonary Nodules. *Computational and Mathematical Methods in Medicine*. PMID:32802147

Ju, W., Xiang, D., Zhang, B., Wang, L., Kopriva, I., & Chen, X. (2015). Random walk and graph cut for co-segmentation of lung tumor on PET-CT images. *IEEE Transactions on Image Processing*, *24*(12), 5854–5867. doi:10.1109/TIP.2015.2488902 PMID:26462198

Kumar, M. V. (2020, July). Detection of Lung Nodules using Convolution Neural Network: A Review. In *2020 Second International Conference on Inventive Research in Computing Applications (ICIRCA)* (pp. 590-594). IEEE. 10.1109/ICIRCA48905.2020.9183183

Li, X., Yang, Y., Xiong, H., Song, S., & Jia, H. (2017, May). Pulmonary nodules detection algorithm based on robust cascade classifier for CT images. In *2017 29th Chinese Control And Decision Conference (CCDC)* (pp. 231-235). IEEE. 10.1109/CCDC.2017.7978097

Li, X. X., Li, B., Tian, L. F., & Zhang, L. (2018). Automatic benign and malignant classification of pulmonary nodules in thoracic computed tomography based on RF algorithm. *IET Image Processing*, *12*(7), 1253–1264. doi:10.1049/iet-ipr.2016.1014

Liu, J., Wang, S., Linguraru, M. G., Yao, J., & Summers, R. M. (2015). Computer-aided detection of exophytic renal lesions on non-contrast CT images. *Medical Image Analysis*, *19*(1), 15–29. doi:10.1016/j.media.2014.07.005 PMID:25189363

Monkam, P., Qi, S., Ma, H., Gao, W., Yao, Y., & Qian, W. (2019). Detection and classification of pulmonary nodules using convolutional neural networks: A survey. *IEEE Access: Practical Innovations, Open Solutions*, *7*, 78075–78091. doi:10.1109/ACCESS.2019.2920980

Rastghalam, R., & Pourghassem, H. (2016). Breast cancer detection using MRF-based probable texture feature and decision-level fusion-based classification using HMM on thermography images. *Pattern Recognition*, *51*, 176–186. doi:10.1016/j.patcog.2015.09.009

Shen, W., Zhou, M., Yang, F., Yu, D., Dong, D., Yang, C., ... Tian, J. (2017). Multi-crop convolutional neural networks for lung nodule malignancy suspiciousness classification. *Pattern Recognition*, *61*, 663–673. doi:10.1016/j.patcog.2016.05.029

Chapter 7
Segmentation of Optic Disc From Fundus Image Based on Morphology and SVM Classifier

Jiamin Luo
Shantou University, China

Alex Noel Joseph Raj
Shantou University, China

Nersisson Ruban
iD https://orcid.org/0000-0003-1695-3618
Vellore Institute of Technology, India

Vijayalakshmi G. V. Mahesh
iD https://orcid.org/0000-0002-1917-7506
BMS Institute of Technology and Management, India

ABSTRACT

Color fundus image is the most basic way to diagnose diabetic retinopathy, papillary edema, and glaucoma. In particular, since observing the morphological changes of the optic disc is conducive to the diagnosis of related diseases, accurate and effective positioning and segmentation of the optic disc is an important process. Optic disc segmentation algorithms are mainly based on template matching, deformable model and learning. According to the character that the shape of the optic disc is approximately circular, this proposed research work uses Kirsch operator to get the edge of the green channel fundus image through morphological operation, and then detects the optic disc by HOUGH circle transformation. In addition, supervised learning in machine learning is also applied in this chapter. First, the vascular mask is obtained by morphological operation for vascular erasure, and then the SVM classifier is segmented by HU moment invariant feature and gray level feature. The test results on the DRIONS fundus image database with expert-labeled optic disc contour show that the two methods have good results and high accuracy in optic disc segmentation. Even though seven different assessment parameters (sensitivity [Se], specificity [Sp], accuracy [Acc], positive predicted value [Ppv], and negative predicted value [Npv]) are used for performance assessment of the algorithm. Accuracy is considered as the criterion of judgment

DOI: 10.4018/978-1-7998-6690-9.ch007

in this chapter. The average accuracy achieved for the nine random test set is 97.7%, which is better than any other classifiers used for segmenting Optical Disc from Fundus Images.

1. INTRODUCTION

1.1 Research Background and Significance

Diabetic retinopathy, hypertension, glaucoma and macular degeneration are the most common causes of visual impairment and blindness (Mariotti,S.P. and Pascolini,D. 2012). The basis for diagnosis of ophthalmic diseases is color fundus image. Through fundus images, experts can directly observe the structure and direction of arteriovenous vessels, the proportion and change of optic disc and cup. This can help doctors to detect the above-mentioned ophthalmic diseases as early as possible, and provide more accurate diagnostic results for patients (Beiji. Z. et al, 2015). Usually, more than 80% of global visual impairment cases can be avoided in advance.

The optic disc is a basic anatomical structure in the fundus of the eye. In color fundus images, it is usually light yellow bright spots similar to circular or elliptic shapes. The gray level of the pixels is higher than other structures. The retinal vessels converge in the center of the optic disc and enter the optic nerve. Hypertension, glaucoma and other diseases can cause optic disc depression and then pathological changes. Analysis of the morphological changes of the optic disc is helpful to the diagnosis of related diseases. Therefore, the location and segmentation of the optic disc has been one of the hot topics of research. However, due to the interference of fundus diseases, non-uniform illumination and contrast, accurate segmentation of the optic disc region is very challenging (Xiaomei . X. et al., 2017).

1.2 Fundus Camera and Fundus Image Structure

Fundus camera is used to take pictures of retina, optic disc, arteriovenous vessels, macula and optic nerve, etc. These structures can be observed directly by fundus images, which can provide auxiliary diagnostic information for fundus diseases caused by various related diseases (Ping . J., 2018).

As shown in Figure 1, there are structures of optic disc, optic cup, macular area and arteriovenous vessels in the fundus of the eye. The optic disc is the place where most of the blood vessels converge in the retina. Its structure is a disc shape which is clearer and brighter than other parts (Fondon, I. et al 2013). Within the optic disc area, arteries and veins are thicker and have many branches. The cup is in the center of the disc, and its brightness is higher than that of other parts of the disc. The macular area is a large circular area with darker color (Zheng.S., et al., 2014). The arteries and veins in the retina begin at the center of the optic disc and extend outward. Retinal artery blood vessels are bright red, because they are rich in oxygen. The venous blood vessel has a lower oxygen content than the arterial blood vessel, showing a dark red color, and it is thicker than the arterial blood vessel (Yuan .Z., 2012).

Figure 1. Fundus structure sketch

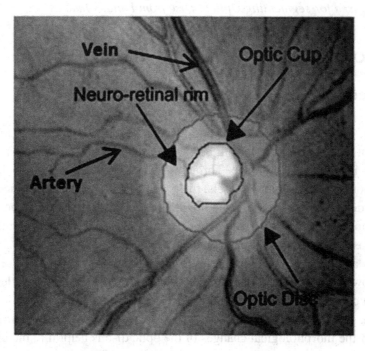

1.3 Research Status of Optic Disc Detection

Over the years, experts and scholars at home and abroad have made many explorations on the location and segmentation of optic discs.

There are mainly three kinds of location algorithms for the optic disc, which focus on the brightness, shape and vascular characteristics of the optic disc. The brightness characteristic is that the optic disc is the brightest part in the fundus image, which is in sharp contrast with the dim part of the non-optic disc. Suero, A. et al., (2013) and other scholars applied morphological operations to fundus images in their literature, then extracted the brightest part and calculated the center of gravity of this area as the position of the optic disc. Shape characteristics refer to the shape of the disc is similar to that of an ellipse or a circle, and the boundary is obvious. Lu S (2011) used HOUGH circular transformation to detect the optic disc in their literature. The characteristics of blood vessels are that the central part of the optic disc is the convergence point of arteries and veins and the starting point of outward extension. The blood vessels are dense and have many branches. In addition, the distribution of blood vessels in the whole image is similar to a parabola, and the vertex of the parabola is located in the center of the disc (Qi Jiajun, 2017). Hoover A and Goldbaum M., (2003) and other scholars in their literature, according to the characteristics that the starting points of the ophthalmic arteries and veins intersect the optic disc, use the fuzzy set to get the number of segments of the blood vessels, and then select the point with the greatest convergence as the detection result. Yin .P et al., (2019) suggested Region Proposal Network (RPN) combined Mask-RCNN algorithm to segment Optic Disc (OD), Optic Cup (OC) and Optic Nerve Head (ONH). Authors claim that by combining this approches, OC and OD overlapping and errors due to partially surrounded proposals can be reduced. Bhat S.H et al., (2019) proposed that Circular Hough Transform (CHT) and localized active contour model (ACM) based image processing operations can be utilized to localize and segmente the Optic Disc (OD). Elbalaoui. A et al., (2018) have presented an approcah to segment the OD by localizing the OD center, and using vesselness filters, eliminating the vascular structure. This approch will segment the OD by the boundary by incorpoating an active contour model. Bhatkalkar, B et al., (2020) have proposed a transfer learning based CNN approch for Fundus Image Quality Assessment.

There are three main methods for disc segmentation: template matching, deformable model and learning. Because of the shape characteristics of the disc, the template method usually models the disc as an ellipse or a circle. Giachetti, A. et al., (2014) used circles and ellipses to approximate the contour of the optic disc in their literature. The method based on deformable model usually starts from the initial disk contour and deforms to the edge of the disk according to various energy terms. These energy terms are usually defined by image intensity, image gradient or edge smoothness. B. Dai et al., (2017) proposed a method of optic disc segmentation which integrates three variational models of energy terms, namely phase boundary energy, shape energy based on principal component analysis and region energy. The learning method usually trains the classifier from the existing label data and divides the pixels into two categories: videodisc pixels or non-videodisc pixels. Abramoff. M. D., et al., (2007) proposed a pixel classification method in his literature, and explored various features used to segment the optic disc and cup, including intensity, gradient, Gauss ambiguity, prior probability.

1.4 Introduction to Database

The database used in this study is DRIONS fundus image database, which consists of 110 color digital retinal images. These images were captured with a color fundus camera. In order to make the image in digital format, the database uses HP-Photosmart-S20 high resolution scanner to digitize the image in RGB format. The resolution of the image is 600 x 400, and the size of each pixel is 8 bits. In this data, the average age of the patients was 53.0 years, of which 46.2% were males and 53.8% were females.

In addition, the database contains the outline of the video disc manually marked by two experts with medical education and rich ophthalmological experience. In this chapter, the manual marking value of the first expert is used as the basis for judgment. Because the image in the database contains interference information such as digital number, this research cuts the image into a fundus image with a resolution of 350 *300 and a optic disc (Feijoo, J. G., 2014)

1.5 Introduction of MATLAB

MATLAB is a programming language developed by MathWorks. It can operate matrix, plot, implement algorithm, create user interface, and interact with other programming languages (MathWorks, Inc. 2005).

All the algorithms in this research are based on MATLAB. They are mainly used in the functions of various morphological algorithms in MATLAB, ginput functions in the manual marking of pixels and other basic functions of the algorithm. In addition, the LIBSVM software package developed by Professor Lin Zhiren is also used in this research work.

1.6 Research Methodology and Structural Arrangement

The main obective of this chapter is to design different algorithms to segment the video disc in the fundus image. The chapter consists of three sections:

The first section mainly describes the composition of fundus image, the purpose, significance and research status of optic disc location and segmentation. In addition, the first chapter also introduces the DRIONS database and MATLAB toolkit used.

Section 2 describes the algorithm of optic disc detection in this chapter. In this chapter, we introduce two disc detection algorithms in detail: disc segmentation based on morphological operation, Kirsch operator edge detection and Hough transform, and disc segmentation based on SVM (support vector machine) classifier. At the same time, this chapter also applies these two algorithms to DRIONS fundus image database for testing and comparison.

Section 3 is the summary of this chapter about the optic disc detection work. In this chapter, the advantages and disadvantages of the two algorithms mentioned above are concluded and the related results are compared. At the same time, the future work of video detection is prospected.

2. OPTIC DISC DETECTION

The most common method of optic disc location and segmentation is using morphological operations. In this chapter, morphological method and machine learning method will be chosen to detect the VCD, and the corresponding VCD segmentation results will be obtained on DRIONS database. Machine learning can be divided into supervised learning and unsupervised learning according to whether or not the data is marked on the training set. The SVM classifier used normally have two classifications in supervised learning.

2.1 Video Disc Detection Based on Morphological Method

In this section, we will introduce a method based on morphological operation, Kirsch operator and Hough transform to obtain the edge information of the optic disc. Figure 2 shows the flow chart of the algorithm for optic disk detection based on this method. In the pre-processing stage, the fundus image of the color fundus camera is obtained from the database, and then the image is passed through the green channel, in which the optic disc and blood vessel are clearer than the red channel and the blue channel. Then, the image is erased and equalized by morphological closure operation and histogram equalization. Finally, according to the brightness characteristics of the video disc, the pixels with the highest

Figure 2. Flow Chart of Optic Disc Detection Based on Morphological Method

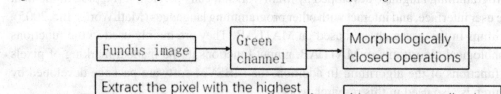

brightness of the first 10% are extracted as the input of edge detection. R. Kirsch invented the Kirsch detection operator in 1971, which is an effective algorithm for edge detection(Kirsch R., 1971, Chen X. F and Wang Y., 2008). This method is based on eight templates in different directions. The selection of edges is based on the part with the greatest directional response. Through this operation, better target edges can be obtained. After the edge of the image is detected, the roughly circular contour of the optic disc is obtained by Hough transform. Next, the author will introduce the method of optic disc detection based on morphology in detail.

2.1.1 Pretreatment

Ophthalmologists use high-resolution fundus cameras to scan the patient's retina to obtain retinal images. Because these images show poor contrast between retinal vascular structure and optic disc and background after scanning, proper preprocessing techniques are needed before accurate segmentation of the retinal disc. In Figure 3, a) is a color fundus image, b), c) and d) are; red channel image, green channel image and blue channel image, respectively. It can be seen that the most abundant and clear detail of the optic disc in various image channels is the green channel, so the color fundus image is processed through this channel first.

Figure 3. Fundus image: a) color fundus image, b) red channel fundus image, c) green channel fundus image, d) blue channel fundus image

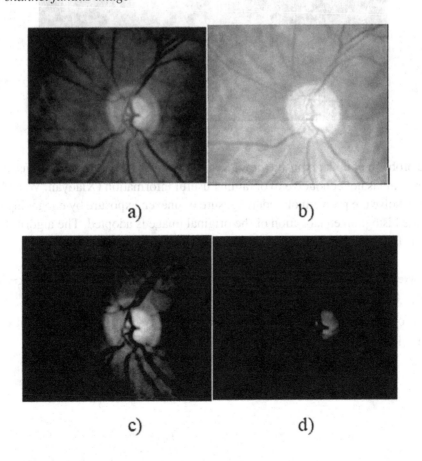

In order to reduce the interference of blood vessels, the image obtained in the previous step will be erased by morphological closure operation. Closed operation can make the fine structure disappear. At the same time, morphological closed operation requires not only the image with slender structure, but also the image with low brightness value. Just the vascular structure and brightness in the fundus of the eye can meet its requirements. Therefore, the removal of blood vessels can be carried out by using closed operation of disc-shaped structural elements. In this chapter, a disc-shaped structure with radius five is selected to erase blood vessels. The results are shown in Figure 4.

Figure 4. Fundus image after morphological closure

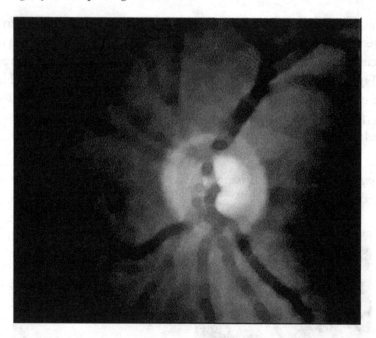

Usually, the problem of underexposure or uneven exposure exists in the fundus image, which makes the image blurred and is not conducive to obtaining useful information (Xiaoyan. W. and Jinggang. X., 2009). In order to solve the problem of underexposure or uneven exposure by enhancing the contrast of fundus image, the histogram equalization of the original image is adopted. The algorithm of histogram equalization is as follows:

1)   The total pixel N of the original image is calculated and the number of pixels n_k .(k= 0, 1, 2,...,255), gray level r_k .is counted respectively.

2)   In order to obtain the original histogram, the probability distribution $p_r . r_k$ .of each gray level should be calculated first. The formula is as follows:

$$p_r\left(r_k\right) = \frac{n_k}{n}, k = 0,1,2\ldots K \cdot \tag{1}$$

3) The histogram cumulative distribution function s_k .of the original image is calculated. The formula is as follows:

$$s_k = T\left(r_k\right) = \sum_{j=0}^{k} p_r(r_j).$$ (2)

4) For integral calculation, the formula is as follows:

$$s_k = \text{int}\left[\left(N-1\right)s_k + 0.5\right], N = 256.$$ (3)

5) Establishment of projective correspondence ($r_k \rightarrow s_k$.(k= 0, 1, 2,..., 255),displaying the equalized image.

Based on the brightness characteristics of the optic disc in the fundus image, the equalized image can basically get the part of the optic disc by extracting the brightest pixels in the first 10%. Figure 5 shows the image after histogram equalization and extraction of the brightest pixels. This image will be used as an input image for edge detection.

Figure 5. Image after histogram equalization and extraction of the brightest pixels

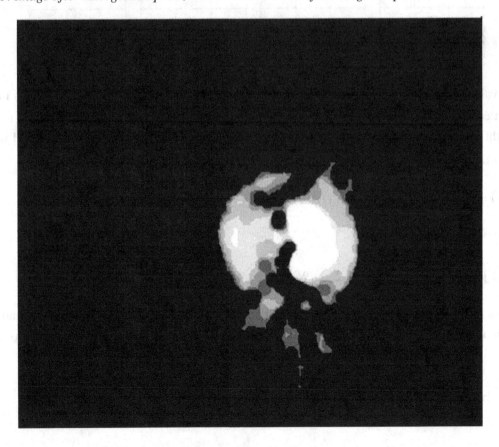

2.1.2 Edge Detection Based on Kirsch Operator

In the 1970s, R. Kirsch put forward a new idea, Kirsch operator, which is used for edge detection: Kirsch operator convolutes the same pixel in the image using eight templates with different directions and 45 degrees of angle between each direction, so as to get the magnitude and direction of the gradient. Among them, the intensity of the edge is the maximum value of direction response, so the direction of the edge is the direction corresponding to it. This method can obtain better image edges and smooth noise. The widely used Kirsch template is shown in Figure 6.

Figure 6. Kirsch Direction Template

5	5	5
-3	0	-3
-3	-3	-3

-3	5	5
-3	0	5
-3	-3	-3

-3	-3	5
-3	0	5
-3	-3	5

-3	-3	-3
-3	0	5
-3	5	5

-3	-3	-3
-3	0	-3
5	5	5

-3	-3	-3
5	0	-3
5	5	-3

5	-3	-3
5	0	-3
5	-3	-3

5	5	-3
5	0	-3
-3	-3	-3

The values in the N direction template (i, j) are represented by $M_n(i,j)$. the input fundus image is represented by I, and the pixel values i n (a, b) are represented by I (a, b). Figure. 2-4 is used to filter I with eight filter templates. Suppose $f_n(a,b)$ .is the filter value at (a, b) obtained by filtering I with the nth filter template. $f_n(a,b)$ .is defined as:

$$f_n(a,b) = \sum_{(i,j)=\tilde{A}} I(a+i,b+j) M_n(i,j).$$

(4)

(i=-1,0,1 j=-1,0,1 a=1,2,…,H b=1,2, …,W)

In this formula, σis the 3*3 region where the template is located, W and H are the width and height of the sample image I respectively, and the maximum $f_{max}(a,b)$ .f the eight filtered values is defined as:

$$f_{max}(a,b) = \max\{f1(a,b), f2(a,b),…,f8(a,b)\}.$$

(5)

The filtered image is composed of $f_{max}(a, b)$. The extremum image FI_{MAX} .ased on its extremum points is defined as:

$$FI_{MAX} = \begin{bmatrix} FI(1,1) & \cdots & FI(1,W) \\ \vdots & \ddots & \vdots \\ FI(H,1) & \cdots & FI(H,W) \end{bmatrix}. \tag{6}$$

In this formula, the pixel value at (a, b) is expressed by FI (a, b). If (a, b) is the extreme point in the image, then FI (a, b) is equal to $f_{max}(a, b)$. otherwise, FI (a, b) is equal to 0. According to FI_{MAX} .and pre-set threshold T, the edge image EI can be obtained, which is defined as:

$$EI = \begin{bmatrix} EI(1,1) & \cdots & EI(1,W) \\ \vdots & \ddots & \vdots \\ EI(H,1) & \cdots & EI(H,W) \end{bmatrix}. \tag{7}$$

In this formula, the pixel value at (a, b) is expressed by EI (a, b). If FI (a, b) is greater than T, the value of EI (a, b) is 1. Otherwise, EI (a, b) is 0.

The contour image obtained by Kirsch edge detection algorithm is shown in Figure 7. The rough region of the optic disc is marked, which is conducive to the next step of the optic disc segmentation.

Figure 7. Edge Detection of Fundus Image Based on Kirsch Operator

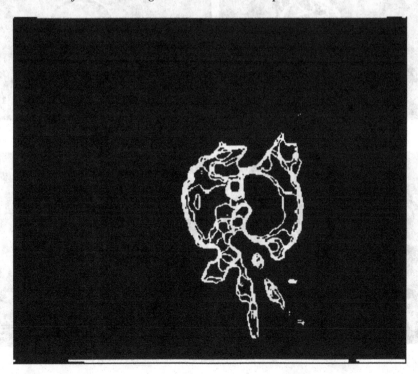

2.1.3 Hough transform

Hough, A., (1962) obtained a patent for the method the transforming technique he proposed which is usually called Hough transform. It is a method that changes the problem of global curve acquisition into an effective peak acquisition problem in parameter space by calculating a certain formula (Mukhopadhyay, P., and Chaudhuri, B. B. 2015, Alioua, N. et al., 2011). It can be effectively recognized as the line in the Figure. 8.

When the form of a circle is taken into account, the transformation formula of the equation is as follows:

$$r^2 = (x-a)^2 + (y-b)^2 . \qquad (8)$$

In this formula, the radius of the circle is expressed in r, and the abscissa and ordinate of the center of the circle are expressed in a and B respectively. After Hough transform, the results are shown in Figure 8. From (a) we can see that this method can depict the contour of the optic disc approximate to the circle, and from (b) we can see that the optic disc segmented by this method is very similar to the expert marker.

Figure 8. Optic Disk Segmentation Results: a) & c)Images after Using Hough Transform, b) & d)Result Images by this method with Expert Markers

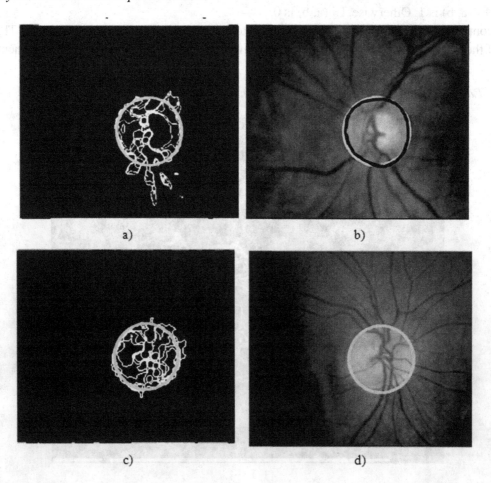

a)

b)

c)

d)

2.1.4 Result Analysis

In this chapter, Hough transform is used to obtain the circular boundary similar to the edge of the optic disc, and then the center of the circle is used as the central coordinate of the optic disc. If the coordinates of the center of the circle are located in the boundary of the optic disc, the result of the positioning is considered correct, otherwise it is considered wrong. In order to verify the feasibility of this algorithm, the morphological algorithm is tested in DRIONS fundus image database. In 110 fundus images tested, the accuracy rate of optic disc location is 99.19%, which shows that the algorithm works well.

Figure 9. Schematic diagram for calculating area overlap rate

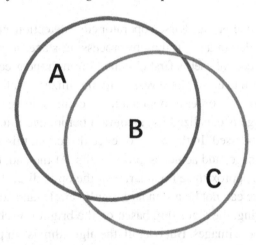

In order to further test the accuracy of this method for optic disc segmentation, this chapter adopts the method of detecting area overlap rate. As shown in Figure 9, the blue coil represents the result of the optic disc obtained by the algorithm in this section, and the red coil represents the result of the optic disc manually marked by experts provided by the database. Then the area of the optic disc obtained by the algorithm is A+B, the area of the optic disc labeled by experts is B+C, and the formula for calculating the area coincidence rate S is as follows:

$$S = B / (A + B + C). \tag{9}$$

According to the formula, the higher the area overlap rate S, the higher the accuracy of optic disk segmentation.

As shown in Table 1, the results of this algorithm are comparable with those of Morales et al. (2013) based on morphological operations and PCA. Table 2 shows the results of specific area overlap rates

Table 1. Comparison of area overlap rate

Algorithm	Area overlap rate
proposed Hough transform based algorithm	0.83
Morphological operations and PCA algorithm (Morales et al. 2013)	0.84

Table 2. Statistics of area overlap rate

Area overlap rate	Number of Images Overlap
≥ 0.9 .	4
	36
	70
	82

2.1.5 Summary and Discussion

In this section, morphological operations, Kirsch operator edge detection and Hough transform are used to detect the optic disc of fundus image. In the pre-processing stage, in order to get the clearest image, the image obtained from the data set is first obtained through the green channel; this section uses morphological closure operation to erase blood vessels to minimize the interference of blood vessels on the optic disc segmentation; then, in order to obtain a more contrast image and obtain the approximate area of the optic disc, the image is equalized by histogram before and after. The method of extracting the brightest pixel points is processed. In the phase of edge detection, this section uses Kirsch operator to detect the edge of fundus image, and achieves good results. At the end, the image is transformed by Hough transform to obtain the approximate boundaries of the optic disc.

In practice, because the disc can not be a standard regular circle, and some images are overexposed or underexposed during shooting, the algorithm based on the brightness characteristics of the disc has poor segmentation effect on these images. But overall, the algorithm is simple, convenient and effective for most images.

In the future work, we can get better results by further improving the brightness and replacing the regular circle with ellipse.

2.2 Optic Disc Detection Based on SVM Classifier

In this section, we will introduce the method of video disc detection based on SVM classifier. Figure 10 shows the flow chart of the algorithm for video disk detection based on this method. In the pre-processing stage, the basic contour of the blood vessel is obtained by the bottom cap operation of the fundus image through the green channel, and then the error of blood vessel acquisition is reduced by the morphological expansion operation. Finally, it is transformed into a binary image as a mask. On the other hand, the fundus image through the green channel is closed morphologically. Then, the pixel value of the vascular part in the closed image is extracted by using the mask mentioned above, and then the image is superimposed on the image which removes the vascular part, so as to achieve the purpose of eliminating the blood vessel. After preprocessing, HU moment invariant feature and gray level feature are extracted from the image pixels to obtain useful information. In order to solve the problem of class imbalance, this chapter uses manual labeling to obtain training pixels, which account for half of all the pixels of the disc and the non-disc, because the pixels of the disc are far less than those of the non-disc. Secondly, the training set adopts the support vector machine classifier with kernel function, and then operates on the classification results, and finally evaluates the performance of the classification. Next, the author will give a detailed introduction to this method of VCD segmentation based on machine learning.

2.2.1 Pretreatment

As we know before, the vascular part should be removed before optic disc segmentation. This is because when the optic disc is extracted, the blood vessel part of the optic disc is dark, which is in sharp contrast to the brightness of the optic disc. This contrast will make the blood vessel part become serious interference. Therefore, it is necessary to remove the blood vessels and segment the optic disc.

As in the previous section, this section takes the green channel with obvious contrast as the input image (Figure 11.a). In order to remove the blood vessel, the first step is to extract the blood vessel. In this chapter, the method of morphological cap transformation is used to extract the vascular pixels in the image, which is introduced in the literature "Research on the Location and Segmentation of the Optic Disk in the Eye Fundus Image" (Jiajun. Q., 2017).

Bottom cap transformation is a method that uses the difference between the result image of morphological closed operation and the original image to achieve the enhancement effect. The morphological closed operation can remove the small structure with low brightness value in the image, and then subtract the result image of the small structure from the original image by the closed operation, which can show these structures, and at the same time can restrain the part of the region that does not change significantly. The expression of the bottom cap transformation is as follows:

$$h = \left(f \bullet b\right) - f.$$ (10)

The working condition of the bottom cap operation is that the object structure is small, and the brightness value of the object can not be too high. In the fundus of the eye, the blood vessel is just the slender part of the image structure and the brightness is not high, so it can be obtained by the bottom cap operation. The result of bottom cap calculation is directly related to the shape and size of the selected structural elements. In fundus image, because the diameter of the thickest blood vessel accounts for about 6 pixels, a disc structure with radius of 6 is used to enhance the partial pixels of blood vessel. The result of the cap transform is shown in Figure 11.b. The cap transform erases the rest of the optic disc and extracts the required vascular structure.

After extracting the blood vessel information, the blood vessel segmentation image is used as a mask (Figure 11.c). In this chapter, a disc structure is used to expand the mask morphologically in order to avoid the effect of the wrong segmentation on the removal of blood vessels as far as possible. The obtained vascular mask image is shown in Figure 11.d.

In this chapter, a disc-shaped structure with radius of 5 is adopted in the morphological closure operation of the image through the green channel to obtain the image of morphological vascular removal. As shown in Figure 11.(e), although the vascular part is removed to a certain extent, the optic disc part is blurred. Thus, using a vascular mask (Figure 11.d) to cover the morphological vascular removal image (Figure 11.e), the pixel values only in the vascular part can be obtained. Finally, the final image can be obtained by adding only the image of blood vessel and the image of removing blood vessel, as shown in Figure 11.f. Results Compared with the original image, the vascular components were erased a lot, and some details of the optic disc were retained, which provided convenience for the next feature extraction operation.

Figure 10. Flow Chart of Optic Disk Segmentation Based on SVM Classifier

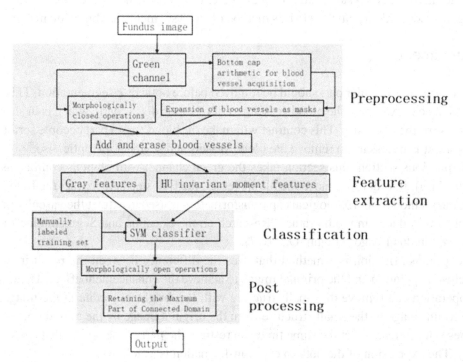

Figure 11. Preprocessing: a) Green Channel Fundus Image, b) Bottom Cap Transform to Obtain Vessels, c) Vascular Mask, d) Vascular Mask Expansion, e) Morphological Closure of Green Channel Image, f) Mask Erasion Effect

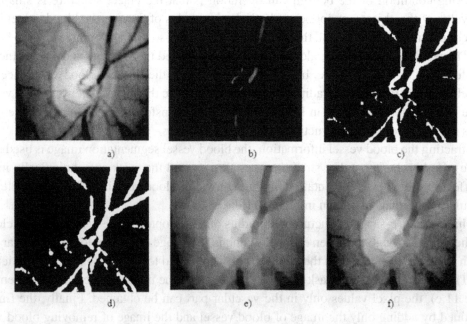

2.2.2 Acquisition of Training Sets

Fundus images contain more non-optic disc pixels than optic disc pixels. If all the pixels in the image are used as training data, an unbalanced data set will be obtained. When the neural network is tested, the classifier's ability to classify non-disc pixels is better than that of disc pixels. Therefore, a training data set is needed, which has the same distribution of optic disk and non-optic disk pixels, in order to obtain the best classification effect. For this purpose, the first eight fundus images in the database are labeled manually as training. Each image has 2000 labeled optic disk pixels and 2000 non-optic disk pixels. Some of the labeled images are shown in Figure 12.

Figure 12. Hand-labeled training set (blue dots represent optic disc pixels and yellow dots represent non-optic disc pixels)

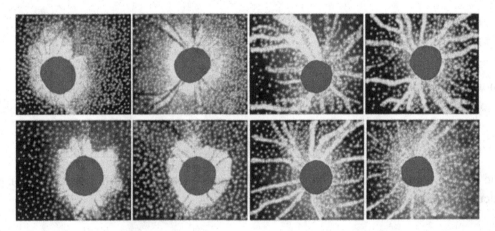

2.2.3 Feature Extraction

Feature extraction represents each pixel of retinal image in the form of feature vectors. The feature vectors contain useful information, which can distinguish between the two categories of optic disk pixels and non-optic disk pixels. In this method, feature vectors are represented by a set of features based on HU invariant moments and a set of gray features. The following two groups of characteristics are introduced.

2.2.3.1 HU Invariant Moment Characteristics

Invariant moments are very important for image recognition or classification, and are widely used as recognition features in many areas of image processing. In the 1960s, Hu.M.K. proved that HU invariant moment has the characteristics of rotation, scaling and translation invariance (Flusser, J., and Suk, T. 2006). The geometric moment m_{pq} .f image f (x, y) is defined as:

$$m_{pq} = \sum_x \sum_y x^p x^q f(x,y), p,q = 0,1,2\ldots. \tag{11}$$

In this formula, pis the order of the image in the x direction and q is the order of the image in the y direction.

The geometric moment of image f (x, y) μ_{pq} .s defined as:

$$\mu_{pq} = \sum_{y=1}^{N} \sum_{x=1}^{M} (x - \bar{x})^p (y - \bar{y})^q f(x,y), p,q = 0,1,2 \ldots. \tag{12}$$

In this formula, N represents the height of the image and M represents the width. Among them, $\bar{x}$ .and $\bar{y}$ .re the centers of gravity of images, and the formulas are as follows:

$$\bar{x} = m_{10} / m_{00}. \tag{13}$$

$$\bar{y} = m_{01} / m_{00}. \tag{14}$$

The normalized center distance is defined as:

$$\eta_{pq} = \mu_{pq} / (\mu_{00}^{\rho}., \rho = \frac{p+q}{2} + 1. \tag{15}$$

On the basis of normalized central moments, HU defines a set of seven different moment invariants. Their calculation methods are as follows:

$$\phi 1 = \eta_{20} + \eta_{02}. \tag{16}$$

$$\phi 2 = (\eta_{20} + \eta_{02})^2 + 4\eta_{11}^2. \tag{17}$$

$$\phi 3 = (\eta_{30} - 3\eta_{12})^2 + (3\eta_{21} - \eta_{03})^2. \tag{18}$$

$$\phi 4 = (\eta_{30} + \eta_{12})^2 + (\eta_{21} + \eta_{03})^2. \tag{19}$$

$$\phi 5 = (\eta_{30} - 3\eta_{12})(\eta_{30} + \eta_{12})\left[(\eta_{30} + \eta_{12})^2 - 3(\eta_{21} + \eta_{03})^2\right]$$
$$+3(\eta_{21} - \eta_{03})(\eta_{21} + \eta_{03})\left[3(\eta_{30} + \eta_{12})^2 - (\eta_{21} + \eta_{03})^2\right]. \tag{20}$$

$$\Phi6 = (\eta_{20} - \eta_{02})\left[(\eta_{30} + \eta_{12})^2 - (\eta_{21} + \eta_{03})^2\right].$$

(21)

$$\Phi7 = 3(\eta_{21} - \eta_{03})(\eta_{30} + \eta_{12})\left[(\eta_{30} + \eta_{12})^2 - 3(\eta_{21} + \eta_{03})^2\right]$$
$$-(\eta_{30} - 3\eta_{12})(\eta_{21} + \eta_{03})\left[3(\eta_{30} + \eta_{12})^2 - (\eta_{21} + \eta_{03})^2\right].$$

(22)

The first two invariants are enough to get the best performance by testing different feature collocation methods in MATLAB. Therefore, this chapter takes $\phi1$ .and $\phi2$ .as HU invariant moment features, which reduces the computational complexity (Huang, Z., and Leng, J. 2010).

As shown in Figure 13, the first two HU invariant moment eigenvalues corresponding to the optic disk pixels and non-optic disk pixels are compared. The left image is $\phi1$. the right image is $\phi2$. the blue dot represents the non-optic disk pixels, and the red dot represents the optic disk pixels. It can be seen that HU invariant moments can distinguish the two kinds of pixels very well.

Figure 13. Plots of Magnitudes for HU Features: Blue dots represent non Optic Disk Pixels and Red Dots Represent Optic Disk Pixels

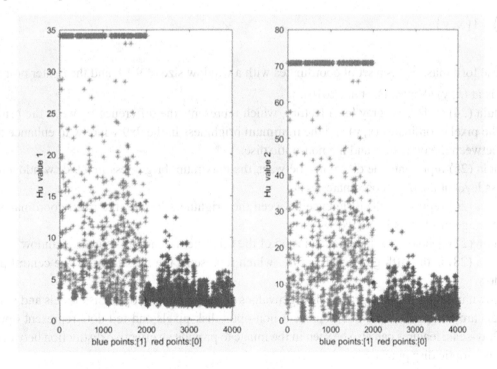

2.2.3.2 Gray Level Characteristics

The disc is usually brighter than the non-disc part of the green channel image. Therefore, the gray value of the pixels in the optic disc is higher than that of other parts of the pixels, and these gray information can be used as features. The gray features reflect the statistical distribution of brightness in the neighborhood of a particular pixel. The pre-processed image I after contrast enhancement is used as the initial image, and (x, y) is used as the center to operate on a 9*9 window. A set of gray-based features is generated for each image pixel (x, y). The eigenvectors are calculated as follows:

$$f_1(x,y) = I(x,y) - \min_{(s,t) \in S_{x,y}^9} \{I_h(s,t)\}.$$ (23)

$$f_2(x,y) = \max_{(s,t) \in S_{x,y}^9} \{I_h(s,t)\} - I(x,y).$$ (24)

$$f_3(x,y) = I(x,y) - \text{mean}_{(s,t) \in S_{x,y}^9} \{I_h(s,t)\}.$$ (25)

$$f_4(x,y) = \text{std}_{(s,t) \in S_{x,y}^9} \{I_h(s,t)\}.$$ (26)

$$f_5(x,y) = I(x,y).$$ (27)

In these formulas, $S_{x,y}^9$ .s a set of coordinates with a window size of 9 *9, and the center point of the window is at (x, y) (Marín, D. et al., 2010).

Formula (24) is the first gray level feature, which represents the difference between the brightness level at the pixel coordinates (x, y) and the minimum brightness in the 9x9 window to enhance the difference between the optic disc and the non-optic disc.

Formula (25) represents the difference between the maximum brightness in a 9x9 window and the brightness level at the pixel coordinates (x, y).

Formula (26) represents the difference between the brightness level at the pixel coordinates (x, y) and the average brightness in the 9x9 window.

Formula (27) denotes the standard deviation of the brightness of all pixels in the window.

Formula (28) is the fifth gray level feature, which represents the brightness of the central pixel of the window.

As shown in Figure 14, five gray-scale eigenvalues corresponding to optic disk pixels and non-optic disk pixels are compared. Blue dots represent non-optic disk pixels and red dots represent optic disk pixels. Gray-scale features can also be seen in the image to provide an effective distinction between optic disc and non-optic disc pixels.

Figure 14. Plots of Magnitudes for Gray Features: Blue dots represent non Optic Disk Pixels and Red Dots Represent Optic Disk Pixels

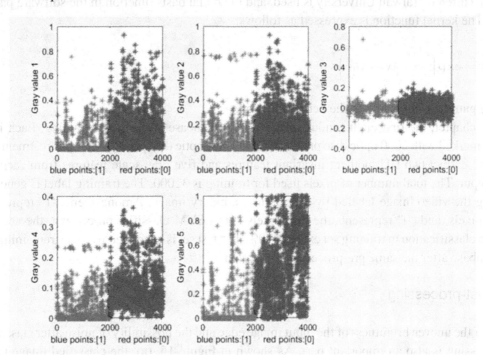

2.2.4 Classification using SVM

Vapnik, V. N. (1999) proposed a support vector machine (SVM) model, which is a machine learning tool for classifying data. The implementation of SVM divides the data into two categories by constructing N-dimensional hyperplane. The classifier is used because of its strong generalization ability and fewer training samples. The problem solved by the support vector machine model is a convex quadratic programming problem, which can obtain the global optimal solution.

In support vector machines, finding the maximum separation hyperplane between classes is the focus of research (Ding, S.F., 2011). Given the training sample set $\{(x1, y1), (x2, y2), \ldots, (xn, yn)\}, yi \in \{-1, +1\}$. to find the existence of a "maximum interval" in the division of hyperplanes, that is to say:

$$\min_{w,b} \frac{1}{2} w^2 . \tag{28}$$

$$\text{s.t.} yi\left(w^T xi + b\right) \geq 1, i = 1, 2, \ldots, n . \tag{29}$$

In this formula, the direction of the hyperplane depends on the normal vector, which is denoted as w; the distance between the origin and the hyperplane depends on the displacement, which is denoted as B. Zhihua, Z., and Jue, W. (2007) proposed a desing of a basic type of SVM.

In this chapter, LIBSVM (Chang, C. C., and Lin, C. J.. 2011) a software package developed by Professor Lin Zhiren of Taiwan University is used, and the radial basis function in the software package is selected. The kernel function is expressed as follows:

$$K\left(x, xi\right) = \exp\left[-\gamma * \|x - xi\|^2\right] \cdot$$

(30)

Where gamma is the width of the kernel function.

In this chapter, the first eight fundus images in the database are used for training. Each image is manually marked with 2000 optic disc pixels and 2000 non-optic disc pixels. After pretreatment of these images, we extract two HU moment invariant features and five gray-scale features from each labeled pixel as input. The total number of pixels used for training is 32000. The training label is generated by converting the video image labeled by experts into a binary image. Among them, "1" represents the non-disc pixels, and "0" represents the disc pixels. After SVM classifier processing, the accuracy of prediction classification in training set exceeds 90%. The test set is generated from the remaining images in the database after the same pre-processing operation.

2.2.5 Post-processing

Because of the uneven brightness of the input image edge and the possibility of noise after classification, post-processing is also an important part. As shown in Figure 15. (a), the classified image has noise and gaps in the optic disc. In order to solve this problem, first of all, the image is directly opened by disc structure elements, so as to remove the small connected pixels such as noise. As shown in Figure 15. (b), the error classified pixels at the top and bottom of the image are removed, and the noise around the disc is also removed to a certain extent. Then, some of the pixels of the disc are filled by the filling operation of the image. The filled image after processing is shown in Figure 15. (c). The post-processing image will be used to compare with the expert tagged video image.

Figure 15. Image Post-processing: a) Classified image, b) Noise-removed image, c) Filled image

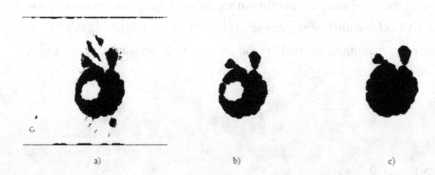

a)   b)   c)

3. RESULT ANALYSIS

In this section, the machine learning algorithm is tested in DRIONS public database, and the results are compared with the corresponding expert marker images. The real examples (TP), false positive examples (FP), false negative examples (FN) and true negative examples (TN) of the algorithm are calculated. The specific methods for calculating these performance indicators are shown in Table 3.

Table 3. Calculation Method of Performance Indicators

	Real Optic Disk Pixels	**Real Non-Optic Disk Pixels**
Predicted Optic Disk pixels	TP	FP
Predicted Non-Optic Disk pixels	FN	TN

According to these indicators, we can get a comparative basis: sensitivity (Se), specificity (Sp), positive predictive value (Ppv), negative predictive value (Npv) and accuracy (Acc). The methods for calculating these indicators are as follows: .

$$Se = \frac{TP}{TP + FN} . \tag{31}$$

$$Sp = \frac{TN}{TN + FP} . \tag{32}$$

$$Ppv = \frac{TP}{TP + FP} . \tag{33}$$

$$Npv = \frac{TN}{TN + FN} . \tag{34}$$

$$Acc = \frac{TP + TN}{TP + FN + TN + FP} . \tag{35}$$

Among these indicators, Se is also called recall ratio, which seeks the ratio of correctly classified videodisc pixels to all real videodisc pixels. Ppv, also known as the accuracy rate, seeks the ratio of correctly categorized videodisc pixels to all classified videodisc pixels. These two are a pair of contradictory measures. When one side is higher, the other side is lower. The value of the two increases and decreases.

Sp and Npv are similar indicators for correctly classified non-optic disk pixels. Ultimately, this chapter uses Accuracy as the criterion of judgment.

Table 4 (a-c) shows the classification results of nine groups of randomly selected test sets, including expert labeling results, SVM segmentation results, the display of segmentation results on the original

Table 4a. Comparisons of optic disc results

	Test1	Test2	Test3
Groud True			
SVM results			
Segmentation results on the original image			
Se	0.9469	0.9865	0.5796
Sp	0.9869	0.9818	0.9936
Ppv	0.8486	0.8314	0.8670
Npv	0.9959	0.9988	0.9704
Acc	0.9841	0.9822	0.9657

Table 4b. Comparisons of optic disc results

	Test4	Test5	Test6
Groud True			
SVM results			
Segmentation results on the original image			
Se	0.9920	0.7792	0.8130
Sp	0.9671	0.9922	0.9902
Ppv	0.7532	0.8939	0.8720
Npv	0.9992	0.9815	0.9847
Acc	0.9671	0.9756	0.9767

map and the above five indicators. The values of the performance assessment parameters of these nine classification results are also shown in Table 4. The average of all the assessment parameters are shown in Table 5.

Table 4c. Comparisons of optic disc results

	Test7	Test8	Test9
Groud True			
SVM results			
Segmentation results on the original image			
Se	0.7450	0.7371	0.8727
Sp	0.9991	0.9985	0.9976
Ppv	0.9830	0.9827	0.9696
Npv	0.9819	0.9714	0.9890
Acc	0.9820	0.9723	0.9876

The results show that the accuracy of the algorithm is high, which shows that the overall classification effect of this algorithm for real optic disk pixels is better. As shown in test sets 2 and 4, their positive predictive values are low. The algorithm detects the lighter non-optic disc part as the optic disc part. The low negative predictive values of test set 3, 7 and 8 indicate that the area of the detected part of the optic disc is smaller than that of the actual part of the optic disc. From the numerical point of view, although

Table 5. Average Indicators

Se	0.8280
Sp	0.9897
Ppv	0.8890
Npv	0.9859
Acc	0.9770

the specificity and negative predictive value are higher than the sensitivity and positive predictive value, the reason is that the proportion of non-optic disk pixels is much larger than that of optic disk pixels.

From the shape of the classification results, the part that goes into the concave is exactly where the blood vessels diverge, while the part that protrudes out is the part of the adjacent blood vessels whose brightness is close to the optic disc. This shows that the distribution of blood vessels has a great impact on the classification effect, and the algorithm of removing blood vessels in pretreatment needs to be improved.

In the aspect of algorithm improvement. In addition to improving the effect of removing blood vessels, increasing the number of training sets, trying other features and using other kernel functions in SVM are also possible improvements in the future.

3.1 Summary and Discussion

In this section, machine learning is used to segment the optic disc of fundus image. In the pretreatment stage, in order to erase the blood vessels, the vascular mask method is used to remove the blood vessels without changing the details of the optic disc. In order to solve the problem of unbalanced number of optic disc pixels and non-optic disc pixels, this chapter uses the method of labeling pixels artificially to obtain two kinds of pixels with the same number. In feature extraction, HU moment feature with invariance and gray level feature sensitive to brightness are adopted. Then, the labeled training set is trained by SVM classifier and tested on DRIONS fundus image data set. Finally, the classified images are processed to reduce noise and fill up the pixels in the region of the disc.

Because the blood vessels are not completely erased in the pretreatment stage, the segmentation results are easily affected by the distribution of blood vessels, and also by the background points of the adjacent brightness of the optic disc. Although the method based on machine learning is cumbersome, on the whole, if the model can be further strengthened, it will play a role and effect in the process of disc segmentation of a large part of fundus images.

In the future, better results can be obtained by strengthening the vessel erasure algorithm and trying to debug the parameters of SVM classifier.

4. CONCLUSION

In this chapter, we focus on the technology of segmentation of fundus image, and test it on the DIONS fundus image database with the contour of the optic disc labeled by experts. In this chapter, we use the characteristics of optic disc approximation circle. First, we erase the interfering blood vessels through morphological closure operation. Then we get the outline of the optic disc by Kirsch edge detection operator. Finally, we use HOUGH circle transform to detect the image, and then segment the optic disc. This morphological method has the characteristics of simple algorithm and low complexity. In addition, this chapter also proposes a method of dividing videos based on supervised learning in machine learning. In the pretreatment stage, we use the vascular mask method to erase the blood vessels while preserving the complete details of the optic disc. In the acquisition of training set, this chapter uses manual labeling of training pixels for each image to label the same number of optic disk pixels and non-optic disk pixels, in order to solve the class imbalance problem and make the classification effect of optic disk pixels better. In feature extraction, we adopt HU moment feature with invariance of translation, rotation and scaling, and gray feature based on brighter optic disc. In this chapter, the classical SVM classifier which solves the binary classification problem is used to classify the optic disc pixels. The average assessment parameters are given in table 5, accoring to that the sensitivity (Se) is 82.8% and accuracy is 97.7%. After removing noise and filling the disc, the position of the disc segmented by the algorithm coincides with that of the manually labeled disc by experts, but it is still affected by the distribution of blood vessels. Therefore, in the future, the pre-processing stage, feature selection stage and parameter debugging stage of the algorithm can be improved.

FUNDING

This research was financially supported by the Scientific Research Grant of Shantou University, China, Grant No: NTF17016.

ACKNOWLEDGMENT

We would like to acknowledge the funding and the support given by Shantou University China.

REFERENCES

Abramoff, M. D., Alward, W. L., Greenlee, E. C., Shuba, L., Kim, C. Y., Fingert, J. H., & Kwon, Y. H. (2007). Automated segmentation of the optic disc from stereo color photographs using physiologically plausible features. *Investigative Ophthalmology & Visual Science*, 48(4), 1665–1673. doi:10.1167/iovs.06-1081 PMID:17389498

Alioua, N., Amine, A., Rziza, M., & Aboutajdine, D. (2011, April). Eye state analysis using iris detection based on Circular Hough Transform. In *2011 International Conference on Multimedia Computing and Systems* (pp. 1-5). IEEE. 10.1109/ICMCS.2011.5945576

Beiji, Z., Sijian, Z., & Chengzhang, Z. (2015). Automatic positioning and segmentation of color fundus image discs. *Optics and Precision Engineering*, 23(4), 1187–1195. doi:10.3788/OPE.20152304.1187

Bhat, S. H., & Kumar, P. (2019). Segmentation of optic disc by localized active contour model in retinal fundus image. In *Smart Innovations in Communication and Computational Sciences* (pp. 35–44). Singapore: Springer. doi:10.1007/978-981-13-2414-7_4

Bhatkalkar, B., Joshi, A., Prabhu, S., & Bhandary, S. (2020). Automated fundus image quality assessment and segmentation of optic disc using convolutional neural networks. *International Journal of Electrical & Computer Engineering, 10.*

Chang, C. C., & Lin, C. J. (2011). LIBSVM: A library for support vector machines. *ACM Transactions on Intelligent Systems and Technology, 2*(3), 1–27. doi:10.1145/1961189.1961199

Dai, B., Wu, X., & Bu, W. (2017). Optic disc segmentation based on variational model with multiple energies. *Pattern Recognition, 64,* 226–235. doi:10.1016/j.patcog.2016.11.017

Ding, S. F., Qi, B. J., & Tan, H. Y. (2011). An overview on theory and algorithm of support vector machines. *Journal of University of Electronic Science and Technology of China, 40*(1), 2–10.

Elbalaoui, A., Ouadid, Y., & Fakir, M. (2018, March). Segmentation of optic disc from fundus images. In *2018 International Conference on Computing Sciences and Engineering (ICCSE)* (pp. 1-7). IEEE. 10.1109/ICCSE1.2018.8374223

Feijoo, J. G., de la Casa, J. M. M., Servet, H. M., Zamorano, M. R., Mayoral, M. B., & Suárez, E. J. C. (2014). *DRIONS-DB: digital retinal images for optic nerve segmentation database.* Academic Press.

Flusser, J., & Suk, T. (2006). Rotation moment invariants for recognition of symmetric objects. *IEEE Transactions on Image Processing, 15*(12), 3784–3790. doi:10.1109/TIP.2006.884913 PMID:17153951

Fondon, I., van Grinsven, M. J., Sanchez, C. I., & Saez, A. (2013, June). Perceptually adapted method for optic disc detection on retinal fundus images. In *Proceedings of the 26th IEEE International Symposium on Computer-Based Medical Systems* (pp. 279-284). IEEE. 10.1109/CBMS.2013.6627802

Giachetti, A., Ballerini, L., & Trucco, E. (2014). Accurate and reliable segmentation of the optic disc in digital fundus images. *Journal of Medical Imaging (Bellingham, Wash.), 1*(2), 024001. doi:10.1117/1.JMI.1.2.024001 PMID:26158034

Hoover, A., & Goldbaum, M. (2003). Locating the optic nerve in a retinal image using the fuzzy convergence of the blood vessels. *IEEE Transactions on Medical Imaging, 22*(8), 951–958. doi:10.1109/TMI.2003.815900 PMID:12906249

Hough, P. V. (1962). *U.S. Patent No. 3,069,654.* Washington, DC: U.S. Patent and Trademark Office.

Huang, Z., & Leng, J. (2010, April). Analysis of Hu's moment invariants on image scaling and rotation. In *2010 2nd International Conference on Computer Engineering and Technology* (Vol. 7, pp. V7-476). IEEE.

Jiajun, Q. (2017). *Research on the positioning and segmentation method of the optic disc in the fundus image* (Master's thesis). Shenyang University of Technology.

Kitsch, R. (1971). Computer detection of the constituent structure of biological image, Compute. *Biomod.*

Lu, S. (2011). Accurate and efficient optic disc detection and segmentation by a circular transformation. *IEEE Transactions on Medical Imaging*, *30*(12), 2126–2133. doi:10.1109/TMI.2011.2164261 PMID:21843983

Marín, D., Aquino, A., Gegúndez-Arias, M. E., & Bravo, J. M. (2010). A new supervised method for blood vessel segmentation in retinal images by using gray-level and moment invariants-based features. *IEEE Transactions on Medical Imaging*, *30*(1), 146–158. doi:10.1109/TMI.2010.2064333 PMID:20699207

Mariotti, A., & Pascolini, D. (2012). Global estimates of visual impairment. *The British Journal of Ophthalmology*, *96*(5), 614–618. doi:10.1136/bjophthalmol-2011-300539 PMID:22133988

MathWorks, Inc. (2005). *MATLAB: the language of technical computing. Desktop tools and development environment, version 7* (Vol. 9). MathWorks.

Morales, S., Naranjo, V., Angulo, J., & Alcañiz, M. (2013). Automatic detection of optic disc based on PCA and mathematical morphology. *IEEE Transactions on Medical Imaging*, *32*(4), 786–796. doi:10.1109/TMI.2013.2238244 PMID:23314772

Mukhopadhyay, P., & Chaudhuri, B. B. (2015). A survey of Hough Transform. *Pattern Recognition*, *48*(3), 993–1010. doi:10.1016/j.patcog.2014.08.027

Ping, J. (2018). *Research on segmentation method of fundus image* (Master's thesis). Jilin University of China.

Shaohua, Z., Jian, C., Lin, P., Jian, G., & Lun, Y. (2014). New method for automatic detection of macular center and optic disc in fundus images. *Dianzi Yu Xinxi Xuebao*, *36*(11), 2586–2592.

Suero, A., Marin, D., Gegúndez-Arias, M. E., & Bravo, J. M. (2013, March). Locating the Optic Disc in Retinal Images Using Morphological Techniques. In IWBBIO (pp. 593-600). Academic Press.

Vapnik, V. N. (1999). An overview of statistical learning theory. *IEEE Transactions on Neural Networks*, *10*(5), 988–999. doi:10.1109/72.788640 PMID:18252602

Wang, X. Y., & Xu, J. G. (2009). Fundus Oculi Images Enhancement Based on Histograms Equalization and Its Simulation with MATLAB. *Journal of Hebei North University (Natural Science Edition), 4*.

Xiaofen, C., & Yuecun, W. (2008). *Color image edge detection* (Doctoral dissertation).

Xiaomei, X., Xiaobo, L., & Yanli, L. (2017). Video disc automatic segmentation algorithm. *Chinese Science and Technology Papers*, *12*(20), 2349–2354.

Yin, P., Wu, Q., Xu, Y., Min, H., Yang, M., Zhang, Y., & Tan, M. (2019, October). PM-Net: Pyramid Multi-label Network for Joint Optic Disc and Cup Segmentation. In *International Conference on Medical Image Computing and Computer-Assisted Intervention* (pp. 129-137). Springer. 10.1007/978-3-030-32239-7_15

Yuan, Z. (2012). *Research on key technologies in fundus retinal vascular segmentation* (Master's thesis). University of Electronic Science and Technology of China.

Zhihua, Z., & Jue, W. (2007). Machine learning and its application. Tsinghua University Press.

Chapter 8
Performance Analysis of VGG19 Deep Learning Network Based Brain Image Fusion

Vijayarajan Rajangam

iD https://orcid.org/0000-0003-0562-4472

Vellore Institute of Technology, Chennai, India

Sangeetha N.

Jerusalem College of Engineering, Chennai, India

Karthik R.

iD https://orcid.org/0000-0002-5250-4337

Centre for Cyber Physical Systems, Vellore Institute of Technology, Chennai, India

Kethepalli Mallikarjuna

iD https://orcid.org/0000-0001-9500-9187

RGM College of Engineering and Technology, Nandyal, India

ABSTRACT

Multimodal imaging systems assist medical practitioners in cost-effective diagnostic methods in clinical pathologies. Multimodal imaging of the same organ or the region of interest reveals complementing anatomical and functional details. Multimodal image fusion algorithms integrate complementary image details into a composite image that reduces clinician's time for effective diagnosis. Deep learning networks have their role in feature extraction for the fusion of multimodal images. This chapter analyzes the performance of a pre-trained VGG19 deep learning network that extracts features from the base and detail layers of the source images for constructing a weight map to fuse the source image details. Maximum and averaging fusion rules are adopted for base layer fusion. The performance of the fusion algorithm for multimodal medical image fusion is analyzed by peak signal to noise ratio, structural similarity index, fusion factor, and figure of merit. Performance analysis of the fusion algorithms is also carried out for the source images with the presence of impulse and Gaussian noise.

DOI: 10.4018/978-1-7998-6690-9.ch008

INTRODUCTION

With the astonishing development of fast computing technologies and medical imaging systems, health care to mankind has evolved tremendously. The rapid development of the fast computing systems over the decade paves the way for advanced machine learning and deep learning concepts in medical image processing. This development directs medical diagnosis towards e-diagnosis that aids medical practitioners in fast diagnostic procedures. Over the decade, medical image processing has evolved manifold with the help of deep learning networks handling a huge volume of complex data. Deep learning models learn high-level features from the medical dataset without complex feature extraction. The evolution of GPU with computing libraries also makes learning faster. Deep learning networks (DLN) have become more effective for image processing due to the availability of public datasets and optimization techniques. Deep networks have their role in computer-aided diagnosis, multimodal image registration, fusion, segmentation, and classification of a region of interest (ROI), image-guided therapy, image analysis, image retrieval, and so on. Deep networks can be trained for specific clinical applications with the intended dataset, fast computing system, and a huge volume of data. Pre-trained networks can also be used for medical image processing towards specific clinical applications. The deep networks surpass machine learning strategies due to their ability to handle a huge volume of complex data. Various deep learning networks have evolved over the years for different applications. Multiple layers of the neuron, stacked for feature representation, can recognize various possible mappings after effective training with a vast knowledge database. There are different types of deep learning networks with a modification in the basic architecture. Deep neural networks (DNN) have more than two layers to analyze the complex non-linear relationship among the input variables. This network is widely employed for classification and regression-based applications. The accuracy of DNN is good. But, the network is very slow in learning. Convolution neural networks (CNN), consisting of convolution layers, are good for a two-dimensional dataset. CNN has the advantage of fast learning but needs a labeled dataset for classification. Recurrent neural networks (RNN) find applications in natural language processing, speech recognition, and character recognition with good accuracy. RNN is capable of learning sequences and the weights are shared across all neurons. Training for RNN needs a very big dataset and also suffering from gradient vanishing. Deep convolutional extreme learning machine (DCELM) uses Gaussian probability functions for the sampling of local connections between the input variables. Deep Boltzmann machine (DBM) achieves robust inference about the input dataset through top-down feedback and unidirectional connection between the hidden layers. But, this network lacks optimization of parameters for a big dataset. Deep belief network (DBN) uses an initialization process that makes a computationally expensive training process. Each hidden layer in this network acts as visible layers to the next layer in the hierarchy. On the top layers, the two layers have a unidirectional connection. The accuracy of DLN largely depends on the quality and size of the dataset. The success of various DLNs in medical imaging applications are suffered by the non-availability of quality dataset and volume of data. This requirement leads to data annotation which requires extensive time from the medical practitioners. Another trivial factor is the reliability of the annotated dataset that needs to be ensured by multiple expert opinions. Non-availability of sufficient data in certain clinical pathologies and ethical guidelines of the patient data restricts the application of deep learning strategies.

Image fusion is a technique that integrates two or more images from the same modality or from different modalities to yield a composite image of complementary details (Chen et al., 2020). This helps medical practitioners for better diagnosis and reduces human error. Image fusion strategies have also evolved due to the rapid development of deep network architecture. Deep networks play the role of feature or detail selection for fusion. An effective decision map regarding the details to be fused from the source images can be derived from the deep learning networks. Deep learning networks have also been suggested for weight map generation and effective activity level measurement for fusion.

The most suggested modalities for clinical diagnosis are X-ray, Computed Tomography (CT), Magnetic Resonance Imaging (MRI), function MRI, Positron Emission Tomography (PET) and Single Photon Emission Computed Tomography (SPECT) (Wang et al. 2020). Multimodal medical images deliver pathological details in different resolution and contrast. CT images provide anatomical details whereas MR images present functional details by contrast variations. On the other hand, SPECT provides functional and metabolic information but lacks in anatomical details. The fusion of multimodal medical images brings complementary pathological aspects into a composite image for a better diagnosis. Fusion methods suggested earlier concentrated more on the fusion of image details without analyzing the relationship between various modalities. Spatial domain methods often result in spectral distortion. Local principal component averaging (LPCA) has the ambiguity in block size selection which is determined by trial and error method. Fuzzy C-Means based principal component averaging (FCMPCA) method is affected by the number of pixels in the relevant clusters. If the clusters don't have an equal number of pixels, it will be compensated by zero padding that affects the evaluation of linear weights. Whereas, frequency-domain methods are influenced by the level of decomposition, frequency subbands, and fusion strategy for various frequency subbands. The decision on the features to be fused in the frequency domain is quite complex and hence requires an automatic feature extraction and feature map generation technique for image fusion. Deep learning networks analyze complex fusion problems to derive decision maps for fusion. This chapter analyzes the performance of a pre-trained VGG19 deep learning network (Huang et al., 2017) for CT-MRI, MRI proton density (PD)-MRI T2, and SPECT-MRI T2 fusion using quantitative and qualitative metrics. For base layer fusion averaging fusion rule is suggested in this chapter. The performance of a pre-trained VGG19 DLN is analyzed using the Whole Brain Atlas dataset. The performance metrics considered for analysis are peak signal to noise ratio (PSNR) in dB, structural similarity index (SSIM), fusion factor (FF), and figure of merit (FOM). PSNR and FF are known as quantitative metrics. Whereas, SSIM is a quality metric based on illumination, contrast, and variance. FOM measures the edge preservation capability using the Sobel operator.

This chapter is organized as follows. Section 2 elaborates image fusion methods and the requirement for medical image fusion. VGG19 DLN based fusion is presented in Section 3. Fusion metrics and performance analysis are discussed in Section 4. This is followed by a conclusion in Section 5.

BACKGROUND

Image Fusion

Image fusion algorithms are classified into pixel, feature, and decision level fusion. Pixel level fusion is employed over the raw values of the source images (Jianwen & Shutao, 2012). The fusion of the raw values can be carried out by scaling factors, weight maps, and so on. Evaluation of scaling factor and weights are the key in pixel-level fusion. Feature level fusion is carried out on the features extracted from the source images such as edges, structural information, key points, mean, standard deviation, variance, contrast, and so on (Lewis et al., 2004). Features can be extracted by feature extraction filters and deep learning networks. Decision level fusion algorithms work on region maps, descriptors, relational graphs, voting, and prediction for making a decision. The fusion rules are used to fuse the decisions derived from the source images (Zhao et al., 2008 & Williams et al., 1999).

The above-mentioned fusion algorithms are carried out in a spatial or transformed domain. Spatial domain methods are vulnerable to spectral distortions and artifacts. Whereas, transform domain methods do suffer from directionality and shift sensitivity. Appropriate transform needs to be selected for avoiding the above-said issues. In this chapter, VGG19 DLN extracts features from the base and detail contents of the source images.

The Requirement for Medical Image Fusion

1. Fusion algorithm need to preserve the pattern existing in the source images (Mitchell, 2010)
2. Fusion algorithm should be free of inconsistencies and artifacts. They should be rotational and shift-invariant.
3. Multimodal medical imaging provides complementary details of the ROI. Medical practitioners may exhaust with the multiple images and the redundancy of details may lead to human errors and a large volume of redundant data (Sabalan & Hassan, 2010).

Multimodal Medical Imaging for Fusion

Computed tomography is the advanced version of X-ray imaging. When a beam of X-rays is directed towards dense living brain tissues, the density of the brain tissues attenuates the X-rays leading to slight blunting. The amount of blunting depends on the type of tissues. Different fluids present in the brain blocks less amount of X-rays. Grey matter blocks some more X-rays and very dense bone blocks more amount. The final CT image is constructed by a software algorithm using the collected X-rays by the X-ray detectors mounted on the circumference of the scanner.

Whenever the brain protons are subjected to a magnetic field, then the electromagnetic energy is received and transmitted by the magnetized protons. The number of photons in the tissue decides the strength of the transmitted energy. The local homogeneous environment and mobility of the magnetic field influence the signal strength. The MR image is reconstructed by superimposing an additional magnetic field. This magnetic field is varied in strength at different space points which have a unique radio frequency for signal transmission and reception. The main advantages of MR are multilayer display of pathoanatomy, multiparametric nature of MR, and sensitivity to the chemical degradation of blood. The three standard planes of view for MR imaging are transaxial, coronal, and sagittal. The examples for the three planes of view are presented in Figure 1.

MR imaging produces high or low signals based on the tissues in the ROI and the sequence of pulses. Dark levels in an MR T1 weighted image represents tumor, increased water, inflammation, infarction, infection, hemorrhage, low proton density, calcification. On the other hand, bright levels reveal the details about subacute hemorrhage, fat, melanin, protein-rich fluid, cerebral infarction, slowly flowing blood, and paramagnetic substances such as manganese and copper. MR T2 weighted images produce bright levels for increased water, infarction, inflammation, tumor, methemoglobin in subacute hemorrhage, subdural collection. Whereas, dark levels represent calcification, fibrous tissue, low proton density, protein-rich fluid, flow void, paramagnetic substances such as deoxyhemoglobin, methemoglobin, iron, ferritin, hemosiderin, and melanin.

Figure 1. Three standard planes of view

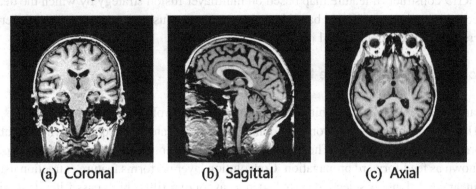

| (a) Coronal | (b) Sagittal | (c) Axial |

In SPECT imaging, the photons are emitted from the tissues, when tracer amounts of radiolabeled compounds are injected. The accumulation of the labeled compounds is represented by the images. SPECT images reveal oxygen metabolism, blood flow, and dopamine transporter concentration.

Deep Learning Networks for Image Fusion

DLN comprises of nonlinear processing units which are arranged in multiple layers (Tongxue Zhou et al., 2019). The network can extract complex features by the multiple layers from a large amount of input information. The output of each layer is fed as input to the successive layers. The early invention of convolution neural network (CNN) (LeCun et al., 1998) and subsequent improvements such as VGGNet (Simonyan & Zisserman, 2015), ResidualNet (He et al., 2016) and GoogleNet (Szegedy et al., 2015) have been used in different image processing applications. CNN is a multilayer neural network consisting of the convolution layer, pooling layer, activation layer, and fully connected layers. Convolution layers are responsible for extracting feature maps from a large volume of input data using filters. Dimensionality reduction of feature maps is carried out in the pooling layer through downsampling. A nonlinear rectified layer and its modified versions are used as activation functions (He et al., 2015). Each neuron in the fully connected layer is connected with all the activation functions in the previous layer.

Due to the rapid development of deep learning architectures for various image processing applications, features extracted at the layers of DLN can be used to construct activity level maps which can be used to frame a scaling strategy for the fusion rule. Convolution sparse representation, a method to extract deep features, can be used to get the fused image (Liu et al., 2016). Image patches containing the blurred version of the input images can be used to train the network for getting the decision map for fusion. This method can fuse multifocus images. The VGG19 DLN works on base and detail contents of the input images and generates an activity map for the fusion of the detail contents (Liu et al., 2017). This network is used for the fusion of multiresolution images and pre-trained using ImageNet. In this chapter, the VGG19 DLN is tested on multimodal medical images and the performance is analyzed using the objective metrics. VGG19 is a pretrained network from ImageNet dataset which has been structured to extract multilayer features from the detail content of the source images. VGG19 (Huang et al., 2017) uses adaptive instance normalization to construct a new style image from the source images. This method is faster than the previous VGG (Gatys et al., 2016) by three orders of magnitude. VGG19 based fusion reconstructs the fused detail image from the multilayer features using weighted and L1 norms. VGG19 constructs a feature map based on multilayer fusion strategy by which the detail fused image is reconstructed. Since VGG19 based fusion uses adaptive fusion strategies for multilayer features, it is preferred for multimodal medical image fusion.

CNN Architecture for Feature Extraction

The CNN architecture (Rikiya Yamashita, 2018) comprises of convolution layers, pooling layers, and fully connected layers. A stack of convolution and pooling layers is repeated subsequently which is followed by one or more fully connected layers. The process of forwarding input data through the above-mentioned layers is known as feed-forward propagation. Convolution layer performs feature extraction using linear and non-linear operations. A selective kernel such as averaging filter, high pass filter, Gaussian filter, bilateral filter, guided filter, etc. can be applied to the input tensor to generate a feature map. Multiple numbers of feature maps can be obtained by applying different kernels. The types and size of the kernels decide the depth of the features which are extracted from the input tensors. Convolution operations tend to detect local patterns, larger field of view, and increased model efficiency through less number of parameters. The output of convolution layers is given to a non-linear activation function known as a rectified linear unit (ReLU).

Pooling layer reduces the dimensionality of the feature maps and also reduces variance due to distortions and minor shifts. Max pooling also reduces the number of learnable parameters. It is commonly employed using a kernel of a size of 2×2 and stride of two.

The feature maps from the convolution and pooling layer are converted into a one-dimensional array of values which is further connected to fully connected layers. The features extracted by the convolution layers are downsampled by the pooling layers and further mapped to the final outputs by the fully connected layers. The nodes in the fully connected layers are equal to the number of classes in the classification strategy.

The activation function, used in the fully connected layer, maps the real values delivered by the last fully connected layer to the probabilities of target classes ranging from zero to one. Softmax function is the most common one to carry out this task.

VGG19 DLN based image fusion

Deep learning networks are well known for extracting different image features at different layers (Hui Li et al., 2018). VGG network (Simonyan & Zisserman, 2014) works on the image features extracted from the three images, known as, content image, style image, and a generated image. Hence, this method is based on image style transfer. Adaptive instance normalization (Xun & Serge, 2017) is used in the VGG network with a new style transfer. The fixed VGG19 is a pre-trained network with ImageNet for feature extraction, thus effectively used in VGG19 based fusion framework. The architecture diagram is presented in Figure 2.

The pre-trained VGG19 network processes base and detailed parts of the source images which are obtained using two-scale decomposition (Hui Li et al. 2018). The base parts are fused by maximum and averaging fusion rules, whereas, detail parts are fused by an activity level map extracted from the feature maps of the jth detail content of the kth layer. Softmax operator is used for initial weight map generation (W_j^k)

Figure 2. VGG19 architecture

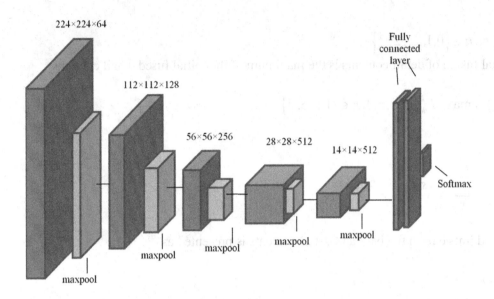

$$\hat{W}_j^k = \frac{\hat{C}_j^k\left(s,t\right)}{\sum_{n=1}^{J}\hat{C}_n^k\left(s,t\right)}\;;\;\text{where J – number of activity level map} = 2 \tag{1}$$

$$\hat{C}_j^k\left(s,t\right) = \frac{\sum_{\beta=-l}^{l}\sum_{\theta=-l}^{i}\hat{C}_j^k\left(s+\beta,t+\theta\right)}{\left(2l+1\right)^2} \tag{2}$$

$\left(2l+1\right)$ is the block size, for $l=-1$ block size is 3×3

$\hat{C}_i^k$ is the final activity level map calculated using a block-based average operator. The initial activity level map is determined as follows.

$$\hat{C}_j^k\left(s,t\right) = \varphi_j^{k,1:P}\left(s,t\right) \tag{3}$$

$$\varphi_j^{k,p} = \varnothing_k\left(I_j^d\right) \tag{4}$$

$\varnothing_k$ is a layer of VGG network and $\varphi_j^{k,1:P}$ represents the contents of $\varphi_j^{k,p}$ at (s,t), where $p \in \left\{1,2,3,\ldots,P=64\times 2^{k-1}\right\}$. The initial weight map is subjected to an upsampling operator to derive the final weight map. The final weight map, W_j^k, is obtained as follows.

$$\hat{W}_j^k\left(s+m,y+n\right) = W_j^k\left(s,t\right) \tag{5}$$

Where $m,n \in \left\{0,1,\ldots,2^{k-1}\right\}$

The final fusion of detail contents is the maximum of the initial fused detail contents

$$F_{detail}\left(s,t\right) = \max\left[F_{detail}^k\left(s,t\right)\right]; k \in \left\{1,2,3,4\right\} \tag{6}$$

$$F_{detail}^k\left(s,t\right) = \sum_q^{J=2}\hat{W}_q^k\left(s,t\right) \times I_q^{detail}\left(s,t\right) \tag{7}$$

The fused image from the base and detail contents is presented as

$$FI\left(s,t\right) = F_{base}\left(s,t\right) + F_{detail}\left(s,t\right) \tag{8}$$

Two-Scale Decomposition

The source images are decomposed into base and detail layers using two-scale decomposition (Shutao li, 2013). Base layer is obtained by employing an averaging filter on the source image. Large scale variations are represented by the base layer image. Detail layer image is obtained by subtracting the base layer image from the source image. To have large scale variations in the base layer, an averaging filter of larger size is preferred. Let I(i,j) denote the source image; i,j=1,2,…,n. The base layer image is obtained as follows.

$$I_{base}\left(i,j\right) = \sum_{k=-m}^{m}\sum_{l=-m}^{m}I\left(i+k,j+l\right) * Z\left(k,l\right) \tag{9}$$

Z(k,l) is the averaging kernel of size (2m+1)×(2m+1)
The detail image is obtained by

$$I_{detail} = I - I_{base} \tag{10}$$

VGG19 DLN based Medical Image Fusion

Multimodal medical images, CT-MRI T2, MRI PD-MRI T2, and SPECT-MRI T2, are the source images to the pre-trained VGG19 DLN. The multimodal medical image fusion is presented in Figure 3. The fusion algorithm is stated as follows.

1.   Source images, IM1 and IM2, are decomposed into base and detail parts using two-scale segmentation.

2.   2. Base parts of IM1 and IM2 are fused using a maximum fusion and averaging fusion rules.

$$F\left(base\right) = Max\left(IM1\left(base\right) + IM2\left(base\right)\right) \tag{11}$$

$$F\left(base\right) = \frac{1}{2}\left(IM1\left(base\right) + IM2\left(base\right)\right) \tag{12}$$

3.   The final weight map is evaluated as stated in Equation (5).
4.   Fused detail parts are evaluated as given in Equations (6) and (7).
5.   5. The final fused image is obtained as follows.

$$FI = F\left(base\right) + F\left(detail\right) \tag{13}$$

Figure 3. VGG19 DLN based multimodal medical image fusion

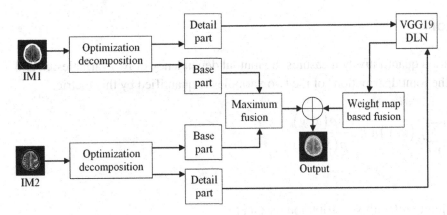

EXPERIMENTAL ANALYSIS

The performance of the VGG19 based medical image fusion is compared with the fusion algorithms based on Standard Wavelet Transform (SWT), Discrete Wavelet Transform (DWT), Dual-Tree Complex Wavelet Transform (DTCWT), Non-Subsampled Contourlet Transform (NSCT), Principal Component Analysis (PCA)(Senthil Kumar et al., 2006), LPCA (Vijayarajan & Muttan 2014a) and FCMPCA (Vijayarajan & Muttan 2014b). The first four methods are transform domain methods. Fusion is employed on the transformed values. The last three methods are spatial domain methods. In VGG19 based method, fusion is employed for the base and detail contents derived from two-scale decomposition. Max and averaging fusion rules are adopted for the base content fusion and activity map is used for the detail content fusion.

Source images are available in The Whole Brain Atlas hosted by www.harvardmed.edu providing free access for research. All the source images are registered which is the prerequisite for fusion. The source images are of spatial resolution 256×256×3. The modalities are CT, MRI, and SPECT. Three experiments were conducted for the performance analysis of VGG19 based medical image fusion. The first experiment is on the fusion of CT and MRI T2 images. The second experiment is employed on MRI PD and MRI T2 images. The third experiment is on SPECT and MRI T2 images.

Fusion Metrics

Objective and subjective analysis are the most common methods for estimating the performance of the image fusion algorithms. There are two categories of objective metrics, known as, reference-based and non-reference based metrics. The first category of metrics is appropriate when the ground truth for the fusion output is available. The metrics are evaluated between the fusion output and ground truth. The multimodal medical image fusion carried out in real-time does not have ground truth and hence non-reference based metrics are prepared. In this case, metrics are evaluated between each one of the source images and the fusion output. The objective metrics can be further classified into quantitative and qualitative metrics. The first case of metrics quantifies the source details fused into the fusion output. Whereas, qualitative metrics analyze the quality transfer happening between the source and fusion output images. The qualitative analysis can be described in terms of contrast, illumination, structural content, edge preservation capability, and so on.

Fusion Factor

Mutual information quantitatively measures the mutual dependency of two variables, x, and y. The distance between the joint distributions of the two variables is quantified by this metric.

$$MI(x,y) = \sum_{x \in X} \sum_{y \in Y} p(x,y) log_2 \frac{p(x,y)}{p(x)p(y)} \tag{14}$$

Where p(x,y) - joint probability distribution of x and y
P(x) and p(y) - marginal probability distribution

Fusion factor (FF) is the summation of mutual information evaluated between two source images, IM1 and IM2, and a fused image, FI.

$$FF = MI(IM_1, FI) + MI(IM_2, FI) \tag{15}$$

Structural Similarity Index

SSIM measures the amount of structural information present in the images. The perceived distortion of images can be approximated by the loss of structural information.

$$SSIM(x,y) = \left(\frac{2\mu_x\mu_y + C_1}{\mu_x^2 + \mu_y^2 + C_1}\right)^{\propto} \left(\frac{2\sigma_x\sigma_y + C_2}{\sigma_x^2 + \sigma_y^2 + C_2}\right)^{\beta} \left(\frac{\sigma_{xy} + C_3}{\sigma_x\sigma_y + C_3}\right)^{\gamma} \tag{16}$$

μ_x and μ_y are the mean of the images x and y. σ_x and σ_y are the variances. σ_{xy} is the covariance. The first and second terms represent luminance and contrast respectively, whereas the third term illustrates correlation. The relative significance of the above said terms are adjusted by α, β, and γ. The stability of the metric is maintained by the constants C1, C2, and C3 when the denominator terms are very close to zero. Average SSIM between the two source images and the fused image is evaluated as follows.

$$SSIM_{av} = \frac{1}{2}\left(SSIM(IM_1, FI) + SSIM(IM_2, FI)\right) \tag{17}$$

$SSIM_{av}$ – Average SSIM

$SSIM(IM_1, FI)$ – SSIM between source image 1 and fused image

$SSIM(IM_2, FI)$ - SSIM between source image 2 and fused image

Peak Signal to Noise Ratio

PSNR quantifies the difference between the two variables x and y

$$PSNR \text{ } in \text{ } dB = 10log_{10}\frac{255^2}{\sqrt{\sum_x\sum_y(x-y)^2}} \tag{18}$$

For fusion performance analysis, PSNR is evaluated between the two source images and the fused image.

$$PSNR_{av} = \frac{1}{2}\left(PSNR(IM_1, FI) + PSNR(IM_2, FI)\right) \tag{19}$$

Figure of Merit

Figure of merit estimates the edge preservation performance of the fusion algorithm using the Sobel operator (Bhutada et al., 2011).

$$FOM = \frac{1}{M}\sum_{i=1}^{M}\frac{1}{1 + \gamma d_i^2} \tag{20}$$

d_i is the Euclidean distance, M is the maximum number of edge pixels among the two images and γ is the scaling factor which is taken as 1/9 (Pratt, 2006).

$$\text{FOM}_{av} = \frac{1}{2}\Big(\text{FOM}\big(\text{IM}_1, FI\big) + \text{FOM}\big(\text{IM}_2, FI\big)\Big) \tag{21}$$

CT - MRI T2 Image Fusion

CT images reveal the anatomical and structural details of the ROI in low resolution. Whereas, MRI-T2 images provide functional details in high resolution. The fusion of CT-MRI T2 images combines the details present in the source images as per the fusion strategy. The three sets of source images for experiments are shown in Figure 4. Fusion outputs from various algorithms are presented in Figure 5. Fusion performance is evaluated and presented in Table 1. Upon analyzing the values, it is observed that the VGG19 fusion using Max rule for base layer delivers competitive results whereas averaging rule-based fusion delivers good results compared to other methods. FF and PSNR in dB reveal that the averaging

Table 1. Performance metrics for CT-MRI T2 fusion

Methods	FF			$SSIM_{av}$		
	Set1	Set2	Set3	Set1	Set2	Set3
SWT	4.008431	6.678998	6.491569	0.999772	0.999737	0.999657
DWT	2.253601	1.796632	1.860186	0.999575	0.999508	0.999346
DTCWT	3.159027	2.279152	3.06194	0.999752	0.999709	0.999624
NSCT	3.191528	6.931229	2.478112	0.999583	0.999556	0.99945
PCA	5.264229	4.208256	4.225463	0.999748	0.999708	0.999619
LPACA	11.51084	3.871332	4.353717	0.99963	0.999686	0.999594
FCMPCA	4.339688	3.881401	4.367759	0.999774	0.999739	0.999646
VGG19(Max)	4.401327	3.804563	3.619372	0.999595	0.999472	0.999307
VGG19(Av)	5.729216	8.539153	6.749026	0.999521	0.999847	0.999734
Methods	$PSNR_{av}$ in dB			FOM_{av}		
	Set1	Set2	Set3	Set1	Set2	Set3
SWT	64.92416	64.35001	63.44189	0.99946	0.999257	0.999002
DWT	62.36919	61.69224	60.93194	0.99886	0.998576	0.998026
DTCWT	64.49447	63.87351	62.99144	0.999286	0.999065	0.998744
NSCT	63.48088	61.89635	61.07489	0.999118	0.9987	0.9982
PCA	65.58551	65.06824	64.12506	0.999498	0.999319	0.999063
LPACA	69.4599	65.50805	64.51552	0.999197	0.999264	0.998989
FCMPCA	65.05828	64.51146	63.74831	0.999566	0.999417	0.999145
VGG19(Max)	64.48553	63.46921	62.74582	0.999361	0.999123	0.998785
VGG19(Av)	67.75129	66.89312	68.81542	0.999723	0.999845	0.999923

Figure 4. Source images (CT-MRI T2)

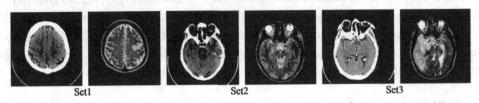

Set1   Set2   Set3

Figure 5. Fusion outputs for (a) Set1 (b) Set2 (c) Set3 source images

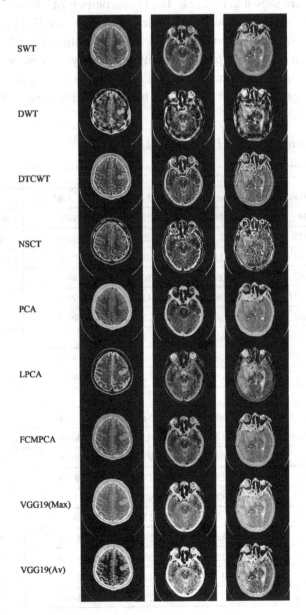

rule based fusion transfers more details to the fused image quantitatively. Whereas qualitative metrics, SSIM and FOM, prove the edge preservation capability and structural similarity of VGG19 method. When the images are subjectively verified, one can observe that PCA are FCMPCA methods incline towards any one of the source images. Wavelet-based methods do suffer from sampling, truncation of coefficients, selection of wavelets, and fusion strategy for different frequency subbands.

MRI PD – MRI T2 Image Fusion

Different modes of MRI tend to present white matter, black matter, cerebrospinal fluid, and tissues of the brain by varying contrast in high resolution. The fusion of MRI PD – T2 images fuse complementary details of the above-mentioned regions. In this experiment, three sets of MRI PD-T2 images are fused. The source images are shown in Figure 6. The fusion outputs of various methods are presented in Figure 7. The evaluated values are, presented in Table 2. It is observed that the VGG19 DLN performs well objectively and subjectively. PCA and FCMPCA methods incline towards one of the source images due to scaling factors obtained through principal component analysis. Wavelet-based methods perform similar to CT-MRIT2 fusion. Among the two fusion rules for the base layer in VGG19, the averaging fusion rule performs better than the max rule. It can be observed from the metrics, FOM and PSNR in

Table 2. Performance metrics for (MRI PD – MRI T2) fusion

Methods	FF			SSIM$_{av}$		
	Set4	Set5	Set6	Set4	Set5	Set6
SWT	3.28938	4.574324	3.321586	0.999934	0.999955	0.999823
DWT	2.911477	3.14122	3.171266	0.999874	0.999908	0.999651
DTCWT	3.157741	4.034433	3.15101	0.999926	0.999947	0.999818
NSCT	3.189467	3.477709	3.098768	0.999894	0.999919	0.999772
PCA	3.904942	5.067706	4.443439	0.999934	0.999955	0.999818
LPACA	4.333652	5.312236	4.586251	0.999913	0.999911	0.999778
FCMPCA	3.903476	4.023365	4.44969	0.999933	0.999953	0.999793
VGG19(Max)	4.097607	5.148576	3.979901	0.999654	0.999282	0.999276
VGG19(Av)	5.832417	7.673418	4.955612	0.999912	0.999734	0.999961
Methods	PSNR$_{av}$ in dB			FOM$_{av}$		
	Set4	Set5	Set6	Set4	Set5	Set6
SWT	70.7955	72.83417	70.22424	0.999806	0.999905	0.999833
DWT	68.40373	70.07359	69.02939	0.999635	0.999805	0.999649
DTCWT	70.15348	71.93919	69.85286	0.999758	0.999877	0.999797
NSCT	68.63192	70.36712	67.83925	0.999618	0.999814	0.999641
PCA	70.96128	72.96048	70.48574	0.999827	0.999919	0.999849
LPACA	72.75601	90.54583	71.63592	0.999752	0.999801	0.999803
FCMPCA	71.02926	73.14528	71.16599	0.999823	0.999914	0.99982
VGG19(Max)	67.26545	65.6767	65.93449	0.999577	0.999546	0.999455
VGG19(Av)	74.91274	82.67419	72.83294	0.999891	0.999528	0.999241

Figure 6. Source images (MRI PD – MRI T2)

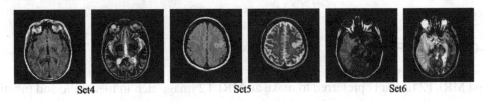

Set4 Set5 Set6

Figure 7. Fusion outputs for (a) Set4 (b) Set5 (c) Set6 source images

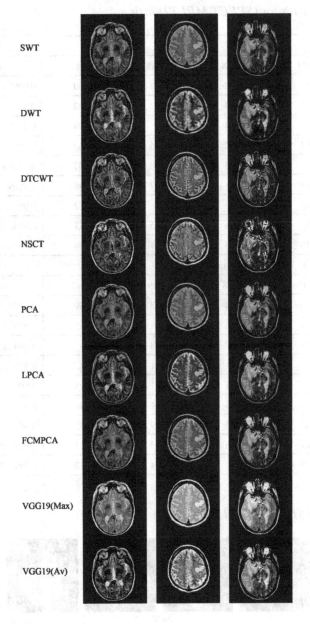

dB, that the averaging rule-based VGG19 delivers better information transfer from the source images to the fused image.

SPECT-CT Image Fusion

SPECT and MRI T2 fusion is preferred to make an MRI T2 image rich in metabolic and functional details. SPECT provides metabolic details in low resolution which can be fused with high-resolution MRI T2 images. To analyze the performance, three sets of the source images are experimented and shown in

Table 3. Performance metrics for (SPECT-MRI T2) fusion

Methods	FF			$SSIM_{av}$		
	Set7	Set8	Set9	Set7	Set8	Set9
SWT	2.68355	2.376143	2.655428	0.999909	0.99994	0.999915
DWT	2.636557	2.308174	2.752773	0.999822	0.999881	0.999835
DTCWT	4.73367	2.450174	2.50818	0.999899	0.99993	0.999904
NSCT	2.725364	2.410942	2.698216	0.99986	0.999896	0.999862
PCA	3.83419	3.449915	3.844248	0.999907	0.99994	0.999915
LPACA	3.858493	3.503605	4.526237	0.999898	0.999935	0.999862
FCMPCA	3.985362	3.502485	4.07857	0.999882	0.999929	0.999894
VGG19(Max)	4.115572	3.699258	4.020915	0.998371	0.998376	0.99857
VGG19(Av)	5.027816	4.164358	4.937281	0.999314	0.999945	0.999156
Methods	$PSNR_{av}$ in dB			FOM_{av}		
	Set7	Set8	Set9	Set7	Set8	Set9
SWT	70.59275	70.84654	69.97673	0.999889	0.999892	0.999872
DWT	70.70621	70.84586	70.7414	0.999765	0.999778	0.999746
DTCWT	70.17694	70.45057	69.58258	0.99986	0.999865	0.999843
NSCT	68.11723	68.41921	67.53181	0.999742	0.999752	0.999689
PCA	70.76124	71.00291	70.16601	0.999911	0.999915	0.9999
LPACA	71.20626	71.37064	74.67754	0.999899	0.999907	0.999812
FCMPCA	72.22169	71.94045	71.40179	0.999875	0.999895	0.999869
VGG19(Max)	61.96069	61.95776	62.15503	0.999251	0.999135	0.999203
VGG19(Av)	72.45689	74.82512	70.87934	0.999932	0.999178	0.999638

Figure 8. Source images (SPECT – MRI T2)

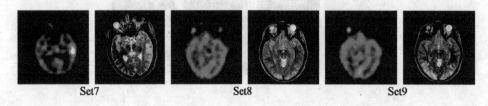

| Set7 | Set8 | Set9 |

Figure 9. Fusion outputs for (a) Set7 (b) Set8 (c) Set9 source images

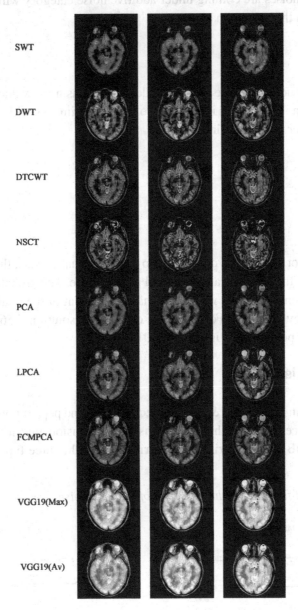

Figure 8. The fusion outputs are shown in Figure 9. The evaluated metrics are presented in Table 3. It is observed that the averaging rule-based VGG19 DLN repeats a similar performance for SPECT-CT fusion.

Performance of Fusion with the Presence of Noise

The performance of the fusion methods can be analyzed in the presence of noise. If the images are corrupted by noise, the fusion rule for integrating the source image details will also fuse the noise details present in the source images. The presence of noise in the source image will have an impact on fusion performance. For conducting this experiment, the source images are subjected to impulse noise and

Gaussian noise. The two noises are coming under additive noise category which is getting added with the pixel values present in the source images

Impulse Noise

Impulse noise is a type of additive noise that has sudden spikes as noise values. Salt and pepper noise is also known as impulse noise which is introduced to the source images with the density ranging from 0.01 to 0.1. Salt and pepper noise is defined as

$$p(z) = \begin{cases} p_a & \text{for} & z = a \\ p_b & \text{for} & z = b \\ 0 & \text{otherwise} \end{cases} \qquad (22)$$

Where 'a' is a bright dot and 'b' is a dark dot. If p_a or p_b is equal to zero, the noise will be unipolar. If neither p_a nor p_b is zero, the noise is called salt and pepper noise. The probability of the level z is denoted as p(z). The noise density of 0.01 represents that one percent of the total number of pixel values in an image is corrupted by the noise. For an image of spatial resolution, 256 × 256, the pixel values corrupted by either salt or pepper noise is $(256)^2 \times 0.01$.

Performance Analysis

The source images shown in Figures 4, 6 & 8 are subjected to salt and pepper noise with densities ranging from 0.01 to 0.1. The source images with noise are fused by the fusion algorithms and the performance is analyzed by PSNR in dB. This experiment is carried out for the three types of multimodal fusion.

Figure 10. Performance of fusion with the presence of impulse noise

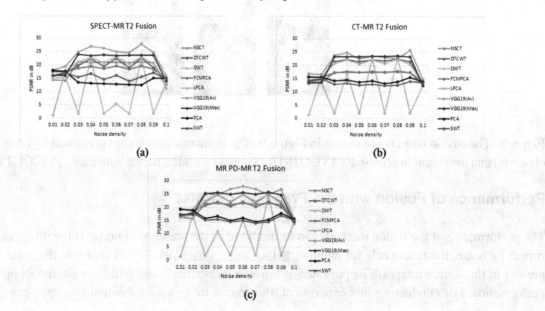

In CT-MRT2 image fusion, the three sets of source images are subjected to salt and pepper noise with varying noise densities. The source image pairs with the noise density are fused and PSNR is calculated. This is repeated for MR PD-T2 and SPECT-MR T2 fusion. Fusion performance in all three categories is presented in Figure 10. It is observed that the averaging rule-based VGG19 based fusion for multimodal medical image fusion can deliver good performance compared to other methods. The performance of DWT fusion is inconsistent due to the presence of noise. It is also interesting to note that the performance of the max rule-based VGG 19 method is consistent with increasing noise densities.

Gaussian Noise

If the noise probability density function satisfies Gaussian distribution, then the noise is known as Gaussian noise. Gaussian distribution is given as

$$p(z) = \frac{1}{\sqrt{2\pi}\sigma} e^{\frac{-(z-\bar{z})^2}{2\sigma^2}} \tag{22}$$

Where z – noise intensity, $\bar{z}$ - mean value of z, σ – *standard deviation*

Performance Analysis

Similar to the previous experiment, all the source images are subjected to Gaussian noise with variance ranging from 0.01 to 0.1. The performance evaluation of the fusion methods is carried out as elaborated in the previous section. PSNR in dB evaluated for all the three cases of the multimodal fusion are pre-

Figure 11. Performance of fusion with the presence of Gaussian noise

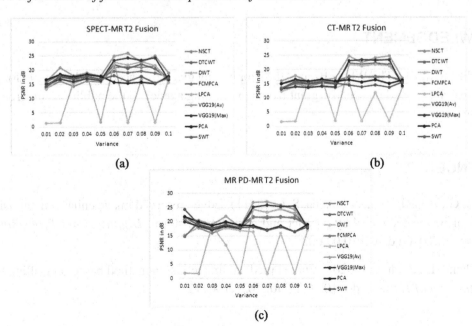

sented in Figure 11. it is observed that the PSNR is around 17dB for the Gaussian noise with the variance ranging from 0.01 to 0.05. For higher noise variances, PSNR values increase for VGG19, DTCWT, and LPCA methods. But, DWT delivers poor performance for high noise variances. Other methods deliver consistent performance for the entire range of noise variance. Among the two fusion rules for base layers in VGG19, averaging fusion works out well in the presence of Gaussian noise.

FUTURE RESEARCH DIRECTIONS

Deep learning algorithms can be employed for specific clinical applications with expert opinion. Dataset creation for a specific clinical application is also a trivial task for deep learning applications. Various deep learning networks can be tested on the brain dataset.

CONCLUSION

The fusion of multimodal images reduces the redundancy of information present in the medical images. Image fusion also reduces the burden of analyzing multiple images of the same ROI and hence, effectively reducing the medical practitioner's time and storage requirement. This chapter has analyzed the performance of VGG19 DLN for the fusion of multimodal images. The pre-trained VGG19 network is employed on the base and detail contents of the source images. Base contents are fused by averaging and maximum fusion rule and the detail contents are fused by the final activity map. The performance of the max rule-based VGG19 network is competitive as compared to other methods. Subjective verification of the outputs proves to be better than other methods. The performance of the averaging rule based VGG19 proved better than the existing fusion methods for multimodal medical image fusion. The performance of the VGG19 network is better in the presence of impulse and Gaussian noise.

ACKNOWLEDGEMENT

We would like to thank "The Whole Brain Atlas" for having given free access to the dataset for research.

This research received no specific grant from any funding agency in the public, commercial, or not-for-profit sectors.

REFERENCES

Bhutada, G. G., Anand, R. S., & Saxena, S. C. (2011). Edge preserved image enhancement using adaptive fusion of images denoised by wavelet and curvelet transform. *Digital Signal Processing*, *21*(1), 118–130. doi:10.1016/j.dsp.2010.09.002

Chen, J., Zhang, L., & Lu, L. (2020). A novel medical image fusion method based on Rolling Guidance Filtering. *Internet of Things*. . doi:10.1016/j.iot.2020.100172

Daneshvar, S., & Ghassemian, H. (2010). MRI and PET image fusion by combining IHS and retina inspired models. *Information Fusion, 11*(2), 114–123. doi:10.1016/j.inffus.2009.05.003

Gatys, L. A., Ecker, A. S., & Bethge, M. (2016). Image style transfer using convolutional neural networks. *Proceedings of the IEEE Conference on Computer Vision and Pattern Recognition,* 2414-2423. 10.1109/CVPR.2016.265

He, K., Zhang, X., Ren, S., & Sun, J. (2015). Delving deep into rectifiers: surpassing human-level performance on ImageNet classification. *Proceedings of the IEEE international conference on computer vision,* 1026–34. 10.1109/ICCV.2015.123

He, K., Zhang, X., Ren, S., & Sun, J. (2016). Identity mappings in deep residual networks. *European conference on computer vision.* 630–45.

Hu, J., & Li, S. (2012). The multiscale directional bilateral filter and its application for multisensory image fusion. *Information Fusion, 13*(3), 196–206. doi:10.1016/j.inffus.2011.01.002

Huang, X., & Serge Belongie. (2017). Arbitrary Style Transfer in Real-Time With Adaptive Instance Normalization. *The IEEE International Conference on Computer Vision (ICCV),* 1501-1510. 10.1109/ICCV.2017.167

LeCun, Y., Bottou, L., Bengio, Y., & Haffner, P. (1998). Gradient-based learning applied to document recognition. *Proceedings of the IEEE, 86*(11), 2278–2324. doi:10.1109/5.726791

Lewis, J. J., O'Callaghan, R. J., Nikolov, S. G., Bull, D. R., & Canagarajah, C. N. (2004). Region-based image fusion using complex wavelets. *Proceedings of the 7th International Conference on Information Fusion (FUSION '04),* 555-562.

Li, H., Wu, X.-J., & Kittler, J. (2018). Infrared and Visible Image Fusion using a Deep Learning Framework. *Conference Paper.* 10.1109/ICPR.2018.8546006

Li, S., Kang, X., & Hu, J. (2013, July). Image Fusion with Guided Filtering. *IEEE Transactions on Image Processing, 22*(7), 2864–2875. doi:10.1109/TIP.2013.2244222 PMID:23372084

Liu, Y., Chen, X., Peng, H., & Wang, Z. (2017). Multi-focus image fusion with a deep convolutional neural network. *Information Fusion, 36,* 191–207. doi:10.1016/j.inffus.2016.12.001

Liu, Y., Chen, X., Ward, R. K., & Jane Wang, Z. (2016). Image fusion with convolutional sparse representation. *IEEE Signal Processing Letters, 23*(12), 1882–1886. doi:10.1109/LSP.2016.2618776

Mitchell, H. B. (2010). *Image Fusion-Theories, Techniques and Applications.* Berlin: Springer-Verlag.

Pratt, W. K. (2006). *Digital Image Processing.* John Wiley and Sons.

Senthil Kumar, S., & Muttan, S. (2006). PCA based image fusion. *Proceedings of SPIE, 6233.*

Simonyan, K., & Zisserman, A. (2015). *Very deep convolutional networks for largescale image Recognition.* arXiv preprint arXiv:1409.1556

Szegedy, C., Liu, W., Jia, Y., Sermanet, P., Reed, S., Anguelov, D., ... Rabinovich, A. (2105). Going deeper with convolutions. *Proceedings of the IEEE conference on computer vision and pattern recognition,* 1–9.

Vijayarajan, R., & Muttan, S. (2014). Fuzzy C-Means clustering based principal component averaging fusion. *International Journal of Fuzzy Systems*, *16*(2), 153–159.

Vijayarajan, R., & Muttan, S. (2014). Local principal component averaging image fusion. *International Journal of Imaging and Robotics*, *13*(2), 94–103.

Wang, Z., Cuia, Z., & Zhu, Y. (2020). Multi-modal medical image fusion by Laplacian pyramid and adaptive sparse representation. *Computers in Biology and Medicine*, *123*, 103823. doi:10.1016/j.compbiomed.2020.103823 PMID:32658780

Williams, M. L., Wilson, R. C., & Hancock, E. R. (1999). Deterministic search for relational graph matching. *Pattern Recognition*, *32*(7), 1255–1271. doi:10.1016/S0031-3203(98)00152-6

Yamashita, R., Nishio, M., Richard, K. G. D., & Togashi, K. (2018). Convolutional neural networks: An overview and application in radiology. *Insights Into Imaging*, *9*(4), 611–629. doi:10.100713244-018-0639-9 PMID:29934920

Zhao, Y., Yin, Y., & Fu, D. (2008). Decision level fusion of infrared and visible images for face recognition. *Proceedings of the Chinese Control and Decision Conference*, 2411-2414.

Zhou, T., Ruan, S., & Canu, S. (2019). A review: Deep learning for medical image segmentation usingmulti-modality fusion. *Array*, *3-4*, 100004. doi:10.1016/j.array.2019.100004

KEY TERMS AND DEFINITIONS

Figure of Merit: Figure of merit estimates the edge preservation performance of the fusion algorithm using Sobel operator.

Fusion Factor: It is the summation of mutual information evaluated between two source images.

Image Fusion: Integration of complementary image details from two or more image details.

Peak Signal to Noise Ratio: PSNR quantifies the difference between the two variables x and y.

Structural Similarity Index: SSIM measures the amount of structural information present in the images. The perceived distortion of images can be approximated by the loss of structural information.

Chapter 9
Apple Leaf Disease Identification Based on Optimized Deep Neural Network

Anitha Ruth J.
SRM Institute of Science and Technology, India

Uma R.
Sri Sairam Engineering College, India

Meenakshi A.
SRM Institute of Science and Technology, India

ABSTRACT

Apples are the most productive fruits in the world with a lot of medicinal and nutritional value. Significant economic losses occur frequently due to various diseases that occur on a huge scale of apple production. Consequently, the effective and timely discovery of apple leaf infection becomes compulsory. The proposed work uses optimal deep neural network for effectively identifying the diseases of apple trees. This work utilizes a convolution neural network to capture the features of Apple leaves. Extracted features are optimized with the help of the optimization algorithm. The optimized features are utilized in the leaf disease identification process. Here the traditional DNN algorithm is modified by means of weight optimization using adaptive monarch butterfly optimization (AMBO) algorithm. The experimental results show that the proposed disease identification methodology based on the optimized deep neural network accomplishes an overall accuracy of 98.42%.

DOI: 10.4018/978-1-7998-6690-9.ch009

INTRODUCTION

Apple trees are mostly affected by pests and diseases that are caused by bacterial and viral infections which lead to the reduction in apple cultivation. Diseases affecting apple trees are of great concern, since they affect the productivity and quality to a large extent. Apple diseases detected so far exceeds more than hundred in number, increase in apple diseases affects the apple production to a great extent. The three common type of disease which affects the apple leaves which are considered in this work are Black Rot, Rust and Apple Scap. The apple diseases can be controlled, only if it is properly identified (Arora & Singh, 2019). This work concentrates on identifying the diseased leaves rather than the tree. Manual identification of the diseased apple leaves is incompetent and costly .The pattern change in apple leaves due to the disease is very minor, this minor variation cannot be effectively monitored by human beings. Computer Vision techniques are efficient in detecting the apple leaf diseases effectively. There is a color and texture change in the affected leaves which are different from normal leaves that can be detected to identify the disease. Many technologies have emerged by considering the colour, texture and shape as differentiating factors to diagnose the plant disease with a threshold between normal and pathological sections using a single feature. The existing technologies use single feature which is not effective. Conventionally the disease diagnosis in the apple leaves are done using machine learning techniques such as k-Nearest Neighbour, Random Forest, and Support Vector Machine, with enhanced recognition rate. The recognition rate is less and is still susceptible. Deep Convolution Neural Network approach which has developed in the recent years is an end-to-end pipeline which automatically determines the discriminative features for image classification. Convolution Neural Network is considered as one of the most excellent classification technique for pattern recognition task. Stimulated with the development of the convolution neural networks in image based recognition, the need of CNN in identifying early diseases has been a new research in recognition of diseases in apple trees (Prasad et al., 2019). This work uses CNN for feature extraction. Developed in the recent years CNNs are highly useful in the field of disease recognition for crops. This work proposes a CNN based approach for identifying the disease features from the affected apple leaves. The investigation of Convolution Neural Networks has not only decreased the need for image pre-processing, but also improves the detection accuracy. The proposed work uses more than thirty features of colour, shape and texture. At first, the input leaf disease image is pre-processed. In pre-processing stage, the quality of the input image is enhanced. Then the resultant pre-processing output is fed to the feature extraction process. For that, the suggested method utilizes the Convolutional Neural Network (CNN). A Convolutional Neural Network is a type of Deep Neural Network, normally applied for analyzing visual images. An Artificial Neural Network (ANN) with several layers between the output and input layers is termed as the Deep Neural Network (DNN). The DNN turns the input into output by finding the correct mathematical manipulation, even if the relationship is a linear one or a non-linear one. The effective leaf infection detection is done with the support of ODNN. As of late, meta-heuristic algorithms have proven to be efficient when compared to the other optimization algorithms. A meta-heuristic algorithm solves the conventional optimization problems such as Particle Swarm Optimization, Genetic Algorithms etc. Generally, meta-heuristic optimization methods aids in providing a suitable solution by trial and error method in a given exact designated time. Here the traditional DNN algorithm is modified by means of weight optimization using Adaptive Monarch Butterfly Optimization (AMBO) algorithm. The Monarch Butterfly Optimization (MBO) mimics the immigration behaviour of the monarch butterflies, to solve global optimization problems. The majority of metaheuristic algorithms, neglects the process of updating the information available from the previous iterations .The proposed

Adaptive Monarch Butterfly Optimization algorithm initialize an initial solution and an opposite solution is obtained for both lower and upper values .This improves the optimization process significantly .To improve the accuracy most important features are selected using the Adaptive Monarch Butterfly Optimization (AMBO) algorithm (Arora & Singh, 2019), and disease detection is done with Optimal Deep Neural Networks(ODNN). A Deep Neural Network (DNN) is a type of Artificial Neural Networks with several connections linking the input and output nodes form a directed graph next to a temporal sequence. Bio-inspired meta-heuristics perform better in selecting better features than the traditional approaches. This chapter uses the Adaptive Monarch Butterfly Optimization (AMBO) algorithm which is a bio-inspired algorithm that mimics the migration behaviour of the monarch butterflies, to solve the feature optimization problem (Ibrahim & Tawhid, 2019). The weight optimization in the traditional DNN algorithm is done with the help of the Adaptive Monarch Butterfly Optimization (AMBO) algorithm. Optimal features are selected by employing AMBO and disease identification is done with the help of ODNN. In this research, efficient apple leaf disease identification is done by Optimal Deep Learning Approach. Performance of the proposed technique is estimated by accuracy, sensitivity and specificity. The implementation work of the proposed method has been done in MATLAB. From the results it is evident that the proposed method proves to be a better technique than the existing methodologies for disease identification

The experimental results show that the suggested method has higher accuracy in comparison with the existing system. The proposed technique efficiently, successfully detects and classifies the examined diseases with best accuracy. This work is organized as follows, background section which describes the related work, main focus of the Chapter which introduces the feature extraction with CNN and feature selection with the Adaptive Monarch Butterfly Optimization (AMBO) algorithm, in addition to pattern classification with ODNN, solutions and recommendations section with the experimental results done with MATLAB and the final section with future scope and conclusion.

BACKGROUND

(Chen et al., 2017) analyzed different regions and found that machine learning algorithms are effectual in forecasting long-standing disease in regions which are subject to diseases. Based on the statistic available in the hospital, the authors have suggested the use of deep learning models to predict the risk factor of disease in the infected regions. The experimental results proves that the new model predicts accurately the diseases when compared with other CNN based risk prediction models.(Cheng et al., 2017) developed a model for detection of pest using deep residual learning method. It was compared with support vector machine and conventional Back propagation NN. This method provides an accurate detection of pest in crop cultivation. Further, in comparison to the normal deep convolution neural network, the recognition performance in this method was improved by optimized deep residual learning method. (Coulibaly et al., 2019)suggested a method to identify mildew disease in pearl millets. Here, transfer learning and feature extraction approach is used to build disease identification system. The application of deep learning methods provides support to the farmers in identifying the diseases found in pearl millets. The results prove to be better than other models. (Hu et al, 2018) identified the drawbacks of the existing monarch butterfly algorithm and found that the basic algorithm does not provide best function values. So they introduced self adaptive and greedy strategy methods which can dynamically decide the number of butterflies in each region. The performance of the new method provides faster convergence which outperformed the basic monarch butterfly algorithm.(Ibrahim &Tawhid, 2019) proposed a hybrid algorithm which combines meta-heuristic algorithms namely, differential evolution and monarch butterfly optimization. The suggested method solves the limitations of both the algorithms and was tested for nonlinear systems.(Jiang et al., 2019) presented a deep learning model based on enhanced CNN for detecting infected apple leafs in real time. The pre-trained CNN model was used in designing the novel method. The results prove that the novel model provides an efficient early identification of apple leaf diseases with high accuracy than previous models.(Liu et al., 2018) designed deep CNN model based on AlexNet to identify infected apple leafs .The model automatically finds selective aspects of infected apple leaf and the experimental results provide better solution to control the diseases in apple leaf. (Mohanty et al., 2016) suggested a method using deep learning to support smart phones for diagnosing the diseases in crops. The use of deep learning models opens a gate to use smart in diagnosing the crop disease on massive global scale. (Park et al., 2018) suggested deep neural network for classification of the hyper spectral data with less dimension .The CNN is used in feature selection of hyper spectral data provides better classification accuracy than RGB image for classification.(Wang & Tan,2019) analyzed a few existing meta-heuristic algorithm to design six information feedback models. These feedback models were then amalgamated into the basic algorithm. In this method the current iteration of the individual was updated based on the previous individuals fitness weight. The outcome of the experiment proves to be efficient in finding the fitness compared to other models

MAIN FOCUS OF THE CHAPTER

The main focus of this chapter is summarized as follows:

1. The diseased leaf images are pre-processed were by the quality of the image is enhanced.
2. The insufficient pathological images of apple leaves, has been overcome with the dataset used. The dataset is further expanded by adjusting the brightness and rotating the images. Investigation of the results on the database, confirms the firmness of the suggested approach.
3. Analysis of the visual image is done with deep neural networks, leaf disease identification is done with the help of Optimal Deep Neural Network(ODNN)
4. Discriminative feature selection is also a challenge to increase the accuracy. This proposed work utilizes the Adaptive Monarch Butterfly Optimization (AMBO) technique which is used to optimize the weights in DNN. Bio-inspired meta-heuristics perform better in selecting better features than the traditional approaches. This chapter uses the Adaptive Monarch Butterfly Optimization (AMBO) which is a bio-inspired algorithm that imitates the migration behaviour of the monarch butterflies, to solve the feature optimization problem.
5. Optimal Deep Neural Network (ODNN) is used for automatically classifying images based on discriminative features.

In this research, efficient apple leaf disease identification is done by optimal deep learning approach. At first, the input leaf disease image is pre-processed. In pre-processing stage, the quality of the input image is enhanced. Then the resultant pre-processing output is fed to the feature extraction process. Convolution Neural Network (CNN) based on Deep learning approach is suggested for feature extraction. After selecting the features, the selected features are given to leaf disease identification process. In our suggested method, leaf disease identification is done by way of Optimal Deep Neural Network (ODNN). Here the traditional DNN algorithm is modified by means of weight optimization using Adaptive Monarch Butterfly Optimization (AMBO) algorithm. Based on the above process, the effective leaf disease detection is done here. The proposed flow diagram of the leaf disease detection is shown in figure1,

The proposed framework flows through the following stages,

- Pre-processing
- Feature extraction using CNN
- Disease identification using ODNN

Pre-processing

Direct observation of colour images is often difficult because human visual perception calculates conscious representation. Therefore, the quality of the input image is improved in the proposed method. Image enrichment enhances the interpretability of information from images by human observers, or to offer "better" input to various automated image processing approaches. Here image enrichment is the process of fine tuning digital images, and the results are more relevant to image analysis and simple to identify key features. Then the resultant pre-processing output is fed to the process of feature extraction.

Figure 1.General flow diagram of the proposed leaf disease detection

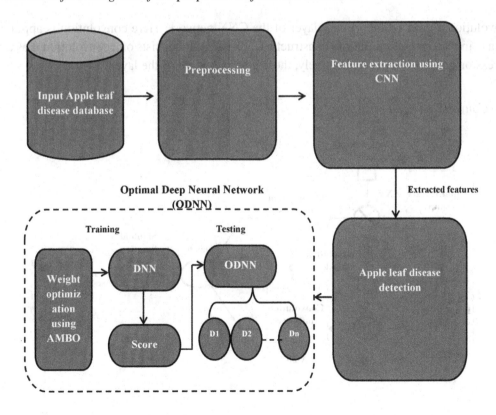

Feature Extraction

Feature extraction is process of finding and extracting the features that can be used to determine the significance of the given sample. This process is attained by utilizing the deep learning approach based on Convolutional Neural Network (CNN). A Convolution Neural Network is a sort of Deep Neural Network commonly used in analyzing visual images. The detailed explanation of CNN is described in following section.

Convolutional Neural Network (CNN)

Convolutional Neural Networks (CNN) is normally is a set of layers that are arranged by their functionalities. Convolution Neural Network can be used to a extensive variety of computational tasks. The network has an input layer, succeeded by three convolutional and max pooling layers succeeded by a soft max fully connected output layer to extract features. CNN has proven to be competent in all image processing applications such as face recognition and pattern recognition. In the proposed framework the input image is given to the initial transformation layer and the consequent output is processed in different layers. The unwanted pixels are eliminated by giving the output from the converter layer to the input of the maximum pooling layer.CNN extracts the features of the image and reduces the dimensions without losing its properties. The clear explanation of each layer is described below,

Convolutional Layer

The Convolutional layer is the primary layer of the CNN network. Here convolution is applied to the input data using a convolution filter to construct a feature map.It consists of a convolution mask, a function expression and bias terms. Collectively, these generate yield of the layer.

Figure 2. Convolution layer structure

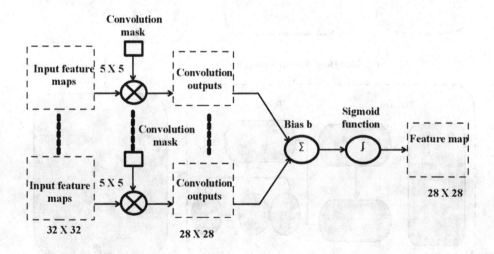

Figure 2 illustrates a 5x5 convolution mask that achieve convolution over a 32x32 input feature map. The resulting output is a 28x28 matrix. The bias and the sigmoid function are connected at the output on the matrix. Mathematically, if W_{ij}^m and b_i^m denote the weights and bias of the ith filter of the mth convolutional layer and A_i^m be its activation map,

$$A_i^m = \sum_{j \in F_i} A_j^{m-1} \otimes W_{ij}^m + b_i^m \tag{1}$$

Where, $\otimes$ is the convolution operator

Max Pooling Layer

The max pooling layer is next to the convolutional layer. The number planes of the max pooling layer are same as that of the convolutional layer. The size of the feature map is reduced by use of this layer. The image is divided into blocks of 2x2 and averaging is performed. The relative information between the features is preserved by the pooling layer and not the correct relation. The structure of pooling layer is shown below,

Figure 3. The Structure of Pooling Layer

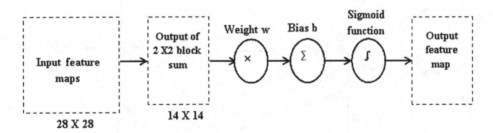

A pooled feature map P is produced as the output, as soon as the feature map A is given to the max-pooling layer and max operation is enforced to the feature map A

$$P_i = \underset{j \in R_j}{Max}\ A_i \tag{2}$$

Output Layer

In fully connected layer, every neuron is connected with every neuron of previous layer. A soft max function is used to convert the output of neural network into probability for each class. Based on the above process the features are extracted from the input leaf image, and then the selected features are fed to the disease detection phase.

Disease Identification Using ODNN

The proposed apple leaf disease identification or detection is done by optimal deep neural network algorithm. The core aim of the ODNN is detect whether the apple leaves are healthy or diseased. If diseased, then to identify whether the disease is black rot, rust and apple scap; here the conventional DNN algorithm is customized by means of weight optimization using the Adaptive Monarch Butterfly Optimization (AMBO) algorithm. The step by step process of ODNN algorithm is explained in following section,

Deep Neural Network (DNN)

Artificial neural network (ANN) with several layers between the input and output layers is called the deep neural network (DNN).

Figure 4. Structure of DNN

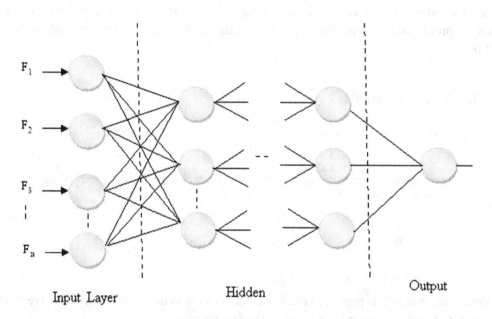

Even if the relationship is a linear relationship or a non-linear relationship DNN uses the exact mathematical operations to turn the input into output. The main aim of this method is to discover the apple leaf disease. DNN includes two phases: pre-training (utilizing generative deep belief network) and fine-tuning stages in its parameter learning. The structure of deep neural network is shown in Figure4.

DNN Pre-Training

Deep feed forward neural network (DNN) is a prototypical deep learning (DL) model. The architecture of the DNN includes three parts, namely, the input layer, output layer and the hidden layer .Each layer has a numerous interrelated processing units. A representative architecture of the DNN is indicated in

Figure 4. The DNN provides a representation in its output by utilizing a nonlinear transformation at each layer on its input. The output of the DNNs is the decision vector while the input of the network is vectorization. Considering 'F$_i$' being the input features where $1 \leq i \leq N$ and 'O' denotes the output data sets. A brief model of the neural network can be given as 'O' the number of times for the yield of the entire network and 'O_H' the time for the yield of the hidden layer. In DNN, hidden layers are more, and load on the main hidden layer increases the individual hidden information sources. Correspondingly second hidden layer weights are multiplied by first hidden element outputs.

In the first hidden layer, the weighted values of the information are enhanced with the ability to add to the neuron's gradient as in condition (3):

$$O_{H\_1}(n = 1, 2.., N) = \left(\sum_{n=1}^{N} w_{nm} f_m \right) + B_n \tag{3}$$

Where, B_x represents the constant value known as bias, w_{nm} is the weight associated between the first hidden layer and input feature were F and N denote the quantity of hidden and input nodes in the main hidden layer.

Activation function of the first hidden layer output is denoted as,

$$A\left(O_{H\_1}(n)\right) = \frac{1}{\left(1 + e^{-O_{H\_1}(n)}\right)} \tag{4}$$

Where, $A\left(\cdot\right)$ is the twisted activation function.

The operation of kth hidden layer can be specified as,

$$O_{H\_n}(k) = \left(\sum_{k=1}^{K} w_{nk} F\left(O_{H\_(n-1)}(k)\right) \right) + B_k \tag{5}$$

Where B_k specifies the bias of kth hidden node, w_{nk} is the associated weight between the $\left(k\right)^{th}$ hidden layer and $\left(n-1\right)^{th}$ hidden layer with K hidden nodes. The actuation effort which is the yield of the kth hidden layer is explained as,

$$A\left(O_{H\_n}(k)\right) = \frac{1}{\left(1 + e^{-O_{H\_n}(k)}\right)} \tag{6}$$

At the output layer, the output of kth hidden layer is again duplicated with the correlation weights (i.e. weight between the kth output layer and hidden layer) then summarized with the bias B_k as

$$O(p) = A\left(\sum_{p=1}^{K} w_{pq} A\left(O_{H\_n}(k)\right) + B_k\right) \tag{7}$$

Where w_{pq} represents the correlation weight at the kth hidden layer and output layer with p^{th} and q^{th} individually. The initialization work at the output layer becomes the output of the entire model.

Currently, the model differs from the target output and the output of the model is achieved to improve the error. Calculation of the error is defined in equation (8)

$$Error = \frac{1}{M}\sum_{m=1}^{M}\left(Actual(O_m) - Target(O_T)\right)^2 \tag{8}$$

Where, $Target(O_T)$ denotes the target output and $Actual(O_m)$ is the factual output. DNN can be improved by decreasing the error. As a result, the values of weight must be balanced to decrease the error in each iteration.

Fine-tuning Phase

At this point, the weight parameters of the DNN are adjusted or improved using the Adaptive Monarch Butterfly Optimization (AMBO).An innovative nature-inspired meta-heuristic algorithm, called MBO has been proposed for continuous optimization in this work, by simulating the migrating behaviour found in nature with the monarch butterflies. In MBO, all the monarch butterflies are idealized and found in two lands such as land one and land two. Positions of the butterflies are modified in two ways. First the migration operator is used to generate the off springs, which can further be updated using the migration ratio. Butterfly adjusting operator is used to tune the positions of the other butterflies. Migration operator and Butterfly adjusting operator are mainly used to determine the search direction of the monarch butterfly individuals in MBO algorithm. The basic MBO algorithm, the search strategy effortlessly falls into local optima, providing premature convergence and poor performance on numerous complex optimization problems. To solve these issues, this paper develops a novel MBO algorithm based on opposition-based learning (OBL).The detailed explanation of AMBO algorithm is shown in further process,

Step by Step Procedure of AMBO Algorithm:

Initialization: For all optimization problem initialization is an important process. This section optimizes the weight value in DNN. Here the input weight values (w) are randomly initialized.

$$W_i = \left[w_1, w_2, ... w_n\right] \tag{9}$$

Opposition based learning (OBL): OBL considers the present weight value and its inverse weight value for a present hopeful arrangement. In this way, the idea of OBL might be used to improve the execution of the population based calculations. Here the opposite agent's positions (OW_i) are completely defined by components of w_i.

$$OW_i = \left[ow_1, ow_2, ...ow_n \right] \tag{10}$$

Where $OW_i = Low_i + Up_i - W_i$ with $OW_i \in \left[Low_i, Up_i \right]$ is the position of ith opposite agent OW_i in the dth dimension of oppositional population.

Fitness calculation: After initializing the weight value, fitness of each weight values are calculated. The maximum accuracy is considered as fitness values. The fitness calculation is given by,

$$Fitness = Max\ Accuracy \tag{11}$$

Updating using AMBO algorithm: Here the updating can be done in two stages. If the weight value belongs to land one then AMBO updates the solution with the help of the movement operator. Similarly, if the weight values belong to land two then the solutions are updated by means of adjusting operator.

Migration Operator

When monarch butterflies remain at Land one and Land two, their values in Land one and Land two can be expressed as $ceil(z * SP)$ (SP_1, $Subpopulation1$) and $SP - SP_1$ (SP_2, $Subpopulation2$), respectively with time. Here, $ceil(y)$ rounds y to the closest integer greater than or equal to y; SP denotes the population size; z denote the ratio monarch butterflies in Land one.

Step 1: Randomly generate a number r by uniform distribution r=rand*period (here period set to 1.2 (12 months a year)).

Step 2: if r>z, generate the nth element of y_u^{v+1},

$$y_{u,n}^{v+1} = y_{r_1,n}^{v} \tag{12}$$

Where $y_{u,n}^{v+1}$ signifies the nth element of y_u at generation $v + 1$. Likewise, $y_{r_1,n}^{v}$ stands for the nth element of y_{r_1}. The current generation number is v. Butterfly r_1 is randomly chosen from $Subpopulation1$.

Step 3: Else, randomly selects the butterfly. Generate the nth element of $y_{r_1,n}^{v}$ is generated by,

$$y_{u,n}^{v+1} = y_{r_2,n}^{v} \tag{13}$$

Where $y_{r_2,n}^{v}$ stands for nth element of y_{r_2}, and butterfly r_2 is randomly selected from $Subpopulation2$.

Butterfly Adjusting Operator

Butterfly adjusting operator can be used to update the locations of monarch butterflies except migration operator. The procedure of butterfly adjusting operator is described as follows

Step 1: Randomly generate a number r by uniform distribution.

Step 2: if $r \le z$, generate the nth element of y_u^{v+1},

$$y_{u,n}^{v+1} = y_{best,n}^{v} \tag{14}$$

Where, $y_{t,n}^{v+1}$ stands for the nth element of y_t at generation $v+1$. Similarly, $y_{best,n}^{v}$ expresses the nth element of the fittest butterfly y_{best}.

Step 3:   Else, randomly selects the butterfly r_3.
Step 4:   Generate the nth element of $y_{u,n}^{v+1}$,

$$y_{u,n}^{v+1} = y_{r_3,n}^{v} \tag{15}$$

Where $y_{r_3,n}^{v}$ expresses the nth element of y_{r_3}. Here, $r_3 \in \{1,2,...,SP_2\}$.

Under this condition, if $rando > BAR$, updating can be performed as follows,

$$y_{u,n}^{v+1} = y_{u,n}^{v+1} + \alpha(dy_n - 0.5) \tag{16}$$

BAR denotes the butterfly adjusting rate. dy is the walk step of butterfly u is calculated with the following equation,

$$dy = (y_u^v) \tag{17}$$

α is the weighting factor in equation (16), which is calculated using equation (18),

$$\alpha = S_{max} / v^2 \tag{18}$$

Where, S_{max} is the maximum walk and v is the current generation.

Termination criteria: The algorithm terminates when the best solution is reached. Algorithm terminates only when the highest number of iterations are attained .The solution with best fitness value is chosen using the AMBO which is presented as the best solution to DNN. Based on the optimal weight value, the proposed ODNN effectively detects the apple leaf disease. Finally, the performance of the suggested method is evaluated and the performance of the proposed technique is compared with the other techniques in result and discussion.

SOLUTIONS AND RECOMMENDATIONS

The proposed optimal apple leaf disease detection method is developed using MATLAB (version 2015a). Here, Apple leaf features taken as input is extracted using CNN and an Optimal Deep NN perform disease identification process. The recommended strategy considers apple leaf disease dataset as input. The sample input leaf disease image is shown below,

Figure 5 .Sample apple leaf disease image (a) healthy image (b) Rust (c) Black rot and (d) Apple scap

(a)

(b)

(c)

(d)

The dataset is available at https://www.kaggle.com/vipooooool/new-plant-diseases-dataset. The test results are presented in the segments following the leaf images.

Performance Metrics

The proposed technique needs different assessment metric qualities to be determined so as to analyse the proposed optimal apple leaf disease detection.

Table 1. Performance metrics using in the proposed method

Measure	Equation	Definition
Positive Predictive Value (PPV)	$PPV = \dfrac{TP}{FP + TP}$	It determines the number of pixels in the input leaf disease image is identified to be positive are actually positive
Negative Predictive Value (NPV)	$NPV = \dfrac{TN}{FN + TN}$	The negative predictive value estimates how many of the pixels in the input leaf disease image is identified to be negative
False Positive Rate (FPR)	$FPR = \dfrac{FP}{FP + TN}$	The proportion of cases that result in identifing correctly the input leaf disease image, but in fact, it was not successful
False Negative Rate (FNR)	$FNR = \dfrac{FN}{FN + TP}$	The cases where the result shows the input leaf disease image is not correctly identified, but it was actually successful
Sensitivity	$Sensitivity = \dfrac{TP}{FN + TP}$	It determines the ratio of input leaf disease that is exactly recognized for positive
Specificity	$Specificity = \dfrac{TN}{TN + FP}$	It determines the proportion of input leaf disease that is exactly identified for negative results
Accuracy	$Accuracy = \dfrac{TP + TN}{TP + TN + FP + FN}$	It determines the percentage of correctly classified instances

The measurement values are found dependent on True Positive (TP), True Negative (TN), False Positive (FP) and False Negative (FN) with the alternative of pixel differences. The performance of this technique is examined by Positive Predictive Value (PPV), Negative Predictive Value (NPV), False Positive Rate (FPR), False Negative Rate (FNR), Sensitivity, Specificity, and Accuracy. The confusion matrix value for the proposed method is tabulated in Table.2. The expected result of the classification problem is represented in a confusion matrix. It represents the numerals of true and false with their count and class group.

Table 2. Confusion matrix of the proposed method

	Apple_scab	Black_rot	Cedar_apple_rust	healthy
Apple_scab	504	0	0	0
Black_rot	0	497	0	0
Cedar_apple_rust	0	0	440	0
healthy	100	0	0	402

In this confusion matrix, the 502 actual healthy leafs, the proposed system predicted that 100 were apple scab, and it predicted that 402 were healthy leafs. Likewise, the proposed system predicted the remaining leaf disease from the database.

Analysis of Proposed Method

Performance analysis of the recommend method is represented in the Table.3. Here the proposed method considers the performance measures are PPV, NPV, FPR, FNR, Sensitivity, Specificity and Accuracy. The results are tabulated below,

Table 3. The performance analysis of proposed model

Metrics	Sensitivity	Specificity	Accuracy	PPV	NPV	FPR	FNR
Proposed method (ODNN)	0.948	0.982	0.984	0.948	0.982	0.0171	0.0514

From the table.3, the suggested method attains the overall Accuracy, Sensitivity and Specificity value as 0.984, 0.948 and 0.982. The overall PPV and NPV value of the proposed method is 0.948 and 0.982 FPR and FNR value of the proposed method is 0.0171 and 0.0514. The effectiveness of the proposed technique is examined and the outcomes are contrasted with the existing methods in the following segment.

Effectiveness of the Proposed Apple Leaf Disease Detection

To determine the efficiency suggested method is related with the current algorithms. The proposed method is the Deep Neural Network with Adaptive Monarch Butterfly Optimization (AMBO) is associated with the existing Monarch Butterfly Optimization(MBO), Particle Swarm Optimization (PSO) and Genetic Algorithm (GA), which is represented as DNN+AMBO, DNN+MBO, DNN+PSO, DNN+GA and DNN without optimization. The results are plotted below,

Figure 6. Effectiveness of proposed apple leaf disease detection using Accuracy, Sensitivity, Specificity, PPV and NPV

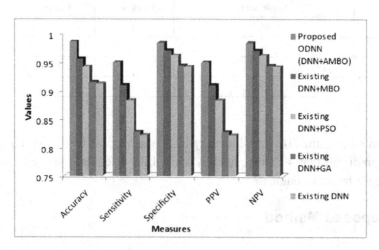

As shown in the above Figure 6, the proposed ODNN (DNN+AMBO) method attains the 0.984 for accuracy value but the existing method attains the 0.954 for DNN+MBO, 0.94 for DNN+PSO, 0.913 for DNN+GA and 0.94 for DNN, that are less compared to the implemented method. The suggested method ODNN attains the maximum accuracy, due to effective feature selection done by CNN from the input apple leaf disease image. The sensitivity value of the suggested method is 0.948. The specificity of the suggested method is 0.982 which is greater when compared to the existing methods. The PPV and NPV of the suggested method are also high when compared to the other methods.

Figure 7. Effectiveness of proposed apple leaf disease detection using FPR and FNR

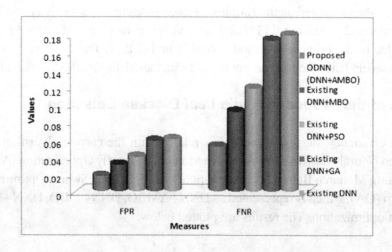

The graphical representation of the comparison of FPR and FNR is shown in Fig.7, when analyzing the above figure, the proposed technique reaches the lowest FPR and FNR value compared to the current methods. Here the proposed ODNN (DNN+AMBO) method gets the FPR and FNR value as 0.0171 and 0.0514 is less when related to the current methods. From the results, it is absolute that the suggested ODNN (DNN+AMBO) method detects the healthy and diseased leaf with the maximum accuracy and minimum FPR and FNR value. The ROC plot comparison of the proposed method is shown below,

Figure 8. ROC considered is plot comparison of proposed ODNN (DNN+AMBO)

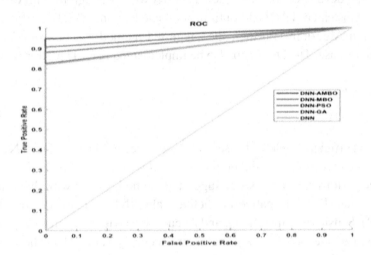

When analyzing the above ROC comparison plot, the suggested method achieves the maximum true positive rate compared to the existing algorithms. The proposed ODNN (DNN+AMBO) method also compares the detection performance with various researches; the results are tabulated below,

Table 4. Comparison of disease detection performance of various Techniques

Methods	Detection Accuracy (%)
Proposed ODNN	98.42
CNN+NAG	97.62
ICNN (VGGNet-16)	97.14
Multi label classification	93.31

All the research works considered above uses the input apple leaf disease dataset. To perform comparison, the suggested method considers existing Convolutional Neural Network method with various training algorithm such as Nesterov's Accelerated Gradient (NAG) Liu et al., 2018, VGGNet-16 et al., 2019 and Multi-label classification Zhong et al 2020. When analyzing the above methods for accuracy the proposed method achieves the maximum value compared to the other methods. Here, the proposed method uses CNN for efficient feature selection, and then the selected features are fed to the detection process using ODNN algorithm. In the proposed method deep learning based algorithm is efficiently used for both feature selection and disease detection process so the suggested method achieves high detection performance when compared to the existing methods. The results prove that the proposed ODNN achieves better disease detection accuracy when related to the present methods.

FUTURE RESEARCH DIRECTIONS

In future, the upcoming developed methods such as Faster RCNN (Regions with Convolutional Neural Network) can be used instead of DNN and optimization can be done with the help of IBOA (Improved Butterfly Optimization Algorithm).Further, the suggested method can be extended to identify more samples of apple leaf disease. The DNN can also be implemented in GPU platform with a large dataset.

CONCLUSION

This work proposes an efficient apple leaf disease detection technique with Deep Neural Network. The appropriate features are extracted with the help of CNN algorithm and finally disease identification is done by ODNN. The performance analysis of suggested method is done with the following metrics the Positive Predictive Value (PPV), Negative Predictive Value (NPV), False Positive Rate (FPR), False Negative Rate (FNR), Sensitivity, Specificity, and Accuracy. The test outcomes depict the effectiveness of the apple leaf disease detection with the maximum accuracy value. Here the proposed ODNN accomplishes 98.42% classification accuracy. From above outcomes it is evident that the suggested method proves that in real time it can detect diseases in apple leaf with better accurateness. It also delivers a real time viable result for the detection of diseases in apple leaves.

REFERENCES

Arora, S., & Singh, S. (2019). Butterfly optimization algorithm: A novel approach for global optimization. *Soft Computing*, *23*(3), 715–734. doi:10.100700500-018-3102-4

Chen, M., Hao, Y., Hwang, K., Wang, L., & Wang, L. (2017). Disease Prediction by Machine Learning over Big Data from Healthcare Communities. *IEEE Access: Practical Innovations, Open Solutions*, *5*(c), 8869–8879. doi:10.1109/ACCESS.2017.2694446

Cheng, X., Zhang, Y., Chen, Y., Wu, Y., & Yue, Y. (2017). Pest identification via deep residual learning in complex background. *Computers and Electronics in Agriculture*, *141*, 351–356. doi:10.1016/j.compag.2017.08.005

Coulibaly, S., Kamsu-Foguem, B., Kamissoko, D., & Traore, D. (2019). Deep neural networks with transfer learning in millet crop images. *Computers in Industry*, *108*, 115–120. doi:10.1016/j.compind.2019.02.003

Hu, H., Cai, Z., Hu, S., Cai, Y., Chen, J., & Huang, S. (2018). Improving monarch butterfly optimization algorithm with self-adaptive population. *Algorithms*, *11*(5), 1–19. doi:10.3390/a11050071

Ibrahim, A. M., & Tawhid, M. A. (2019). A hybridization of differential evolution and monarch butterfly optimization for solving systems of nonlinear equations. *Journal of Computational Design and Engineering, 6*(3), 354–367. doi:10.1016/j.jcde.2018.10.006

Jiang, P., Chen, Y., Liu, B., He, D., & Liang, C. (2019). Real-Time Detection of Apple Leaf Diseases Using Deep Learning Approach Based on Improved Convolutional Neural Networks. *IEEE Access: Practical Innovations, Open Solutions, 7*, 59069–59080. doi:10.1109/ACCESS.2019.2914929

Kaya, A., Keceli, A. S., Catal, C., Yalic, H. Y., Temucin, H., & Tekinerdogan, B. (2019). Analysis of transfer learning for deep neural network based plant classification models. *Computers and Electronics in Agriculture, 158*(January), 20–29. doi:10.1016/j.compag.2019.01.041

Liu, B., Zhang, Y., He, D. J., & Li, Y. (2018). Identification of apple leaf diseases based on deep convolutional neural networks. *Symmetry, 10*(1), 11. doi:10.3390ym10010011

Manzak, D., Cetinel, G., & Manzak, A. (2019). Automated Classification of Alzheimer's Disease using Deep Neural Network (DNN) by Random Forest Feature Elimination. *14th International Conference on Computer Science and Education, ICCSE 2019, Iccse*, 1050–1053. 10.1109/ICCSE.2019.8845325

Mohanty, S. P., Hughes, D. P., & Salathé, M. (2016). Using deep learning for image-based plant disease detection. *Frontiers in Plant Science, 7*(September), 1–10. doi:10.3389/fpls.2016.01419 PMID:27713752

Nachtigall, L. G., Araujo, R. M., & Nachtigall, G. R. (2017). Classification of apple tree disorders using convolutional neural networks. *Proceedings - 2016 IEEE 28th International Conference on Tools with Artificial Intelligence, ICTAI 2016*, 472–476. 10.1109/ICTAI.2016.75

Park, K., Hong, Y., Kim, G., & Lee, J. (2018). Classification of apple leaf conditions in hyper-spectral images for diagnosis of Marssonina blotch using mRMR and deep neural network. *Computers and Electronics in Agriculture, 148*(February), 179–187. doi:10.1016/j.compag.2018.02.025

Prasad, K., Sajith, P. S., Neema, M., Madhu, L., & Priya, P. N. (2019). Multiple eye disease detection using Deep Neural Network. *IEEE Region 10 Annual International Conference, Proceedings/TENCON, 2019-Octob*, 2148–2153. 10.1109/TENCON.2019.8929666

Wang, G. G., Deb, S., & Cui, Z. (2019). Monarch butterfly optimization. *Neural Computing & Applications, 31*(7), 1995–2014. doi:10.100700521-015-1923-y

Wang, G. G., & Tan, Y. (2019). Improving Metaheuristic Algorithms With Information Feedback Models. *IEEE Transactions on Cybernetics, 49*(2), 542–555. doi:10.1109/TCYB.2017.2780274 PMID:29990274

Zhong, Y., & Zhao, M. (2020). Research on deep learning in apple leaf disease recognition. *Computers and Electronics in Agriculture, 168*, 105146. doi:10.1016/j.compag.2019.105146

Chapter 10
A New Approach of Deep Learning–Based Tamil Vowels Prediction Using Segmentation and U–Net Architecture

Julius Fusic S.
ⓘ https://orcid.org/0000-0001-9572-4025
Thiagarajar College of Engineering, India

Karthikeyan S.
Thiagarajar College of Engineering, India

Sheik Masthan S. A. R.
Thiagarajar College of Engineering, India

ABSTRACT

In this chapter, 500 different images of Tamil vowels that are hand written (அ ஆ இ ஈ உ ஊ எ ஏ ஐ ஒ ஓ ஔ ஃ) interprets that the Tamil alphabets model has trained about 75% accuracy with proposed U-net model algorithm. The introduction of various segmentation proportions was discussed for English and Tamil language text identification was explained. In this work, the selection of image is split into four segments and read the data during training itself. Thus, the Tamil and English font prediction accuracy of the model was improved about 85% using U-net architecture was explained.

INTRODUCTION

Machine learning has now become the most famous problem-solving tool for any criteria yet the models are not effective to handle cognitive data and process to yield the optimum solution. Some researchers worked towards making the machine model effective and to enable its extraordinary by preferring other optimum solutions in the field of computation, neural networks. The development of neural networks

DOI: 10.4018/978-1-7998-6690-9.ch010

and its various problem-solving optimization techniques gives birth to Deep learning. The investigation of neural networks is still an oceanic research area especially the selection of hidden layers and the number of neurons for the selected application. The neural network structural performance may differ from one application model to another.

Deep learning allows a computation model to represent certain details of parameters to be processed. This method brought breakthroughs in image processing, video, speech recognition and in other notable research fields. Applying deep neural networks to a variety of data types are complicated in the selection process, preprocessing and segmentation process to yield a high efficiency model. Moreover, the appropriate selection of filters and type of cost function yield good results in the final structure. Many comparative studies and literature reviews results end up with a single architecture model with their own data type. All these data types are having their own functions that cannot be specified.

Natural Language Processing was established in favor of Artificial Intelligence and specifically to process human language for computers. NLP too showcases extensive development after applying deep neural networks. Thus, Deep learning has now become more evolved computation in language related tasks.

HISTORY OF OCR

Fournier Optophone and the Tauschek's reading machine was developed during 1870 to 1931 to help the visually impaired people in their optical character recognition ideas. Gismo was invented in the year 1950 by Harvey Cook and David. H. Shepard stated that Gismo is a machine that translates printed text messages to machine codes which would be easy for the computer processing and also capable of reading the text aloud. The first company to sell out of these OCR devices is Intelligent Machines Research Corporation. The consumers of these OCR devices at the time were Standard Oil Company of California, Reader's Digest and the Telephone Company and in 1954, Optacon arrived at the market. It is a device used to scan and digitize the postal address. The price tag scanners and passport scanners were developed with the help of the OCR technology during the period of 1980's. The companies such as Caere Corporation, Kurzweil Computer Products Inc and ABBYY began during 1980's and 1990's. These are some of the famous companies in the OCR field. The OCR technology has developed immensely during the period of 2000 to 2019.Technologies such as web OCR and applications that translate foreign language have been developed. Tesseract developed by Hewlett Packard and the University of Nevada, Las Vegas is a famous OCR engine. There are other numerous OCR software developed by Adobe and Google which are accessible by all. Now, the OCR research is directed towards the non-cursive scripts such as the Arabic, Urdu, Tamil, Kannada.

DEEP LEARNING

Deep learning was developed mainly to process the images where the parameters will be huge especially when it comes to video segments. Furthermore, deep neural networks have paved a way through these by applying various algorithm models. The research related with any field like image processing, data analytics, Industry 4.0, Image segmentation, video segmentation, data visualization can go ahead with deep neural networks. This chapter will be mainly focusing on the processing of an image through deep neural networks. Like any machine learning model deep neural networks require training. It is essential to know about different kinds of neural networks and cost functions that can yield specific output models for text recognition.

In deep learning fundamentally the neural networks are classified into four main types as follows:

- Unsupervised pre-trained networks
- Convolutional neural networks
- Recurrent neural networks
- Recursive neural networks

In this chapter we will be only discussing supervised neural network models which is widely practiced in the present times.

Convolutional Neural Networks

The Convolutional neural networks are extensively used in the image processing-based machine learning models. In CNN, the authors take a dive into the linkage relation between the input and output. To derive specific output a layer consists of a number of artificial neurons or perceptrons to communicate about various parameters. This layer is called a hidden layer, which looks for a specific input from the number of inputs and based on the latter, it will give a bias. The bias value is based on the weightage value of the inputs. The bias will activate or trigger the function corresponding to the input like true or false based on the conditions given. The typical artificial neuron or perceptron which was developed by Frank Rosenblatt. A layer in CNN will have a number of perceptron's based on the input and parameters specified.

Recurrent Neural Network:

The recurrent neural networks are similar to neural networks but the functions will be repeated with a feedback loop until the corresponding bias is activated in a particular layer. The recurrent networks are specialized for sequential inputs. The networks will be able to train for sequential applications like word predictions and speech recognition. During the process the network forms a continuous chain like structure in order to achieve the specific value which yields results for the sequential process.

Figure 1. A typical recurrent information passing structure

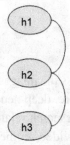

Recursive Neural Network

The recursive neural networks are developed from the recurrent neural networks only. Moreover, it will function the same as recurrent networks but the structure formed at the end will be in the form of a tree in order to branch and predict the next iteration in the sequential inputs. These RNNs end up with vanishing gradient problems.

Figure 2. A typical recursive information passing structure

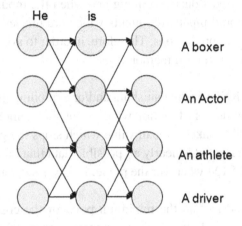

Weight:
In neural networks, the weight is the very basic term. Weight is defined as the real value which is a measure of input to a neuron. Weight will have the information about the input and it compares with a threshold value in order to pass the information further to the networks.
Bias:
Bias is like a condition element, if it receives the suitable weight then it will activate the neuron. It can be said that bias will have condition statements to pass the weight through it and to alter the weights for the next set of neurons. A bias will decide where the information has to pass.

Figure 3. Weight and bias representation for a single neuron

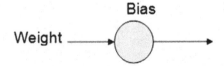

Cross entropy function:
The cross-entropy function is used to fix the learning slowdown problem. The output of the function will be non-negative and if the actual output and desired output is close for all the training inputs, then

the results will be zero. So, it will be easier to compute the desired output. The cross-entropy function is given by,

$$C = -\frac{1}{n}\sum_x \left[y \ln a + (1-y)\ln(1-a) \right].$$

Vanishing Gradient Problem:

Vanishing gradient problems occur only in repetitive functioning networks like RNN. RNNs will remember the large amount of inputs during training and when the model is subjected to predictions, it will be using only specific stored inputs; the inputs which are unused will vanish as it is no longer required. This in turn affects future predictions. Therefore, in order to avoid this problem people offered a solution which is called Long-short term memory.

LSTM:

One challenge in the use of RNNs is the vanishing and/or exploding gradient problem which can be reduced to the Long-short term memory function which gains the memory even when the trained data is not utilised many times. LSTM makes a recall value which stops the gradients vanishing which can be termed as forgotten data. LSTM holds nearly all possible data that have been trained so far. Thus, it becomes advantageous to use LSTM wherever the model involves sequential data.

Gradient descent:

Gradient descent is a method to find the minimum point of the cost function. The efficiency of gradient descent does not change with the number of neurons but certain cases do show some chaotic values due to many class variables in the network. By updating the position of the vector v repeatedly the minimum cost function can be calculated. The gradient descent depends on the learning rate of the model, to make it work correctly; the learning rate should be small enough.

Stochastic gradient descent:

Stochastic gradient descent is the commonly used powerful technique for learning in neural networks. It actually speeds up the learning for the minimum batch size chosen. These are widely used optimizers for classification problems to reduce the loss and it works perfectly if the mini batch size is small.

Back propagation:

Back propagation algorithm is the most widely used method to do classification purposes in deep learning. Back propagation will reduce the error by repeatedly changing the weight and bias according to the previous error calculation. It is like adjusting to the information passed repeatedly by comparing it with loss. So initially the chance of having error will be high and it will gradually decrease as it changes values to compensate for the error.

Figure 4. Comparison of back propagation and Learning vector quantization methods

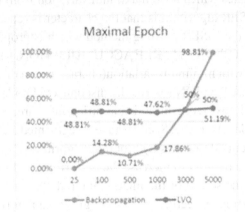

Literature review:

Qixiang Ye et.al (2015) stated that the classification of text falls under two categories namely Graphic text and scene text. The graphic text is digitally written text and the scene texts are those texts which are derived from the scene images. Most of the ongoing research relates to the scene text detection. The common challenges on the text detection are lighting problems, image blur, and variation in fonts, environment and complexity in computation. The two commonly used methodologies are stepwise and integrated methodologies The stepwise methodology consists of common four steps namely localization (classifies the text region and group them), verification (verify whether the grouped region is text or non-text region), segmentation (separate the characters from the text region and make them as image blocks), recognition (converts the image blocks to characters).While the integrated methodology consists of character classification (which involves differentiation of a word from the environment as well as the other characters), along with the detection and recognition steps. The integrated methodology is preferable for the small dictionary of words as the character classification is a tedious process. From the survey of the commonly used methods, it has been found that processing the multilingual text is a quite difficult process especially for the Asian languages due to the variety of characters, complicated structure, and multiple strokes. The suggested possible solution is to use a common trainable method to specify a model for each language of its kind.

Jon almazan (2014) pointed out the recognition of the whole word instead of recognizing each character and formation of words based upon the recognized characters. It consists of three layers namely, Attribute space, Label space and common space. The word images are sent to the attribute space where it is attribute embedded with the help of the embedded function. At the same time in parallel the label words which are aided by the dictionary are sent to the label space where it is label embedded with the help of the pyramidal histogram of characters (PHOC). The PHOC is developed based upon the bag of words algorithm. The attribute embedded word images and the label embedded labels are sent to the common space. The common space compares the labels and the word image. If a label and word space is close together, then it is recognized.

Xuwang Yin et.al (2014) analyzed that a maximally stable extreme regions [MSER] algorithm is the most effective algorithm when compared to the previous traditional algorithms. The MSER is a tree-based parent – child algorithm. From the tree, the candidates which are likely to be characters are chosen as characters, whereas the candidates which have maximum variation from the characters are eliminated. The major drawback of the MSER algorithm is that the character is repeating with each other. The repeating defect is reduced with the MSER pruning method which is proposed in his publication. It has two algorithms LINEAR REDUCTION and TREE ACCUMULATION. LINEAR REDUCTION returns one child from the parent node with minimum variation(character) as a disconnected node and works on the other child. TREE ACCUMULATION returns the disconnected nodes and clusters it together. The work done by Shuohao Li et.al Text recognition is classified into three stages. First stage is character extraction and segmentation from the image. Second stage is segmented characters are under recognition. The last stage is to combine them into groups by grouping algorithms. There are some text recognition problems which are to be solved in order to increase the performance of the scene text detection. Scene text is the text that appears on the screen or the image captured by camera. Text recognition problems are the grouping of more characters, selecting the correct grouping algorithm, sequencing the data and its performance. Therefore, in order to solve this problem CNN cannot be used. Since it is used for single label detection, DNN can be employed as it can recognize the scene text. DNN comprises CNN and RNN. Hence, to solve this problem, DNN with an attention model is used.

This model consists of three parts. The first part deals with extraction of features by CNN acting as an encoder. The second part deals with the attention of feature by feature vector taken from feature sequence using the attention model. The last part deals with the recognition of sequences using the LSTM network by which LSTM acts as decoder. It decodes the above vector into text, through which a complete text of DNN with an attention model is represented as a DANN model. The DANN model does not use grouping algorithms and performs better than the state of art methods.

Xiao hang Ren et al. (2017) noted that Extraction of text information consists of two processes: text detection and text recognition. In Text detection, challenges like variations in text font, size, style, noise, complex background and lightning conditions take place. In Text recognition, challenges like orientation or position of text, layout of text, geometric distortions and partial occlusions happen. Usually, text detection and text recognition of English words are done due to its simplicity. But Chinese words were difficult to use for text detection and text recognition. Since, Chinese words have thirty types of strokes when compared to English words. English words have ten types of strokes and are more complex than English words. Therefore, in order to detect and recognize the Chinese texts in images, Novel Text Structure Feature Extractor is proposed. It is based on a TSCD layer, residual network for detecting and recognizing Chinese texts in images. It is also based on a three-layer cognition model of humans; the TSCD layer and residual network are joined for Chinese text extraction. Here, TSCD is converted into a TSCD block and in the three-layer model the bidirectional connections among layers are stimulated by a residual network. Text Structure Component Detector is used to enhance the accuracy and the uniqueness of feature descriptors by extracting multiple text structure components in various ways. TSCD block based Chinese test structure feature extractor is used to detect and recognize Chinese texts.

Basavaraj and Kumuda (2015) proposed a method which is used to detect and localize the text from natural scene images. The method is divided into two sections- Text detection and text localization based upon the texture features. The text detection involves preprocessing and texture analysis. The preprocessing is used to increase the quality of the texture analysis. In the preprocessing step, the input color image is changed to intensity image from the RGB. Every 8×8 block of the image is computed with the direct cosine transform (DCT) coefficient values. The 8×8 array contains the pixel's gray scale value.

The DCT coefficient and high pass filters are used to suppress the constant background. Only discontinuities in the pixel's gray scale value are allowed for further processing. There are always certain regularities in the texture of an object and hence it is used in the texture analysis section. To calculate the variations in gray first order statistics is used and to include the spatial distribution and local variance in gray second order statistics is used. The second order statistical features are derived from the gray level co-occurrence matrix, which stores the pixel neighborhoods that have grayscale combination at a distance d and direction theta. The extracted features are then stored in a feature matrix. The blocks are then classified into text and Non-text using the discriminant functions. The vectors which satisfy the threshold value are classified as text blocks and those which do not satisfy are classified as Non text blocks. This process of classification is known as the Text localization. The text regions are obtained by merging the satisfied text blocks.

Md Zahangir Alom et al made 96% efficiency on using the Resnet Model with HPL-Tamil-IsoChar database and classification was based on the normal size of the text as they have given in training. But in order to recognize the text in any size requires a better trained model with precision techniques. It used to perform text identification using Convnets for the tamil database IWFHR-10 by HP labs India and able to achieve good results yet discussed the reliability of the model while pooling and using huge amounts of data. This shows Convnets are not enough to produce the prominent results for a long time.

Furthermore, Peng liu et.al (2019) proposed the hand written high precision gesture recognition using Single-Shot Multi-box Detector paved a 19-layer NN which interface human actions with computer as the advancement of communication platform.

BACKGROUND WORK

In this chapter, the dataset for a specific language will be created which would be the handwritten text content from different persons. These data are then used to train the network in order to predict the texts of the language. The deep learning model will be using an RNN network type and SoftMax as the final classifier function. The RNNs are used for text recognition widely since it has the ability to match with the next iteration of words and predict subsequent words in such a way that a line can be easily detected and predicted with less error.

The character recognition of a foreign language is not as easy as it is for English language. Besides English the structure of a single letter is difficult to recognize. Like in the case of Chinese letters, the letters have too many patterns and it is difficult to extract as a feature. This makes it a tedious process and takes a huge amount of time for recognition.

Xiao hang Ren et.al (2017) made a layer before training where they have to segment a single letter into 3:3 ratio patterns. Further, they classify them into thirteen other categories in order to recognize the word, hence, there will be thirteen labels. The thirteen labels will give an easy way to recognize the letters based on the content in their segmented ratios. The synthesizing of these labels gives the pre-trained networks by sparse encoders enabling them to recognize the character in an image as shown in figure 5.

Figure 5. Text segmentation ratios used to detect Chinese letters

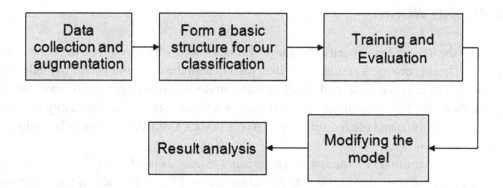

DATA COLLECTION AND AUGMENTATION

For any deep learning model, data collection is the hard process. Collecting data from different sources is not easy. The data has to have different features which are very necessary, so the pre-process of creating a deep learning model is time consuming. If there is the same or similar featured data in the dataset it is difficult to get the best result. After all, the very purpose of creating the model would become a failure here. So, here it is required that a distinct and large amount of data is trained in order to predict good results.

Figure 6. Proposed work Block Diagram

```
Data collection and augmentation  →  Form a basic structure for our classification  →  Training and Evaluation
                                                                                              ↓
Result analysis  ←  Modifying the model  ←
```

The next thing is data augmentation; it is the preparing of the collected data for training and evaluating the model. The augmentation of the data should be in such a way that the researcher can give input for the predictions. If not, the model will show error or the resulting prediction will be wrong. This is an important factor for training and evaluation as well.

This research has eminist data which will be available on the internet. Since, it will take more time to get data and process it for training this dataset has been chosen. This is an extended data set of a famous eminist dataset (which contains 0-9 handwritten digits). The eminist dataset has handwritten alphabets from a to z and also digits. This research has imported the data into the proposed model of this study for training and evaluating.

Neural networks model:

The selection of neural networks can be messy because mostly the neural networks concept was inspired from the human brain. So, in practical terms consider a class of students in a school wherein not every student is able to grasp the concept, only few can get. Moreover, each individual will have a different aspect of learning in their own way. Likewise, in artificial neural networks not every neural network model gives a good result for the required output. The team of the famous Alex net classifier has been asked for how they chose the architecture to give better results. The Perceptron convergence theorem states that,

Rosenblatt (1961), *"The perceptron algorithm finds a linear discriminant function in finite iterations if the training set is linearly separable"*.

Figure 7. A typical Neural network system

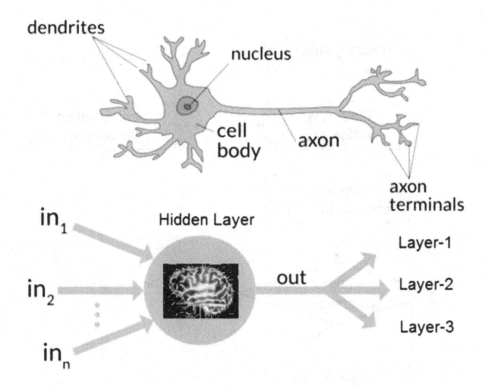

The study explained that they trained the model in various conditions and they chose the final model based on the trial and error methods. The selection of the neurons for text extraction was not accurate and selection may vary from one researcher to another. So, the selection of neurons and selection of hidden layers will not be compared with other work. This criterion varies with person to person depending on application and feature extraction.

Initially the random selection of the system was developed using trial and error methods and checks for accuracy. As the accuracy varies, then the modification is required to improve the efficiency and reduce the model error in step by step basis. In this proposed work, the step by step improvement was explained for high efficiency structure development to identify and read the alphabets. No matter what, the last layer should contain a number of labels that are supposed to make predictions. In this study, 42 have been chosen as it contains labels of both upper case and lower case of alphabets and digits as well.

The compilation of the model with commonly used Adam optimizer and categorical cross entropy loss function has been conducted. Thus, the first neural network model was selected based on the tensor board results and that gives the basic model to extract the application required in the current research work. The tensor board may vary from applications and hardware you run it.

Figure 8. Proposed work flow diagram

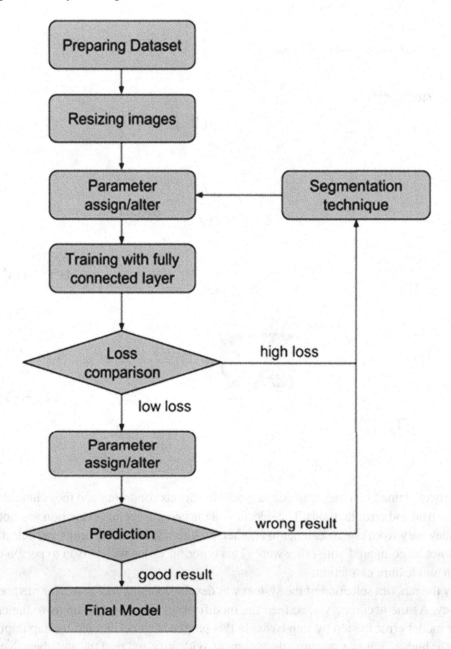

Model Evaluation and Optimization:

The selection of the best model to be picked that suited the classification for this study. This resembles the same as the case discussed previously. The checking of the performance analysis for various possible conditions will be conducted. Initially there are four fully connected layers with a smaller number of neurons in each layer and as it is said the final layer contains neurons which would be equal to the number of labels about to classify. This resembles the same as the case discussed previously. The performance analysis processed in this work in various possible conditions is shown in figure 9. The basic model has four fully connected layers with a smaller number of neurons in each layer and as it is said the final layer contains neurons which would be equal to the number of labels which is to be classified. The evaluation between train and test shows a significant difference that the model needs to improvise.

The results obtained in the training and test will not attain best results. But it was suggested to be best while compared to other results. The evaluation between train and test shows significant differences depicting that the model needs to improvise.

Figure 9. a) Model loss vs Epoch b) Accuracy vs Epoch plots for Adam optimizer

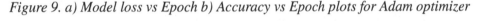

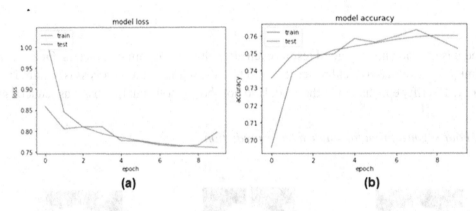

From the results it can be interpreted that the model has trained about 75% accuracy and the results provided will have prediction errors. Among the eight predictions one prediction of "4" resulted as "Class V". Based on that, the resulting model has to train further to improve the efficiency and reduce the model error which was shown in the figure 10.

Figure 10. Results showing correct and incorrect predictions

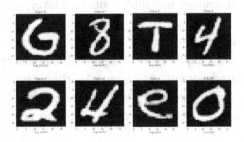

Segmentation:

Now the modification of the network model for a better technique to classify the features for text classification is discussed in various literature surveys. The implementation of stochastic gradient descent optimizer and segmented image features have been used to classify precisely.

Figure 11. Final structure of layer for proposed work

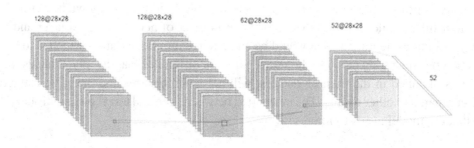

The model is not showing any good results even after altering certain parameters. One can apply any sort of techniques on models to yield better results. Thus, the segmentation process is required to improve the efficiency. The fifty epochs run of the model did not show results but the loss was reduced gradually.

Figure 12. Four segmentation for English letter prediction

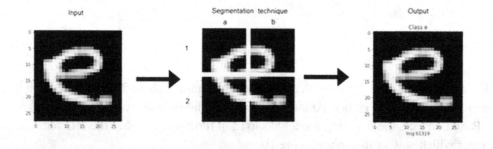

After so many trial and errors on improvising the model and altering various parameters like learning rate, optimizers and number of neurons in a fully connected layer, better results depict an accuracy of about 85%.

It is said that a deep learning model should be trained with a very distinct unique featured number of models. To improvise further there is a requirement to segment the image by four regions of interest. The region was equally divided into four quadrants. As discussed earlier in the text identification process, the model's ability can be improvised by segmenting a text and train along. But the segmentation also has some constraints like, the more it is segmented the more it requires processing the data. Furthermore,

Figure 13. Results of Model loss and accuracy vs Epoch before segmentation

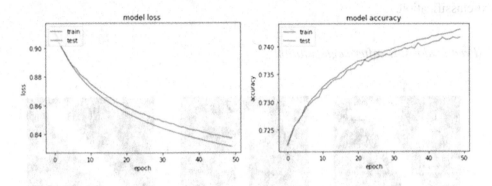

Figure 14. Results of Model loss and accuracy vs Epoch final segmentation

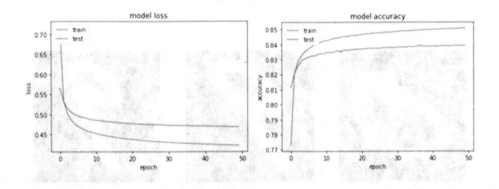

the texts must contain such features that it should be worthwhile to classify them in such a way. In the case of English alphabets which have less curves and features compared to the Chinese texts. The Table 1 explained about the step by step algorithm procedure for segmentation process.

Table 1. Algorithm steps for Normal segmentation process.

Algorithm 1: Segmentation
Input: text image
Output: Classified text
Step 1: Import image
Step 2: resize ()
Step 3: def (layers):
def (activation function):
Step 4: training parameters No. of epochs: 10 Images per GPU: 1 Weight: random Segmentation Type:(2/2)
Step 5: Model save
Step 6: Predicting raw image
Step 7: Evaluation of model

So, the research did a 2 by 2, four quadrant technique to classify which yielded good results. This will also give better results when feature extraction was achieved from an image where text will be of abnormal size and pattern. So, one can use segmenting techniques to improve their model efficiency in case of text classification.

Figure 15. Predicted results after segmentation

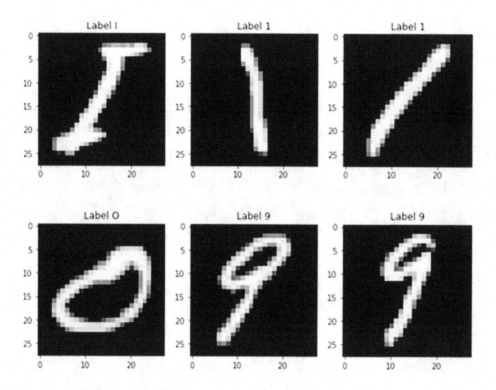

Figure 16. Sample results of text reorganization after segmentation

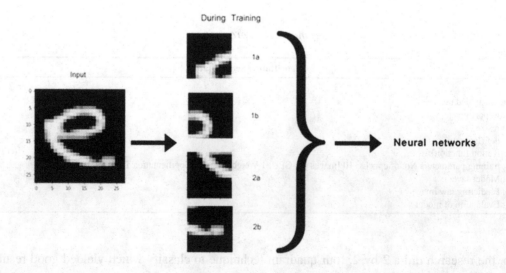

To improvise further there is a need to iterate the model for each possible parameter to yield a better result. The bias, weights, number of layers, type of layers, cost functions, loss functions, pooling, padding, batch size, epochs, and metrics and so on can be altered. The only problem will be the hardware; for which a good set of GPUs can be used to run such different iterations of all parameters to know the best model for classification. This study used NVIDIA GeForce GTX 1050 graphics card to perform all the tests. When it comes to deep learning models, the hardware dependent is more to train and evaluate it and Time becomes a real factor here.

Even after that there is a need to compile each and every sort of results in a single place to review it better. If not, there will be a need for repetitive analysis tests like in the old-fashioned way, conducting experiments and observing details in a document. There is a tool called Tensor Board where it can analyze the entire model by just creating logs for the results. These logs in Tensor Board will represent visualization for the model and best result for the definite parameter can be reviewed and upgraded subsequently for best efficiency. The maximum accuracy for a model can be achieved by using similar techniques to find out the best architecture for the application. The table 2 details about the step by step procedure for U net semantic segmentation process.

Table 2. Algorithm steps for U-net semantic segmentation process.

Algorithm 2: U-net semantic Segmentation
Input: Augmented image + mask
Output: Segmented image + results in graph
Step1: Import Augmented data
Step2: resize of original
Step3: Neural network model define
def (layers):
layers for contraction
def (activation function):
layers for expansion
def (activation function):
Step4: parameter configuration No.of epochs: 10 Images per GPU: 1 Weight: random
Step5: Model save
Step6: Predicting raw image
Step7: Evaluation of model

Similarly, for Tamil font, in the U-net based text predicting algorithm the sample images considered for training Tamil vowels of 500 different hand written images (அ ஆ இ ஈ உ ஊ எ ஏ ஐ ஒ ஓ ஔ ஃ). The overall block diagram of the process is shown in the figure 17. From the results it can be interpreted that the Tamil letter model has trained about 75% accuracy as shown in figure 18.

Figure 17. Block diagram of Tamil font model algorithm

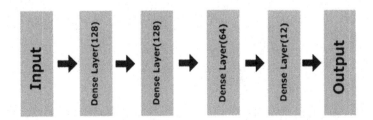

Figure 18. Model loss and accuracy plots for selected architecture

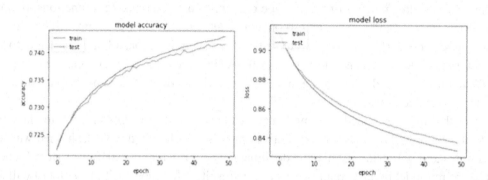

The semantic segmentation technique was one of the highly used in terms of text identification. U-Net architecture as displayed in figure 19 which provides the semantic segmentation for any input. The difference between previous architecture and the U-Net is that the input in U-net will be accompanied with masks of the same image on which the class has been labelled. The sample Tamil letter image and its mask is shown in figure 20.

Figure 19. U-Net Tamil letter prediction layer architecture

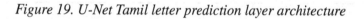

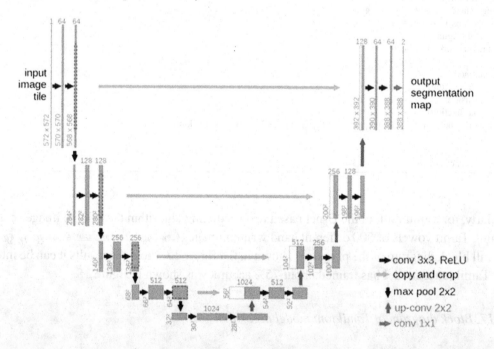

Figure 20. Sample Tamil letter Image and its Mask

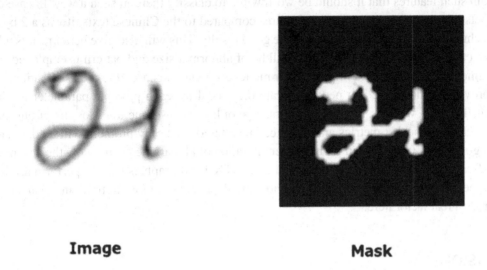

Image   **Mask**

During model segmentation up to fifty epochs the run of the model did not show results but the loss was reduced gradually. After so many trial and errors on improvising the model and altering various parameters like learning rate, optimizers and number of neurons in a fully connected layer better results of about 85% accuracy were achieved as shown in figure 21.

The same architecture cannot be applied to different applications even though it has the same amount of class or datasets. A model's behavior is dependent on the hardware that is used. So, to analyze any model in the desired parameter iterations it is best to choose the best model suited as per the research's requirements.

Figure 21. Final results for Tamil letter prediction

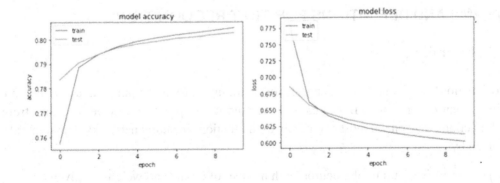

It is said that a deep learning model should be trained with a very distinct unique featured number of models. To improvise further the image was segmented by four regions of interest. The region was equally divided into four quadrants. As discussed earlier in the text identification process, the model ability by segmenting a text and train along can be improvised. But the segmentation also has some constraints like, the more it is segmented the more it requires to process the data. To add to it, the texts must contain such features that it should be worthwhile to classify them in such a way. In case of English alphabets which have less curves and features compared to the Chinese texts, it was a 2 by 2, four quadrant technique for classification which gave good results. This will also give better results when the feature extraction from an image where text will be of abnormal size and pattern is employed. So, one can use segmenting techniques to improve their model efficiency in case of text classification.

To improvise further there is a need to iterate the model for each possible parameter to yield the better result. The bias, weights, number of layers, type of layers, cost functions, loss functions, pooling, padding, batch size, epochs, metrics and so on can be altered. The only problem will be the hardware, you need a good set of GPUs to run such different iteration of all parameters to know the best model for your classification. Here we used NVIDIA GeForce GTX 1050 graphics card to perform all the tests. When it comes to deep learning models, the hardware dependent is more to train and evaluate it. The time becomes a real factor here.

CONCLUSION

In the presented chapter, an implementation of a step by step process to identify text through segmentation technique has been used. The selection of segmentation techniques made the structure to increase the capability of the machine learning model for all foreign language's texts. The many curved letters are also identified using our designed model and the efficiency graphs were displayed. A trial and error method used to select neurons to identify the suitable model for the classifier was performed. The introduction of various segmentation proportions was discussed for English and Tamil language text identification was explained. In this work the selection of images is splitted into four segments and reads the data during training itself. By doing so the accuracy of the model was improved by about 85%. In future the selection of segmentation for Tamil words identification will perform for road safety cloud awareness projects, based on identification the model which automatically identifies the language.

KEY TERMS AND DEFINITIONS FOR TEXT RECOGNITION:

Sigmoid Function:

Sigmoid function is the function which transforms the input to an output. The actual neuron will be delivering output either 0 or 1. But in case of sigmoid it will produce a range of values from 0 to 1. Sigmoid functions were one of most commonly used functions in neural networks. The sigmoid function (σ . is given by,

$$\sigma(z) \equiv \frac{1}{1+e^{-z}}$$ .The output of a neuron with number of inputs and weights is given by,

$$\frac{1}{1+exp\left(-\sum_j w_j x_j - b\right)}.$$

Hyperbolic Tangent Function:

The hyperbolic tangent function for a neuron is given by,

$$tanh(w.x + b).tanh(z) \equiv \frac{e^z - e^{-z}}{e^z + e^{-z}}$$ .The range of output will be from -1 to 1. While using tanh function there is a need to normalize the outputs for real values.

ReLU:

Rectified linear units can be used to compute any functions. The range of the function will vary from 0 to z. ReLu is defined by,

$$max(0, w.x + b).$$

Softmax:

Softmax is the excellent function to be used for a classification problem involving more than two labels. The softmax for neuron activation is given by,

$$a_j^L = \frac{e^{x_j^L}}{\sum_k e^{x_k^L}}$$

REFERENCES

Almazan, J., Gordo, A., Fornes, A., & Valveny, E. (2014). Word Spotting and Recognition with Embedded Attributes. *IEEE Transactions on Pattern Analysis and Machine Intelligence, 36*(12), 2552–2566. doi:10.1109/TPAMI.2014.2339814 PMID:26353157

Alom, M. Z., Sidike, P., Hasan, M., Taha, T. M., & Asari, V. K. (2018). Handwritten Bangla Character Recognition Using the State-of-the-Art Deep Convolutional Neural Networks. *Computational Intelligence and Neuroscience, 2018*, 1–13. doi:10.1155/2018/6747098 PMID:30224913

Cohen, Afshar, Tapson, & van Schaik. (2017). EMNIST: an extension of MNIST to handwritten letters. *Computer Vision and Pattern Recognition.*

Cutter, M. P., & Manduchi, R. (2015). Towards Mobile OCR: How to Take a Good Picture of a Document Without Sight. *Proceedings of the 2015 ACM Symposium on Document Engineering.* 10.1145/2682571.2797066

Gibson, A., & Patterson, J. (2017). Deep Learning. O'Reilly Media, Inc.

Hochreiter, S., & Schmidhuber, J. (1997). Long short-term memory. *Neural Computation, 9*(8), 1735–1780. doi:10.1162/neco.1997.9.8.1735 PMID:9377276

HP Labs India Indic Handwriting Datasets IWFHR. (2006). http://lipitk.sourceforge.net/hpl-datasets.htm

Khan, N. H., & Adnan, A. (2018). Urdu Optical Character Recognition Systems: Present Contributions and Future Directions. *IEEE Access : Practical Innovations, Open Solutions, 6*, 46019–46046. doi:10.1109/ACCESS.2018.2865532

Kumuda, T., & Basavaraj, L. (2015). Detection and localization of text from natural scene images using texture features. *2015 IEEE International Conference on Computational Intelligence and Computing Research (ICCIC)*, 1-4. 10.1109/ICCIC.2015.7435688

Li, Tang, Guo, Lei, & Zhang. (2017). Deep neural network with attention model for scene text recognition. *IET Computer Vision, 11*(7), 605-612.

Liu, P., Li, X., Cui, H., Li, S., & Yuan, Y. (2019). *Hand Gesture Recognition Based on Single-Shot Multibox Detector Deep Learning*. Mobile Information Systems. doi:10.1155/2019/3410348

Long, J., Shelhamer, E., & Darrell, T. (2015). Fully convolutional networks for semantic segmentation. *Proceedings of the IEEE Conference on Computer Vision and Pattern Recognition*, 3431–3440.

Nielsen. (2015). *Neural Networks and Deep Learning*. Determination Press.

Ramakrishnan, A., Urala, B., Sundaram, S., & Harshitha, P. (2014). *Development of OHWR System for Tamil*. Academic Press.

Ren, X., Zhou, Y., He, J., Chen, K., Yang, X., & Sun, J. (2017). A Convolutional Neural Network-Based Chinese Text Detection Algorithm via Text Structure Modeling. *IEEE Transactions on Multimedia, 19*(3), 506–518. doi:10.1109/TMM.2016.2625259

Ren, X., Zhou, Y., Huang, Z., Sun, J., Yang, X., & Chen, K. (2017). A Novel Text Structure Feature Extractor for Chinese Scene Text Detection and Recognition. *IEEE Access : Practical Innovations, Open Solutions, 5*, 3193–3204. doi:10.1109/ACCESS.2017.2676158

Rosenblatt, F. (1961). *Principles of neurodynamics: Perceptions and the theory of brain mechanism*. Washington, DC: Spartan Books. doi:10.21236/AD0256582

Watanabe, T., & Iima, H. (2018). Nonlinear Optimization Method Based on Stochastic Gradient Descent for Fast Convergence. *2018 IEEE International Conference on Systems, Man, and Cybernetics*. 10.1109/SMC.2018.00711

Ye, Q., & Doermann, D. (2015). Text Detection and Recognition in Imagery: A Survey. *IEEE Transactions on Pattern Analysis and Machine Intelligence, 37*(7), 1480–1500. doi:10.1109/TPAMI.2014.2366765 PMID:26352454

Yin, X., Yin, X., Huang, K., & Hao, H. (2014). Robust Text Detection in Natural Scene Images. *IEEE Transactions on Pattern Analysis and Machine Intelligence, 36*(5), 970–983. doi:10.1109/TPAMI.2013.182 PMID:26353230

Chapter 11
Edge Enhancement Method for Detection of Text From Handwritten Documents

Chandrakala H. T.
https://orcid.org/0000-0002-2727-8593
Government First Grade College, Madhugiri, India & Tumkur University, India

Thippeswamy G.
BMS Institute of Technology, India

ABSTRACT

Edge detection from handwritten text documents, particularly of Kannada language, is a challenging task. Kannada has a huge character set, amounting to 17,340 character combinations. Moreover, in handwritten Kannada, the character strokes are highly variable in size and shape due to varying handwriting styles. This chapter presents a solution for edge detection of Kannada handwritten documents. Sobel edge detection method, which efficiently enhances the image contrast and detects the character edges, is proposed. Experimentation of this edge detection approach yielded high F-measure and global contrast factor values.

INTRODUCTION

In today's digital era, text documents both printed and handwritten are maintained as digital images, either by scanning or camera capturing them. Unlike their hard copies, these digital documents not only have longer shelf life but are also easily accessible and sharable on the internet. Moreover these documents can be made editable using an OCR (Optical Character Recognition) tool.OCR converts a digital text document image from human readable form to machine editable codes [Chandrakala etal: 2016] Detection of text edges in the document is the key prerequisite step to be performed before employing an OCR for their interpretation. Edges are significant intensity changes that distinguish the different regions of an image. Edge Detection is a fundamental process which separates the background and foreground text

DOI: 10.4018/978-1-7998-6690-9.ch011

in the document image based on the consequential gray level discontinuities. The edge representation of the document contains significantly less amount of data to be handled, while retaining vital information about the shape of the text in the document. Moreover it enhances and highlights the text contours which can serve the further steps of text processing like segmentation and character recognition.

The process of digitization of text documents adds noise artifacts thus reducing the legibility of the foreground text. Edge detection of the digital text documents is a difficult task, because the image noise as well as text edges are of high frequency. Noise removal from these images would lead to blurred and distorted edges. Furthermore in handwritten documents, not all edges involve sharp changes in intensity owing to the inherent variability of individual handwriting styles. The quality of handwriting and the language in which the text is written majorly influences the accuracy of various text image processing phases like edge detection, segmentation and character recognition. This chapter presents an efficient edge detection methodology which not only increases the image contrast by noise removal but also enhances the text edges in handwritten text documents. The method is tested for its efficacy on the Kannada Handwritten Text Document (KHTD) Dataset. The only published Kannada Document Dataset till date is KHTD dataset. *Figure 1* shows a sample KHTD image. This dataset was published in ICDAR2011 and is not available publically. It consists of 204 handwritten Kannada documents. These documents are written by 51 writers and are divided into four categories [Alireza etal; 2011]. Each document contains 21 text lines on an average.

Figure 1. Sample image from KHTD dataset

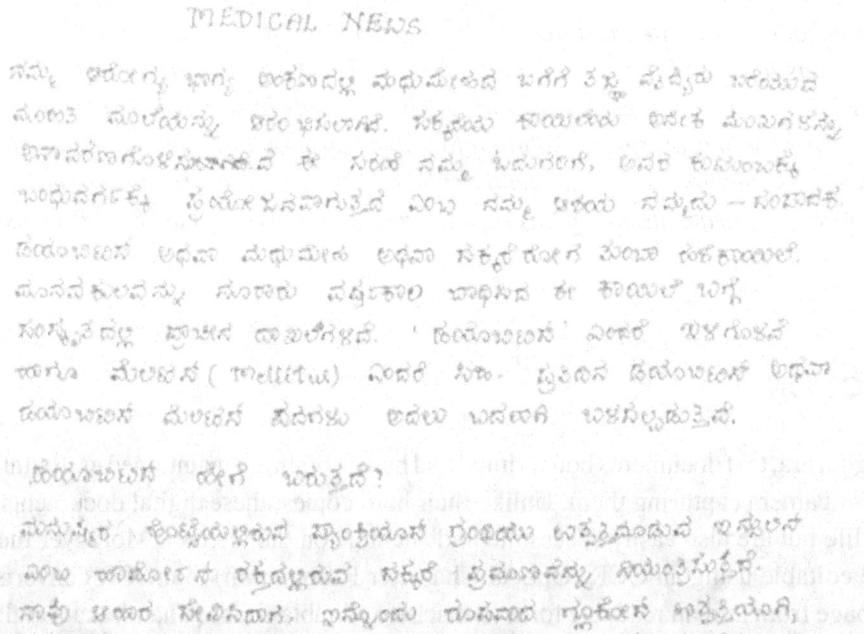

Further, the chapter is organized as follows: The edge detection methods prevalent currently for handwritten documents are summarized in the *Literature review* section. The *Methodology* section gives a detailed explanation of the proposed Sobel algorithm for edge detection. This is followed by the *Results and Discussion* section which demonstrates the results achieved by the proposed system. A summary of the proposed research is given in the *Conclusion* section.

LITERATURE REVIEW

As reported in the literature, edge detection has been utilized in many research works. The main edge detection methods used in practice are Sobel, Canny, Roberts, Prewitt, and Laplacian of Gaussian(LoG). Out of these Sobel is the more extensively used method. [Chew etal; 2000] performed edge detection for text extraction from historical handwritten documents of National Archives of Singapore using Canny method. [Matti etal; 2001] employed Sobel edge for text extraction from Oulu University database document images. Edge detection using Sobel operator and Zernike moments is proposed by [Qu etal; 2005]. [Zhang etal; 2009] used a combination of Sobel operator and genetic algorithm for edge detection in real images. [Gao etal; 2010] proposed a soft threshold wavelet and Sobel operator for edge detection of white Gaussian noise effected images. [Chen etal; 2011] in their proposed Edge Enhanced Maximally Stable Extremal Regions algorithm, make use of canny edge detection on ICDAR2003 and ICDAR2005 natural scene text image dataset. [Revati etal; 2012] used Sobel and Canny edge detectors to identify disease spots in the cotton leaf images. [Samta etal; 2013] evaluated the efficiency of Sobel edge detection operator on images of various resolutions.

Some of the works on edge detection from bilingual and multilingual documents are:- [Aradya etal:2011] used wavelet transform and gabor filter to extract text edges from ICDAR multilingual dataset. On ICDAR 2001, KIAST and MSRA-TD500 datasets a Nonlinear neural network was employed by [Lin etal; 2015] for multilingual text detection based on language independent stroke feature learning approach. [Wen etal: 2015] employed Canny edge detector and maximally stable extremal region techniques to detect Chinese and English text from books and natural scenes. For text detection and recognition of ICDAR 2015 and 2017 MLT datasets OctShuffleMLT method was employed by [Antonio etal; 2019]. Stroke width transform was used by [Ramanathan etal; 2018] for text detection in multilingual Indian Signage board documents comprising of Kannada, Hindi and English text. A CNN model of text detection for Chinese characters was developed by [Xiahong etal; 2016] and was experimented on ICDAR 2011 and 2013 datasets. Chinese and English Bilingual Scene text detection was performed on MSRA-TD500 dataset by [Yaun etal; 2017] using pretrained VGG16 CNN.

METHODOLOGY

In the Kannada Handwritten Text Document (KHTD) images as shown in *Figure 1*, the character strokes are not very sharp and the overall image contrast is poor due to the effect of noise artifacts. So an edge detection method which can enhance the image contrast as well as detect the text edges effectively is required to facilitate the further document image processing phases like segmentation, feature extraction and character recognition. Therefore Sobel edge detection algorithm is employed for the enhancement and detection of character edges in the KHTD images. Sobel Edge Detector finds the edge strength

Figure 2. (a) Original Image (b) Gradient Magnitude (c) Gradient Direction (d) Detected Edges

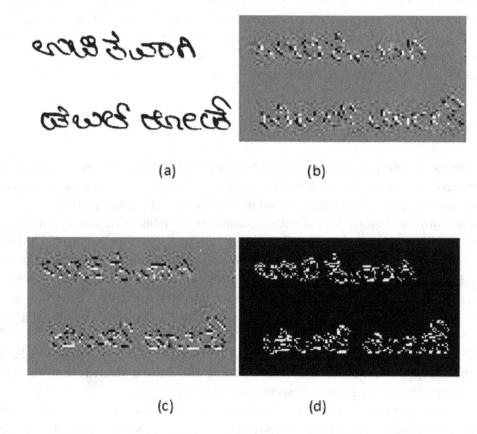

(a)   (b)

(c)   (d)

and direction using the gradient operator. It performs double thresholding using the magnitude of the gradient which represents the edge strength, thus detecting the character edges in the image foreground. The direction of the gradient is used to separate the image background and foreground. *Figure 2* shows the gradient magnitude, direction and detected edges for a zoomed part of a gray scale KHTD image.

For a location (x, y).f an image f .the gradient is represented as a vector [13] given by:

$$\nabla f = \begin{bmatrix} g_x \\ g_y \end{bmatrix} = \begin{bmatrix} \dfrac{\partial f}{\partial x} \\ \dfrac{\partial f}{\partial y} \end{bmatrix}. \tag{1}$$

The magnitude of the vector ∇f .is:

$$M(x, y) = \sqrt{g_x^2 + g_y^2}. \tag{2}$$

The direction of the gradient vector is given by the angle:

$$\alpha(x, y) = tan^{-1}\left[\frac{g_y}{g_x}\right].$$ (3)

The gradient of an image can be obtained by computing the partial derivatives $\frac{\partial f}{\partial x}$ .and $\frac{\partial f}{\partial y}$ .at every pixel of the image. The Sobel edge detector makes use of the following digital approximations of these partial derivatives using 3×3 .mask:

$$g_{x=}\frac{\partial f}{\partial x} = (z_7 + 2z_8 + z_9) - (z_1 + 2z_2 + z_3)$$ (4)

$$g_{y=}\frac{\partial f}{\partial y} = (z_3 + 2z_6 + z_9) - (z_1 + 2z_4 + z_7)$$ (5)

These masks take into account the data on the opposite side of the center pixel, hence carry more information about the direction of an edge. The weight of 2 in the center coefficient of the mask provides better noise suppression thus enhancing the image contrast as well .The masks used to implement the above equations are shown in *Figure 3* .

Figure 3. (a) A 3×3 region of an image where z's are the pixel intensity values (b) Mask for Equation 4 (c) Mask for Equation 5.

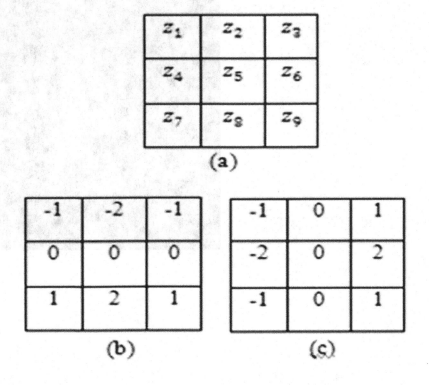

RESULTS AND DISCUSSION

The Sobel edge detection method is evaluated on the entire KHTD dataset. Two sample outputs are shown in *Figure 4* and *Figure 5* .

Figure 4. (a) Original KHTD Image (b) Sobel edge detected image

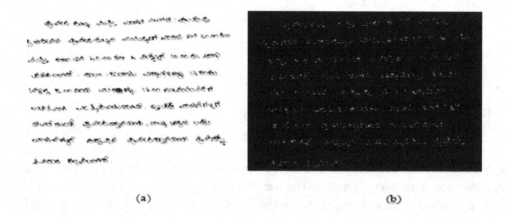

(a)   (b)

Figure 5. (a) Original KHTD Image (b) Sobel edge detected image

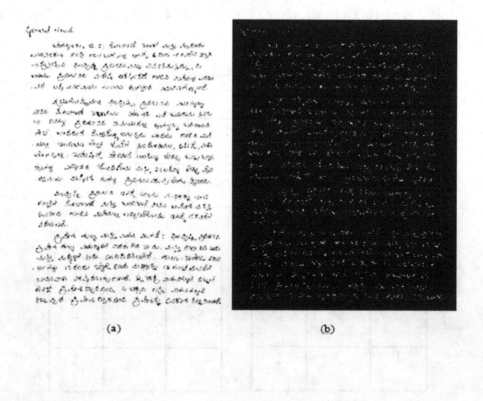

(a)   (b)

The proposed method is tested for its efficiency using two performance metrics namely: Global Contrast Factor (GCF) and F-measure. GCF uses perceptual luminance to measure the contrast instead of linear luminance, hence it is very close to the perception of contrast by humans. It uses local contrasts at different resolutions to compute overall contrast. F- Measure is a better rated measure to rank edge detection results for handwritten text image. A higher F-measure indicates more broken characters and false alarms. Hence lower F- measure is desirable. The performance of the proposed Sobel method was evaluated in comparison to other methods like Prewitt, Canny, Roberts, Log (Laplacian of Gaussian). The average GCF of the original KHTD dataset is 0.174. As tabulated in the *Table 1*, the proposed method could achieve better average GCF and F-measure on the KHTD dataset, compared to all the other methods.

Table 1. Performance evaluation of the proposed method

Edge Detection Method	GCF	F-measure
Canny	0.2633	95.13
Roberts	0.2706	95.42
Log	0.2706	95.42
Prewitt	0.3047	96.45
Sobel	0.3369	94.20

CONCLUSION

The chapter presented a method for edge detection and enhancement from handwritten text documents. The method was tested on the KHTD (Kannada Handwritten Text Document) image dataset. These images suffer from low contrast due to the effect of noise artifacts and also the handwritten Kannada character strokes are not very sharp and uniform. The proposed Sobel edge detection algorithm improved the global contrast by 0.1629 and achieved a good edge detection rate of 94.2 F-measure. Exploration of the effect of proposed edge detection methodology on the subsequent segmentation and recognition phases of handwritten documents is a future direction to this work.

ACKNOWLEDGMENT

The authors thank the creators of the KHTD dataset, Prof. P Nagabhushan, Prof. Alireza Alaei, Prof. Umapada Pal for providing us the dataset for experimentation.

REFERENCES

Alaei, Nagabhushan, & Pal. (2011). A benchmark Kannada Handwritten Document Dataset and its Segmentation. *Proceedings of International Conference on Document Analysis and Recognition*, 1520-5363.

Chandrakala, Thippeswamy, & Sahana. (2018). Enhancement of degraded document images using Retinex and Morphological operations. *International Journal of Computer Science and Information Security*, *16*(4).

Chandrakala, H. T., & Thippeswamy, G. (2016). A Comprehensive Survey on OCR techniques for Kannada Script. *International Journal of Science and Research*, *5*(4).

Chandrakala, H. T., & Thippeswamy, G. (2017). Epigraphic Document image enhancement using Retinex method. *Proceedings of 3rd international symposium of signal processing and intelligent recognition systems, Book chapter in Advanced in signal processing and intelligent recognition systems*.

Chen, H., Tsai, S. S., Schroth, G., Chen, D. M., Grzeszczuk, R., & Girod, B. (2011). Robust Text Detection in Natural Images with Edge-Enhanced Maximally Stable Extremal Regions. *18th IEEE International Conference on Image Processing*. 10.1109/ICIP.2011.6116200

Chew, Tan, Cao, Shen, Chee, & Chang. (2000). Text extraction from historical handwritten documents by edge detection. *6th International Conference on Control, Automation, Robotics and Vision, ICARCV2000*.

Gao, W., Zhang, X., Yang, L., & Liu, H. (2010). An Improved Sobel Edge Detection. *3rd International Conference on Computer Science and Information Technology*.

Gonzalez & Woods. (2008). Digital Image Processing. Pearson Education, Inc.

Gupta & Mazumdar. (2013). Sobel Edge Detection Algorithm. *International Journal of Computer Science and Management Research*, *2*(2).

Li, L., Yu, S., Zhong, L., & Li, X. (2015). Multilingual Text Detection with Nonlinear Neural Network. *Mathematical Problems in Engineering*, *2015*. doi:10.1155/2015/431608

Liao, Liang, & Wu. (2015). An Integrated Approach for Multilingual Scene Text Detection. *Seventh International Conference of Soft Computing and Pattern Recognition*.

Lundgren, A., Castro, D., Lima, E., & Bezerra, B. (2019). OctShuffleMLT: A Compact Octave Based Neural Network for End-to-End Multilingual Text Detection and Recognition. *International Conference on Document Analysis and Recognition Workshops*. 10.1109/ICDARW.2019.30062

Manjunath Aradhya, V. N., Pavithra, M. S., & Naveena, C. (2011). *A Robust Multilingual Text Detection Approach Based on Transforms and Wavelet Entropy. Procedia Technology, 4(2012), 232 – 237*.

Pietik¨ainen, M., & Okun, O. (2001). Edge-Based Method for Text Detection from Complex Document Images. *Proceedings of Sixth International Conference on Document Analysis and Recognition*. 10.1109/ICDAR.2001.953800

Qu, Y.-D., Cui, C.-S., Chen, S.-B., & Li, J.-Q. (2005). A fast subpixel edge detection method using Sobel–Zernike moments operator. *Image and Vision Computing*, *23*(1), 11–17. doi:10.1016/j.imavis.2004.07.003

Rahul, B., Amudha, & Gupta. (2018). Multilingual Text Detection and Identification from Indian Signage Boards. *International Conference on Advances in Computing, Communications and Informatics*.

Ren, X., Zhou, Y., He, J., Chen, K., Yang, X., & Sun, J. (2016). A Convolutional Neural Network Based Chinese Text Detection Algorithm via Text Structure Modeling. *IEEE Transactions on Multimedia.* doi:10.1109/TMM.2016.2625259

Revathi, P., & Hemalatha, M. (2012). Classification of Cotton Leaf Spot Diseases Using Image Processing Edge Detection Techniques. *International Conference on Emerging Trends in Science, Engineering and Technology.* 10.1109/INCOSET.2012.6513900

Sha, Y., Shi, P., You, J., Bao, X., Fu, S., & Zeng, G. (2017). Chinese And English Bilingual Scene Text Detection. *IEEE 3rd Information Technology and Mechatronics Engineering Conference.*

Zhang, J.-Y., Yan, C., & Huang, X.-X. (2009). Edge Detection of Images Based on Improved Sobel Operator and Genetic Algorithms. *2009 International Conference on Image Analysis and Signal Processing.* 10.1109/IASP.2009.5054605

Chapter 12
A Deep Learning–Based Framework for Accurate Facial Ethnicity Classification and Efficient Query Retrieval

Geraldine Amali
Vellore Institute of Technology, India

Keerthana K. S. V.
Oracle, India

Jaiesh Sunil Pahlajani
Grofers, India

ABSTRACT

Facial images carry important demographic information such as ethnicity and gender. Ethnicity is an essential part of human identity and serves as a useful identifier for numerous applications ranging from biometric recognition, targeted advertising to social media profiling. Recent years have seen a huge spike in the use of convolutional neural networks (CNNs) for various visual, face recognition problems. The ability of the CNN to take advantage of the hierarchical pattern in data makes it a suitable model for facial ethnicity classification. As facial datasets lack ethnicity information it becomes extremely difficult to classify images. In this chapter a deep learning framework is proposed that classifies the individual into their respective ethnicities which are Asian, African, Latino, and White. The performances of various deep learning techniques are documented and compared for accuracy of classification. Also, a simple efficient face retrieval model is built which retrieves similar faces. The aim of this model is to reduce the search time by 1/3 of the original retrieval model.

DOI: 10.4018/978-1-7998-6690-9.ch012

INTRODUCTION

"Faces" have always been an intriguing area of research. Scientists have been digging into human abilities to grasp a lot of information by just looking into someone's face (Kennedy & Eberhart, 1995). According to psychology whenever a human encounters a stranger the first thing he does is evaluate the other person based on his facial features. The brain intercepts rich data just from a glance at the other person's face and classifies their gender, ethnicity, in some cases even their economic background. Facial Recognition is another highly complex activity .The brain performs it with almost 100% accuracy. All these are done in just a matter of few seconds. And this has consequential effects on the perceiver and the perceived.

In the field of Artificial Intelligence, technologists are taking interest in this field now more than ever. The upsurge of facial recognition apps is the proof. And truly, facial recognition technology now occupies a strategic position in the defence sector. It has eliminated the mundane job and the time consuming task of manually searching through files. With the CCTVs installed everywhere, literally scanning every person in every video frame, it has become a challenging task for illegal immigrants or terrorists to operate. But what if the targeted person has disguised himself, or his picture isn't in the database, or it isn't a recent one. These are the circumstances where the current facial recognition technology might fail.

To address the above impediments, a mechanism is devised where similar pictures of the targeted person are retrieved from the database instead of replicas. Hence the objectives of the chapter are

- To solve the ethnicity classification problem
- Identify a novel approach that results in enhancing global convergence in the initial stages
- Compare this approach with multiple optimization techniques. Test the hypothesis that meta-heuristic optimization techniques are better than gradient descent optimization techniques
- To retrieve faces based on the texture and colour features of the face from the database of its classified ethnicity

It isn't a secret anymore that the coming ages will be dominated by robots, cyborgs, humanoids, super Computers etc. Every innovation or a novel approach in AI today is ultimately going to help us program them. Advances in computer vision, computer graphics and machine learning based on racial face analysis has started to become popular. It is safe to say that learned features are better for Ethnicity Classification (Muthiah-Nakarajan & Noel, 2016). Hence it is a necessity for us to explore various global optimization techniques that can help a fully connected neural network classify a face into either Asian or Caucasian or Latino or African.

BACKGROUND:

Anthropometric statistics show the racial and ethnic morphometric differences in the craniofacial complex. 25 identified measurements on the face were used to examine three racial groups Caucasian, African-American, and Chinese. The three groups exhibited significant differences. For example, the Chinese group had the widest faces. Also, the soft nose is wider in the Chinese group and it had the highest upper lip in relation to mouth width.

Figure 1. Statistical Assessment of a face as done in "Assessment of facial analysis measurements by golden proportion"

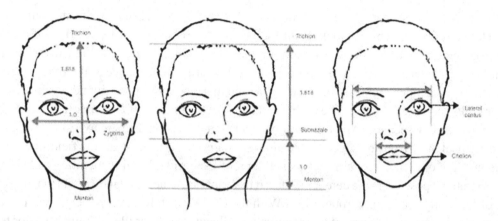

With the help of such measurements, one can train a model which subjects each and every picture in the database to check the similarity ratio with the query picture. But for the model to iterate through such a huge database is again a time consuming task. The most efficient method to do this would be to classify the query picture's ethnicity into one among the four groups(Asian, Latino, Caucasian, African) and then subject the trained model to the corresponding database's faces.

Taking such measurements as the base several methods are being explored in the ethnicity classification field. The most elaborate paper which surveyed and learnt race and ethnicity from facial features Is the "Learning Race from Face: A Survey" (Fu, He & Hou, 2014). The paper provides a comprehensive and critical review of the state of art advances in face race perception, principles, algorithms and applications. Formulation of the race perception problem is discussed here. The factors humans use to percept and recognise a face are modelled and inferred quantitatively in theoretical concepts. They are formulated and tested in a systematic environment, hence conceptualising the features a machine should be fed in order to perceive race.

There is a common misconception that color can be used as a dominant feature. Take the case in which a machine is classifying between Hispanic and Asian. Color feature isn't optimal to proceed with. For example, in an attempt to distinguish faces among 3 ethnicities (Hispanic Chinese White) Trivedi et al (2017) used supervised ML models, logistic regression and SVM models, to train the images per class. From each training image of dimensions 200X250, 86 feature points were extracted. Out of these 86 feature points, they reduced to only 10 features. These 10 features were:

- Chin Size
- Measurement between mouth and chin
- Measurement between eyeballs
- Measurement between inner corners of the eyes
- Measurement between outer corners of the eyes
- Measurement between inner corners of the eyebrows
- Distance between outer corner of the eyebrows
- Nose's size

- Mouth's size
- Measurement between mouth and nose

SVM classifier when compared to logistic classifiers; results have shown that the latter is more precise. As said in the beginning of the section, many more landmarks and measurements are conceptualised; among them few were considered. Masood, Wajid, Shubham and Suhani Gupta(2017) instead of using the traditional RGB values, have calculated geometry features of the Negros, Mongolian and Caucasian and have inputted the values to a neural network received an accuracy of 82.4%. Interestingly, University of Bradford, extracted geometric facial features to feed into their learning algorithms(Jilani, Ugail, Bukar, Logan, & Munshi, 2017). We will learn their approach shortly.

Though a lot of experiments were done to classify people based on their ethnicities, most of them were classified on a broader basis, for instance Latino, White, African, Asian. To narrow it down to a particular nation or a specific nation's race is a huge advancement. The binary classification of whether a "British Pakistani or not" (Jilani, Ugail, Bukar, Logan, & Munshi, 2017) is one such example. Another development this research has produced is the use of profile images. Current literature uses frontal images. From profile silhouettes geometrical measurements were taken and trained using a supervised algorithm. There were 135 participants in the study and the database was made up of 5 pictures of each participant from different angles; totalling 675 images. The 5 different angles were frontal, right view at 45°, right Profile, left view at 45° and left Profile. Every facial image carried a neutral expression. Geometric Feature Extraction included eyes, nose, chin etc,, i.e., primary facial features and the relation between them, like distances between one another and relative angles. This is done right after the first step to remove deflecting variances. Feature Transformation included in the training set is a 2Dvector, having (x,y) coordinates for each facial landmark. For efficient computation and removal of redundancy this vector's dimensionality was reduced using the PCA algorithm, and PLS (Partial Least Square, to encapsulate the variance between independent and dependent variables) algorithm. The input is then reduced to 10 anthropometric facial landmarks or 10 distinguished features. Finally the classes of images were optimally separated by a hyperplane constructed by a Support Vector Machine Model as a linear classifier.

The headway in the field came when Chen, Deng and Zhang (2016) tried to classify Japanese, Chinese and Koreans based on their facial features. Though people from these nationalities look strikingly similar, we humans can tell them apart. This means that there are facial landmarks that our cognition can calculate. To teach AI to classify into the 3 categories, they approached this problem in the following manner. Stage 1 was collection of raw images .These included images from search engines, photos of colleagues, friends and family etc. This had to be done since there was no dataset available made specifically for their objective. Stage 2 was face Cropping. Stage 3 was augmentation of images. Since the size of the database was only 1380 images, they used data/image augmentation techniques to quadruple the database size. We will discuss more about this in Section 4 of the chapter. Stage 4 is training the classifier for ethnicity classification. This is a new challenge altogether to differentiate individuals based on nations. Hence they experimented with 2 Layer fully neural network classifiers, KNN, SVM, KNN and CNN. Interestingly, they have scaled the dimensions of the pre-processed image to 64X64 to input into the CNN classifier, but to 128X128 for the other classifiers. CNN is a Deep Learning model that we will be discussing in the upcoming sections thoroughly. Of all these models, CNN achieved the highest accuracy(89.2%).Stage V is prediction. Given the query image which nationality (Chinese, Japanese, Korean) does it belong to. Though CNN seems to have the highest accuracy in predicting the ethnicity of a person, a limitation was overlooked. CNN often looked at ethnicity as a multi-class problem and never was the intermediate functions which provide rich hierarchical features utilised. It was only in "Hybrid Supervised Deep Learning for Ethnicity Classification using Face Images'' (Heng, Dipu & Yap, 2018) this limitation was worked upon. Their method combines the soft likelihood of CNN classification output with an image ranking engine that leverages on matching of the hierarchical features between the query and dataset images. A supervised Support Vector Machine (SVM) hybrid learning is developed to train the combined feature vectors to perform ethnicity classification. A consolidated report on the ethnicity classification techniques used this far has been presented in Table 1.

Table 1. Review of Existing Models for Ethnicity Classification

AUTHOR/ YEAR	TITLE	CONTRIBUTION	DRAWBACKS
Haoxuan Chan, Yiran Deng and Shuying Zhang (2016)	Where am I from? – East Asian Ethnicity Classification from Facial Recognition	Classified Japanese, Korean and Chinese faces	Despite using CNN, achieved an accuracy of only 89.2%
Advait Trivedi and Geraldine Amali Bessie D (2017)	A comparative study of machine learning models for ethnicity classification	Showcased that logistic classifier acts as a better classifier for images as SVM overfits or under-fits the data.	Logistic classifiers performed well on models trained to identify Chinese faces but had a mediocre accuracy of just 57% for Hispanic faces.
Siyao Fu, Haibo He and Zeng-Guang Hou (2014)	Learning Race from Face: A Survey	Provides a comprehensive and critical review of state-of-art advances in facial based race perception	The paper is a survey of different techniques present to extract the facial features in order to input them into a ML framework. There are no cons here.
Sarfaraz Masood, Abdul Wajid, Shubham Gupta and Suhnai Gupta (2018)	Prediction of Human Ethnicity from Facial Images Using Neural Networks	Accuracy achieved using CNN was 98.6% which is far superior than any previous traditional ML model.	Time required for training and feature extraction for CNN was much more than Artificial Neural Networks.
Shelina Khalid Jilani, Hassan Ugail, Ali M. Bukar, Andrew Logan and Tasnim Munshi (2017)	A Machine Learning Approach for Ethnic Classification: The British Pakistani Face	Addressed the challenge of binary ethnicity classification(combining 2 classes) using SVM as it acts as a good separator. Uses PCA for dimensionality reduction.	Despite a promising accuracy of 72%, the results can be improved using LDA instead of PCA.
Zhano Heng, Manandhar Dipu and Kim-Hui Yap (2018)	Hybrid Supervised Deep Learning for Ethnicity Classification using Face Images	Addresses the problem of finding differentiating Indians, Bangladeshis and Chinese.Uses intermediate CNN features to train a SVM classifier	Accuracy just improved by 4% compared to previous works. Instead of using gradient optimisation techniques, meta heuristics can be explored

FRAMEWORK FOR ACCURATE FACIAL ETHNICITY CLASSIFICATION AND EFFICIENT RETRIEVAL

The system we have proposed contains of 2 modules –

I.   Facial Ethnicity Image Classification

Ethnicity classification problem is a supervised learning problem which contains 4 classes, namely – Asian, African, Latino and White. The database has over 5000 images distributed among the 4 classes. This database is subjected to a Convolutional Neural Network and is tested with different optimizers. The output passed is then passed to the retrieval module.

II.   Texture and Colour based Efficient Facial Image Retrieval

Once the ethnicity is obtained from the Ethnicity Classification module the test image is then compared to all the images of that class using a similarity measure, i.e., Euclidean Distance. This improves searching efficiency as the test image is only compared to images of that class and not the entire database.

Figure 2. High Level Design of the proposed deep learning framework for ethnicity classification

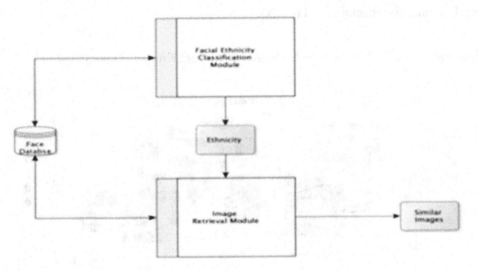

I. Facial Ethnicity Classification Module

Present practices to classify images on a large scale, use traditional machine learning techniques to achieve this. To classify images, features are extracted of each type during the preprocessing period. These features are extracted using Computer vision or any other feature extraction algorithms. During the training a feature matrix is fed to the algorithm where upon excessive training a classifier is created. Now the test image is again subjected to the same preprocessing technique and the features, in a matrix form, are inputted to the classifier which predicts the output based on probability.

The major disadvantage with this approach is construction of the feature matrix. Appropriate features should be extracted, otherwise the resultant classifier would be flawed, and hence the prediction. A lot of features of the images are next to impossible to figure out for the naked eye. Hence after a series of consuming trial and error proceedings scientists and engineers have come up with 'unique features' for the corresponding image classes. And later on, to construct the best algorithm, that iterates through a huge database is another tedious work. The present era saw the rise of Deep learning, which overcomes all the above shortcomings. Deep Learning is a subfield of machine learning concerned with algorithms, inspired by the structure and function of the brain called artificial neural networks. Deep Learning Algorithms has demonstrated state-of-art performance on image classification . A few known Deep Learning Algorithms are:

1. Convolutional Neural Network (CNN)
2. Recurrent Neural Networks (RNNs)
3. Long Short-Term Memory Networks (LSTMs)
4. Stacked Auto-Encoders.
5. Deep Boltzmann Machine (DBM)
6. Deep Belief Networks (DBN)

In this work the authors have proceeded with Convolution Neural Network.

a. Deep Learning Architecture used (CNN).

Figure 3. Demonstration of a complete CNN Model [source: Towards Data Science (33)]

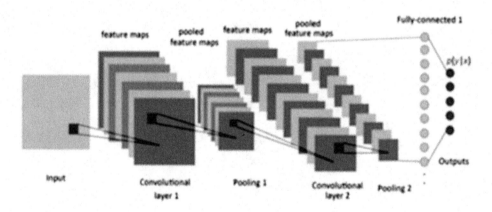

Deep Convolutional Network created by Alex Krizhevsky, Ilya Sutskever, Geoffrey E. Hinton (2017) classified images from imageNet into 1000 classes. They have used five convolutional layers which consist of 60 million parameters and 650,000 neurons. For a given input x, the neurons' output, f is modelled as f(x) = tanh(x). Neurons with non linearity are referred to as Rectified Linear Units by Nair and Hinton(as cited in Muthiah-Nakarajan & Noel, 2016). Rectified Linear units have been used in CNN instead of tanh because the training is done faster. The Convolution layer is later followed by max pooling layers .For pooling we will set size s < z(where z is the unit's size) as described in the former paper, to obtain max pooling, every value is taken into consideration equal number of times. The net comprises 8 layers. After parameters have been transformed into feasible computational forms they are fully connected in the last three layers with the activation function as softmax. The probability of each hidden neuron is set to 0.5 and this technique is called 'dropout'. These neurons do not participate in forward or in backward propagation. A different architecture is sampled every time an input is fed into the neural network. All these architectures share weights. The Error Percentage Performed on the Imagenet is in between 17.0% and 37.5%. Referring to the architecture in this paper we have implemented

ReLU function rather than tanh. To classify images into labels we have used the softmax function at the output layer. On the other hand Karen Simonyan & Andrew Zisserman(2015), stretched the depth of the Neural Network by incorporating (3X3) Convolution Filters. Architecture used in this paper is based on the idea above, but before 3D-training the images, they were cropped randomly and every training image was rescaled(1 crop per image SGD iteration). Also the cropped images undergo random flipping and Color shift. The paper written by by Maxime Oquab, Leon Bottou, Ivan Laptev, Josef Sivic(2014) has made the same architecture as above. The key idea in their work is that mid-level image representation of any image can be generically extracted from the hidden layers of Convolutional Neural Networks. This data is initially used train on a dataset and later, the same is used again on other target tasks. This paper has confirmed the architecture to proceed with. In the proposed framework, this architecture will be exploited to extract facial features which are later given as input to a fully connected neural network that uses various meta heuristic algorithms to optimize the weights.

b.   Working of the CNN

1.   <u>Face Database</u>: Collect images of different ethnicities (Asian, African, Latino, African). Make sure one image has only one person in it.
2.   <u>Pre-Process the image</u>: Subject the image to Viola-Jones face detection algorithm and crop out the faces accordingly. This is done to ensure that during retrieval background hue and colour mean isn't considered during face retrieval.

Figure 4. Preprocessing using Viola Jones Algorithm

Often in image recognition systems there is a need for a larger dataset..There aren't a lot of datasets available for ethnicity classification. Deep learning requires large data sets. This is where data augmentation techniques come to rescue. It increases the number of images by performing various operations on it and this is how it curbs the problem of data scarcity.

Data augmentation techniques used here are:

- *Mirroring*: In this technique of data augmentation each image if flipped horizontally such that we get similar images from a totally opposite angle.

Figure 5. A sample image and its mirror image after preprocessing [source: Data Set and Data Augmentation for Face Detection and Recognition (34)]

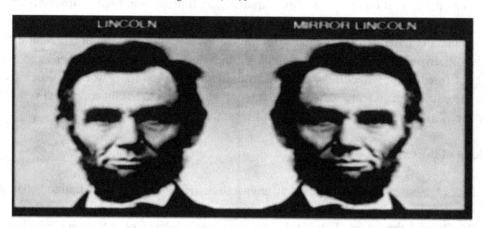

- *Shearing:* It is a mapping function which displaces each pixel of the image in a fixed direction such that multiple copies of the image are generated in different angles and are trained which significantly contributes to a highly accurate classifier.

Figure 6. Sample Shearing of an image [source:MathWorks (36)]

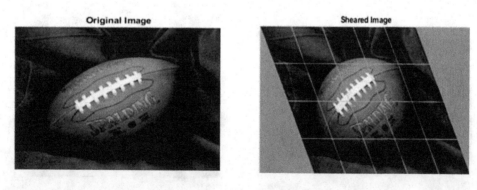

- *Random cropping:* Each image is randomly zoomed and cropped in multiple permutations and combinations which is then fed into the training model. This too impacts the accuracy of the classifier.

Figure 7. Process of random cropping demonstrated [source: github(35)]

3. <u>Feature Extraction:</u> *Convolutional Layer* extracts the features of the input image through a convolutional operation. This preserves the spatial relationship between by learning the image features using small squares of input data.

In our convolutional neural network architecture we have 2 convolutional layers. To the first convolutional layer an input image of size 64 x 64 x 5 was applied to 32 different filters. Each filter had a size of 5 x 5 . 32 different convolutional operations between the filter and a given image are performed and 32 different feature maps were generated. Those features map undergo pooling operation and with reduced dimensionality, the features were fed into the second convolutional layer which also had 32 filters with a size of 5x5.

4. <u>Dimension Reduction:</u> (i). Apply dimension reduction algorithms (Pooling, Partial Least Square Regression/ t- Stochastic Neighbour Embedding,PCA). In our model we have used the Max Pooling and PCA algorithm.

Pooling is nothing but sub sampling of the feature maps. It is done after the convolutional operation. It is responsible for dimensionality reduction of features but at the same time retains spatial information.

Figure 8. Demonstration of max pooling

Input Matrix

-4	20	55	100
-60	2	-10	39
19	-43	6	76
22	-47	57	119

Output Matrix

20	100
22	119

With each pooling operation the dimensionality of the features will be reduced. Another advantage is that distortions will not affect the classification of the output. Principal Component Analysis is a linear transformation algorithm. Given 'x' points in the nD coordinate system, PCA finds the dimension, where these x points have the maximum variance, thereby eliminating closest values, and hence reducing the dimensions. In the demonstration section(Section 6) you can see how PCA was used to reduce no:of features from 4096 to 576. All the dimensions areorthogonal to each other.

5. Fully Connected Artificial Neural Network: After successive convolutional and pooling operations, the features are then fed into a fully connected neural network layer.

Figure 9. Representation of fully connected neural network

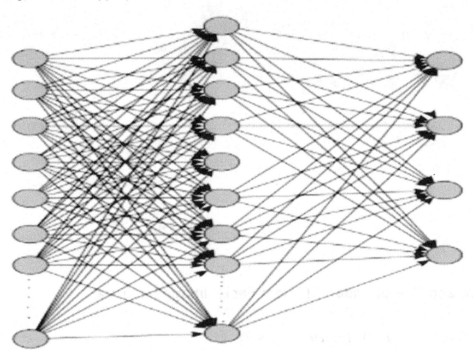

(i). The neural network classifier which uses gradient descent algorithms for optimising the weights. (ii). Subject the acquired dimensions to the neural network classifier and train it using ***adam optimizer, RMS prop and SGDM optimizer.***

6.   Activation Functions Used

Rectified Linear Unit is an activation function used in the convolutional layer and also in the hidden layer of the dense and fully connected neural network. After the convolution operation a feature map is generated. If any value on the feature map is negative, it is converted to 0 and remains the same if the values are positive. The same activation function is applied to the generated output of the hidden layer such that there are no negative values.

Sigmoid Activation Function *is* Also known as logistic function, is used in the cases of binary classification. Sigmoid function is basically a probability function, i.e., all the values lie between 0 and 1 that tells us how likely the query input belongs to a particular class.

Softmax Activation Function is another activation function that is applied only to the output layer. Softmax is used for categorical prediction rather than binary. Softmax is also a probability function, but unlike sigmoid function all the logits(raw values, without being subjected to weights or activation functions) when subjected to the formula in Figure8, the output elements of the output vector sum to 1.

7.   Testing:Repeat steps 2-6 to the image/face that you want to retrieve from the database. Classify it using the Trained Neural Network.

Figure 10. Low Level Design of the classification module

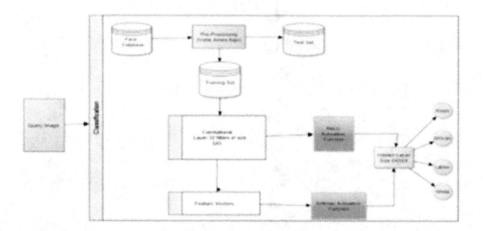

II. Texture and Colour based Efficient Facial Image Retrieval

Figure 11. Low Level of the Design retrieval module

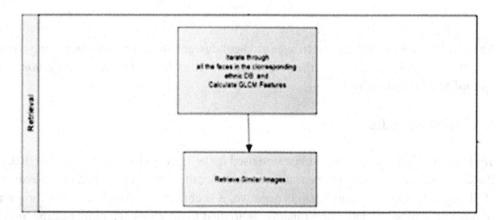

(i)   Get the label of the classified test image.
(ii) Search for the folder with that label.
(iii) Take Euclidean distance of 'contrast','homogeneity','correlation','energy', i.e., Texture features and Colour moment features of the first order of all the faces in the folder with the test face.
(iv) Get the top 3 images with the least Euclidean distance.

PROBLEMS

The framework uses gradient descent optimization techniques. The problem is, when optimizing, the weights may fall into the trap of local optima. That is why we explore meta-heuristics. Meta-heuristics are advanced optimization techniques. They address the problem of local optimums; and are far more simple, and flexible. Hence we explore these algorithms.

a.   Metaheuristics as essential tools in training machine learning models

All meta heuristic algorithms can be classified under 3 categories: Evolutionary, Physics Based, Swarm Intelligence. Evolutionary algorithms are based on Darwin's theory of evolution. Genetic Algorithm is the most popular evolutionary algorithm. SI was initially proposed in 1993 (Beni, & Wang, 1993). The origin of SI algorithms are mostly derived from the pattern and behaviour of natural colonies, flock, herds, and schools. Among the S optimisation techniques PSO is the most well-known optimization algorithm due to its simple update formula and good performance on wide search spaces. Physics based algorithms like the Gravitational search algorithm is based on laws of physics.

In "Particle Swarm Optimization", Kennedy and Eberhart(1995) introduced the concept of optimizing non linear functions using swarm theory. This technique was inspired from the real life behavior of bird flocking and fish schooling. It is initialized with a random group of particles called swarm. With each iteration for searching the optima, each particle is updated with its personal best fitness value that it has achieved and this value is called the 'pbest' value and there is a global best value 'gbest' which is the best fitness value achieved by any particle so far. Based on these values, the velocity of the particle is calculated and its new position is updated. Particle swarm optimization algorithm has been used to train artificial neural networks. Training a neural network requires adjusting the weights to reduce the mean square error.

Issue with the PSO algorithm is that it is hard to find a balance between the exploration and exploitation stage. If the algorithm converges to a poor local minimum during exploration stage it results in suboptimal solution. To address this issue Nakarajan and Noel (2016) introduced Galactic Swarm Optimization which is inspired by the motion of stars and galaxies. Here a subpopulation of particles are taken into account, i.e., sub-swarm. If there are 'm' subswarms in population, best solution for each subswarm is found and those are called the super-swarm. PSO is performed 'm' times to find out the best solution in each sub-swarm, although any other swarm optimization technique could have been used. This modification prevents premature convergence and allows multi-modal surfaces to be efficiently explored. Galactic swarm optimization was used to train a feedforward neural network for ethnicity classification in their research experiment.

D.Amali and Dinakaran(2018) introduced the concept of Quantum Tunneling PSO. In classical mechanics a particle cannot cross a barrier with less energy but in quantum mechanics the particle can penetrate the barrier without sufficient energy. The personal best solution can tunnel through peaks and avoid getting trapped in the local minima, thus, overcoming the greedy search heuristic of the classical PSO. This technique significantly increases the explorative ability of the PSO algorithm. The authors have used the proposed algorithm to train a neural network for function approximation.

The ABC algorithm developed by Karaboga(2005) was inspired intelligent foraging behavior of honey bee swarm. There are three types of bees used – employee bees, onlooker bees and scout bees. The employed bees search for food and share the information to onlooker bees. The onlooker bees tend to select the best food sources from the given information. The scout bees are those which abandon their food source and look for a new one. Kaya, Uymaz and Kocer (2018)proposed a variant of the original ABC called GSO_ABC very similar to GSO_PSO but GSO uses the ABC swarm algorithm instead of the PSO. Results have shown that GSO_ABC had faster convergence compared to GSO_PSO. This new algorithm is used for training a CNN in this chapter.

An other SI algorithm introduced recently is the Grey Wolf Optimizer (Mirjalili, Mirjalili, & Lewis, 2014). Grey wolves are at the apex of the food chain and are always seen in packs. The wolves in the pack belong to a very strict social dominant hierarchy with the alphas at the top, betas at the second level, delta and omega at the third and fourth level respectively. The pack follows the alpha wolf and has a ritual to hunt its prey. First it tracks the prey, then it encircles and harasses the prey till gives up and then the pack attacks the prey. Viewing prey as the global optimum poin,t a group of points are initialised in the plane and following the alpha wolf or the point with the best fitness value is followed by the other points. But the convergence speed of GWO is also an issue in some cases. The reason for this issue is that it is too difficult for GWO to well coordinate between the exploitation and exploration. Wen Long and Songjin Xu (2016) presented a modified GWO (denoted by MGWO) algorithm to enhance the global convergence, further improve the solution precision and the convergence speed of GWO. The method employed in order to achieve this is called the good-point-set method, where the points are scattered evenly all over the exploratory region. In GWO alpha is decreased from 2 to 0. In MGWO alpha decreases at a rate proportional to the number of iterations.

The above modification couldn't still force the GWO algorithm to get away from the local optima. HenceGrey Wolf Optimization Algorithm with Invasion-based Migration Operation(Jitkongchuen, Phaidang, & Pongtawevirat, 2016) is being adopted . The Invasion-based Migration Operation technique will come into play only when the GWO or the MGWO gets stuck in a local optimum. The initialisation, distribution of points and the updation of alpha remain the same as in MGWO. But the only difference is instead of exploring with one pack we explore with multiple packs. And in case we get stuck in a local optimum the wolves from all the existing packs whose fitness values are greater than their respective pack's average fitness value migrate to the best pack. After immigration operation, the best pack would have more individual wolves so the selection operation is performed to reduce wolf amounts of the best pack.

Swarm Intelligence has been used to solve various mathematical problems but hasn't been much explored in supervised learning classification. To test our hypothesis that meta-heuristics can perform better than gradient descent optimization techniques, we have tested the features using a pre trained CNN called Alexnet and have subjected those features to a fully connected neural network which are optimised by Swarm Intelligence algorithms such as ABC, PSO, GSO_PSO and GSO_ABC. The highest accuracy achieved via CNN is only 92%. The convolutional features extracted from the images can also be subjected to SVM. They work by creating one or more hyperplanes that separate the data clusters. Without using the kernel trick, the hyperplanes are strictly linear which are roughly equivalent to feed forward neural networks without an activation function. With the kernel trick, SVMs are roughly equivalent to feed forward neural networks with a non-linear activation function. Other Supervised ML models to which the features were subjected were – KNN, Decision Tree and Naïve Bayes. The highest accuracy was achieved via CNN.

DEMONSTRATION

Figure 12. Sample Features extracted: Convolved features of the pre-processed face is subjected PCA algorithm giving us an input matrix of 20000*4096.

	4087	4088	4089	4090	4091	4092	4093	4094	4095	4096	4097	409
3	-0.1610	0.8755	1.0184	0.3965	0.1452	0.0028	1.4007	-0.0095	0.1676	2.1190		
4	-0.4110	-1.0110	-0.2840	-0.3053	0.0286	0.5022	-0.4521	-0.2284	-1.5262	-0.4805		
5	0.4789	-0.3409	-1.7416	-0.5579	0.5120	0.8736	-0.0958	-0.3478	1.0332	-5.0794		
6	0.4068	0.8604	-1.0456	-0.2647	0.8084	0.8574	-0.1910	-0.4324	2.0273	-2.1358		
7	0.3539	2.1096	-0.4837	0.1307	0.4917	0.2103	2.1514	0.0298	0.6087	-0.3454		
8	0.3540	0.0562	-0.0755	0.0586	0.6426	0.3380	0.2968	-0.2604	2.4914	1.8674		
9	-0.0272	1.6575	0.6851	0.2926	0.5607	0.0606	2.7374	0.5190	3.4746	1.9907		
10	0.6297	0.5480	-1.9735	-0.7285	0.3480	0.7698	-0.8724	-0.3531	1.4595	0.1377		
11	-0.2074	-1.0825	-1.3953	-0.0899	-0.6704	0.1577	-2.1672	-0.3213	-4.4464	-2.4778		
12	-0.1139	-0.4215	-0.7824	0.2029	-0.5175	0.0932	-1.6314	-0.0464	-4.1038	1.4695		
13	-0.3204	-1.3604	-0.7230	-0.2199	-0.4454	-0.0549	-0.8452	-0.2548	-2.1244	1.8967		

Figure 13. Classification of Jackie Chan as Asian

Figure 14. Classification of Michelle Rodriguez as Latino

Figure 15. Classification of Will Smith as African

Figure 16. Classification of Emma Watson as White

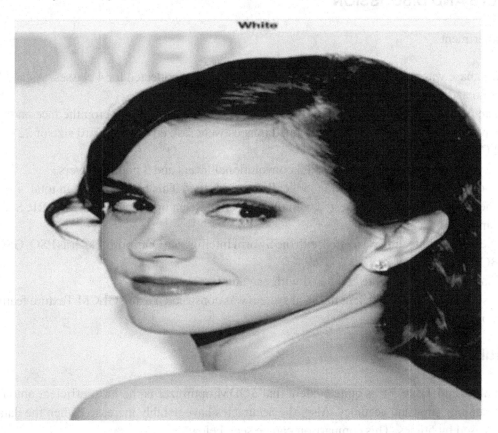

Figure 17. Facial Retrieval based on Texture and Colour Features- Retrieval of similar pictures not replicas (as said in the beginning of the chapter).

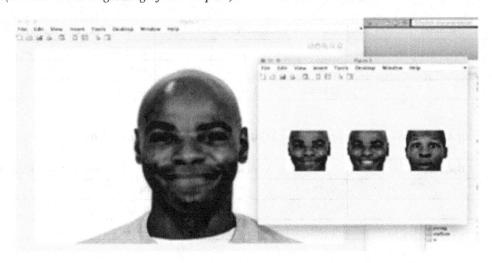

RESULTS AND DISCUSSION

1. Experiment

Step1: Database was built using face images. 4000 images were collected for 4 classes- Asian, African, Latino and White. Each class has 1000 images.

Step2: The database images were subjected to the Voila Jones algorithm to crop the face and ignoring the rest of the background. These cropped images were resized to a standard size of 227*227.

Step3: 2 CNN models were used .

One was a custom model which had 3 convolutional layers and 3 pooling layers.

The other one was a pre-trained model called the Alexnet. This had 17 layers in total.

Step4: The CNN architecture was tested with the gradient descent optimizers – RMSPORP, SGDM and Adams optimizer

Step5: The CNN architecture was tested with the Swarm Intelligence Optimizers such as PSO, GSO_PSO, ABC, GSO_ABC

Step6: Classification results are compared with one another

Step7: A simple yet highly efficient retrieval system was constructed using GLCM Texture features and Colour moments

2. Results

From Table 2 and Table 3 it is quite evident that SGDM optimizer is the most efficient among the 3, given its running time and accuracy. Also, the accuracies have notably increased when the dataset has been increased by 5times. This comparison can be seen below

Table 2. Accuracy of CNN using gradient descent optimizers - 4000 training images

Optimizer	Accuracy	Time taken to Train (HH:MM:SS)
RSMPROP	74.73%	00:07:02
SGDM	81.58%	00:06:01
Adam	75.44%	00:05:47

Table 3. Accuracy of CNN using gradient descent optimizers - 20000 training images

Optimizer	Accuracy	Time taken to Train (HH:MM:SS)
RSMPROP	89.75%	04:00:24
SGDM	93.55%	01:46:24
Adam	91.75%	04:22:21

Greater the size of training images, higher the accuracy.

Figure 18. Comparing performance of optimizers on different size of training images.

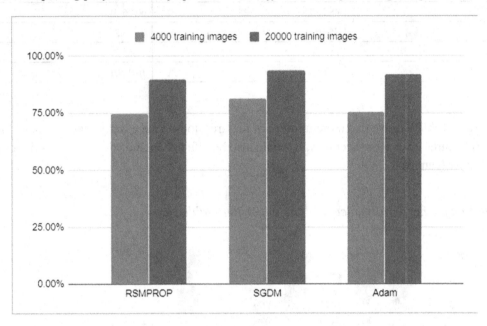

The only trade-off is that the training time has also exponentially increased.

Table 4. Accuracy of Convolutional features tested against traditional ML models

Model	Accuracy	Time taken to Fit (HH:MM:SS)
Decision Tree	92.35%	00:01:35
K-NN(5 neighbours)	84.07%	00:13:20
Naive Bayes	52.92%	00:00:11
SVM	98.57%	00:13:13

The above models are known to perform poorly in the domain of image classification. Table4 shows otherwise. As a result of using CNN features, it is seen that SVM and Decision Tree have performed well as compared to KNN and Naïve Bayes.

Table 5. Accuracy of Convolutional features tested against Meta-Heuristics before using PCA (4096 features per image)

Optimizer	Accuracy	Time taken to Train (HH:MM:SS)
ABC	46.90%	08:50:02
PSO	64.93%	06:13:41

Table 6. Accuracy of Convolutional features tested against Meta-Heuristics after using PCA (576 features per image)

Optimizer	Accuracy	Time taken to Train (HH:MM:SS)
ABC	48.28%	00:26:04
PSO	75.10%	01:28:23
GSO_ABC	55.30%	12:53:24
GSO_PSO	58.67%	10:26:01

Table 5 and Table 6 prove that more number of features doesn't necessarily have to mean higher accuracy. 576 features gives more accuracy. It would also be safe to conclude that meta-heuristics perform well with fewer features.

Figure 19. Comparing performance of all the algorithms tabled above

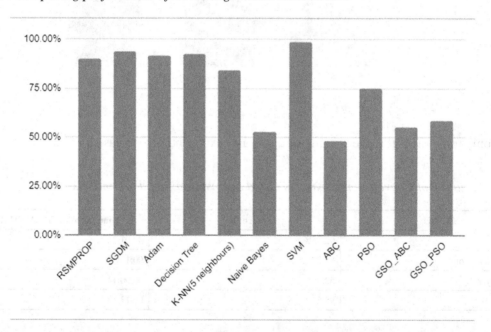

Table 7. Comparison of efficiency of performance of Image Retrieval with standard database and classified database

Type of Database	Time Taken to Retrieve (Seconds)
Full Database	86.564608
Classified Database	23.418109

Figure 20. The graph clearly shows that the time has decreased significantly

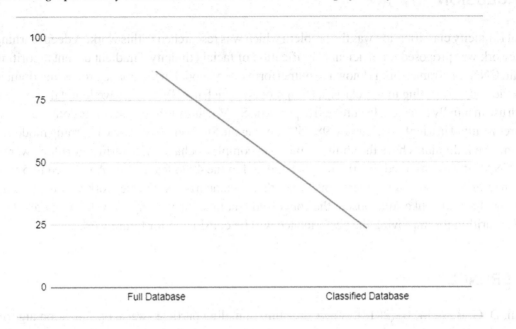

when the retrieval operation is done on the database of the identified ethnicity, rather than on the entire database .

The target of the project is achieved. Retrieving from labelled classified Ethnic folders takes 3 times less time than retrieving similar faces from a folder of 20000 images .

FUTURE WORKS:

There is a lot of scope to the proposed framework. So far, faces have been broadly classified into Asian, African, Latino and Caucasian. To reduce the retrieval time further, the algorithm can be developed to identify African-American, African-Indian etc,. Also, classification can be performed on a secondary level. For instance, if primarily classified as Asian, we can further narrow down to Korean, Indian, Chinese etc.

Metaheuristics involves particles finding their individual best values and later on finding the global best among these particles. An interesting approach would be to parallelize this process, since finding independent best values is an independent process. This approach would drastically reduce the training time. One should note that both the sub swarm and the super swarm in the GSO algorithm discussed here underwent via PSO optimization or ABC optimization. Instead subjecting sub-swarm to PSO and Super Swarm to ABC will boost the results exponentially. We can also fine tune ABC, GSO and PSO velocity parameters to perform secondary level classification. Further, there are many other meta heuristic models such as AAA and GWO to explore. Applying Adaboost to Convolved features is an other area to investigate in order to improve accuracy. The scope is endless.

CONCLUSION

Facial Ethnicity classification was the problem which was researched in this work. A deep learning based framework was proposed for efficient classification of facial ethnicity. Gradient decent algorithms used to train CNN, the framework is known to outperform every model in the image processing domain. Having reviewed the existing image classification models which use SVM, we have found that these models which use manually extracted features fail to perform. SVM using the highly accurate convoluted extracted features resulted in a highest accuracy(98.75%) among the Supervised Machine Learning models. Swarm of primitive individuals have the ability to perform complex behaviour. Swarm algorithms were used to train CNNS it was observed that the weights updated in the 4096 features PCA reduced to 576 features fitted neural network, PSO outperformed the other metaheuristics. Future work will explore applying boosting algorithms like Adaboost to the convolved features. Fine tuning the velocity parameters of the GSO algorithm for improving the performance will be considered for future work.

REFERENCES

Amali, D. G. B., & M, D. (2018). A new quantum tunneling particle swarm optimization algorithm for training Feedforward neural networks. *International Journal of Intelligent Systems and Applications, 10*(11), 64-75. doi:10.5815/ijisa.2018.11.07

Bagchi, C., Amali, D. G. B., & Dinakaran, M. (2019). Accurate Facial Ethnicity Classification Using Artificial Neural Networks Trained with Galactic Swarm Optimization Algorithm. In *Information Systems Design and Intelligent Applications* (pp. 123–132). Singapore: Springer. doi:10.1007/978-981-13-3329-3_12

Balci, K., & Atalay, V. (n.d.). PCA for gender estimation: Which eigenvectors contribute? *Object recognition supported by user interaction for service robots*. doi:10.1109/icpr.2002.1047869

Beni, G., & Wang, J. (1993). Swarm intelligence in cellular robotic systems. *Robots and Biological Systems: Towards a New Bionics*, 703-712. doi:10.1007/978-3-642-58069-7_38

Criollo, Mestizo, Mulato, LatiNegro, Indigena, White, or Black? The US Hispanic/Latino population and multiple responses in the 2000 census. (2000). *American Journal of Public Health, 90*(11). doi:10.2105/ajph.90.11.1724 PMID:11076239

Fu, S., He, H., & Hou, Z. (2014). Learning race from face: A survey. *IEEE Transactions on Pattern Analysis and Machine Intelligence, 36*(12), 2483–2509. doi:10.1109/TPAMI.2014.2321570 PMID:26353153

Gao, W., & Ai, H. (2009). Face gender classification on consumer images in a multiethnic environment. *Advances in Biometrics*, 169-178. doi:10.1007/978-3-642-01793-3_18

Gutta, S., Wechsler, H., & Phillips, P. (n.d.). Gender and ethnic classification of face images. *Proceedings Third IEEE International Conference on Automatic Face and Gesture Recognition*. doi:10.1109/afgr.1998.670948

Heng, Z., Dipu, M., & Yap, K. (2018). Hybrid supervised deep learning for ethnicity classification using face images. *2018 IEEE International Symposium on Circuits and Systems (ISCAS).* 10.1109/ISCAS.2018.8351370

Jacobs, D., Swyngedouw, M., & Hanquinet, L. (2009). Int. *Migraciones Internacionales, 10,* 67. doi:10.100712134-009-0091-2

Jilani, S. K., Ugail, H., Bukar, A. M., Logan, A., & Munshi, T. (2017). A machine learning approach for ethnic classification: The British Pakistani face. *2017 International Conference on Cyberworlds (CW).* 10.1109/CW.2017.27

Jitkongchuen, D., Phaidang, P., & Pongtawevirat, P. (2016). Grey wolf optimization algorithm with invasion-based migration operation. *2016 IEEE/ACIS 15th International Conference on Computer and Information Science (ICIS).* doi:10.1109/icis.2016.7550769

Karaboga, D., & Basturk, B. (2007). A powerful and efficient algorithm for numerical function optimization: Artificial bee colony (ABC) algorithm. *Journal of Global Optimization, 39*(3), 459–471. doi:10.100710898-007-9149-x

Kaya, E., Uymaz, S. A., & Kocer, B. (2018). Boosting galactic swarm optimization with ABC. *International Journal of Machine Learning and Cybernetics, 10*(9), 2401–2419. doi:10.100713042-018-0878-6

Kennedy, J., & Eberhart, R. (1994). Particle swarm optimization. *Proceedings of ICNN'95 - International Conference on Neural Networks.* doi:10.1109/icnn.1995.488968

Krizhevsky, A., Sutskever, I., & Hinton, G. E. (2017). ImageNet classification with deep convolutional neural networks. *Communications of the ACM, 60*(6), 84–90. doi:10.1145/3065386

Lapedriza, A., Masip, D., & Vitria, J. (n.d.). Are external face features useful for automatic face classification? *2005 IEEE Computer Society Conference on Computer Vision and Pattern Recognition (CVPR'05) - Workshops.* doi:10.1109/cvpr.2005.569

Long, W., & Xu, S. (2016). A novel grey wolf optimizer for global optimization problems. *2016 IEEE Advanced Information Management, Communicates, Electronic and Automation Control Conference (IMCEC).* doi:10.1109/imcec.2016.7867415

Lu, X., Chen, H., & Jain, A. K. (2005). Multimodal facial gender and ethnicity identification. *Advances in Biometrics,* 554-561. doi:10.1007/11608288_74

Lu, X., & Jain, A. K. (2004). *Ethnicity identification from face images.* Biometric Technology for Human Identification. doi:10.1117/12.542847

Masood, S., Gupta, S., Wajid, A., Gupta, S., & Ahmed, M. (2017). Prediction of human ethnicity from facial images using neural networks. *Advances in Intelligent Systems and Computing,* 217-226. doi:10.1007/978-981-10-3223-3_200

Mirjalili, S., Mirjalili, S. M., & Lewis, A. (2014). Grey wolf optimizer. *Advances in Engineering Software, 69,* 46–61. doi:10.1016/j.advengsoft.2013.12.007

Muthiah-Nakarajan, V., & Noel, M. M. (2016). Galactic swarm optimization: A new global optimization metaheuristic inspired by galactic motion. *Applied Soft Computing*, *38*, 771–787. doi:10.1016/j.asoc.2015.10.034

Oquab, M., Bottou, L., Laptev, I., & Sivic, J. (2014). Learning and Transferring Mid-Level Image Representations using Convolutional Neural Networks. *The IEEE Conference on Computer Vision and Pattern Recognition (CVPR)*, 1717-1724. 10.1109/CVPR.2014.222

Perez, L., & Wang, J. (2017, December 13). *The effectiveness of data augmentation in image classification using deep learning*. Retrieved from https://arxiv.org/abs/1712.04621

Shakhnarovich, G., Viola, P., & Moghaddam, B. (n.d.). A unified learning framework for real time face detection and classification. *Proceedings of Fifth IEEE International Conference on Automatic Face Gesture Recognition*. doi:10.1109/afgr.2002.1004124

Simonyan, K., & Zisserman, A. (2015, April 10). *Very deep Convolutional networks for large-scale image recognition*. Retrieved from https://arxiv.org/abs/1409.1556

Springenberg, J. T., Dosovitskiy, A., Brox, T., & Riedmiller, M. (2015, April 13). *Striving for simplicity: The all Convolutional net*. Retrieved from https://arxiv.org/abs/1412.6806

Trivedi, A., & Geraldine Bessie Amali, D. (2017). A comparative study of machine learning models for ethnicity classification. *IOP Conference Series. Materials Science and Engineering*, *263*, 042091. doi:10.1088/1757-899X/263/4/042091

Wang, W., He, F., & Zhao, Q. (2016). Facial ethnicity classification with deep Convolutional neural networks. *Biometric Recognition*, 176-185. doi:10.1007/978-3-319-46654-5_20

Yang, Z., & Ai, H. (n.d.). Demographic classification with local binary patterns. *Advances in Biometrics*, 464-473. doi:10.1007/978-3-540-74549-5_49

Chapter 13
Finding Facial Emotions From the Clutter Scenes Using Zernike Moments–Based Convolutional Neural Networks

Wencan Zhong
Shantou University, China

Vijayalakshmi G. V. Mahesh
https://orcid.org/0000-0002-1917-7506
BMS Institute of Technology and Management, India

Alex Noel Joseph Raj
Shantou University, China

Nersisson Ruban
https://orcid.org/0000-0003-1695-3618
Vellore Institute of Technology, India

ABSTRACT

Finding faces in the clutter scenes is a challenging task in automatic face recognition systems as facial images are subjected to changes in the illumination, facial expression, orientation, and occlusions. Also, in the cluttered scenes, faces are not completely visible and detecting them is essential as it is significant in surveillance applications to study the mood of the crowd. This chapter utilizes the deep learning methods to understand the cluttered scenes to find the faces and discriminate them into partial and full faces. The work proves that MTCNN used for detecting the faces and Zernike moments-based kernels employed in CNN for classifying the faces into partial and full takes advantage in delivering a notable performance as compared to the other techniques. Considering the limitation of recognition on partial face emotions, only the full faces are preserved, and further, the KDEF dataset is modified by MTCNN to detect only faces and classify them into four emotions. PatternNet is utilized to train and test the modified dataset to improve the accuracy of the results.

DOI: 10.4018/978-1-7998-6690-9.ch013

INTRODUCTION

The recent years are witnessing an emerging interest in the area of computer vision due to its ability to provide the solutions for the tasks where traditional image processing techniques cannot meet the requirements. Thus crowd monitoring is paying interest in computer vision systems to monitor a group of people in crowded environments.

Crowd monitoring includes examining the patterns of crowd movement to identify the mood or type of a crowd. Crowd monitoring systems are normally installed in the areas that attract a large group of people. It can be used to support law enforcement in identifying and recognizing the crowd that may trigger public chaos in a region. Identifying the mood of a crowd in real time can assist in alerting the officials to take necessary procedures to prevent further violence and aggression. The system utilizes facial expression recognition to detect and classify the emotion of an individual's face in a crowd for monitoring the crowded environments.

Detecting or finding faces in a crowd is a huge challenge for computer vision systems as the scenes are cluttered, and there exist a large and unpredictable variations in the appearance of facial images. Also, partial faces usually occur in cluttered scenes due to variations in pose and occlusion which is difficult for the systems to detect. This chapter deals with utilizing deep learning methods in detecting the faces in the cluttered scenes and classifying them into full and partial faces which are further used to recognize the emotions.

The rest of the chapter is organized as follows. Section 2 describes face detection using a multistage CNN architecture (MTCNN). Section 3 presents a Zernike kernel based CNN for classifying facial images into full and partial faces to recognize the emotion. Finally, section 4 concludes the chapter.

METHODOLOGY

This section describes the complete frame work for finding facial emotions from the clutter scenes using Zernike moments based CNN. The methodology includes (i) Face detection (ii) Classification of full and partial faces and (iii) Recognition of facial emotions from full faces.

FACE DETECTION

Finding human face in a cluttered scene is difficult and is also of prime importance in face-related applications. Face detection could be considered as a specific case of object detection. Object detection aims at finding the locations and dimensions of all the objects present in an image and categorize them into different classes. Cluttered images contain not only human faces but also other objects and background as displayed in Fig.1. Thus given a cluttered image, the task of the face detection system is to detect, locate the facial regions and separate or segment them in the cluttered images ignoring the other objects.

Figure 1. Cluttered image with human faces and background

It is an undeniable fact that human faces appear with a different orientation, head poses and scales, making face detection a demanding task.

Additionally, the illumination conditions, facial expressions variation, the nonrigidity of faces, and the occlusions of objects such as glasses, beards, mustache scarves, hats and one person hiding the other add considerably to the variations in appearance of faces in an image. These added conditions increase the variability of the face patterns that face detection system should handle. Accordingly, these parameters should be taken into consideration while designing a face detection system. To get the best results it requires good algorithms and design. In recent years, there is a large increase in the number and variety of methods attributed to face detection.

A review of the related works find several methods proposed and presented on face detection using appearance-based, template matching and structural methods. The basic face detection algorithms focused on the detection of frontal faces whereas newer algorithms attempt to solve the more general and difficult problem of multiview face detection.

One of the popular face detector based on template matching is the Viola-Jones method (Viola and Jones, 2001) that utilized Haar-like features with Adaboost learning. This method motivated many of the recent advancements in face detection. The Haar-like features provided very good performance for the frontal faces. Further, several variants of Haar-like features were proposed like co-occurrence of multiple Haar-like features(Mita, Kaneko and Hori, 2005) and single Haar-like feature with Real boost learning algorithm(Wu, Haizhou, Huang, and Lao, 2004).

Also, the basic Haar-like features were not robust when the faces were subjected to variations in illumination conditions(Viola and Jones, 2001). The advanced features help in more accurate classification but with computation complexity. The local binary patterns(LBP)(Ojala, Pietikainen, and Maenpaa, 2002; Ahonen, Hadid, and Pietikäinen, 2004; Zhang, Huang, Li, Wang and Wu, 2004) and census transform (Froba and Ernst, 2004) were adopted which showed an improvement in the performance of face detection even under illumination variations. As compared to LBP the local gradient patterns(LGP)[8] was robust in handling the background variations. The methods based on regional statistics such as Histogram of oriented gradients(HoG), binary HoGs are also popular in handling face detection tasks. Further, the performance was improved by combining or fusing the features such as HoG and LBP(Jun, Choi and Kim, 2013) which achieved a noteworthy performance and was able to handle occlusions. These features were combined with various classifiers that included Adaboost classifier, Bayesian classifier, support vector machines(SVM) and neural networks(NN).

Neural networks were earlier employed in (Vaillant, Monrocq and Le Cun, 1994; Rowley, Baluja and Kanade, 1998) for face detection. (Rowley, Baluja and Kanade, 1998; Rowley, Baluja and Kanade, 1998) presented a method to detect frontal and semi frontal faces in the cluttered image. Later shape-based features(Chen, Ren, Wei, Cao and Sun, 2014) were found to be powerful in distinguishing the face and non-face patterns. Further, the idea of multi-resolution based networks motivated(Zhang, Zelinsky and Samaras, 2007) and (Park, Ramanan and Fowlkes, 2010) for object detection. Additionally, part based methods (Zhu and Ramanan, 2012; Yan, Zhang, Lei and Li, 2014; Mathias, Benenson, Pedersoli and Van Gool, 2014) showed that the methods achieved better detection accuracy.

The traditional face detection systems are based on hand crafted features briefly described above. These are effective in representing and detecting the faces, but they fail in real-time applications with faces under visual variations of pose, illumination, occlusion, and facial expression. The hand crafted features also convey the little amount of semantic information. This is overcome by shifting from hand tailored algorithms to the algorithms that perform cognition by using the deep networks. These networks are designed with multiple layered architectures for learning the features to provide semantic information. As compared to the handcrafted features the convolutional neural network(CNN), one of the deep learning methods automatically learns the features and extracts the visual variations in the images.

CNNs(Phung and Bouzerdoum, 2009; Gu, Wang, Kuen, Ma, Shahroudy, Shuai, and Chen, 2018; Le Cun, Bengio and Hinton, 2015) are deep neural networks with hierarchical learning. These networks have multistage architecture and process two-dimensional data. The structure of CNN is based on three architectural characteristics: local receptive fields, weight sharing, and sub-sampling in the spatial domain. The network combines feature extraction with classification into one structure and is invariant to translation and geometrical distortions in the images. Each stage of the architecture is a collection of three layers: convolution layer, subsampling layer, and nonlinear layer. Each convolution layer is followed by a subsampling layer, and the last convolution layer is followed by an output layer or classification layer. All the layers of CNN process 2D data whereas the output layer processes 1D data.

CNN is successful and finds applications in various areas such as speech recognition(Nassif, A. B., Shahin, I., Attili, I., Azzeh, M., & Shaalan, K. (2019), image processing(Long, Jonathan, Evan Shelhamer, and Trevor Darrell.2015), image classification(He, Zhang.Z, Zhang.H, Zhang. Z, Xie and Li, 2019; Krizhevsky, Sutskever and Hinton, 2012), human action recognition(Zhang, Lan, Xing, Zeng, Xue, J and Zheng, 2019), sentence modeling(Zhang.Y, Zhang.Z,Miao and Wang, 2019), scene labeling(Le, Duong, Han, Luu, Quach and Savvides, 2018), matching natural language sentences(Hu, Lu, Li and Chen, 2014), health care(Rasti, Teshnehlab and Phung, 2017), hand gesture recognition(Barros, Magg, Weber and Wermter, 2014) and face recognition(Deng, Peng, Li and Qiao, 2019).

Thus this chapter presents a face detection method based on multitasking cascaded convolutional networks(MTCNN)(Zhang.K, Zhang.Z, Li, and Qiao, 2016; Li, Lin, Shen, Brandt and Hua, 2015)with very high discrimination ability and good performance in differentiating the faces from non-faces(background). The requirement of the proposed CNN method is to reduce or reject the number of false positives.

MTCNN is a cascaded convolutional neural network that utilizes multi-task learning has achieved significant progress in a wide range of computer vision tasks such as object recognition and classification, face recognition, facial expression recognition. MTCNN provides better performance by combining face detection with face alignment which other methods failed to do and hence this method have been applied in face detection approaches. The next section presents a detailed description of MTCNN.

Facial expression recognition is a biometric recognition technology which can express and analyze human facial expressions, and then enable computers to recognize and even understand human emotions. Facial expression recognition was first used by psychologists to study national psychology in crisis situations. With the integration of computer science, this technology has gradually made a series of attempts in the fields of human-computer interaction such as fatigue driving, smiling detection, network video analysis and mobile phone service, and extended its antennae to the fields of emotional robots, vehicular assistant systems, intelligent mobile terminals and instant messaging on the Internet. Although researchers are eager to put facial expression recognition technology into practical application as soon as possible, there are still many technical constraints on the exploration of effective facial expression recognition.

In 2015, Sariyanidi et al. wrote on PAMI that facial expression recognition research faces five major challenges: head deflection, illumination change, registration error, facial occlusion and identity difference. Among these problems, head deflection is an important cause of registration error and facial occlusion. Psychological studies have shown that head deflection can interfere with human emotional cognition, and plays an important role in emotional expression. Therefore, non-positive facial expression recognition derived from head deflection has become an unavoidable focus and difficulty in the practical development of facial expression recognition.

In recent years, non-positive facial expression recognition has attracted the attention of the National Natural Science Foundation of China. The IEEE International Conference on Automatic Face and Gesture Recognition (IEEEFG2017) was held in Washington, USA, in May 2017. The third Facial Expression Recognition and Analysis Challenge is the theme of facial expression recognition under head deflection. Although the research on this issue is increasing, there is still a lack of comprehensive articles on this issue in the field of non-positive expression recognition, which has caused many difficulties for the research in this field.

It is found that references focus on the problem of facial expression recognition in both positive (or near-positive) face images and videos, without considering the recognition of non-positive facial expression samples. Document focuses on five difficult problems in the field of facial expression recognition, and lists non-positive facial expression recognition as a sub-topic, but it has not been systematically discussed. Reference focuses on the changes of facial expression samples, and takes RGB images, three-dimensional images and thermal images as the important basis of classification and recognition methods. The effect of large-angle head deflection on recognition is mentioned in document, but obviously this is not the main concern.

In this chapter, we focus on full face which contains complete face information with two eyes, one nose and one mouth. These faces contain more detailed information than partial faces which only contain partial details like one eye, one side of nose and one side of mouth. We utilize Zernike Moments to classify the faces extracted from crowded images. And then, do emotion recognitions only on the full faces.

MTCNN Approach to Face Detection

The overall structure of the **MTCNN** approach is as shown in the Fig.2. As shown, the input image is preprocessed initially to build an image pyramid which is the collection of different size

Figure 2. Structure of MTCNN

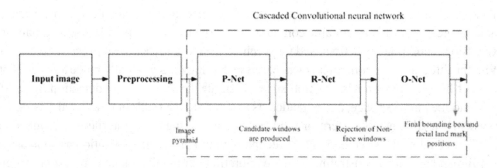

Images of the input image. The obtained images pyramid will be used as the input image to the cascaded convolutional neural network which is a multilevel network structure for face detection. MTCNN uses Proposal network (P-Net), Refine network(R-Net) and Output network(O-Net) separately in three stages and utilizes the input pyramid images to implement the multiscale detection. The architecture of P-Net, R-Net, and O-Net employed here for face detection is as displayed in Fig.3. The combination of these three low complexity convolution networks reduces the running time of the detection task.

1.   P-Net

P-Net is the first stage network of MTCNN. The purpose of this layer network is to obtain candidate windows of the face area and the regression vector of the corresponding face boxes. It utilizes convolution network to do the face detection on the input image pyramid firstly. Then, obtain the face boundary windows of the input image through regression to align the detected candidate face windows. At last, merge the highly overlapping face windows by non maximum suppression(NMS).

2.   R-Net

R-Net is the second stage network of MTCNN. The purpose of this layer is to further restrain face area candidate windows with the wrong decision. Input all the face area candidate windows obtained in P-Net into R-Net. Then, remove the wrong face area candidate windows similarly through regression boundary boxes and NMS. However, comparing to P-Net, R-Net adds one more full-connected layer to achieve far better inhibition effects. Therefore, it can obtain candidate face windows with more accuracy.

3.   O-Net

O-Net is the third stage network of MTCNN. O-Net adds one more convolution layer based on the R-Net so that the results disposed of can be more refined. The function of O-Net is the same to the R-Net, but O-Net does more supervisions on the face area. It outputs five face feature points while restraining wrong candidate windows.

As indicated in Fig.3, the architecture of P-Net, R-Net, and O-Net is composed of convolution layer (C), subsampling layer (S) and nonlinear layer. The architecture utilizes Parametric ReLU(Barros, Magg, Weber and Wermter, 2014) as the non linear activation function. Each convolution layer is followed by a subsampling layer, and the last convolution layer is followed by an output layer or classification layer. The convolution layer is a 2D layer with various planes. In each plane, the neurons are arranged in a 2D array, and the output of each plane is termed as feature map. The feature map of a convolutional layer is computed by convolving the input to the layer with the convolutional kernel. The convolutional kernel is a matrix of learnable weights. Also, each feature map is given an additive bias term b. The output of a convolution layer 'l' is given by

$$y_j^l = \sum_{i \in P_j^l} y_i^{l-1} * k_{ij}^l + b_j^l \qquad (1)$$

where y_i^{l-1} .s the input to the layer(feature map of the preceding layer), k_{ij}^l . is the convolution kernel, P_j^l . is the list of all planes that connects the preceding layer to the current layer and b_j^l . is the bias term. If the size of the input is H x W and the size of the convolution kernel is R x C, then the size of the feature map is (H - R + 1) x (W - C +1). Every plane in a convolutional layer is connected to one or more feature maps of the previous layer but connected to one plane of the subsampling layer.

A subsampling layer down samples the inputs provided to it by the convolution layer. The number of outputs from the layer is the same as its input. The layer divides the input feature map into distinct blocks of size n x n and is averaged or summed to generate an output that is n times smaller than the original along both the dimensions in the spatial domain. Later each output is multiplied with connecting weights, and a learnable bias term is then added to complete the process. The output of the subsampling layer is computed as shown below.

$$y_j^l = z_j^{l-1} . w_j^l + b_j^l \qquad (2)$$

where, z_j^{l-1} .is the resultant matrix of averaging or summing up of n x n blocks of input, w_j^l .are the connecting weights and b_j^l .is the associated bias term of the layer.

Figure 3. Architecture of (a)P-Net (b) R-Net and (c) O-Net

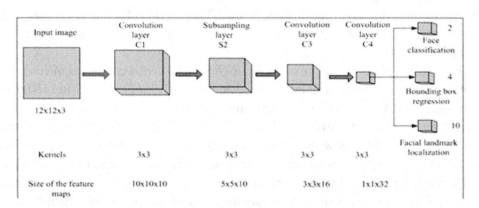

As indicated in Fig.3, the output of the last convolution layer is fed to the fully connected layer for classification.

MTCNN Learning

After selecting the appropriate architecture of the network, the network is trained using stochastic gradient descent algorithm to detect the faces. The training process includes three tasks (a) Face classification (b) Bounding box regression and (c)Facial landmark localization. Before training, for each of the task, the ground truth label(or target) is defined. During the process of training, the output obtained from the network is compared with the ground truth label for a gradual convergence of the loss function intended for accurate learning.

1.   Face classification

Face classification is a two-class classification problem, where the network is trained to learn the discrimination between a face and a non-face. In this task, for every input sample xi, the cross-entropy loss function is computed for convergence. The entropy is computed as shown below

$$E_i = -(y_i^E \log(P_i) + (1 - y_i^E).(1 - \log(P_i.)) \tag{3}$$

where, P_i .is the output probability that indicated whether a given sample is a face or not and y_i^E .is the ground truth label such that $y_i^E \in \{0,1\}$ .2. Bounding box regression

Bounding box regression is devised as a regression problem. Here the network learns to predict the regression output that includes the following co-ordinates: left top, height, and width of the bounding box. During training, for each candidate window, the error between the regression output and the regression ground truth co-ordinates is computed. The Euclidean loss function is utilized here which is computed as,

$$B_i = \hat{y}_i^B - y_i^{B2} \tag{4}$$

where, $\hat{y}_i^B$ .is the regression output of the network and y_i^B .is the ground truth co-ordinates such that $y_i^B \in R^4$.

3. Facial land mark localization

Facial land mark localization produces co-ordinates of five facial landmarks that include left eye, right eye, nose, left eye cornet and right eye corner which contribute for face detection. This task is also designed to be a regression problem similar to the bounding box regression. During training, the Euclidean loss is minimized for reliable learning. The Euclidean loss is computed as shown below,

$$L_i = \hat{y}_i^L - y_i^{L2} \tag{5}$$

where, $\hat{y}_i^L$ .is the facial landmark co-ordinates output from the network and y_i^L .is the ground truth co-ordinates such that $y_i^L \in R^{10}$.

As specified earlier, the P-Net, R-Net, and O-Net are designed to perform the different process and to produce distinguished outputs. Thus the above-mentioned loss functions are not suitable for all the tasks. Hence the loss functions are appropriately selected as specified in(Zhang.K, Zhang.Z, Li and Qiao, 2016).

This work presents a face detection scheme for crowded images that utilizes MTCNN to achieve a noteworthy performance as compared to the methods that rely on handcrafted features. For evaluation 61 crowded images were considered with facial variations. Few sample output images of the face detection are illustrated in Fig.4.

Figure 4. Face detection using (a) Viola-Jones method and (b) MTCNN

The performance of MTCNN is compared with the Viola-Jones method. From Fig.4.a, it is seen that the Viola-Jones method utilizing the Haar-like features and Adaboost learning performs significantly well in detecting the frontal faces whereas it fails to detect the partial faces and faces with variations in pose and facial expressions. From Fig.4.b it can be observed that MTCNN with cascaded CNN networks is successful in detecting all the faces in the images irrespective of the presence of facial variations in them. It can also be observed that the method can detect even the partial faces by providing appropriate landmark positions as represented in Fig.5.

Figure 5. Face detection in the presence of facial variations (a) Occlusion (b) & (c) Pose and facial expressions (c) & (d) Partial faces

Accordingly, the cascaded CNN structure was able to detect all the full and partial faces in 60 images which we picked up from clutter scenes randomly with 100% as displayed in Fig.6. But, due to complex background, low contrast and non-uniform illumination, MTCNN doesn't perform well on some specific clutter scene group face images(Fig.7). We extract all the faces from these images and define them as MTCNN dataset.

Figure 6. Face detection in by MTCNN with 100% accuracy on clutter scene images (a) & (b) & (c) & (d)

Identifying partial faces is important as most of the facial images that are captured in the unconstrained environment for crowd monitoring are partial and these faces have to be further processed to be used in different applications. The next section describes the classification of faces into partial and full using Zernike based convolutional neural networks(Z-CNN).

Figure 7. Face detection on clutter scene face images (a) & (b) with low accuracy due to specific limitations

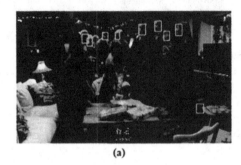 

(a)   (b)

CLASSIFICATION OF PARTIAL AND FULL FACES USING Z-CNN

CNN is a deep neural network with multiple stages adopting hierarchical learning. The network can learn multiple features in the hierarchy from each stage. The output from each stage is a feature map. Feature map represents the feature extracted from all the locations of the input. As described earlier CNN is a sequence of layers where each layer is made of neurons that has trainable biases and weights. Also, CNN combines the feature extraction with classification. Thus the inputs to the network get transformed layer by layer to the final score values. Various methods based on CNN have achieved a significant amount of accuracy by choosing the initial parameters for convolution kernels randomly from a normal distribution. These convolutional kernels are trained to achieve optimization.

Further, they are not hierarchical to suit the multilayered architecture of CNN. Besides, the orthogonal Zernike Moments(ZM) with better shape description possess a hierarchical architecture, where the lower order moments represent the global shape characteristics of the image and higher order moments provide detailed or finer shape information of the image(Mahesh and Raj, 2015; Tahmasbi, Saki and Shokouhi, 2011). Thus ZM can be utilized to derive the initial trainable parameters for convolution kernels by varying the moment orders as applicable to the different layers of CNN to achieve hierarchical feature learning.

Architecture of Z-CNN

The overall structure of the CNN approach based on Zernike moments(Mahesh, Raj and Fan, 2017; Phung and Bouzerdoum, 2009)is as displayed in the Fig.8. The working principle of convolutional and subsampling layers remains similar to that explained in section 2.1 whereas the nonlinear layers use the Pureline, Tan sigmoid or Log sigmoid activation functions. The CNN network is comprised of six layers, and the input to the network is an image of dimension 32x32 which has to be classified as a full face or partial face. The first convolution layer C1 produces two feature maps of resolution 28x28 by performing convolution on input using kernels of magnitude 5x5. Next, the subsampling layer S2 down samples the output of C1 by a factor of two producing two feature maps of 14x14 pixels. The layers C1 and S2 have one to one connection. Likewise, the convolution layer C3 using kernels of size 3x3 produces five feature maps with dimension 12x12.

Figure 8. Architecture of Z-CNN

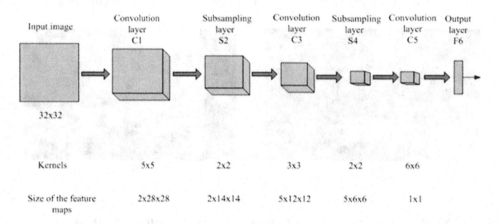

The layer S2 is connected to C3 in a similar mode as described in(Mahesh, Raj and Fan, 2017) . The sub sampling layer S4 also produces five feature maps of size 6x6. Finally, C5 uses kernels of size 6x6 to produce six scalar outputs for each of its input. So the features for training and classification are presented by C5. Later the features are provided to the fully connected output layer F6 to produce the class label of the input image, i.e., full face or partial face. The output of layer F6 is obtained as shown

$$y_j^l = \sum_{i=1}^{N} y_i^{l-1} . w_{ij}^l + b_j^l \qquad (6)$$

where N is the number of neurons in the output layer.

As mentioned, the work presents Z-CNN where the initial trainable parameters for convolution kernels are derived by varying the Zernike moment orders as applicable to the different layers of CNN. The ZM is selected as they have the multi-level structure to match with multi-layered architecture of CNN. The next section describes the acquisition and selection of the elements for convolution kernels based on ZM.

ZM Based Convolution Kernels and Classification of Full and Partial Faces

ZM(Mahesh and Raj, 2015; Khotanzad, Alireza and Yaw Hua Hong, 1990; Tahmasbi, Saki and Shokouhi, 2011) are projections of the image function $f(x, y)$ on to set of complex Zernike polynomials defined on the unit circle. The Zernike polynomials are given by,

$$V_{nm}(x,y) = V_{nm}(\rho,\theta) = R_{nm}(\rho)\exp(jm\theta) \qquad (7)$$

where

n is the order of the polynomial

m is the repetition factor such that $|m| \leq n$, and $n-|m|$ is even

ρ is the length of the vector from the origin to the pixel located at a spatial location

(x, y)and is given by $\rho = \sqrt{x^2 + y^2}$. θ . angle of the vector from the origin to the pixel located at a spatial location,

(x, y) from the x-axis in counter-clockwise direction and

$R_{mn}(\rho)$ is the radial polynomial defined as

$$R_{nm}(\rho) = \sum_{s=0}^{n-|m|} (-1)^s \frac{(2n+1-s)!}{s!(n-|m|-s)!(n+|m|+1-s)!} \rho^{n-s} \qquad (8)$$

The ZM of an image is obtained as below

The ZM so obtained are orthogonal and are invariant to rotation, scale and, translation. These moments make the best shape descriptors and hence the appropriate elements of the kernels can be obtained for C1, C3 and C5 layers of Z-CNN. The convolution kernels as required for the presented architecture are determined as described in [36].

At first, as per the required size, an image $f(x,y)$ is assumed, and each of the image points is mapped into the internal region of the unit circle. Later the ZM integral is evaluated over each pixel assuming $f(x,y)$ to be constant over that pixel using equation (9) with the moment order n and repetition factor m to produce the convolution kernels k_{nm}. Following the procedure of (Mahesh, Raj and Fan, 2017), 22 kernels were obtained by varying the moment order from 1 to 18. Finally, these kernels are assigned to the convolution layers C1, C3, and C5 appropriately. The kernel assignment to the layers is as shown in Table.1.

Table 1. Kernel assignment to convolution layers

Convolution layers	Number of kernels	Convolution kernels k_{nm} with order n and repetition factor m
C1	5	$k_{11} k_{22} k_{42} k_{62} k_{66}$
C2	8	$K_{82} k_{86} k_{10,2} k_{10,6} k_{10,10} k_{12,2} k_{12,6} k_{12,10}$
C3	9	$K_{14,2} k_{14,4} k_{14,6} k_{14,10} k_{16,2} k_{16,6} k_{16,10} k_{16,14} k_{18,2}$

The kernels are assigned in a such a way that, each kernel when selected during the training process should get an equal probability of getting trained. As illustrated in Table.1 two kernels when selected out of five for C1 get 40% chance in getting trained. Similarly, five out of eight and five out of nine kernels when selected randomly for C2 and C5 respectively indicates 60% and 50% chance of getting trained. The assigned kernels, when convolved with the input image, gives out edge map for further processing.

With the designed architecture the Z-CNN network is trained under supervision with gradient descent back propagation algorithm to classify the input facial images into full faces and partial faces. During training, the elements of the convolution kernels and bias are modified to achieve faster convergence by reducing the loss function as computed below.

$$E = \frac{1}{P.N} \sum_{p=1}^{P} \sum_{j=1}^{N} \left(y_j^p - d_j^p \right)^2.$$

(10)

where P is the number of input images, N is the number of neurons in the output layer, y^p .s the network output and d^p .is the desired output.

The performance of Z-CNN in classifying the detected faces from the crowded scenes into partial and full faces is evaluated by network convergence and accuracy. Besides, the implementation is also compared with the CNN that uses randomly selected initial parameters for convolution kernels(R-CNN). Thus for evaluation four datasets: AR(Martinez and Benavente, 1998), IMFDB(Setty, Husain, Beham, Gudavalli, Kandasamy, Vaddi, Hemadri, Karure, Raju, Rajan, and Kumar, 2013), KDEF(Lundqvist, Flykt and Öhman,1998) and UMIST(http://images.ee.umist.ac.uk/danny/database.html) were considered. The total images in the datasets are divided into training set and testing set using the hold-out 60-40 method(Han, Pei and Kamber, 2011). Accordingly, the training set has 60% of the total images, and testing has 40% of the total images. The details about the datasets and its division are provided in Table.2 and corresponding sample images are displayed in Fig.7.

Table 2. Dataset and its division using the hold-out method

Dataset	Number of images	Number of training images	Number of testing images
AR	2600	1560	1040
IMFDB	1740	1045	697
KDEF	1980	1188	792
UMIST	509	306	203

The sample images presented in Fig.9 indicates the presence of both full faces and partial faces obtained due to occlusions and pose variations in the considered datasets. So the devised Z-CNN should provide strong discrimination between them to get the classified output.

The presented Z-CNN network is now trained by providing the training images from the training sets from all the datasets each at a time. During training 316 network parameters are trained by setting the epoch limit to 1000 and loss function to 0. The training process has to reduce the loss function for optimization; The results thus obtained from the training process are furnished in Fig.10 to Fig.13. The performance curves depicts the training process and indicate the path in which the network is learning. The curves displayed in Fig.10 to Fig.13 indicate the learning curves with good fit. Later the learned network is tested by providing the samples from the testing test for measuring its accuracy.

The performance curves presented in Figs (10 - 13) clearly indicate that the Z-CNN converged faster with lesser number of epochs to meet the designated loss function as compared to R-CNN for all the

Figure 9. Sample images from (a) AR (b) IMFDB (c)KDEF and (d) UMIST datasets

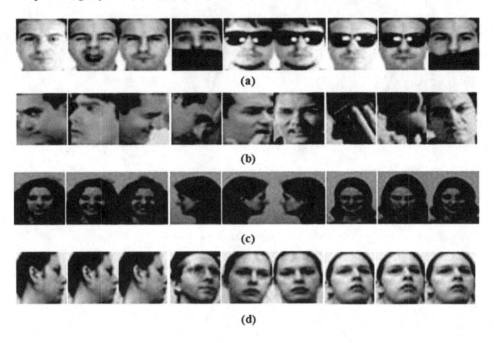

Figure 10. Performance curve obtained for AR dataset from (a) R-CNN and (b) Z-CNN

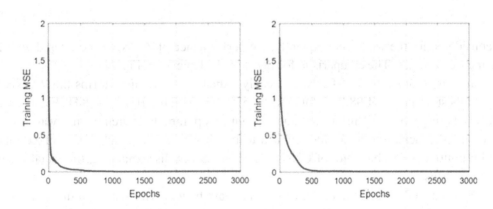

Figure 11. Performance curve obtained for IMFDB dataset from (a) R-CNN and (b) Z-CNN

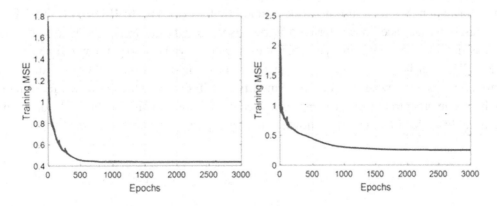

Figure 12. Performance curve obtained for KDEF dataset from (a) R-CNN and (b) Z-CNN

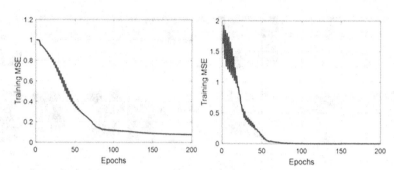

Figure 13. Performance curve obtained for UMIST dataset from (a) R-CNN and (b) Z-CNN

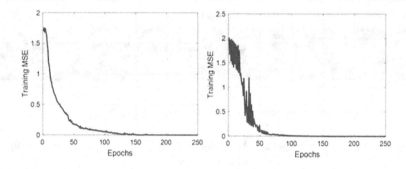

datasets considered for the work. Subsequently, the performance of Z-CNN is compared with R-CNN using the metric accuracy. The comparison for the same is depicted in Fig.14.

The accuracies obtained from Z-CNN noticeably indicates that it outperforms the R-CNN by providing the highest accuracy of 98.92% for AR, 81.67% for IMFDB, 100% for KDEF and 99.14% for UMIST datasets respectively. This shows that ZM with its pyramidical architecture was best suitable for representing the facial images for hierarchical feature learning. The combination of Zernike based kernels with multi-stage architecture of CNN was successful in discriminating the facial images into partial and full faces.

The CNN based on Zernike Moments are proved to have better performance on full and partial faces classification than the Random kernel. So, we utilize it to classify the full and partial faces of our own crowded faces dataset extracted from group face images and we name it as MTCNN dataset.

Considering face images extracted by MTCNN that have only faces without any backgrounds with irrelevant information. So, if we use networks trained by four **(a) AR (b) IMFDB (c)KDEF and (d) UMIST** datasets whose face images have backgrounds to classify our MTCNN dataset, it's no doubt that the classification accuracy is just passable or even worse. We need to get new training dataset that matches MTCNN. Further, we are aimed at finding full face emotions from clutter face images. Taking these factors into account, we use MTCNN to modify KDEF dataset which contains face emotions to extract only face in order to make sure to get better accuracy from the classification. The original KDEF dataset and modified KDEF dataset are shown below in Fig.15.

Figure 14. Accuracies of Z-CNN and R-CNN for all the datasets

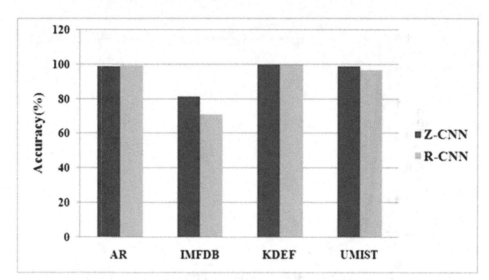

Figure 15. KDEF dataset (a) with background and (b) modified KDEF dataset without background

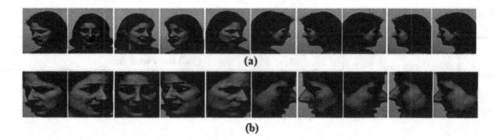

We use modified KDEF dataset to train the network that 60% of the total modified images for training and 40% of the total for testing(total modified image number is 688). Finally, we get satisfactory results that the training classification rate is 100% and testing classification rate is 97.81%. The training MSE result is furnished in Fig.16. The training MSE converges to 0 for 1100 epochs.

The trained network that used Zernike moment based CNN is now utilized to test faces extracted from the clutter scenes group face images (MTCNN dataset). A part of MTCNN dataset is shown in Fig.17. The confusion matrix for classification results are shown in Table.3. From the matrix, the total classification rate is found to be 98.83%. Nearly all the faces are classified into full faces and partial faces correctly which confirms that CNN based on Zernike moment has good performance on classification with MTCNN dataset. Some classified full and partial faces are furnished in Fig.19, 20.

Figure 16. Performance curve obtained for modified KDEF dataset from R-CNN

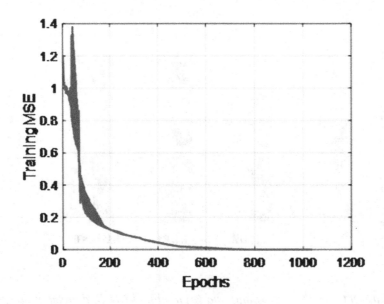

Table 3. Confusion matrix of classification results

Actual class	Full face Partial face	Predicted class Full face Partial face	
		146	1
		2	108

Figure 17. Sample Faces extracted from the clutter scenes group face images(MTCNN dataset)

Figure 18. (a) Full faces classified by Z-CNN on MTCNN dataset and (b) Partial faces classified by Z-CNN on MTCNN dataset

(a)

(b)

CLASSIFICATION OF FULL FACES OF MTCNN DATASET INTO FOUR FACIAL EMOTIONS USING PATTERNNET

We have managed to extract faces from clutter scene group face images with high accuracy to create MTCNN dataset. Besides, the full faces and partial faces in this dataset are separated by Z-CNN effectively. Based on these positive results, we proceed to recognize facial expressions further. Due to some influence of realistic factors as mentioned in the Introduction, this work focuses on full face emotion recognition.

In the previous section, we had modified KDEF dataset to obtain a more appropriate database without redundant backgrounds. Now, we divide the modified full face KDEF dataset into four emotions which are happiness(HA), neutral(NE), sadness(SA), surprise(SU). Here, we utilize pattern recognition concept to classify four emotions.

Figure 19. Four emotions of modified full face KDEF dataset (a) Happiness (b) Neutral (c) Sadness (d) Surprise

To give a definition of the pattern recognition, interpose a set of K input vectors as columns to constitute a matrix. Then, in order to indicate the classes to which the input vectors are assigned, another set of K target vectors is arranged.

When there are only two classes; you set each scalar target value to either 0 or 1, indicating which class the corresponding input belongs to. When inputs are to be classified into N different classes, the target vectors have N elements. For each target vector, one element is 1 and the others are 0.

We have found that ZM have satisfactory performance on facial recognition as discussed in previous section. Besides, when we convert original facial images of modified full face KDEF dataset into feature vectors, every column possess extensive features. Most of these features contain superfluous information which probably obstruct the final results and increase much training time. To avoid this situation, we utilize 72-feature ZM sliding window to go through every face images by pixel so that to retain 72 features per face image which almost have 95% reference value information.

Now a shallow neural network is used to train the modified full face KDEF dataset. The input is a 72x232 matrix, representing static data: 232 samples of 72 elements. The target is a 4x232 matrix, representing static data: 232 samples of 4 elements. The 4 elements are the class labels: Happiness, Neutral, Sad and Surprise. Next, a pattern recognition neural network: PatternNet is defined. The number of hidden neurons for the PatternNet is chosen to be 71 in order to make better use of all 72 features of every column. The structure of PatternNet is shown in Fig.20. For validation and testing, the data sets are each set to 15% of the original training data. With these settings, the input vectors and target vectors will be randomly divided into three sets as follows: (i) 70% for training (ii) 15% to validate that the network is generalizing and to stop training before overfitting and (iii) the last 15% are used as a completely independent test of network generalization.

Figure 20. The structure of PatternNet

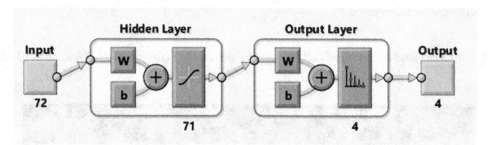

The performance of the training process on the training samples are evaluated using the confusion matrix and Receiver operating characteristics(ROC). Table 4 shows the confusion matrix of training process for classifying facial emotions. The network outputs are very accurate, as it is noticed by the high numbers of correct responses in the green squares and the low numbers of incorrect responses in the red squares. The lower right blue squares illustrate the overall accuracies.

Table 4. Confusion matrix of training process

			Actual class HA NE SA SU				
Predicted class		HA NE SA SU	44 25.6%	4 2.3%	2 1.2%	0 0.0%	88.0% 12.0%
			0 0.0%	35 20.3%	11 6.4%	1 0.6%	74.5% 25.5%
			1 0.6%	4 2.3%	30 17.4%	1 0.6%	83.3% 16.7%
			0 0.0%	2 1.2%	2 1.2%	35 20.3%	89.7% 10.3%
			97.8% 2.2%	77.8% 22.2%	66.7% 33.3%	94.6% 5.4%	83.7% 16.3%

Figure 21. The receiver operating characteristic for the training results

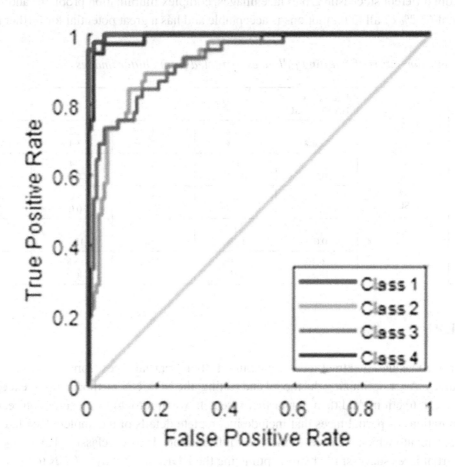

Fig.21 represent the ROC curves for training. The colored lines in each axis in Fig.21 represent the ROC curves. The ROC curve is a plot of the true positive rate (sensitivity) versus the false positive rate (1 - specificity) as the threshold is varied. A perfect test would show points in the upper-left corner, with high sensitivity and specificity. The plot shows that the network performs well in classifying all the four emotions.

After evaluating the performance on training samples, we test the model on full faces extracted from clutter images. Each time a neural network is trained, it can result in a different solution due to different initial weights and bias values and different divisions of data into training, validation, and test sets. As a result, different neural networks trained on the same problem can give different outputs for the same input. To ensure that an optimized neural network classifier with good accuracy has been found, we retrained the network several times. The confusion matrix of the testing result is shown in Table 5. The diagonal cells in the matrix show the number of cases that were correctly classified, and the off-diagonal cells show the misclassified cases. The blue cell in the bottom right shows the total percent of correctly classified cases (in green) and the total percent of misclassified cases (in red). Due to uncontrollable factors in random clutter scene images, like the attitude changes of full faces extracted, contrast difference of all the faces from different stochastic group face images, complex illumination problems and so on, the final accuracy of 67.2% of all four emotions is acceptable and has a great potential for further research.

Table 5. The confusion matrix for testing full faces extracted from clutter images

		Actual class HA NE SA SU				
Predicted class	HA NE SA SU	13 22.4%	1 1.7%	1 1.7%	2 3.4%	76.5% 23.5%
		0 0.0%	11 19.0%	4 6.9%	4 6.9%	57.9% 42.1%
		2 3.4%	2 3.4%	8 13.8%	0 0.0%	66.7% 33.3%
		0 0.0%	1 1.7%	2 3.4%	7 12.1%	70.0% 30.0%
		86.7% 13.3%	73.3% 26.7%	53.3% 46.7%	53.8% 46.2%	67.2% 32.8%

CONCLUSION

In this chapter, we manage to extract faces containing full and partial faces from clutter scene images with high accuracy. After optimizing the model and testing, the MTCNN method showed excellent performance on face extraction. And then, for further research, we aim to do face expression recognition. Because of limitations of partial faces that include incomplete details of a complete face like one eye, one nose and one mouth which means extremely few information. Thus we classified all extracted faces into full and partial faces successfully before optimizing the KDEF dataset by Z-CNN to retain only the full faces for emotion recognition. These full faces were used for emotion recognition and classification by defining PatternNet a pattern recognition network with appropriate parameters to get a better trained network model. With this network, four emotions of the extracted full faces from random crowded group face images are recognized with acceptable accuracy.

ACKNOWLEDGMENTS

The project is supported by Scientific Research Grant of Shantou University, China Grant No: NTF17016. The National Science Foundation of China, Grant. No: 61471228 and the Key Project of Guangdong Province Science and Technology Plan, Grant. No: 2015B020233018.

REFERENCES

Ahonen, T., Hadid, A., & Pietikäinen, M. (2004). Face recognition with local binary patterns. In *European conference on computer vision* (pp. 469-481). Springer.

Barros, P., Magg, S., Weber, C., & Wermter, S. (2014). A multichannel convolutional neural network for hand posture recognition. In *International Conference on Artificial Neural Networks*. Springer International Publishing. 10.1007/978-3-319-11179-7_51

Chen, D., Ren, S., Wei, Y., Cao, X., & Sun, J. (2014). Joint cascade face detection and alignment. In *European Conference on Computer Vision* (pp. 109-122). Springer.

Deng, Z., Peng, X., Li, Z., & Qiao, Y. (2019). Mutual component convolutional neural networks for heterogeneous face recognition. *IEEE Transactions on Image Processing*, 28(6), 3102–3114. doi:10.1109/TIP.2019.2894272 PMID:30676957

Froba, B., & Ernst, A. (2004). Face detection with the modified census transform. In *Automatic Face and Gesture Recognition, 2004. Proceedings. Sixth IEEE International Conference on* (pp. 91-96). IEEE. 10.1109/AFGR.2004.1301514

Gu, J., Wang, Z., Kuen, J., Ma, L., Shahroudy, A., Shuai, B., ... Chen, T. (2018). Recent advances in convolutional neural networks. *Pattern Recognition*, 77, 354–377. doi:10.1016/j.patcog.2017.10.013

Han, J., Pei, J., & Kamber, M. (2011). *Data mining: concepts and techniques*. Elsevier.

He, T., Zhang, Z., Zhang, H., Zhang, Z., Xie, J., & Li, M. (2019). Bag of tricks for image classification with convolutional neural networks. In *Proceedings of the IEEE Conference on Computer Vision and Pattern Recognition* (pp. 558-567). 10.1109/CVPR.2019.00065

Hu, B., Lu, Z., Li, H., & Chen, Q. (2014). Convolutional neural network architectures for matching natural language sentences. Advances in Neural Information Processing Systems, 2042-2050.

Jun, B., Choi, I., & Kim, D. (2013). Local transform features and hybridization for accurate face and human detection. *IEEE Transactions on Pattern Analysis and Machine Intelligence*, 35(6), 1423–1436. doi:10.1109/TPAMI.2012.219 PMID:23599056

Khotanzad, A., & Hong, Y. H. (1990). Invariant image recognition by Zernike moments. Pattern Analysis and Machine Intelligence. *IEEE Transactions on*, 12(5), 489–497.

Krizhevsky, A., Sutskever, I., & Hinton, G. E. (2012). Imagenet classification with deep convolutional neural networks. Advances in neural information processing systems, 1097-1105.

Le, T. H. N., Duong, C. N., Han, L., Luu, K., Quach, K. G., & Savvides, M. (2018). Deep contextual recurrent residual networks for scene labeling. *Pattern Recognition*, 80, 32–41. doi:10.1016/j.patcog.2018.01.005

LeCun, Y., Bengio, Y., & Hinton, G. (2015). Deep learning. *Nature*, 521(7553), 436–444. doi:10.1038/nature14539 PMID:26017442

Li, H., Lin, Z., Shen, X., Brandt, J., & Hua, G. (2015). A convolutional neural network cascade for face detection. In *Proceedings of the IEEE Conference on Computer Vision and Pattern Recognition* (pp. 5325-5334). 10.1109/CVPR.2015.7299170

Long, J., Shelhamer, E., & Darrell, T. (2015). Fully convolutional networks for semantic segmentation. *Proceedings of the IEEE Conference on Computer Vision and Pattern Recognition*.

Lundqvist, D., Flykt, A., & Öhman, A. (1998). *The Karolinska Directed Emotional Faces -KDEF, CD ROM from Department of Clinical Neuroscience, Psychology section.* Karolinska Institutet.

Mahesh, V. G., & Raj, A. N. J. (2015). Invariant face recognition using Zernike moments combined with feed forward neural network. *International Journal of Biometrics, 7*(3), 286–307. doi:10.1504/IJBM.2015.071950

Mahesh, V. G., Raj, A. N. J., & Fan, Z. (2017). Invariant moments based convolutional neural networks for image analysis. *International Journal of Computational Intelligence Systems, 10*(1), 936–950. doi:10.2991/ijcis.2017.10.1.62

Martinez & Benavente. (1998). *The AR Face Database.* CVC Technical Report #24.

Mathias, M., Benenson, R., Pedersoli, M., & Van Gool, L. (2014, September). Face detection without bells and whistles. In *European conference on computer vision* (pp. 720-735). Springer.

Mita, T., Kaneko, T., & Hori, O. (2005). Joint haar-like features for face detection. In *Computer Vision, 2005. ICCV 2005. Tenth IEEE International Conference on* (Vol. 2, pp. 1619-1626). IEEE. 10.1109/ICCV.2005.129

Nassif, A. B., Shahin, I., Attili, I., Azzeh, M., & Shaalan, K. (2019). Speech recognition using deep neural networks: A systematic review. *IEEE Access : Practical Innovations, Open Solutions, 7*, 19143–19165. doi:10.1109/ACCESS.2019.2896880

Ojala, T., Pietikainen, M., & Maenpaa, T. (2002). Multiresolution gray-scale and rotation invariant texture classification with local binary patterns. *IEEE Transactions on Pattern Analysis and Machine Intelligence, 24*(7), 971–987. doi:10.1109/TPAMI.2002.1017623

Park, D., Ramanan, D., & Fowlkes, C. (2010). Multiresolution models for object detection. *European conference.*

Phung, S. L., & Bouzerdoum, A. (2009). *MATLAB library for convolutional neural networks.* University of Wollongong, Tech. Rep. http://www. elec. uow. edu.au/staff/sphung

Rasti, R., Teshnehlab, M., & Phung, S. L. (2017). Breast cancer diagnosis in DCE-MRI using mixture ensemble of convolutional neural networks. *Pattern Recognition, 72*, 381–390. doi:10.1016/j.patcog.2017.08.004

Rowley, H., Baluja, S., & Kanade, T. (1998). Rotation invariant neural network-based face detection. In *Proceedings of IEEE Conference on Computer Vision and Pattern Recognition* (p. 38). IEEE.

Rowley, H. A., Baluja, S., & Kanade, T. (1998). Neural network-based face detection. *IEEE Transactions on Pattern Analysis and Machine Intelligence, 20*(1), 23–38. doi:10.1109/34.655647

Setty, S., Husain, M., Beham, P., Gudavalli, J., Kandasamy, M., Vaddi, R., . . . Kumar, V. (2013, December). Indian movie face database: a benchmark for face recognition under wide variations. In *2013 fourth national conference on computer vision, pattern recognition, image processing and graphics (NCVPRIPG)* (pp. 1-5). IEEE. 10.1109/NCVPRIPG.2013.6776225

Tahmasbi, A., Saki, F., & Shokouhi, S. B. (2011). Classification of benign and malignant masses based on Zernike moments. *Computers in Biology and Medicine, 41*(8), 726–735. doi:10.1016/j.comp-biomed.2011.06.009 PMID:21722886

Vaillant, R., Monrocq, C., & Le Cun, Y. (1994). Original approach for the localisation of objects in images. *IEE Proceedings. Vision Image and Signal Processing, 141*(4), 245–250. doi:10.1049/ip-vis:19941301

Viola, P., & Jones, M. (2001). Rapid object detection using a boosted cascade of simple features. In *Computer Vision and Pattern Recognition, 2001. CVPR 2001. Proceedings of the 2001 IEEE Computer Society Conference on* (*Vol. 1*, pp. I-I). IEEE. 10.1109/CVPR.2001.990517

Wu, B., Haizhou, A. I., Huang, C., & Lao, S. (2004). *Fast rotation invariant multi-view face detection based on real adaboost. In Null* (p. 79). IEEE.

Yan, J., Zhang, X., Lei, Z., & Li, S. Z. (2014). Face detection by structural models. *Image and Vision Computing, 32*(10), 790–799. doi:10.1016/j.imavis.2013.12.004

Zhang, G., Huang, X., Li, S. Z., Wang, Y., & Wu, X. (2004). Boosting local binary pattern (LBP)-based face recognition. In *Advances in biometric person authentication* (pp. 179–186). Berlin: Springer. doi:10.1007/978-3-540-30548-4_21

Zhang, K., Zhang, Z., Li, Z., & Qiao, Y. (2016). Joint face detection and alignment using multitask cascaded convolutional networks. *IEEE Signal Processing Letters, 23*(10), 1499–1503. doi:10.1109/LSP.2016.2603342

Zhang, P., Lan, C., Xing, J., Zeng, W., Xue, J., & Zheng, N. (2019). View adaptive neural networks for high performance skeleton-based human action recognition. *IEEE Transactions on Pattern Analysis and Machine Intelligence, 41*(8), 1963–1978. doi:10.1109/TPAMI.2019.2896631 PMID:30714909

Zhang, W., Zelinsky, G., & Samaras, D. (2007). Real-time accurate object detection using multiple resolutions. In *Computer Vision, 2007. ICCV 2007. IEEE 11th International Conference on* (pp. 1-8). IEEE. 10.1109/ICCV.2007.4409057

Zhang, Y., Zhang, Z., Miao, D., & Wang, J. (2019). Three-way enhanced convolutional neural networks for sentence-level sentiment classification. *Information Sciences, 477*, 55–64. doi:10.1016/j.ins.2018.10.030

Zhu, X., & Ramanan, D. (2012). Face detection, pose estimation, and landmark localization in the wild. In *Computer Vision and Pattern Recognition (CVPR), 2012 IEEE Conference on* (pp. 2879-2886). IEEE.

Chapter 14
Facial Expression:
Psychophysiological Study

Elena Lyakso
St. Petersburg State University, Russia

Olga Frolova
St. Petersburg State University, Russia

Yuri Matveev
ITMO University, Russia

ABSTRACT

The description of the results of five psychophysiological studies using automatic coding facial expression in adults and children (from 4 to 16 years) in the FaceReader software version 8.0 is presented. The model situations of reading the emotional text and pronouncing emotional phrases and words, natural interaction in mother-child dyads, child and adult (experimenter), and interaction of children with each other were analyzed. The difficulties of applying the program to analyze the behavior of children in natural conditions, to analyze the emotional facial expressions of the children with autism spectrum disorders and children with Down syndrome are described. The ways to solve them are outlined.

INTRODUCTION

The Chapter presents the results of the psychophysiological study aimed at analyzing the facial expression of adults and children (with typical and atypical development brought up in a family and in an orphanage) in different situations. The Chapter includes the description of the study background: theories of emotions, the physiological basis of the emotion manifestation in the facial expression; the application of automatic systems for analysis of video images: modern technologies, systems and application fields. A more detailed specification of the FaceReader version 8.0 that was used in the study is given. The results, conclusion, and discussion of the results are presented. The aim of the work was to describe the

DOI: 10.4018/978-1-7998-6690-9.ch014

facial expressions in children of different ages and different psychoneurological status, who are brought up in a family and an orphanage in the model situations and natural behavioral situations.

BACKGROUND

Theories of Emotions

Emotion is an active state of specialized brain structures that induces the body to change a behavioral reaction in the direction of minimizing or maximizing this state. Emotion is a special type of mental processes expressing a human's experiences, his attitude to the world around him and himself (Lyakso & Nozdrachev, 2012).

There are many theories of emotions based on different criteria. According to the biological theory of Ch. Darwin, emotions (fear, anger, joy) and accompanying them mimic and pantomimic movements are adaptive. Many of them appear from the moment of birth and are defined as innate emotional reactions. Darwin pointed out the role of the muscular system in body movements and facial expressions specific for emotional states; the meaning of feedback in the regulation of emotions. The strengthening of emotions is associated with their free manifestation. The suppression of external expressions of emotions weakens the emotion.

The James-Lange theory is based on the idea about a connection between emotions and vegetative changes in the human body that accompany emotions. Physical feeling is the emotion itself: "We feel sorry because we cry, angry because we strike, afraid because we tremble" (Lange, 1912; Pace-Schott et al., 2019). "James' theory" at present is discussed mainly into the context of nineteenth century brain research (Wassmann, 2014). It is considered as the basement for future studies that should be aimed at identifying the autonomic and somatic variables that maximally contribute to distinguishing among basic emotions (Friedman, 2010).

According to the Thalamic Cannon-Bard theory, the thalamus is the central brain formation responsible for emotions. At the perception of emotional events, nerve impulses enter the thalamus, then part of the impulses go to the cerebral cortex, where a subjective experience of emotions (fear, joy, etc.) emerges, and some of the impulses go to the hypothalamus, which is responsible for vegetative changes in the body (Izard, 1977).

Lindsley's Activation Theory assigns a central role in providing emotion to the reticular formation of the brain stem. An emotional stimulus excites brain stem neurons that send impulses to the thalamus, hypothalamus, and cortex. An emotional reaction occurs with diffuse activation of the cortex with the simultaneous activation of hypothalamic centers. The condition for the appearance of emotional reactions is the presence of activating influences from the reticular formation while weakening the cortical control of the limbic system (Lindsley, 1951, 1982).

P.K. Simonov's Information Theory considers emotions through the reflection by the human and animal brain of the actual need. The brain evaluates the probability of need satisfaction based on genetic and acquired individual experience. A small probability of need satisfaction leads to negative emotions. A higher probability of need satisfaction compared with prediction leads to positive emotions.

The theories of cognition-emotion relation described that all emotional experiences are associate with cognitive appraisal of environment. The appraisal is rather unintentional (Arnold, 1960). This theory is popular but some questions are still not fully resolved. "Can cognitive emotion theory explain all affective experiences or only a subset of them? What kinds of appraisals (or beliefs and desires) are required for emotions in general, and precisely which appraisal patterns characterize different emotions?" (Reisenzein, 2019, p. 114).

The Theory of Differential Emotions of K. Isard (Izard, 1977) is based on the idea of ten primary emotions: anger, contempt, disgust, distress, fear, guilt, interest, joy, shame, surprise, emotions that cannot be reduced to more basic emotions but that can be combined to produce other emotions. Basic emotions are manifested by specific facial expressions and accompanied by feeling grasped by a person. Emotion includes three interconnected components: neural activity of the brain and peripheral nervous system; activity of striated muscles providing mimic and pantomimic activity; subjective emotional experience. The components have a certain autonomy and can exist independently of others.

Ekman's Neurocultural Theory (Ekman & Friesen, 1978) of emotions takes as a basis the idea of the existence of six basic emotions. According to this theory, the expressive manifestations of basic emotions (anger, fear, sadness, surprise, disgust, happiness) are universal and practically insensitive to environmental factors. Each of the emotions is associated with a genetically determined facial muscle movement program. The external manifestation of emotions is determined by the cultural and historical features of society.

The facial-feedback theory of emotions suggests that facial expressions are connected with experiencing emotions.

By contrast with theories assuming mainly a biological basis of emotions, James Averill (Averill, 1980) views emotions as social constructions. The emotions are defined as socially constituted syndromes or transitory social roles. This conception does not deny the contribution of biological systems to emotional syndromes, but the author supposes that functional significance of emotional responses is to be found largely within the sociocultural system. The book of Rome Harre "Social Construction of Emotions" presented social constructionist approach (Harre, 1989; Parrot, 2019): physiological, cognitive and moral aspects of emotion are examined as part of a social system. Social constructivists consider that the emotions are a product of culture and are conditioned by social norms and cultural norms regulate the rules of who and how can feel and display emotions. Therefore, the emotions manifestations differ in different age and social groups.

It was noted (Reisenzein, 2019) that during the past 30 years, the set of serious contenders for a theory of emotions has been reduced. The research on emotions has made progress in theory, methods and empirical research, but several important issues (for example, about the link between emotions and bodily and facial expressions) are not fully resolved.

Physiological Basis of the Emotion Manifestation in the Facial Expression

The human face is one of the most striking and effective means of communication. By facial expression, people recognize the emotional state of the interlocutors, reacting to the subtle nuances of voice and facial expressions, and build our own behavior. Changing facial expressions is due to the coordinated facial muscle work.

The muscles of facial expression are located in the subcutaneous tissue, originating from bone or fascia, and inserting onto the skin (https://teachmeanatomy.info/head/muscles/facial-expression/). By contracting, the muscles pull on the skin and exert their effects. The muscles and face skin are more closely connected anatomically than the muscles and skin of other areas of the human body. They are the only group of muscles that insert into the skin. The specificity of the facial muscles is that when attached to the skin, they are connected with each other in separate bundles. As a rule, there is a contraction of a whole group of muscles, but only one of the muscles is decisive. The variety of facial expressions depends on the combinations of these abbreviations.

The facial muscles can broadly be split into three groups: orbital, nasal, and oral (Sinelnikov, 2009) (fig. 1). Accordingly, the facial muscles are topographically divided into the muscles of the cranial vault; muscles surrounding the palpebral fissure; the muscles surrounding the nasal openings, the muscles surrounding the oral gap, and the muscles of the auricle.

The orbital group of facial muscles contains two muscles associated with the eye socket. These muscles control the movements of the eyelids. They are both innervated by the facial nerve. The nasal groups of facial muscles are associated with movements of the nose and the skin around it. There are three muscles in this group, and they are all innervated by the facial nerve. The oral group is the most important group of the facial expressors – it is responsible for movements of the mouth and lips. Sometimes a group of chewing muscles is included in the group of facial muscles. Chewing muscles are covered with dense fascia, have a bilateral attachment to the bones. They perform the following functions: closing the mouth, moving the lower jaw forward, back and to the side, articulating movements.

The activity of these muscle groups is the basis for automatic recognition of facial expression systems.

Figure 1. The main groups of facial muscles, modified by https://teachmeanatomy.info/head/muscles/ facial-expression/

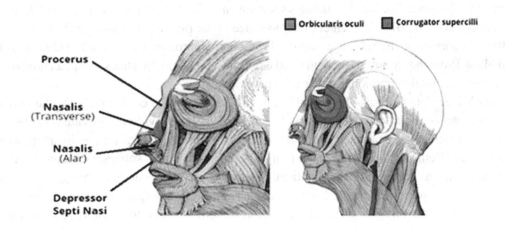

Muscles contract due to the clear motor program in the structures of the brain. This program is based on the processing of information received from the visual sensory system and motivational structures (limbic system).

In typically developing children, the motor program provides the link between the internal (true) state and its external manifestation by facial expression. Thus, the correspondence between links of vegetative, humoral, and nervous factors takes place in the regulation of emotions. The degree of contraction of certain groups of facial muscles is reflected in the force of the emotional expression.

In the case of developmental disorders and / or the child's atypical development, any of the complex links can be violated that leads to a mismatch between the internal state and external manifestation.

The Application of Automatic Systems for Analysis of Video Images: Modern Technologies, Systems, and Application Fields

The analysis of video images has various application areas: market research, health support and medicine, cognitive robotics, psychological research, nonverbal speech recognition, hard and soft biometrics, and much more, that is, the analysis of video images has a wide scope - from cell structures to emotional facial expression of a human.

In the social sphere, the analysis of expression is important. State-of-the-art emotion recognition and psychometric profiling are used to enable investors to objectively understand their own behaviors and how they impact their financial decisions, on the one hand; on the other hand - to assess the formation of the emotional sphere of children, especially children with atypical development, with the aim of further correction and training in the correct (adequate to the situation) emotional response.

Specialized expression analysis software exists. As the most famous, the following can be distinguished:

Amazon Recognition – Amazon Web Services, USA – high-precision face analysis and face recognition from video and images.

Emotion Recognition Software SHORE – Fraunhofer SSD, Germany – real time detection of faces; real time detection on facial features such as eyes and mouth and their state (open/closed); estimation of gender and age; estimation of four facial expressions: "happy – sad – surprised – angry".

Insights Now – NVISO SA, Switzerland - face recognition: face detection, face verification, demographic detection; emotion recognition: facial muscle tracking, emotion classification, action unit detection.

Emodetect – Neurobotics, Russia – defines six main emotions (similar to FaceReader). The company is young, established in 2016, is a center of competence in the field of emotional artificial intelligence; since 2019 - a partner of the robotic company Promobot. Neurodata Lab's neural network technologies will allow Promobot robots to recognize 20 emotions and cognitive states, adapt a communication strategy depending on the emotional state of the participants.

Emotion Miner Data Corpus – Neurodata Lab. LLC, Russia. The corpus contains the multimodal emotion and behavior data for male and female actors, aged 18-28: video (150 videos in the Russian language which include six emotions: joy, anger, sadness, disgust, fear, surprise), audio, motion capture. FaceReader – the Netherlands (on the market for more than 20 years) - software runs on the Microsoft Azure cloud platform. The program automatically identifies six basic emotions "happy – sad – angry – surprised – scared – disgusted", neutral state, and determines gender, age, and ethnicity. Special filters permit to work with the analysis of facial expression of adults and children, starting from the age of four. Automated analysis of facial expressions brings clear insights into the effect of different stimuli on emotions.

Programs differ in terms of accuracy, presence / absence of restrictions (image illumination quality, face position, angle of incidence of light), purpose and price range, and, therefore, accessibility for the user.

The algorithms in the software provided to a user are usually hidden; these algorithms are the know-how of the company producing these programs. Scientific research discusses topic questions in this area more openly. Scientific elaborations are aimed at creating software that can recognize with high accuracy not only basic emotions but also subtle nuances of mood (Martinez, 2017). For example, there is an investigation about which generative model was more suitable to describe the data and the minimum of invariant components required for an accurate approximation of a variety of facial expressions. For this purpose, Nonnegative Matrix Factorization (NMF) and a blind source separation algorithm (FADA) were applied to approximate the temporal profiles of the action units (AU) activation coefficients by superposition of a very small number of source components, defining movement primitives and new Bayesian model selection criterion (Chiovetto, Curio, Endres, & Giese, 2018). A unified probabilistic framework was developed based on the dynamic Bayesian network to simultaneously and coherently represent the facial evolvement in different levels, their interactions and observations (Li, Wang, Zhao, & Ji, 2013).

The history of the use of machine recognition of visual images is fascinating and exciting. The first manuscript on automatic facial recognition was published in 1974 (Parke, 1974). Since then, over 45 years, automated systems have been created with a high level of recognition of video images, including facial expression of a person.

The automatic facial expression/emotion recognition (FER) is a well-known problem in the field of pattern recognition and image analysis (Konar & Chakraborty, 2015), machine learning (Anbarjafari, Rasti, Noroozi, Gorbova, & Haamer, 2018) and constitutes an active research field due to the latest advances in computer vision (Kumar, Jaiswal, Kumar, & Kumar Singh, 2016) and facial biometrics (Kukharev, Kamenskaya, Matveev, & Shchegoleva, 2013).

To solve the problem of automatic FER, two approaches are currently used.

The first is the conventional approach based on classical methods of facial image analysis and recognition (Kukharev et al., 2013), where handcrafted features and traditional methods of machine learning (Anbarjafari et al., 2018) are used. Comprehensive reviews of conventional FERs can been seen in (Huang, Chen, Lv, & Wang, 2019; Ko, 2018; Samadiani et al., 2019).

In the conventional approach, a FER pipeline is composed of the following major steps:

Preprocessing an input facial image. Many practical algorithms for facial image preprocessing can be found in (Konar & Chakraborty, 2015; Anbarjafari et al., 2018; Kumar et al., 2016; Kukharev et al., 2013).

Detecting a face and facial components in an input image. Some practical algorithms for face and facial components detection, especially under varying lighting conditions and complex backgrounds, are given in (Kukharev et al., 2013), including Viola-Jones, color-based and histogram-based approaches. The detected face should be aligned.

Extracting various spatial and temporal features from the detected faces and facial components. Developers of FER algorithms often use such features as AU (Tian, Kanade, & Cohn, 2001) from Ekman's Facial Action Coding System (FACS). This coding technique enables the objective description of facial expressions based on individual muscle activations.

Other key features are key points or facial landmarks, which are potentially more descriptive of faces in unconstrained environments than FACS (Josey & Acharya, 2018). Many different methods have been developed to calculate the coordinates of key points, for example, the Active Appearance Model (AMM) (https://www.menpo.org/menpofit/aam.html). AAM is a generative model which while fitting aims to recover a parametric description of a certain object through optimization. Usually from 5 to 68 points are extracted, tying them to the position of facial components, which allows capturing facial expressions. The resulting feature vector is composed of normalized coordinates of key points or their derivatives.

Simple use of coordinates without a visual component leads to a significant loss of useful information, therefore, to improve the FER system performance, various descriptors of emotions are usually calculated, such as Local Binary Pattern (LBP), Histogram of Oriented Gradient (HOG), scale-invariant feature transform (SIFT), etc. For example, it is possible to concatenate the descriptors, reduce the dimensionality with principal component analysis (PCA), and use the resulting feature vector to classify emotions (Huang et al., 2019; Ko, 2018; Samadiani et al., 2019). Combinations of different models are used not only to enhance the accuracy of the emotion recognition (RBF SVM HOG+LBP model attained the highest average accuracy of 0.94 across the seven emotions, (Kwong, Garcia, Abu, & Reyes, 2018)), also in medical image analysis (for example: Alhindi, Kalra, Hin, Afrin, & Tizhoosh, 2018).

Classifying a predefined set of expression/emotions is based on the use of well-known classifiers such as Random Forest, Support Vector Machine, Artificial Neural Networks, etc.

In contrast to traditional approaches, which use handcrafted features, the second approach is based on deep learning, where the input image is fed directly into the "end-to-end" pipeline, the output of which is an emotion/expression class. The convolutional neural network (CNN), a particular type of deep learning, is the most popular in various pattern recognition applications (Ko, 2018; Li & Deng, 2018).

The advantages of deep neural networks (DNN) are that, having a good generalizing ability, they work in a universal situation and produce results even in poor lighting conditions. This may work well in ordinary applications, but it is not suitable for a deeper analysis of a psychophysiological state. For in-depth psychophysiological research, classical pattern recognition & image processing and such features as landmarks and FACS are used. Under good lighting conditions, they are more accurate than neural networks. In contrast to the traditional approach, large and representative datasets are needed to train deep neural networks that can be an essential limitation in some applications due to the lack of such databases. Deep FER systems might require a considerable dataset to learn each expression of each particular individual at a specific age and with large pose variations (Samadiani et al, 2019).

Let's take the detailed description of the FaceReader version 8.0 program (Noldus, Netherlands) used in this study. FaceReader accurately finds the location and size of faces in arbitrary scenes under varying lighting conditions and complex backgrounds and combines it with eye detection (https://facereader-online.com/technology).

The newest version 8.0 of FaceReader software authors used in the study, therefore, the algorithms and capabilities are consider in more detail. FaceReader classifies the face in three consecutive steps (Noldus Information Technology, the Netherlands. FaceReader 7.1. Technical Specification. 2019): face finding, modeling, classification.

First, an accurate position of the face is found. FaceReader uses the Viola-Jones algorithm to detect the presence of a face. Eye detection is used to store information about the likely rotation of a face in a plane.

The second step – 3D modeling of the face using an algorithmic approach based on the AAM. To build a face model, FaceReader uses AAM. The model describes over 500 key points in the face and the facial texture of the face entangled by these points, where the key points define the global position and the shape of the face, and the texture gives extra information about the state of the face, for example, the presence of wrinkles and the shape of the eyebrows. New faces can be described as deviations from the mean face using a compact vector called the "appearance vector".

The AAM manages to compactly model individual facial variations in addition to variations related to pose/orientation, lighting and facial expression [https://facereader-online.com/technology].

On the next step to classify facial expression, FaceReader uses artificial neural network that is fed with the face model. Over 10000 pictures labeled by experts were used to train the emotional expression classifiers, achieving 89% classification accuracy (Terzis, Moridis, & Economides, 2010).

Another option is the use of CNN to directly detect the facial expressions from the input image. In this case, no face finding or modeling is needed. The advantage of FaceReader is that it can analyze the face in diverse lighting conditions, head poses and if part of a face is hidden. To enhance the accuracy of FER, AMM and CNN can be used jointly. If AMM fails, CNN is used stand-alone (https://facereader-online.com/technology).

FaceReader uses the general face model, which works well under most circumstances for most people, and also models for East Asian people, elderly, children and special – versus – for (babies) infants (6-24 months).

Recognition accuracy is different in different versions of FaceReader software. In 2005, matching scores of 89% were reported for FaceReader version 5. FaceReader version 6 recognized 88% of the target emotional labels in the Warsaw Set of Emotional Facial Expression Pictures (WSEFEP) and Amsterdam Dynamic Facial Expression Set (ADFES). The software reached a FACS index of agreement of 0.67 on average in both datasets (Lewinski, den Uyl, & Butler, 2014). Validation of the software FaceReader v. 7 has been done (Skiendziel, Rosch, & Schultheiss, 2019). FaceReader accomplished correct classifications of the intended emotion expressions in 79% and 80% of the cases without and with calibration, respectively. Compared to emotion classification results obtained with FaceReader version 6 (Lewinski et al., 2014), version 7 (Skiendziel et al., 2019) performed somewhat poorer in certain conditions. The authors explain the differences in software packages and different versions of this package by use different data sets for learning their algorithms, particularly if they are applied to different and novel sets of pictures (Skiendziel et al., 2019). In our study, FaceReader version 8.0 was used, but authors emphasize, worked as users without testing the software.

MAIN FOCUS OF THE CHAPTER

The aim of the study is to identify the state of a person (child and adult) in situations when their behavior is spontaneous. Authors considered the facial expression as the physiological indicator of the human internal state. The facial expression was estimated using the FaceReader program, which is a reliable tool for scientific research. We analyzed several situations in which children and adults showed acting skills for the manifestation of emotions and natural emotions. The situations when adults and children read and utter emotional words and phrases are a fairly standardized situation conducted in a laboratory. It shows the ability of the child and adult to manifest a certain state required by a given text. The situations of interaction between mothers and preschool typically developing (TD) children, children with autism spectrum disorders (ASD) and Down syndrome (DS); between orphans and the adult experimenter, children and their peers – were recorded in a natural condition. These recordings provide us more important information that could be considered when building maternal behavior with atypically developing children. The analysis of the emotional sphere of children brought up in maternal deprivation in an orphanage is no less important. The pilot study on the analysis of facial expression of children with DS was carried out. The difficulties encountered in the study are analyzed and the perspectives are determined.

Experimental Results

Five experimental series were conducted. The videos were filmed with a SONY HDR-CX560E camera (maximal resolution 1920x1080 at 50 frames) in the room of the laboratory (study 1), at home (study 2), in the orphanage and kindergartens (study 3, 4), in Down center and in the orphanage (study 5). The conditions of good illumination of the room observed were only in the laboratory to provide good frontal light on the face of the participant and a look directly into the camera. The recordings were saved as AVI files.

Study 1. Model Situation – Reading and Speaking the Emotional Words and Phrases

The aim of the first experimental series was to determine the facial expression of participants reading and speaking words and phrases in different emotional states: neutral, joy (happy), fear (scare), anger, and sadness. The words and phrases reflecting different emotional states were selected, i.e. the lexical meaning of words was emotionally colored - /fear, anger, sadness, I love when it is beautiful, I am scared, dark and scared /, etc. The participants should pronounce the speech material, manifesting the emotional state. This task was designed to show the "acting skills" of the participants, i.e. how they can demonstrate different states in the characteristics of the voice and facial expressions. An additional task was to use the newest version of the FaceReader program, version 8, for facial expression analysis.

Based on the algorithms of the FaceReader program (see: The application of automatic systems for analysis of video images: modern technologies, systems, and application fields), the time during which the participant manifested the emotional state in facial expression was determined from the total duration of the task (the task is to express the certain emotion). The program automatically counted the duration of each emotional state manifestation in facial expression for all participants.

The participants of study 1 were non-actor adults (n = 10, 7 women, 3 men), the age of participants was 22-33 years (25.1 $\pm$ 4.2 y), and children (n = 6) at the age of 5, 5.5, 8, 8.5, 12 and 14 years.

It was found that adults displayed the neutral state (78.2% of the time – women and 77.9% - men) and happy (43.7% - women and 25.2% – men) better than other states (table 1, 2). The difficulties in manifesting the states of fear (11.2% - women; 0% - men), sadness (9.2% - women; 7.3% - men) were revealed for all adult participants. The text corresponding to the emotion of anger caused in men a better manifestation of the corresponding emotion (15.1%) than in women (5.1%). Men did not show a state of fear (the anger was manifested instead of fear – 5.2%) (table 2).

Table 1. The facial expression of women reading and speaking the emotional speech material (duration, %)

emotional state	neutral	happy	sad	angry	scared	other
neutral	78.2	3.2	5	3.5	2.6	7.5
happy	43.8	43.7	0.6	0.7	3.9	7.3
sad	78.6		9.2	2.6	3.8	5.8
angry	63.3	8.6	3.5	5.1	7.2	12.3
scared	65.5	2.6	3.9	3.5	11.2	13.3

Table 2. The facial expression of men reading and speaking the emotional speech material (duration, %)

emotional state	neutral	happy	sad	angry	scared	other
neutral	77.9	1.1	2.5	10.4		8.1
happy	51.8	25.2	1.4	2.3		19.3
sad	74.8	3.3	7.3	7		7.6
angry	63.7	4.8		15.1	1.2	15.2
scared	65.4	3.9	2.1	5.2		23.4

All the children manifested facial expression corresponding to the happy state (85.6% - 5 years, 94.7% - 8 years, 92.8% - 14 years) better than corresponding to sadness, anger, and fear (fig. 2).

Figure 2. The facial expression of children speaking the emotional speech material

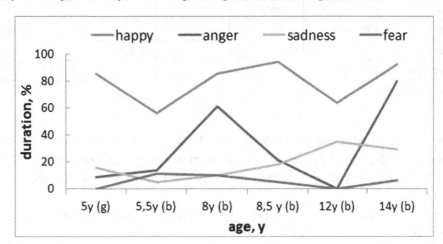

The reflection of different emotional states in the facial expression of children was very individual. 5 year old children manifested the neutral and happy states better than sadness and anger, but they did not demonstrate facial expression corresponding to the state of fear.

8.5 year old boy, like 5 year old children, showed the neutral and happy states more longer than sadness and fear (table 3, fig. 3). 14 year old boy demonstrated the state of anger longer than other children (80% - for 14 year old boy when pronouncing the words).

Figure 3. Program FaceReader v. 8.0 – facial expression corresponding to the happy state (boy, 8.5 years old)

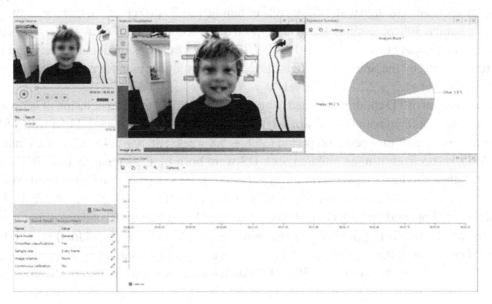

Table 3. The facial expression of 8.5 year old boy uttering the speech material that reflects emotional states (duration, %)

emotional state	neutral	happy	sad	angry	scared	other
neutral	85.6/90					14.4/10
happy		94.7/96.2				5.3/3.8
sad	75.9/70.8	10.4/	/18.3			13.7/10.9
angry	61.2/39.3	/5.5	9.4/26.6	21.3/23.2		8.1/5.4
scared	79.4/32.4				5.3/53.2	15.3/14.4

Note: the data for words / phrases

The gender and age of adults were also determined by the program. The gender of the participants was determined correctly, with the exception of one woman. Her gender was classified as female with the level of 60%. All the ages of adult participants were determined correctly (in the range suggested by the program).

In accordance with the task of study 1, the bright manifestations of emotions in facial expression were not expected.

Study 2. Mother-Child Interaction

Studying the speech behavior strategies of mothers of TD children, children with ASD and children with DS (Lyakso, Frolova, Grigorev, Gorodnyi, & Nikolaev, 2019), one of the tasks is to determine the state of the mother and child in the process of interaction. The participants of the study were 86 mother-child dyads with 4-7 year old children: 40 dyads with TD children, 25 dyads with children with ASD, 21 dyads with children with DS.

The age of mothers of children with DS (36.7 ± 6.4 y) at the time of child's birth was higher than that of TD children's mothers (28.6 ± 5.6 y) and mothers of children with ASD (29.7 ± 5.0 y). Families of children with TD and DS were complete. For 48% of children with ASD, the families were incomplete. In 50% of families with children with DS and 40% of families with ASD children, there were two or three children in a family; 30% of families with TD children had a second child. For mothers of children with ASD, the level of anxiety (26.1 ± 12.7 and 45.1 ± 10.7 - the levels of situational anxiety and personal anxiety, respectively, by the Spielberger-Hanin Inventory) was higher than for mothers of children with DS (21.5 ± 10.6 and 41.2 ± 2.1 – respectively).

The development of TD children matched to age norms according to the conclusion of neonatologists and pediatricians. Children with DS had worse rates of early development than children with ASD. They are characterized by a shorter gestation period (35.8 ± 5.8 weeks; 38.8 ± 3.4 weeks - for children with DS and ASD, respectively); more children with DS were born by Caesarean section (22% and 10%, respectively); they had lower Apgar scores (6.6 ± 1.6/7.2 ± 1.7 – Apgar 1 and 2 for children with DS; 7.5 ± 1.1/8.3 ± 1.0 – for children with ASD), lower weight (2891.1 ± 677 g – for DS; 3581.3 ± 701g – for ASD). 77.8% of children with DS had no cooing; babbling, first words, and gross motor skills appeared later. Mothers report aggression in most children with ASD (79% of children) vs. children with DS (56%). The manifestation of emotions was adequate to the situation in a larger number of children with DS vs. children with ASD (55% and 50% of children – for children with DS and ASD, respectively).

Children with ASD are characterized by regression in the development (73% of children). Mothers of ASD children observed the regression in the child's development at the age of 1 year to 2.5 years (1.9 ± 0.5 years). Mothers of children with DS did not indicate the age of regression in the child's development. Points of CARS scale for children with ASD were 36.3 ± 6.0 points that characterize verbal development were 3.1 ± 0.6.

The perceptual experiment was made. The experts (n = 5 adults) viewed video tests containing fragments of video recording of the mother-child interaction situation in the natural conditions (the duration of each fragment was 1 minute) without a soundtrack. They had to describe for mothers and children if they smile, are satisfied or dissatisfied.

According to the experts' answers, mothers of children with DS were more often dissatisfied with their children vs. mothers of children with ASD and TD. Mothers of children with DS smiled less vs. mothers of TD children and children with ASD (table 4). In the process of interaction with the mother, children with DS more often were dissatisfied than TD children and children with ASD were. Children with ASD smiled less vs. TD and DS children.

Table 4. Experts' answers for mother's and child's states during the interaction,%

participants		smile	satisfied	dissatisfied
mothers of children	TD	51	66	7
	ASD	50	50	3
	DS	36	40	19
children	TD	56	67	1
	ASD	19	31	19
	DS	33	46	47

The automatic analysis of the facial expression of the mother and the child during the interaction in natural conditions was carried out. In contrast to the human perceptual experiment for analysis in the FaceReader program, the video fragments were selected where the mother and child looked at the camera or the rotation of their head did not exceed 45 degrees. Indoor light did not always illuminate the participants' faces.

For each dyad, fragments of video recordings of the child, mother, joint, corresponding to the requirements of the analysis in program FaceReader were identified: sufficient illumination of the face and face location. Video fragments for all children of one diagnosis were combined into a single file, video fragments of their mothers in another, and video fragments of joint interaction in the third file, if separate analysis was impossible.

This approach allowed us to determine for each type of dyad (with TD, ASD, and DS children) the duration of facial expression corresponding to the different emotional states in the mothers and children separately and together.

The analysis of facial expression showed that mothers of children of the three groups displayed mainly the neutral state. Mothers of children with ASD and DS more often showed the neutral facial expression than mothers of TD children did (46.1% - TD, 62% - ASD, 80.3% - DS). In dyads with TD children, the mothers manifested more joy (25.2%), sadness (7.5%), and anger (5.4%) than mothers of children with ASD (11.3% - joy, 5.7% - sadness, 2.6% - anger) and mothers of children with DS (7.1% - joy, 0% - sadness, 3.8% - anger).

TD children showed joy (18.1%) longer than children with ASD (3.6%) and children with DS (2.4%). Children with ASD demonstrated the state of surprise (18.3%) for a long time. Children with DS, according to the analysis, did not show a state of fear, unlike TD children (0.6%) and children with ASD (2%) (table 5).

Table 5. The facial expression of mother and child during the interaction in the dyad (duration, %)

	Facial expression							
	neutral	happy	sad	angry	surprised	scared	disgusted	other
Dyads with TD children								
mother	46.1	25.2	7.5	5.4		3.5	4.1	8.2
child	53.8	18.1	8.4	6.5	3.3	0.6	1.9	7.4
together*	61.5	16.2	9	2.1	1.2			10.2
Dyads with ASD children								
mother	62	11.3	5.7	2.6	1.1	2.5	8.8	6
child	53.4	3.6	6.4	3.8	18.3	2	3.1	9.4
together	60.4	8	9.3	9.1	2.1	1.6	1.7	7.8
Dyads with DS children								
mother	80.3	7.1		3.8	2.5			6.3
child	61.1	2.4	5.3	3.9	12.3		6.8	8.2
together	56.6	13.9	2.8	2.7	12.2	3	1.6	7.2

Note: * together – the change of actions of partners occurred very quickly, so the "Face Reader" program analyzed the facial expression of the mother and the child together

The analysis of emotional behavior of the mother and child in the perceptual experiment, allowed us to determine a neutral and emotional state. Mothers of children with DS longer manifested the neutral state (80.3%). Mothers of TD children expressed the happy state more frequently and the neutral state less frequently vs. mothers of children with DS and ASD. Mothers of children with DS expressed a negative emotional state - sad, fear, disgust, less frequently vs. mothers of children with ASD. The data on emotional states of children obtained in the human perceptual experiment and automatic recognition by the FaceReader program are similar.

The data on children with DS could be corrected in the future because the FaceReader software has not been tested on this type of person. Authors conducted a special study to analyze the facial expression of 4-16 year old children with DS (see study 5).

Study 3. The facial Expression of Orphans and Children Grown up in Families

The analysis of the facial expression of children brought up in families and in an orphanage during the interaction with the adult (experimenter) was made. It is known that children from orphanages have some features of cognitive and emotional development associated with factors of maternal and social deprivation

(Bick et al., 2015; Cameron, Eagleson, Fox, Hensch, & Levitt, 2017). In our study, the analysis of facial expression of emotional state in children from orphanage and families was conducted in the situation of dialogue with the adult. The adult (experimenter) standardized the behavior and asked the same questions about walks, games, and favorite animals during the interaction with all of the children. The purpose of the study is to determine the effect of social deprivation on the emotional manifestations of children.

The participants were 5-7 year old children. Orphans were divided into three groups in accordance with diagnoses: children without psychiatric diagnoses (TD-o, n = 8), with mixed specific developmental disorders (MDD-o, n = 20) and with light intellectual disabilities (ID-o, n = 12). These children were the group of orphans with "light diagnoses", without cerebral palsy and genetic syndromes. Children growing up in families were typically developing (TD, n = 25) and with mixed specific developmental disorders (MDD, n = 13).

On the first step of the study, the perceptual experiment was made. The experts (n=6 adults) viewed video tests containing fragments of video recording of interaction between adult and child (the duration was 1 minute) without a soundtrack. It was the fragments of an adult-child dialogue when the child answers the adult's questions about walks and games. The method is similar to study 2. They had to mark for children only if they smiled, were satisfied or dissatisfied.

According to the experts' answers, TD children from families smiled more vs. other groups of children (table 6); they were more satisfied than children with ID. Experts gave the answers "dissatisfied" for orphans (with TD, MDD, and TD), but not for children from families.

Table 6. Experts' answers for child's states during the interaction with the adult, %

group of children*	Facial expression		
	smile	satisfied	dissatisfied
ID-o	68	60	3
MDD-o	60	64	7
TD-o	64	64	4
MDD	60	60	0
TD	72	66	0

Note:* ID-o – orphans with light intellectual disabilities, MDD – orphans with mixed specific developmental disorders, TD-o – orphans without psychiatric diagnoses, MDD – children from families with mixed specific developmental disorders, TD – children from families without psychiatric diagnoses (typically developing)

For analysis in the FaceReader program the video files were prepared separately for each group of children (see procedure of analysis in Study 2). A similar approach was used in the Studies 4, 5.

Based on the FaceReader data, the children of all the groups more often demonstrated the neutral state: 45.04% in the ID-o group, 54.7% in the MDD-o group, 57% - TD-o, 56.6% - MDD, and 60.2% - TD vs. emotional state.

Orphans more often vs. children from families manifested the facial expression corresponding to a state of joy (17.5%; 15.4%; 11.4%; 13.7%; 11.2% - in groups of ID-o, MDD-o, TD-o, MDD, TD, respectively). Orphans with intellectual disabilities and developmental disorders more often manifested anger (3.7%, 5.5% - ID-o and MDD-o, respectively) than children with TD did (1.9% - TD-o and 1.7% - TD) (table 7).

Table 7. Facial expression of children during the interaction with the adult (duration, %)

group of children	Facial expression							
	neutral	happy	sad	angry	surprised	scared	disgusted	other
ID-o	45	17.5	7.6	3.7	11.9	2.3	4	8
MDD-o	54.7	15.4	7.1	5.5	5.8		5	6.5
TD-o	57	11.4	4.3	1.9	10.3	2.7	6.6	5.8
MDD	56.6	13.7	10.7	2.5	4.7	2.4	2.7	6.7
TD	60.2	11.2	3.9	1.7	11.2	2.3	1.9	7.6

It can be assumed that the manifestation of happy state in orphans is associated with the additional attention shown by the experimenter to them. The effect of the disease factor is shown. Children with developmental disabilities, regardless of their upbringing in a family or orphanage, show more anger vs. TD children. This finding may be verified in future studies.

Study 4. Interaction Between Children

The analysis of the facial expression of the child during the situation of interaction between the children and the peers was made. The participants were children from groups taking part in study 3. Children with ID, MDD and TD from orphanage were combined in the orphans group and their facial expression was analyzed together (table 8).

Most of the time, all children showed a neutral state (50%, 44.5%, and 59.5% of the time - for orphans, children with MDD and TD children from families, respectively). All children showed more facial expression corresponding to a state of joy when interacting with peers than when interacting with an adult. Facial expressions corresponding to the states of fear, anger, and disgust were longer in children from the orphanage (table 8).

Table 8. Facial expression of children during the interaction with peers (duration, %)

group of children	Facial expression							
	neutral	happy	sad	angry	surprised	scared	disgusted	other
orphans	50.0	24.7	5.3	2.3	2.7	0.3	7.2	7.5
MDD	44.5	32.3	6.3	1.8	4.7		3.2	7.2
TD	59.5	22.1	5.3	1.5	2.3		2.7	6.6

If children with ID were included in the interaction between orphans, more facial expressions of aggression and joy were observed. If children with ID were excluded from the interaction, more facial expressions corresponding to sadness and disgust were revealed (table 9).

Table 9. Facial expression of orphans during the interaction with peers (duration, %)

groups of children	Facial expression							
	neutral	happy	sad	angry	surprised	scared	disgusted	other
ID-o, MDD-o, & TD-o	50.7	26.3	3.8	3.4	2.2		6.0	7.6
MDD-o & TD-o	49.3	23.0	6.8	1.1	3.1	0.7	8.5	7.5

The limitations of these studies are established in the program. The situation of video recording caused the difficulties: the feature of the program FaceReader is the ability to analyze images of full faces (not in profile) in good light. The records were made in a natural interaction, which did not allow us to analyze all the video recordings of the interaction.

Study 5. Specificity of the Analysis of Facial Expression of Children with Atypical Development – Down Syndrome

The special study of the facial expression of 4-16 year old children with DS (n=37) during situations of interaction with adults was conducted.

Children with DS are characterized by features in the structure of speech organs: a large folded tongue, a small volume of the oral cavity, a lowered lower jaw, a high, narrow arcuate palate, therefore sounds are sometimes made more "nasal"; shorter length of the vocal cords, muscle hypotension (Markaki & Stylianou, 2011). Most children with DS have an open bite, small, narrower than usual upper jaw. Children are short, their nose and face flattened, eyes slanted. They are good-natured, sociable, and show sympathy for their interlocutor (Kumin, 2003).

16 children with DS (4-16 years old; 8 boys and 8 girls) were brought up in families. All the children have education classes, sports, music and dance lessons in the Child developmental center. The video recordings of the child's behavior and facial expression were made in the Child developmental center in the situations of interaction between the child, experimenter, and parents.

21 children with DS (4-15 years old; 18 boys and 3 girls) were brought up in an orphanage. The video recordings were made in the classroom of the orphanage during the interaction between the child and the experimenter.

The situations of interaction were: dialogues, play with the standard set of toys, picture description. The duration of every situation was 5 minutes (some children stopped interacting themselves up to 5 minutes).

For the following analysis by FaceReader, the 1-minute fragments of video recordings when the child looks directly at the camera were chosen. It was the problem to find such fragments for most children with DS because they often switched their attention from one object to another turning their heads. Data analysis was made for children from families and the orphanage, for boys and girls separately.

According to the data analysis most of the time the children with DS from families were in the neutral emotional state. The girls manifested the neutral state longer than boys; boys demonstrated happy and sad longer vs. girls (table 10). The emotional states of 2 boys (12 and 16 years old) and 2 girls (4.5 and 9 years old) were not determined by the program.

Although the FaceReader program detected the emotions of children with DS, the program is worse at detecting the gender and age of children. The child's gender was defined correctly only for 3 boys

Table 10. Facial expression of children with DS from families during the interaction with the adult (duration, %)

gender	Facial expression							
	neutral	happy	sad	angry	surprised	scared	disgusted	other
f	62.8	12.5	4.9	3.6	4.2	2.5	1.2	8.3
m	59.6	5.9	4.3	5	10.6	4.1	4.5	6

Note: f - female, m - male

(9-15 years old) and for 3 girls (7-13 years old). The age was correctly defined only for two children, for other children the age was determined as older (or not determined at all). Difficulties in determining the emotions, gender, and age of children with DS are caused by the features of DS child's face (the geometric proportions of the faces of children with DS are different from those of TD children).

For the orphans, the situation of interacting with an adult was a bit like a lesson. However, children with DS from the orphanage were more emotional vs. children with DS from families: they demonstrated less facial expression corresponding to the neutral state vs. children brought up with parents. Boys from orphanage demonstrated more the neutral state than girls did. Girls manifested more aggression, fear vs. boys. Boys manifested more surprise and disgust vs. girls (table 11).

Table 11. Facial expression of orphans with DS during the interaction with the adult (duration, %)

gender	Facial expression							
	neutral	happy	sad	angry	surprised	scared	disgusted	other
f	47.6	11.3	2.4	9.5	15.9	6.4		6.9
m	49.8	11.7	4.9	3.7	19.8	1	1.5	7.6

The child's gender was defined correctly only for 6 boys (8-15 years old) and for 2 girls (7, 12 years old). The age range was correctly defined for 5 children (1 girl and 4 boys), for other children the age was determined as older or not determined at all.

CONCLUSION

The results of a model experiment in which adults and children pronounced emotional words and phrases showed the ability to reflect the emotional state caused by the text in their facial expression. Adult participants manifested the neutral state and the happy state better than other emotional states, all the children demonstrated facial expression corresponding to the state of happiness better than corresponding to sadness, anger, and fear.

The analysis of facial expression during the interaction in mother-child dyads with TD children, children with ASD and DS revealed the specificity of emotion manifestation of the mother and the child, depending on the child's diagnosis. Facial expression of mothers of children of the three groups was neutral. An analysis of emotional expression showed that mothers of TD children demonstrated more happiness emotions, facial expressions of mothers of children with DS are characterized by neutral emotional state, mothers of ASD children showed a wide range of emotions with a predominant manifestation of happy and disgust.

Children with ASD demonstrated the facial expression corresponding to the state of surprise more vs. TD children and children with DS. Children with DS, according to the analysis, did not show a state of fear.

Comparison of facial expression of orphans with different diagnoses and children brought up in families showed that during interaction with adult orphans with ID manifested less facial expression corresponding to the neutral state vs. orphans with MDD, TD and children from families (especially TD children from families). Orphans more often manifested the facial expression corresponding to a state of happiness vs. children from families. Orphans with ID and MDD more often manifested anger than children with TD did. Children with developmental disabilities, regardless of their upbringing in a family or orphanage, showed more aggression vs. TD children. All children showed more facial expression corresponding to a state of joy when interacting with peers than when interacting with an adult. Facial expressions corresponding to the states of fear, anger, and disgust in the situation of interaction with peers were more often in orphans.

The specificity of the facial expression in children with DS growing up in orphanage and families during the interaction with adults was described. Orphans with DS expressed less facial expression corresponding to the neutral state and more facial expressions corresponding to the state of happy (boys) and surprise vs. children with DS from families.

DISCUSSION

A brief description of the use of the automated program FaceReader by users for recognition of facial expression in scientific research is presented.

There are various possibilities for evaluating facial expression reflecting emotional states. In studies devoted to the analysis of the cognitive and emotional development of a child, the method of visual perceptual experiment is widely used. The method involves the recognition by groups of people of different gender, age, nationality, experience (professional, household or absence) of various states of children by static and dynamic images. The advantage of this approach is the ability of the human brain to recognize the subtle nuances of a person's state by mimic expression, based on significant signs. Moreover, the significance of the signs is first formed involuntarily, practically, starting with the birth of the child, and as he is socialized and educated, it is supplemented and fixed, leading to an automated fast correct determination of the state. However, despite the fact that this ability is, to one degree or another, inherent in all Homo sapiens, its implementation depends on many factors: motivation, general functional and psychological state, degree of formation of emotional intelligence, and much more. Erroneous interpretations of the interlocutor's facial expressions can lead to a misunderstanding of the situation and can worsen the quality of interaction.

In experiments, as a rule, several people take part as experts. Therefore, in this case, to make a judgment requires that the opinions of experts coincide. For example, the study showed that adults (n = 90 adults) have difficulty in recognizing the emotional state of TD children aged 4-7 years by video images (Lyakso, Frolova, Grigor'ev, Sokolova, & Yarotskaya, 2017). When viewing the TD test containing photographs of TD children in different emotional states, the adults recognized 12% of presented images with probability of 0.75-1.0 and 13.6% of images with probability of 0.5-0.74 as reflecting a state of comfort. They attributed 15.6% of images with probability of 0.75-1.0 and 4% of images with probability of 0.5-0.74 to reflecting a state of discomfort. Women recognized significantly better the state of children than men by facial expression images (Lyakso et al., 2017).

Age is negatively associated with the accuracy of decoding emotional facial expressions. It has been shown that it is more difficult to decode the emotional expressions of older actors than younger actors (Hess, Adams, Simard, Stevenson, & Kleck, 2012), older evaluators are more difficult to decode facial expressions than younger ones (Ruffman, Henry, Livingstone, & Phillips, 2008). For example, happy faces are perceived as younger (Völkle, Ebner, Lindenberger, & Riediger, 2012), old ones are sad (Fölster, Hess, Hühnel, & Werheid, 2015).

A type of material provided to experts for analysis – static or dynamic images – is important. Static images are recognized worse than dynamic ones (video fragments). So, when recognizing the emotional states of children with ASD aged 6-12 years, experts (n = 5) correctly attributed more fragments of videos to the corresponding categories "comfort - neutral - discomfort" than when recognizing by photographs (Lyakso et al., 2017).

The dynamic state is inherent in the human face, facial expressions of a person is mobile because facial muscles are involved not only in emotion reflection but also in conversation. In this regard, part of the limitations caused by human recognition of facial expression is removed if automatic recognition based on pre-selected features is used.

The FaceReader program used in the study was widely used in various studies in the analysis of facial expression of children and adults in solving different problems.

A stratum of research using the FaceReader program is dedicated to lie recognition (for example – Gadea, Aliño, Espert, & Salvador, 2015). In this study, the program classified the video as a neutral or emotional facial expression when analyzing video fragments in which the children told the truth or lies. Lies expressed by emotional facial expressions are easier to recognize than lies expressed by "poker faces". The intensity of the expression of emotion influenced recognition (Gadea et al., 2015).

The ability to manifest emotions was analyzed in 6-8-year-old children with "emotional numbing" as a symptom of post-traumatic stress disorder (Fujiwara, Mizuki, Miki, & Chemtob, 2015). An interesting study was conducted using FaceReader v. 7 to provide empirical data on the production of basic emotional facial expressions in Japanese laypeople. The results of the analysis of target emotions in photography showed that expressions of target emotions were reflected more clearly in facial expression than all other emotions for all facial expressions when participants imitated photographs of prototypical facial expressions. According to the authors' conclusions, the results provide partial support for the theory of universal, prototypical facial expressions for basic emotions (Sato, Hyniewska, Minemoto, & Yoshikawa, 2019).

Authors described the results of five studies using the newest version of the FaceReader program - version 8.0, which allows us to include high recognition accuracy, since each subsequent version of the program is more accurate (Lewinski et al., 2014; Terzis et al., 2010).

The study made it possible to obtain interesting results, but also showed corrections to be made to the research protocol, and in which situations the program works well, and which questions should be referred to developers to improve recognition accuracy.

FUTURE RESEARCH DIRECTIONS

The FaceReader v. 8.0 program has not been tested (and not intended) on the faces of informants with DS, but psychophysiological and psychological studies are needed to assess the state of children with atypical development.

The situation of video recording caused the difficulties: the feature of the program FaceReade is the ability to analyze images of full faces (not in profile) in good light. Most of the video records (excluding study 1) were made in interaction situations. All the children, especially children with DS and ASD, were not ready to look at the camera for a long time, without making head movements and moving in the room that complicated the program work.

To eliminate the problem of non-frontal faces, in (Lai & Lai, 2018) a multi-view FER was proposed that uses the Generative Adversarial Networks (GAN)-based approach to frontalization of non-frontal images while retaining the identity and expression information. This approach demonstrated its effectiveness for FER with visible head pose variations. Later we proceed further and proposed the Identity and Pose Disentangled GAN (IP-GAN) (Zeno, Kalinovskiy, & Matveev, 2019) that learns to disentangle identity and pose representations of the data in an unsupervised mode. IP-GAN can make face frontalization preserving the identity and expression without any assumptions about the pose, expression, or identity of a source face image. We are planning to use this approach as a preprocessing step for FaceReader to enhance the performance of FER for children with DS and ASD.

ACKNOWLEDGMENT

This study is financially supported by the Russian Foundation for Basic Research [grant numbers: 19-57-45008–IND_a; 17-06-00503-OGN, 18-013-01133], Russian Science Foundation [grant number 18-18-00063].

REFERENCES

Alhindi, T. J., Kalra, S., Hin, N. K., Afrin, A., & Tizhoosh, H. R. (2018). Comparing LBP, HOG and deep features for classification of histopathology images. In *2018 International Joint Conference on Neural Networks (IJCNN)* (pp. 1-7). Rio de Janeiro, Brazil: IEEE. 10.1109/IJCNN.2018.8489329

Anbarjafari, G., Rasti, P., Noroozi, F., Gorbova, J., & Haamer, R.E. (2018). *Machine learning for face, emotion, and pain recognition.* SPIE. DOI: doi:10.1117/3.2322572

Arnold, M. B. (1960). *Emotion and personality.* New York: Columbia University Press.

Averill, J. R. (1980). A constructivist view of emotion. In R. Plutchik & H. Kellerman (Eds.), *Theories of emotion* (pp. 305–339). New York: Academic Press. doi:10.1016/B978-0-12-558701-3.50018-1

Bick, J., Zhu, T., Stamoulis, C., Fox, N. A., Zeanah, C., & Nelson, C. A. (2017). Early deprivation, atypical brain development, and internalizing symptoms in late childhood. *Neuroscience, 342,* 140–153. doi:10.1016/j.neuroscience.2015.09.026 PMID:26384960

Cameron, J. L., Eagleson, K. L., Fox, N. A., Hensch, T. K., & Levitt, P. (2017). Social origins of developmental risk for mental and physical illness. *The Journal of Neuroscience*, *37*(45), 10783–10791. doi:10.1523/JNEUROSCI.1822-17.2017 PMID:29118206

Chiovetto, E., Curio, C., Endres, D., & Giese, M. (2018). Perceptual integration of kinematic components in the recognition of emotional facial expressions. *Journal of Vision (Charlottesville, Va.)*, *18*(4), 13. doi:10.1167/18.4.13 PMID:29710303

Ekman, P., & Friesen, W. V. (1978). *Facial action coding system: A technique for the measurement of facial movement.* Palo Alto, CA: Consulting Psychologists Press.

Fölster, M., Hess, U., Hühnel, I., & Werheid, K. (2015). Age-related response bias in the decoding of sad facial expressions. *Behavioral Science*, *5*(4), 443–460. doi:10.3390/bs5040443 PMID:26516920

Friedman, B. H. (2010). Feelings and the body: The Jamesian perspective on autonomic specificity of emotion. *Biological Psychology*, *84*(3), 383–393. doi:10.1016/j.biopsycho.2009.10.006 PMID:19879320

Fujiwara, T., Mizuki, R., Miki, T., & Chemtob, C. (2015). Association between facial expression and PTSD symptoms among young children exposed to the Great East Japan Earthquake: A pilot study. *Frontiers in Psychology*, *6*, 1534. doi:10.3389/fpsyg.2015.01534 PMID:26528206

Gadea, M., Aliño, M., Espert, R., & Salvador, A. (2015). Deceit and facial expression in children: The enabling role of the "poker face" child and the dependent personality of the detector. *Frontiers in Psychology*, *6*, 1089. doi:10.3389/fpsyg.2015.01089 PMID:26284012

Harré, R. (1989). *The Social Construction of Emotions.* Oxford, UK: Blackwell Pub.

Hess, U., Adams, R. B. J. Jr, Simard, A., Stevenson, M. T., & Kleck, R. E. (2012). Smiling and sad wrinkles: Age-related changes in the face and the perception of emotions and intentions. *Journal of Experimental Social Psychology*, *48*(6), 1377–1380. doi:10.1016/j.jesp.2012.05.018 PMID:23144501

Huang, Y., Chen, F., Lv, S., & Wang, X. (2019). Facial expression recognition: A survey. *Symmetry*, *11*(10), 1189. doi:10.3390ym11101189

Izard, C. E. (1977). Theories of emotion and emotion-behavior relationships. In *Human Emotions. Emotions, Personality, and Psychotherapy* (pp. 19–42). Boston, MA: Springer. doi:10.1007/978-1-4899-2209-0_2

Josey, J. D., & Acharya, S. A. (2018). A methodology for automated facial expression recognition using facial landmarks. *Proceedings of 2018 ASEE Annual Conference & Exposition.* https://peer.asee.org/29696

Ko, B. C. (2018). A brief review of facial emotion recognition based on visual information. *Sensors (Basel)*, *18*(2), 401. doi:10.339018020401 PMID:29385749

Konar, A., & Chakraborty, A. (2015). *Emotion recognition: A pattern analysis approach.* John Wiley & Sons, Inc.; doi:10.1002/9781118910566

Kukharev, G. A., Kamenskaya, E. I., Matveev, Y. N., & Shchegoleva, N. L. (2013). *Methods of facial images processing and recognition in biometrics.* St. Petersburg: Politechnika.

Kumar, S., Jaiswal, S., Kumar, R., & Kumar Singh, S. (2016). Emotion recognition using facial expression. In P. Rajarshi P (Ed.), Innovative research in attention modeling and computer vision applications (pp. 327-345). IGI Publication. doi:10.4018/978-1-4666-8723-3.ch013

Kumin, L. (2003). *Early communication skills for children with Down syndrome. A Guide for Parents and Professionals*. Woodbine House.

Kwong, J. C. T., Garcia, F. C., Abu, P. A., & Reyes, R. S. J. (2018). Emotion recognition via facial expression: Utilization of numerous feature descriptors in different machine learning algorithms. *Proceedings of TENCON 2018 - 2018 IEEE Region 10 Conference*. 10.1109/TENCON.2018.8650192

Lai, Y. H., & Lai, S. H. (2018). Emotion-preserving representation learning via generative adversarial network for multi-view facial expression recognition. In *Proceedings of the 13th IEEE International Conference on Automatic Face & Gesture Recognition (FG 2018)* (pp. 263–270). Xi'an, China: IEEE. 10.1109/FG.2018.00046

Lange, C. (1885/1912). The mechanisms of the emotions. In B. Rand (Ed.), *The Classical Psychologists* (pp. 672–684). Houghton.

Lewinski, P., den Uyl, T. M., & Butler, C. (2014). Automated facial coding: Validation of basic emotions and FACS AUs in FaceReader. *Journal of Neuroscience, Psychology, and Economics, 7*(4), 227–236. doi:10.1037/npe0000028

Li, S., & Deng, W. (2018). Deep Facial Expression Recognition: A survey. In *Proceedings of EEE Transactions on Affective Computing* (pp. 99). DOI: 10.1109/TAFFC.2020.2981446

Li, Y., Wang, Sh., Zhao, Y., & Ji, Q. (2013). Simultaneous facial feature tracking and facial expression recognition. *IEEE Transactions on Image Processing, 22*(7), 2559–2573. doi:10.1109/TIP.2013.2253477 PMID:23529088

Lindsley, D. B. (1951). Emotion. In S. S. Stevens (Ed.), *Handbook of experimental psychology*. New York: Wiley.

Lindsley, D. B. (1982). Neural mechanisms of arousal, attention, and information processing. In J. Orbach (Ed.), *Neuropsychology after Lashley*. Erlbaum.

Lyakso, E., Frolova, O., Grigorev, A., Gorodnyi, V., & Nikolaev, A. (2019). Strategies of speech interaction between adults and preschool children with typical and atypical development. *Behavioral Science, 9*(12), 159. doi:10.3390/bs9120159 PMID:31888116

Lyakso, E. E., Frolova, O. V., Grigor'ev, A. S., Sokolova, V. D., & Yarotskaya, K. A. (2017). Recognition by adults of Emotional State in Typically Developing Children and Children with Autism Spectrum Disorders. *Neuroscience and Behavioral Physiology, 47*(9), 1051–1059. doi:10.100711055-017-0511-2

Lyakso, E. E., & Nozdrachev, A. D. (2012). *Psychophysiology. Textbook for students of institutions of higher professional education*. Moscow: Publishing Center "Academy".

Markaki, M., & Stylianou, Y. (2011). Voice pathology detection and discrimination based on modulation spectral features. *IEEE Transactions on Audio, Speech, and Language Processing, 19*(7), 1938–1948. doi:10.1109/TASL.2010.2104141

Martinez, A. M. (2017). Visual perception of facial expressions of emotion. *Current Opinion in Psychology*, *17*, 27–33. doi:10.1016/j.copsyc.2017.06.009 PMID:28950969

Noldus Information Technology. (2019). *FaceReader 7.1*. Technical Specification.

Pace-Schott, E. F., Amole, M. C., Aue, T., Balconi, M., Bysma, L. M., Critchley, H., ... Kotynski, A. (2019). Physiological feelings. *Neuroscience and Biobehavioral Reviews*, *103*, 267–304. doi:10.1016/j.neubiorev.2019.05.002 PMID:31125635

Parke, F. I. (1974). *A parametric model for human faces* (PhD thesis). The University of Utah.

Parrot, W. G. (2019). The Social Construction of Emotions. In B. Christensen (Ed.), *The Second Cognitive Revolution. Theory and History in the Human and Social Sciences* (pp. 131–139). Cham: Springer. doi:10.1007/978-3-030-26680-6_14

Reisenzein, R. (2019). Cognition and emotion: A plea for theory. *Cognition and Emotion*, *33*(1), 109–118. doi:10.1080/02699931.2019.1568968 PMID:30654695

Ruffman, T., Henry, J. D., Livingstone, V., & Phillips, L. H. (2008). A meta-analytic review of emotion recognition and aging: Implications for neuropsychological models of aging. *Neuroscience and Biobehavioral Reviews*, *32*(4), 863–881. doi:10.1016/j.neubiorev.2008.01.001 PMID:18276008

Samadiani, N., Huang, G., Cai, B., Luo, W., Chi, C. H., Xiang, Y., & He, J. (2019). A review on automatic facial expression recognition systems assisted by multimodal sensor data. *Sensors (Basel)*, *19*(8), E1863. doi:10.339019081863 PMID:31003522

Sato, W., Hyniewska, S., Minemoto, K., & Yoshikawa, S. (2019). Facial expressions of basic emotions in Japanese laypeople. *Frontiers in Psychology*, *10*, 259. doi:10.3389/fpsyg.2019.00259 PMID:30809180

Sinelnikov, R. D. (2009). The doctrine of bones, the connection of bones, and muscles. Atlas of human anatomy (7th ed., vol. 1). Moscow: New wave.

Skiendziel, T., Rosch, A. G., & Schultheiss, O. C. (2019). Assessing the convergent validity between the automated emotion recognition software Noldus FaceReader 7 and Facial Action Coding System Scoring. *PLoS One*, *14*(10), e0223905. doi:10.1371/journal.pone.0223905 PMID:31622426

Taha, J., Alhindi, T. J., Kalra, S., Hin, Ng, K., Afrin, A., & Tizhoosh, H. R. (2018). Comparing LBP, HOG and Deep Features for classification of histopathology images. In *Proceedings of 2018 International Joint Conference on Neural Networks (IJCNN)*, Rio de Janeiro, Brazil: IEEE. DOI: 10.1109/IJCNN.2018.8489329

Terzis, V., Moridis, C. N., & Economides, A. A. (2010). Measuring instant emotions during a self-assessment test: The use of FaceReader. In *Proceedings of the 7th International Conference on Methods and Techniques in Behavioral Research* (pp. 192-195). 10.1145/1931344.1931362

Tian, Y. I., Kanade, T., & Cohn, J. F. (2001). Recognizing action units for facial expression analysis. *IEEE Transactions on Pattern Analysis and Machine Intelligence*, *23*(2), 97–115. doi:10.1109/34.908962 PMID:25210210

Völkle, M. C., Ebner, N. C., Lindenberger, U., & Riediger, M. (2012). Let me guess how old you are: Effects of age, gender, and facial expression on perceptions of age. *Psychology and Aging*, *27*(2), 265–277. doi:10.1037/a0025065 PMID:21895379

Wassmann, C. (2014). "Picturesque incisiveness": Explaining the celebrity of James's Theory of Emotion. *Journal of the History of the Behavioral Sciences*, *50*(2), 166–188. doi:10.1002/jhbs.21651 PMID:24615670

Zeno, B., Kalinovskiy, I., & Matveev, Yu. (2019). IP-GAN: Learning identity and pose disentanglement in generative adversarial networks. *Lecture Notes in Computer Science*, *11731*, 535–547. doi:10.1007/978-3-030-30493-5_51

Chapter 15

Performance Analysis of GAN Architecture for Effective Facial Expression Synthesis

Karthik R.

ⓘ https://orcid.org/0000-0002-5250-4337

Centre for Cyber Physical Systems, Vellore Institute of Technology, Chennai, India

Nandana B.

Vellore Institute of Technology, India

Mayuri Patil

Vellore Institute of Technology, India

Chandreyee Basu

Vellore Institute of Technology, India

Vijayarajan R.

ⓘ https://orcid.org/0000-0003-0562-4472

Centre for Cyber Physical Systems, Vellore Institute of Technology, Chennai, India

ABSTRACT

Facial expressions are an important means of communication among human beings, as they convey different meanings in a variety of contexts. All human facial expressions, whether voluntary or involuntary, are formed as a result of movement of different facial muscles. Despite their variety and complexity, certain expressions are universally recognized as representing specific emotions - for instance, raised eyebrows in combination with an open mouth are associated with surprise, whereas a smiling face is generally interpreted as happy. Deep learning-based implementations of expression synthesis have demonstrated their ability to preserve essential features of input images, which is desirable. However, one limitation of using deep learning networks is that their dependence on data distribution and the quality of images used for training purposes. The variation in performance can be studied by changing the optimizer and loss functions, and their effectiveness is analysed based on the quality of output images obtained.

DOI: 10.4018/978-1-7998-6690-9.ch015

INTRODUCTION

Facial expressions are a direct result of the emotions experienced by human beings and a primary component of communication between human beings. Facial expressions produced as a result of emotions are not just involuntary responses to emotional stimuli, but also a means of conveying empathy. Understanding the emotional state of a person is a key aspect of effective interpersonal communication, and has been studied in a variety of fields ranging from human development and psychology to computer science. The cognitive ability of human beings to recognize emotional cues develops early in life, right from infancy. Discerning certain emotions such as fear or disgust from facial expressions can become a complex process, as there is little consistency in the way these emotions are exhibited by different people. However, certain emotions like happiness, surprise, sadness and anger are associated with distinctive modifications of facial features and facial expressions of these emotions can easily be categorized based on these differences. In a rising era of artificial intelligence and deep learning, human-computer interaction has seen significant growth in terms of the quality of interaction, which is the result of contributions from various fields, such as linguistics and industrial disciplines.

Rapid developments in computer interfaces involving computer graphics and programming techniques has improved interaction between humans and computing systems. This process of interaction can be significantly enhanced by introducing emotional recognition ability to machines. The primary purpose of every machine is to serve the needs of human beings, and to help them accomplish certain tasks. New technologies like virtual reality (VR) and augmented reality (AR) make use of facial expression recognition and synthesis to communicate with humans in a nearly-natural manner, and to make applications appear convincing, realistic emulation of facial expressions is important. Facial expression synthesis has a variety of applications including enhancement of facial recognition as well as data augmentation. Often, the need for realistic expression synthesis arises due to lack of available actors for the same purpose, or their lack of conviction. Even when available, involvement of actors is an expensive process, given that there are a variety of alternatives for data collection. Automated emotion recognition has been the subject of extensive research in the fields of science and technology owing to its large potential in a variety of applications. In the era of Industry 4.0, business communities prefer using marketing strategies that elicit emotional responses from customers to attract them towards products and services. Corporate organizations that enforce security by means of biometric data typically employ facial recognition components trained to identify authorized personnel. These facial recognition systems can be significantly enhanced by further training to identify variations in a single person's face that are caused as a result of different emotions.

Emotion synthesis also plays a significant role in multimedia applications such as animation, where human-based models created using software need to be animated with facial expressions as realistic as possible. Models that synthesise images with facial expressions based on a textual description have also been proposed. Traditional methods of animation require complex modelling and computer graphics techniques in order to model different expressions, and the process can be simplified if one can generate the required expressions from a single face. Besides computer animation, emotion detection and synthesis can be incorporated in robots which can then be used as test subjects or assistants in social assignments.

Emotion detection involves two main techniques, i.e. computer vision for extracting essential features from images, and machine learning algorithms to identify and classify expressions depicting different emotions. Traditionally, expression synthesis has been implemented using methods such as geometric manipulation of 3D objects and image processing techniques for extraction of essential features.

Performance based approaches in the field of animation have also been implemented, which involved measurement of parameters from real actors and their replication in synthetic models. 2D morphing of photographs is yet another technique that was used in animation, but it failed to produce accurate results for different positions or points of view of the same object. Subsequently, machine learning based approaches have also been employed for generation of facial expressions. With the advent of deep learning, face detection models based on Convolution Neural Networks (CNNs) and Recurrent Neural Networks (RNNs) have also been proposed. However, one of the major challenges in such implementations is their architectural complexity when compared to other models, and training them can often become computationally expensive – often, a decision has to be made as to whether accuracy should be compromised for performance or vice-versa.

The facial action coding system (FACS) adopted by Ekman and Friesen has played a significant role in influencing research in facial expression classification and synthesis. FACS defines action units (AUs) on human faces on the basis of facial muscles, which, when activated at different levels of intensity, cause changes in facial expression, corresponding to the triggered muscles on actual human faces. Several researchers have attempted to generate facial expressions based on FACS encoded action units, and have achieved satisfactory results. Owing to the relatively standardized nature of this encoding system, the models trained on such systems have produced considerably unbiased results as they rely solely on movement of facial muscles – moreover this system allows one to develop a system that is capable of generating various degrees of intensity for a given expression. However, this in itself is a challenge owing to the limited availability of labelled datasets. Moreover, labelled datasets like the extended Cohn-Kanade database are small in size, consisting of as few as 100 training examples, which is insufficient for supervised learning methods. In addition to this, the computer graphics techniques required to model such systems are often time-consuming and resource-intensive.

Among the deep learning approaches proposed for facial expression synthesis, models with generative adversarial network (GAN) architecture have shown promising results in facial expression recognition and synthesis owing to their high accuracy and high quality output. Compared to existing models, GANs have produced the best results, particularly in terms of image quality. However, a major drawback of most GANs is that the output is not satisfactory unless they are trained on a sufficiently large dataset. Collection of data is laborious – and although there are several datasets publicly available, very few contain good quality images, and even fewer with labels. Moreover, databases with good quality images are proprietary and require authorized access. Nevertheless, experimental results have demonstrated the ability of this architecture to significantly enhance what would have otherwise been unsatisfactory output.

Another key challenge in facial expression synthesis is that it is hard to eliminate bias in a model developed for this application. Most models for facial expression synthesis tend to be biased towards the dataset used for their training. This bias becomes a major drawback for models, especially when the training set is not sufficiently diverse – existing models are known to have been trained on datasets lacking diversity in terms of gender, age, and ethnicity. As a result, they are often unable to produce accurate output when the input provided consists of variations in any of these domains. Deep learning models for most applications are known to perform significantly better than traditional methods only when the system architecture is highly complex along with sufficiently large training datasets – therefore, diversity and large data size are key requirements for improving the performance of deep learning based models.

Owing to its ability to preserve essential features, the GAN architecture is largely dependent on the data it is trained on, and therefore, even with low classification error rates, GAN based models can become prone to overfitting, which is undesirable. Image attribute transfer across multiple domains has been achieved using several GAN architectures but with limited ability – individual models are required for attribute transfer between each pair of domains. Among existing GAN models, StarGAN has demonstrated superior performance, both in terms of image quality as well as classification accuracy and is capable of attribute transfer across multiple domains with a single model. However, when tested with images external to the training dataset used for its demonstration, it was found that the quality of the output images obtained was not as expected. The authors believe that this must be due to the inherent bias developed by training the model on the Radboud Faces Database (RaFD), which primarily comprised emotional expressions of similar ethnicities. Moreover, owing to the limited number of subjects in the RaFD dataset, there is a possibility of the model being unable to distinguish between common facial features and identification parameters unique to a specific human being. In order to validate this, experiments have been conducted with variations in the proposed model of StarGAN, including modification of loss functions. To reduce bias, training of these varied models was done with customized datasets comprising examples from multiple datasets, thereby enhancing the size and diversity.

BACKGROUND

Numerous techniques for facial expression recognition have been studied and analyzed and in some cases, a trade-off between precision and performance has been observed (G. Sailaja, 2019). Existing systems can easily identify basic human emotions, but find it difficult to recognize subtler emotions such as contempt and disgust. Common methods of facial expression recognition have been categorized on the basis of feature extraction methods and closely examined. Several datasets have been widely used for this purpose including the JAFFE dataset and the CK dataset, which provide compiled image samples for a variety of human expressions (Htay & Win, 2019). Michael et al. (2018) did a survey on human face expression recognition techniques. The basic architecture included pre-processing, feature extraction and classification. Performance analysis is done based on the database, complexity rate, recognition accuracy and major contributions. Changxing Ding et al. (2015) propose a novel face identification framework which is capable of handling the full range of pose variations within ±90° of rotation. The model transforms the original pose-invariant face recognition problem into a partial frontal face recognition problem, followed by a robust patch-based face representation scheme to detect the face.

Yihjia Tsai et al. (2017) studied and designed a model in which facial expressions can be generated based on imitation. The difference between shape feature vectors of neutral image and expression image is used to imitate the facial expression. Two post-processing steps were included - adding texture to resulting image; and blending and seamless processing. Computer graphic technology such as 3DMM was used for facial expression synthesis in order to convey specific messages to the viewer. Arbitrary FACS codes were used to generate random facial expressions which could then be validated by responses from naive observers (Yu et al., 2012). Based on these responses, it was possible to determine the parameters that influence human perception of facial expressions, thereby incorporating flexibility as well as validity.

Patel and Agrawal (2016) did a survey on face expression recognition techniques and the basic architecture was observed to be face detection-feature extraction-expression recognition-facial expression classification. Jyoti Kumari et al. (2015) conducted a survey based on facial expression recognition techniques, in which six feature extraction methods were studied. These methods used filters to extract the features. Classification was done using kNN with k=2. It was studied that these techniques are suitable when the input is non dynamic, but needs to be extended for cases for dynamic input, such as in the case of a video - it was also observed that the accuracy rate for expression recognition could be improved. Tairi et al. (2018) worked on methods of face detection using machine learning, a comparative study was done for four methods, namely, Haar-AdaBoost, LBP-AdaBoost, GF-SVM, GF-NN. It was concluded that these techniques differ in their methods of data extraction and adopted learning algorithms.

Facial detection using deep learning was studied by Manik Sharma et al. (2017), and a model was developed for face detection which detected facial features by the given gray level frame, and its fitness is determined by the projection on the Eigen-faces. The advantage of implementing this model is that it recognizes blurred images and side face images also which traditional models fail to do. Comparisons of existing CNN models have been made and have demonstrated significant accuracy in Facial Recognition, the best of which was reported to be AlexNet which was developed in 2012 (Kasim et al., 2018). Jiao et al. (2018) presented a Convolutional Neural Network architecture to convert a facial image into a black and white sketch. End-to-end mapping using a four layer network is done, the first layer scans the image using different filters and returns group of feature maps. An overlapping max-pooling layer is connected to the first layer to relieve the misalignment, followed by a multilayer perceptron convolutional layer. Nguyen et al. (2015) adopted a two-stage training mechanism with smaller datasets to enhance the recognition ability of a CNN and reported a 16% improvement in performance when compared to single stage training with a large hybrid dataset. Sun et al. (2018) employed a decision fusion technique in which three CNNs were trained on three different active regions of the face and use the features learned from each to determine the final expression. Despite the model's performance, the learning process can become time-consuming and is power intensive. Shraddha Arya et al. (2018) worked on face recognition with partial face recognition and Convolutional Neural Networks, in which the proposed idea was to design and implement a face recognition model that can accept a partial image as input, and recognize the face class. The images are partitioned into multiple facial parts, and feature extraction is done using LDA. A neural network is used to train and classify the images.

El Khiyari et al. (2017) worked on a deep learning and set-based approach to face recognition subject to aging. The images for each subject taken at various times are treated as a single set, which is then compared to sets of images belonging to other subjects. Facial features are extracted using a convolutional neural network characteristic of deep learning. Deep face recognition using imperfect data was done by Ali Elmahmudi et al. (2019), in which performance of machine learning methods using partial faces and other changes in face such as rotation, etc. was studied. The results show that individual facial areas have low recognition as compared to recognition of the entire face at once. Researchers have also employed mathematical transformations such as Haar based cascade classifiers and saliency using hyper-complex Fourier transform to incorporate essential details in feature vectors, thus providing a way to utilise the representational power of deep networks (Jothimani et al., 2019). Lee et al. (2013) proposed an approach to expression recognition which involved traditional methods of face detection followed by use of image processing techniques such as feature extraction to create a feature vector from conventional attributes such as eyes, nose, mouth, and even facial muscle streak. This feature vector was then processed using a neural network to classify the expression, i.e. "recognition" of the facial expression.

Research on face detection using neural networks was done by Shukla et al (2019). They studied machine learning approaches for Face Identification using Feed forward networks. This is done first improving the face alignment of detected image, followed by one-to-many or many to one feature extraction, and simultaneously face matching from the available registered database. The feed forward algorithms, which are the basic architecture of the identification process, determine the location of the facial landmarks in this model. Le et al. (2011) proposed a hybrid model combining AdaBoost and artificial neural network, followed by a multi-layer perceptron. In this, feature extraction is done by combining a geometric feature based method with an independent component analysis method. Ashu Kumar et al. (2018) conducted a review on face detection techniques for feature based and image based approaches. It was observed that for image based approaches, the learned characteristics are in the form of distribution models or discriminant functions, used for face detection. Whereas for feature based approach, the features are extracted using edge detectors.

Bozorgtabara et al. (2019) proposed a system with bidirectional learning algorithm using an encoder-decoder technique. The architecture presented can be used for multiple attribute transfer. Peng and Yin (2019) suggested a method in which facial expression is synthesized using GAN, based on appearance – this included a framework, based on geometry to synthesize expression from texture and shape of facial landmark movements. Two generators are used here, shape generator to generate shape deformation and texture generator to generate expression details. This model takes into consideration cycle consistency and mapping losses; it was used to successfully generate expressions using 14 facial sub-regions. Liu et al. (2017) worked on unsupervised image to image translation, which can be performed using GAN architecture. A UNIT framework was proposed such that each image domain was modeled using a GAN model, and the training was done with a weight-sharing constraint, and the image transformation was done using auto-encoders. Sricharan et al. (2017) presented a model to edit the facial expression by controlling the intensity. The Oulu-CASIA dataset having 480 images, 80 subjects and 6 expressions each was used. The Conditional GAN and adversarial auto-encoder(AAE) network form the basis architecture of this model.

Gu et al. (2017) developed a model which generates facial expressions using differential GAN. It studies the difference between the input image (neutral expression) and the ground truth (given expression) and mimics it to get the resulting expression. This method is found to be useful when the training data is small. The concept of a two-stage learning procedure was also employed by researchers who proposed a unified framework for generation and recognition of facial expressions (Xie et al., 2017). The model consisted of two simultaneously trained units - an expression synthesis GAN (generative adversarial network) and a recognition network for recognizing facial expression. By incorporating an intra-class loss which measured variation in images belonging to the same category, this approach minimizes the intrinsic data bias typically found in data generated by GANs and boosts model performance by making use of a real data-guided back-propagation algorithm. Hall et al. conducted a survey of methods of facial expression synthesis using GANs. Texture synthesis, image-to-image translation, image in-painting, image editing and similar topics were studied. CycleGAN and AI-GAN were proposed for unpaired data for training (Wu et al., 2017). It was observed that GANs are not suitable for high resolution images. In a recent study, Zhuang et al. (2020) used RDA-UNET WGAN for lesion segmentation in breast ultrasound images. Wasserstein loss, which is unique to WGANs, was employed to accurately segment tumours in BUS images.

Yunjey Choi et al. (2018) proposed a system for multi domain attribute transfer called the StarGAN model. In traditional methods, a new generator is required for attribute transfer between each pair of domains. This method uses a single generator for training, it takes an image and domain info as input, and gives an output image with required changed attribute. RaFD is used for expression synthesis, using PyTorch and Tensorflow.

MATERIALS AND METHODS

Datasets

The proposed experiments were conducted on a single mixed set of images, derived by combining four benchmark datasets, listed below as follows:

- **Karolinska Directed Emotional Faces (KDEF)** – The Karolinska Directed Emotional Faces dataset is a set of 4900 images of human facial expressions that were originally produced in 1998 and are freely available for non-commercial purposes. This dataset has been used extensively, in over 1500 research publications, including research that investigates effect of cultural factors on emotion recognition. The dataset contains images of 70 different individuals displaying 7 different emotional expressions. The faces in the database are of Swedish amateur actors with ages between 20 and 30 years old, half of whom are women. The average age of the models in the dataset is 25 years.

- **Taiwanese Facial Expression Image Database (TFEID)** – The Taiwanese facial expression image database consists of a total of 7200 images of Taiwanese faces. The images were captured from 40 individuals, 20 of whom are male, and the dataset includes eight facial expressions, i.e. neutral, surprise, anger, disgust, fear, happiness, sadness, contempt. Each expression is depicted at two intensity levels, and it has been open for public access since 2007. The primary reason for including this dataset was its ethnicity, and the even distribution of male and female faces was ideal for removing any gender bias that might have been present in the original model.

- **Radboud Faces Database (RaFD)** – The Radboud Faces Database consists of 8 emotional expressions displayed by 67 models. Eight facial expressions have been displayed by the models, who are either Caucasian or Moroccan. Each model has 120 pictures of facial expressions captured using cameras at different angles. This dataset is a high quality faces database, which refers to the high resolution of the images.

- **Amsterdam Interdisciplinary Centre for Emotion (AICE) database** – This dataset consists primarily of North European and Mediterranean models, containing a total of 648 expressions belonging to 22 models, 10 of whom are female and 12 of whom are male.

METHODOLOGY

As part of the proposed model, enhancements can be introduced by incorporate various combinations of loss functions in order to ensure output quality and classification accuracy. Numerous optimization algorithms have also been proposed for training GAN models. These include Averaged Stochastic Gradient Descent (ASGD), Adadelta, Adam, SparseAdam, and even Adamax. By training models using different combinations of optimizers and loss functions, it is possible to determine the combination that works best for a GAN model, in terms of performance and accuracy. In order to validate the output obtained, PSNR and SSIM are used to compare the quality of original image to that of the modified image. Higher the value of PSNR, better the quality of the generated image. In this case, the input is the original image from the dataset and modified image is the output of trained model. SSIM is a weighted combination of three comparative measures – contrast, luminance and structure. An SSIM index of 0 implies no similarity, while an SSIM index of 1 indicates that the two images are perfectly identical.

For every model, the PSNR and SSIM with optimizer as the varying parameter was calculated, and hence the comparison was done.

Figure 1. GAN block diagram

Figure 1 illustrates the training process used for performance analysis. Each model was trained using a unique combination of optimizers and loss functions – the discriminator network was trained using real images as well as those produced by the generator. Based on the accuracy of the discriminator, the generator learned probability distribution of the training set and produced more convincing images to fool the discriminator.

GAN Overview

Generative Adversarial Networks were introduced in 2014 by Ian Goodfellow and his colleagues when they were proposed as a method for unsupervised learning. However, in recent years, they have proven to be useful in semi-supervised learning as well. GANs have a wide variety of applications in technology, especially when it comes to synthesis of high quality images. They can also be used for voice and video synthesis. The basic architecture of a GAN comprises two neural networks – one is known as the generator, while the other is called the discriminator.

The two neural networks constantly try to outperform each other in order to synthesize superficially authentic images. The primary objective of the GAN is to optimize the function given in eq. (1):

$$V(D,G) = E_{x \sim pdata(x)} \left[loglog D(x) \right] + E_{z \sim p(z)} \left[loglog \left(1 - D(G(z)) \right) \right] \tag{1}$$

Where
$D(x)$ represents the discriminator's estimate of the probability that the given data 'x' is real,
E_x represents the expected value over all real data instances,
$G(z)$ represents the generator's output for a given noise z,
$D(G(z))$ represents the probability that a fake instance $G(z)$ is real,
E_z represents the expected value of all random inputs to the generator

Generator

The main role of the generator is to generate images with features such that it appears as realistic as possible. The output of the generator is directly fed to the input of a discriminator to assess if it is real or fake. Once this has been determined, the weights and loss are updated through back-propagation. This provides an indication to the generator to produce a better image. Therefore, as the training proceeds, the generator learns the probability distribution better, using the feedback from the discriminator, and produces more and more realistic images that confuse the discriminator. The stable state is reached when the discriminator can no longer determine whether the image provided as input is real or fake. Unlike the discriminator training, generator training incorporates the use of discriminator and generator to work together. Back-propagation modifies each weight in the right direction by calculating the impact of each weight on the sample, i.e. how the sample changes with change in weight. However, the effect of the weight of the generator depends primarily on the impact of the weight of the discriminator it feeds into. Thus, the back-propagation begins at output and flows back from the discriminator and into the generator.

Discriminator

The discriminator mainly plays the role of a classifier. It is responsible for determining whether the image given to it as input is real or fake. Training data for the discriminator is obtained from two sources

- in order to provide positive samples for training, real data samples are provided. Secondly, fake data instances produced by the generator are used as the negative examples for training. The two samples are fed into the discriminator from these two sources. Training of generator and discriminator happens independently. The weights are kept constant when it produces the examples to train the discriminator. During training, the discriminator extracts the features from the input image and determines whether these features belong to a given category.

StarGAN

Yunjey Choi et al. (2018) proposed a GAN model for attribute transfer across multiple domains, which they called the StarGAN model. Traditionally, for attribute transfer between two domains, a unique generator is required for transfer from one to the other. Existing models have implemented this between each pair of domains. An example includes the RDA-UNET WGAN used for lesion segmentation in breast ultrasound images (Zhuang et al., 2020). This particular model makes use of Wasserstein distance to accurately segment tumours in the images. StarGAN, in contrast, is capable of performing attribute transfer between multiple domains using a single generator. Compared to other existing models like CycleGAN and IcGAN, StarGAN has demonstrated production of the best output with respect to classification accuracy and image quality. Moreover, it has been shown to preserve essential image characteristics, which was not effectively achieved by other models. Just like Auxiliary classifier GANs (AC-GANs), this model learns how to classify images independent of the class label (corresponding to different domains) assigned to them.

Like most GAN models, the architecture of StarGAN comprises two main units – the generator and the discriminator. The generator network is responsible for learning the probability distribution of the facial features in the training set, and synthesizes new images by sampling this probability distribution. In this unit, two convolutional layers are used for down-sampling, with a stride size of 2, as shown in figure 2. The discriminator network is based on the architecture of the PatchGAN model. Its task is to classify images as real or fake. Instance normalization is not used.

The generator network of StarGAN is described as follows:

1. **Down-sampling unit** – Three convolution operations are performed in this layer:
    a. The input for the convolution operation is a 3-dimensional matrix whose dimensions are dependent on the number of weights 'w' and bias 'h', and the number of domain labels, 'n_c'. These are converted into a (w x h x 64) matrix using a 7x7 kernel with a stride size of 1 and padding size 3. Instance normalization is applied, and the layer uses the ReLU activation function.
    b. The (w x h x 64) matrix generated from the previous step is provided as input into the next convolution layer. The convolution operation is performed with a 4x4 kernel of stride size 2, and padding size 1. Instance normalization is applied, and this operation yields a (w/4) x (h/4) x 128 matrix.
    c. The (w/4) x (h/4) x 128 matrix obtained from the previous step undergoes another convolution operation with a 4x4 kernel with padding size 1, yielding a (w/4) x (h/4) x 256 matrix. Instance normalization is used in this layer.
2. **Bottleneck** – This layer consists of six residual blocks, each of which performs a convolution operation on the values obtained from the previous block, except for the first block which receives the

output matrix from the down-sampling layer as input. Each block produces a (w/4) x (h/4) x 256 matrix using a 3x3 kernel with stride size 1, and padding size 1. Instance normalization is used in each block. The final output is also a matrix of dimensions (w/4) x (h/4) x 256.

3. **Up-sampling unit** – This layer performs two de-convolution operations on the output matrix of the bottleneck layer, and one final convolution operation, as described below:

   a. The output parameters obtained from the bottleneck layer undergo a de-convolution operation with a 4x4 kernel with stride size 2, padding size 1. An output matrix of dimensions (w/2) x (h/2) x 128 is obtained. Instance normalization is used.

   b. The (w/2) x (h/2) x 128 matrix from the previous step is made to undergo another de-convolution operation with a 4x4 kernel, stride size 2, padding size 1. Instance normalisation is used, and this operation yields a (w x h x 64) matrix.

   c. The (w x h x 64) matrix obtained from the previous step is used for a final convolution operation with a 7x7 kernel and stride size 1, padding size 3. Unlike the rest of the convolution layers, instance normalization is not used here, and a tanh activation function is used here instead of ReLU. The final output is an (w x h x 3) matrix.

Figure 2. Generator network architecture

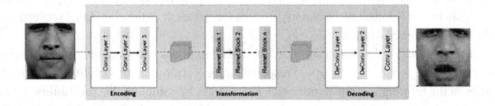

As shown in figure 3, the discriminator network consists of three main units, in the following order:

1. **Input Layer** – This layer receives an (h x w x 3) matrix as input, and produces an output matrix of dimensions (h/2) x (w/2) x 64 after convolution with a 4x4 kernel of stride size 2, padding size 1. Leaky ReLU is used in this layer.

2. **Hidden Layer** – This layer is composed of six inner layers, each of which perform convolution operation on the matrix obtained from the input layer. All layers use Leaky ReLU.

   a. The (h/2) x (w/2) x 64 matrix obtained from the input layer undergoes convolution with a 4x4 kernel of stride size 2 and padding size 1. The output obtained in this step is a matrix of dimensions (h/4) x (w/4) x 128.

   b. A second convolution operation is performed on the (h/4) x (w/4) x 128 matrix from the previous step using a 4x4 kernel of stride size 2 and padding size 1. This step yields a (h/8) x (w/8) x 256 matrix.

   c. The (h/8) x (w/8) x 256 matrix from the previous step is made to undergo another convolution operation which yields a (h/16) x (w/16) x 512 matrix. This is done with the help of a 4x4 kernel with stride size 2 and padding size 1.

    d.   Convolution is performed again on the (h/16) x (w/16) x 512 from the previous step to yield a matrix of dimensions (h/32) x (w/32) x 1024. A 4x4 kernel with stride size 2 and padding size 1 is used.

    e.   The matrix obtained from the previous step undergoes another convolution operation with a 4x4 kernel with stride size 2 and padding size 1. The operation yields a matrix of dimensions (h/64) x (w/64) x 2048. This is the final output of the hidden layer.

3.   **Output Layer** – Two convolution operations are performed on the (h/64) x (w/64) x 2048 input matrix in this layer, which yield 2 different parameters as results, i.e. D_{src} and D_{cls}.

    a. D_{src} is calculated by performing convolution operation on the input matrix using a 3x3 kernel with stride size 1 and padding size 1. The output of this operation is an (h/64) x (w/64) x 1 dimensional matrix.

    b. D_{cls} is calculated by performing convolution on the (h/64) x (w/64) x 2048 matrix with a kernel of dimensions (h/64) x (w/64) with stride size 1 and no padding. This operation produces a $(1 \times 1 \times n_d)$ dimensional output.

Figure 3. Discriminator Network Architecture

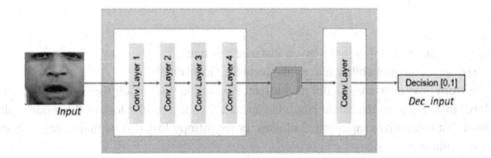

Hyperparameter Tuning

The effectiveness of model training can be determined by the initial configuration of hyper-parameters used for training the model. These include the beta parameters and the learning rate, which are determined by the choice of algorithms, and also by varying the loss functions used. Varying combinations produce varying results with different levels of accuracy.

Loss Functions

Once the discriminator and generator is designed, appropriate loss function is designed. The loss function should be designed such that the discriminator approves all the original images as real and all the generated images that was made to fool it as a fake image. Whereas, generator must strive to make the discriminator approve the generated images and fool the discriminator. Also, the generator should be able to retain the features of the original image when it generates the fake image. The training process is best described as a minimax game between the two networks where each network optimizes the objective function described in eq. (1).

The Hinge loss function is commonly used for training maximum-margin classifiers, such as support vector machines. For wider applications, this loss function can be further extended for use in structured prediction. It is a convex function, which is why it can be used in combination with almost any optimizer of one's choice. Hinge loss is given by the formula for L(y) in eq. (2):

$$L(y) = \{\frac{1}{2} - ty, if \ ty \le 0, \frac{1}{2}(1-ty)^2, if \ 0 < ty \le 1, 0, if 1 \le ty. \tag{2}$$

Here, t represents the expected output label and y represents the classifier output.

Wasserstein Loss is the default loss function that is used and it was introduced in 2017. In this, the discriminator does not really classify the image as real or fake. It outputs a number which does not have to be lesser or greater than 0. It tries to make the output bigger for the real images. It is more of a "critic" than a discriminator.

Critic loss is given by eq. (3):

$$L_{critic} = D(x) - D(G(z)) \tag{3}$$

where

D(x) denotes the probability that a given instance x is real,

D(G(z)) denotes the probability that a fake instance G(z) is real.

Cross entropy loss measures model performance based on how much the estimated probability of a given label diverges from the actual label. Under ideal conditions, the loss of the model will be zero. For a model that categorizes input into 2 classes, cross entropy loss can be mathematically calculated using the formula in eq. (4):

$$L(y) = -(y \log\log(p) + (1-y) \log\log(1-p)) \tag{4}$$

Here, y represents the actual probability of the label, and p represents the estimated probability for that label.

The discriminator tries to maximize the difference between the output on real images and its output on fake images. Wasserstein GANs are however less vulnerable to getting stuck as compared to minimax-based GANs and also avoid the problems with vanishing gradients.

Optimizers

Optimization algorithms are used to optimize model parameters in a fixed number of iterations based on specific learning rates and the rate of weight decay. With different combinations of learning rates and rates of decay, optimization of parameters can be achieved after varying number of iterations. Fewer iterations result in lower accuracy, and large rates of decay can cause gradient optimization to overshoot the minimum. At the same time, if the rate of decay is too small, it may take longer to reach convergence.

Different types of optimization algorithms use different learning rates and different rates of decay to reach the optimum values.

Adam stands for adaptive moment estimation, and is a way of using past gradients to calculate current gradients. Adam also utilizes the concept of momentum by adding fractions of previous gradients to the current one. This optimizer has become pretty widespread, and is practically accepted for use in training neural nets. The default learning rate used by this algorithm is 0.001, and the coefficients used for computing running averages of gradient and its square, known as Betas, are 0.9 and 0.999.

An improved version of Adam is called weighted Adam (AdamW) where the weight decay is performed only after controlling the parameter-wise step size. The weight regularization term does not end up in the moving averages and is thus only proportional to the weight itself. The default learning rate for this optimization algorithm is 0.001, and the Beta values are 0.9 and 0.999.

AdaMax is an adaptive stochastic gradient descent method, and a variant of Adam based on the infinity norm. AdaMax offers the important advantage of being much less sensitive to the choice of the hyper-parameters (for example, the learning rate). This algorithm uses a learning rate of 0.002 and the Beta values chosen are 0.9 and 0.999.

Stochastic Gradient Descent is the most commonly known optimization algorithm, which uses an estimate of the actual gradient, which is calculated from randomly selected instances of data. The principle behind Stochastic Gradient Descent originates from the Robbins Munro algorithm for calculating roots of a given function.

The model was trained with different combinations of hyper parameters, to observe the variation in output.

RESULTS AND DISCUSSION

Environment Setup

The proposed experiments were carried out in Google Colaboratory, a cloud based environment that allows use of Google hardware for machine learning applications and other GPU intensive operations. Code in Google Colab was stored in the form of a Colab notebook, which was run by sequential execution of cells. The datasets used for this experiment were stored in Google Drive, which was then mounted onto the notebook. PyTorch and TensorFlow libraries required for this execution were already existing components of the cloud environment, and therefore, no separate installation was required.

Analysis of Hyperparameter Tuning

Although the efficiency of StarGAN as compared to other models is better, the quality of output images can be improved in different ways by implementing different combinations loss functions and optimizer to obtain maximum accuracy, and also varying the training dataset.

Sample images were generated by the GAN model during the training phase. Initially, the model was trained for 20,000 iterations instead of 200,000. When the model was tested with test images belonging to the RaFD dataset, the quality of images generated was found to be almost state-of-the art – this is evident from the images in figure 4. However, the model was tested with real time data, and the results obtained were not satisfactory. As is evident from the images in figure 5, the expressions generated were found to be visibly distorted rather than convincing or realistic. For this purpose, the model was re-trained with a customized dataset that comprised images of individuals of diverse ethnicities, and with images taken under a wide variety of lighting conditions.

PSNR stands for Peak Signal-to-Noise Ratio, a metric used for measuring the similarity between two images. This metric is often used for measurement of image quality after transmission through a communication channel. PSNR is calculated using the formula given in eq. (5):

$$PSNR = 20\left(\frac{MAX}{\sqrt{MSE}}\right) \tag{5}$$

where,

MAX represents the maximum pixel value based on the image resolution.

MSE is the mean squared error between two images.

SSIM refers to Structural Similarity Index, another full-reference metric which is similar to PSNR. It is calculated based on windows of different regions of the images to be compared. For two such windows x and y of fixed dimensions, SSIM is calculated using the formula given in eq. (6):

$$SSIM\left(x, y\right) = \frac{\left(2\mu_x\mu_y + c_1\right)(2\sigma_{xy} + c_2)}{(\mu_x^2 + \mu_y^2 + c_1)\left(\sigma_x^2 + \sigma_y^2 + c_2\right)} \tag{6}$$

For each combination of optimizers and loss functions, the PSNR and SSIM values of the generated expression images with respect to the original expressions were calculated. As seen in table 1, the maximum PSNR value obtained was from the images generated using the Adam weighted decay optimizer for training.

Table 1. PSNR and SSIM for Each Optimizer with Corresponding Loss Function

Optimizer	Cross Entropy Loss		Hinge Loss	
	PSNR	SSIM	PSNR	SSIM
Adam	29.9567	0.7945	28.3459	0.3516
AdamW	29.9838	0.8267	29.4532	0.6885
Adamax	29.0226	0.4664	27.9031	0.3498
Stochastic Gradient Descent	29.7936	0.5657	28.3645	0.4228

Figure 4. Adam with cross entropy

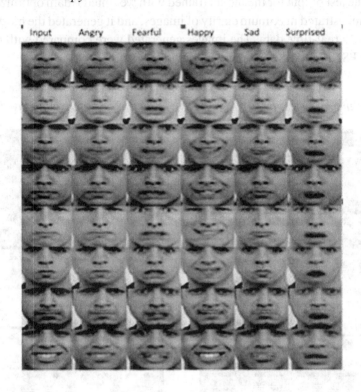

Figure 5. Adam with cross entropy (Real Time)

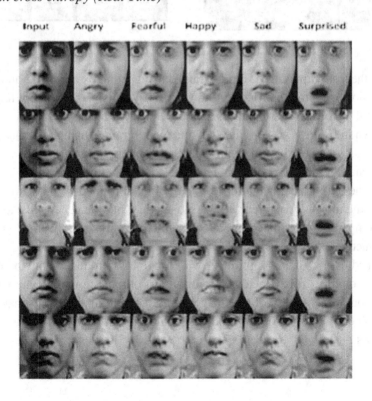

Figure 6 shows the test output for the model trained with weighted Adam optimizer and cross entropy loss. This model demonstrated maximum clarity of images, and it generated the most convincing expressions when tested with real-time data. The images generated were compared with original expressions and had the highest PSNR and SSIM for any model in this study.

Figure 6. AdamW with cross entropy

Figure 7. Adamax with cross entropy

Figure 7 shows the test output for the model trained using Adamax optimizer and cross entropy loss. Most of the expressions generated during testing were fairly satisfactory, except for the happy expression, which appeared distorted for some faces.

The output shown in figure 8 was produced by the model trained using Stochastic Gradient Descent and cross entropy loss. As is evident from the image, the expressions generated were not as expected. Despite the image quality, the expressions generated were barely distinguishable.

Figure 9 shows the output obtained after testing the model trained with Adam optimizer and hinge loss. The quality of the images generated was not satisfactory, but the generated expressions were fairly distinguishable. Compared to the images produced by the other models, this loss – optimizer combination produced distinctive expressions.

The model trained using Adamax optimizer with hinge loss produced convincing expressions, but at the cost of image quality. This is evident from the test output shown in figure 10. It is clear from this image that although the quality of the images is not as high as the input images, the expressions are clearly discernable. The output of this model is similar to that produced by the model trained using Adam and hinge loss.

Figure 8. SGD with cross entropy

Figure 9. Adam with hinge loss

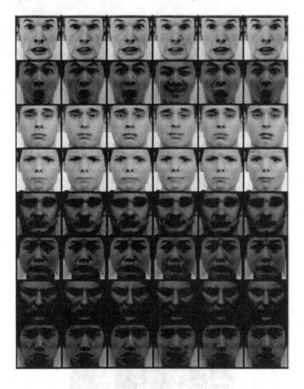

Figure 10. Adamax with hinge loss

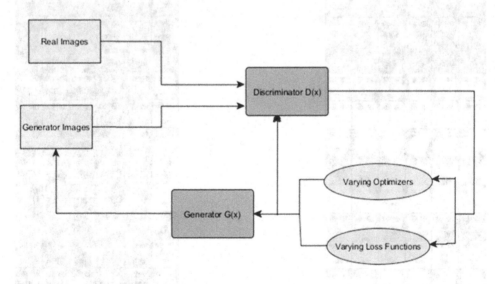

Figure 11 describes the output produced by the model trained using weighted Adam optimizer and hinge loss. The image quality is significantly better than that of other models, and the expressions generated are also distinguishable, although their intensity is lower.

Figure 11. AdamW with hinge loss

Figure 12. SGD with hinge loss

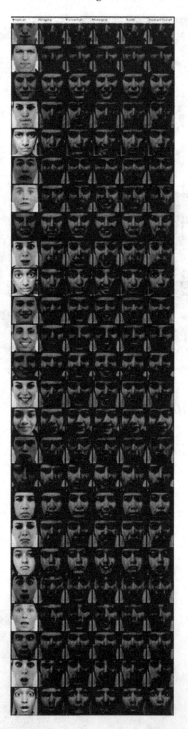

The test output for the model trained with Stochastic Gradient Descent and hinge loss is described in figure 12. This model produced better images than most other models, while the generated expressions were somewhat subtle.

Figure 13. Adam – Cross Entropy plot

Figure 13 and Figure 14 depict plot the generator and discriminator losses for Adam optimizer, using cross entropy and hinge loss respectively. The X-axis denotes the number of iterations, thus plotting the variation in loss over the course of the training process. The losses fluctuate the most at 100,000 iterations. Greater fluctuation is observed in the plot for Hinge loss. In contrast, when we compare the plot for AdamW and cross entropy in figure 15 with that of AdamW and Hinge loss in figure 16, fewer fluctuations are observed for hinge loss.

Figure 17 and Figure 18 depict plot the generator and discriminator losses for Adamax optimizer, using cross entropy and hinge loss respectively. Greater fluctuation is observed in the plot for Hinge loss. Comparing the plot for Stochastic Gradient Descent and cross entropy in figure 19 with that of Stochastic Gradient Descent and Hinge loss in figure 20, the latter fluctuates more.

Figure 14. Adam – Hinge plot

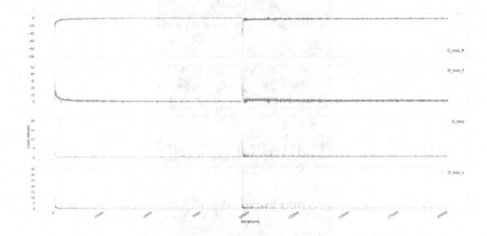

Figure 15. AdamW – Cross Entropy plot

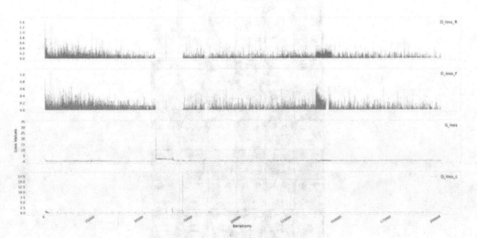

Figure 16. AdamW – Hinge plot

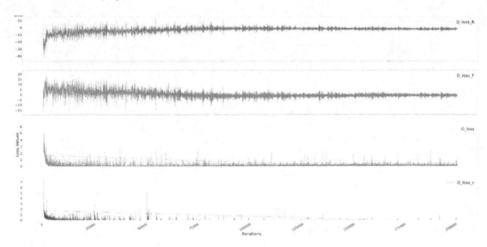

Figure 17. Adamax – Cross Entropy plot

Figure 18. Adamax – Hinge plot

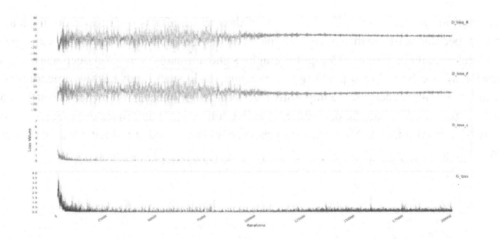

Figure 19. SGD – Cross Entropy plot

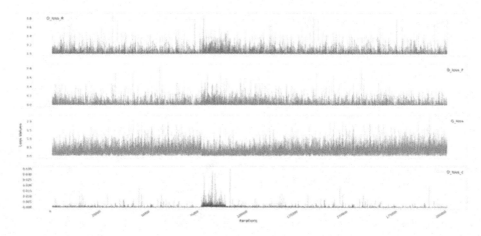

Figure 20. SGD – Hinge plot

FUTURE RESEARCH DIRECTIONS

Facial recognition systems often suffer from lack of data which affects their recognition capacity, and many systems become biased in this process. In such situations, expression synthesis provides significant potential to enhance these systems. Computer graphics and animation rarely on deep learning methods for expression synthesis, and incorporating these techniques in such fields has the potential to achieve better results that might otherwise be impossible. Existing implementations typically suffer from data bias which, at present, can only be overcome by collection of more and more data. Future research in facial expression synthesis or GAN models in general could be aimed at reducing this bias, with lesser risk of overfitting.

Future applications of expression synthesis might involve the use of such techniques in modelling virtual assistants, whose frequency of usage is growing with time. Moreover, expression synthesis may be used in criminal identification processes, where accurate modelling of criminals is critical for justice. In addition to to these, image segmentation for feature analysis in areas such as medicine is also a potential avenue for research using GANs.

CONCLUSION

Compared to existing models for facial expression synthesis, GANs have produced the best results, in terms of image quality, owing to their capacity for semantic manipulation. The images generated by training the model with weighted Adam optimization and cross entropy loss surpassed all other tested combinations, and it is clear from the above data that this algorithm helps the model to generate the most convincing facial expressions. A primary drawback of the model is its reliance on quality of images in the training dataset – it was found that the quality of the images generated from a given expression during testing was slightly lower than that of the training samples. We attribute this to the high resolution of the images in our dataset, most of which were captured using professional photographic equipment, which may not always be the case for a randomly selected image in real time. This is a drawback prevalent in AC-GANs, as well. At present, the only solution for this is increasing the number of training samples, which may produce better results, but at the cost of longer training time. Facial expression synthesis can prove to be useful in enhancing facial recognition systems that are otherwise trained on fewer images per person. The field of computer animation can also benefit from more efficient expression synthesis techniques. Our analysis demonstrates that it is possible to introduce enhancements by incorporating different combinations of loss functions and optimizers in order to improve the quality of output and classification accuracy.

REFERENCES

Arya, S., & Agrawal, A. (2018). Face Recognition with Partial Face Recognition and Convolutional Neural Network. *International Journal of Advanced Research in Computer Engineering & Technology*, *7*(1), 91–94.

Bozorgtabara, B., Rada, M. S., Ekenelb, H. K., & Thiran, J. P. (2019). Learn to synthesize and synthesize to learn. *Computer Vision and Image Understanding*, *185*, 1–11. doi:10.1016/j.cviu.2019.04.010

Choi, Y., Choi, M., Kim, M., Kim, J. H. S., & Choo, J. (2018). *StarGAN: Unified Generative Adversarial Networks for Multi-Domain Image-to-Image Translation*. ArXiv.

Ding, C., Xu, C., & Tao, D. (2015). Multi-Task Pose-Invariant Face Recognition. *IEEE Transactions on Image Processing*, *24*(3), 980–993. doi:10.1109/TIP.2015.2390959 PMID:25594967

El Khiyari, H., & Wechsler, H. (2017). Age Invariant Face Recognition Using Convolutional Neural Networks and Set Distances. *Journal of Information Security*, *8*(3), 174–185. doi:10.4236/jis.2017.83012

Elmahmudi, A., & Ugail, H. (2019). Deep Face recognition using imperfect facial data. *Future Generation Computer Systems, 99*, 213–225. doi:10.1016/j.future.2019.04.025

Filali, H., Riffi, J., Mahraz, A. M., & Tairi, H. (2018). *Multiple face detection based on machine learning.* Paper presented at the Conference on Intelligent Systems and Computer Vision(ISCV), Fez, Morocco. 10.1109/ISACV.2018.8354058

G, S., & V, H. D. (2019). Facial Expression Recognition Complications with the Stages of Face Detection and Recognition. *International Journal of Recent Technology And Engineering, 8*(2), 2728-2740.

Gu, G., Kim, S. T., Kim, K., Baddar, W. J., & Ro, Y. M. (2017). *Differential Generative Adversarial Networks: Synthesizing Non-linear Facial Variations with Limited Number of Training Data.* ArXiv.

Htay, M. M., & Win, Z. M. (2019). Survey on Emotion Recognition Using Facial Expression. *International Journal of Computer, 33*(2), 1–10.

Jiao, L., Zhang, S., Li, L., Liu, F., & Ma, W. (2018). A modified convolutional neural network for face sketch synthesis. *Pattern Recognition, 76*, 125–136. doi:10.1016/j.patcog.2017.10.025

Jothimani, A., Prasanth, P., Anil, S., & Nehru, J. A. (2019). Facial Expression for Emotion Detection using Deep Neural Networks. *International Journal of Recent Technology and Engineering, 8*, 242–248.

Kasim, N. A. B. M., Rahman, N. H. B. A., Ibrahim, Z., & Mangshor, N. N. A. (2018). Celebrity Face Recognition using Deep Learning. *Indonesian Journal of Electrical Engineering and Computer Science, 12*(2), 476–481. doi:10.11591/ijeecs.v12.i2.pp476-481

Kumar, A., Kaur, A., & Kumar, M. (2018). Face Detection Techniques: A Review. *Artificial Intelligence Review, 52*(2), 927–948. doi:10.100710462-018-9650-2

Kumari, J., Rajesh, R., & Pooja, K. (2015). Facial Expression Recognition: A Survey. *Procedia Computer Science, 58*, 486–491. doi:10.1016/j.procs.2015.08.011

Le, T. H. (2011). Applying Artificial Neural Networks for Face Recognition. *Advances in Artificial Neural Systems, 2011*, 1–16. doi:10.1155/2011/673016

Lee, H., Wu, C., & Lin, T. (2013). Facial Expression Recognition Using Image Processing Techniques and Neural Networks. *Advances in Intelligent Systems and Applications, 2*, 259–267.

Liu, M., Breuel, T., & Kautz, J. (2017). Unsupervised Image-to-Image Translation Networks. *Conference on Neural Information Processing Systems (NIPS).* 10.1007/978-3-319-70139-4

Ng, H. W., Nguyen, V. D., Vonikakis, V., & Winkler, S. (2015). Deep Learning for Emotion Recognition on Small Datasets Using Transfer Learning. *ACM International Conference on Multimodal Interaction (ICMI).* 10.1145/2818346.2830593

Patel, M. B., & Agrawal, D. L. (2016). A Survey Paper on Facial Expression Recognition System. *Journal of Emerging Technologies and Innovative Research, 3*(2), 44–46.

Peng, Y., & Yin, H. (2019). ApprGAN: Appearance-Based Generative Adversarial Network for Facial Expression Synthesis. *IET Image Processing, 13*(14), 2706–2715. doi:10.1049/iet-ipr.2018.6576

Revina, I., & Emmanuel, W. (2018). A Survey on Human Face Expression Recognition Techniques. *Journal Of King Saud University - Computer And. Information Sciences.*

Sharma, M. J. A., Manne, H. K., & Kashyap, G. S. C. (2017). Facial detection using deep learning. *IOP Conference Series. Materials Science and Engineering, 263.*

Shukla, R. K., & Tiwari, A. K. (2019). Machine Learning approaches for Face Identification Feed Forward Algorithms. *Proceedings of 2*nd *International Conference on Advanced Computing and Software Engineering.* 10.2139srn.3350264

Sricharan, H. D. K., & Chellappa, R. (2017). ExprGAN: Facial Expression Editing with Controllable Expression Intensity. *The Thirty-Second AAAI Conference on Artificial Intelligence.*

Sun, A., Li, Y., Huang, Y., Li, Q., & Lu, G. (2018). Facial expression recognition using optimized active regions. *Human-centric Computing and Information Sciences, 8*(1).

Tsai, Y., Lin, H., & Yang, F. (2017). Facial Expression Synthesis Based on Imitation. *International Journal of Advanced Robotic Systems, 9*(4), 148. doi:10.5772/51906

Wu, X., Xu, K., & Hall, P. (2017). A Survey of Image Synthesis and Editing with Generative Adversarial Networks. *Tsinghua Science and Technology, 22*(6), 660–674. doi:10.23919/TST.2017.8195348

Xie, W., Shen, L., & Jiang, J. (2017). A novel transient wrinkle detection algorithm and its application for expression synthesis. *IEEE Transactions on Multimedia, 19*(2), 279–292. doi:10.1109/TMM.2016.2614429

Yu, H., Garrod, O., & Schyns, P. (2012). Perception-driven facial expression synthesis. *Computers & Graphics, 36*(3), 152–162. doi:10.1016/j.cag.2011.12.002

Zhuang, Z., Negi, A., Raj, A. N. J., Nersisson, R., & Murugappan, M. (2020). RDA-UNET-WGAN: An Accurate Breast Ultrasound Lesion Segmentation Using Wasserstein Generative Adversarial Networks. *Arabian Journal for Science and Engineering, 45*(8), 6399–6410. doi:10.100713369-020-04480-z

ADDITIONAL READING

Ertuğrul, I., Jeni, L. A., & Dibeklioğlu, H. (2018). Modelling and Synthesis of Kinship Patterns of Facial Expressions. *Image and Vision Computing, 79*, 133–143. doi:10.1016/j.imavis.2018.09.012

Goodfellow, I. J., Pouget-Abadie, J., Mirza, M., Xu, B., Warde-Farley, D., Ozair, S., . . . Bengio, Y. (2014). Generative Adversarial Nets. In *Advances in Neural Information Processing Systems (NIPS), 27*, arXiv:1406.2661.

Isola, P., Zhu, J., Zhou, T., & Efros, A. A. (2018). Image-to-Image Translation with Conditional Adversarial Networks. Retrieved from https://arxiv.org/pdf/1611.07004.pdf

Langner, O., Dotsch, R., Bijlstra, G., Wigboldus, D. H. J., Hawk, S. T., & Knippenberg, A. (2010). Presentation and validation of the Radboud Faces Database. *Cognition and Emotion, 24*(8), 1377–1388. doi:10.1080/02699930903485076

Odena, A., Olah, C., & Shlens, J. (2017). Conditional Image Synthesis With Auxiliary Classifier GANs. In *Proceedings of the 34th International Conference of Machine Learning*, 70, arXiv:1610.09585v4.

Radford, A., Metz, L., & Chintala, S. (2016). Unsupervised Representation Learning with Deep Convolutional Generative Adversarial Networks. In *International Conference on Learning Representations*, arXiv:1511.06434v2.

Springenberg, J. T. (2016). Unsupervised and Semi-supervised Learning with Categorical Generative Adversarial Networks. Published as a conference paper in *International Conference on Learning Representations*, arXiv:1511.06390v2.

Viola, P., & Jones, M. J. (2004). Robust Real-Time Face Detection. *International Journal of Computer Vision*, 57(2), 137–154. doi:10.1023/B:VISI.0000013087.49260.fb

Yan, Y., Huang, Y., Chen, S., Shen, C., & Wang, H. (2020). Joint Deep Learning of Facial Expression Synthesis and Recognition. *IEEE Transactions on Multimedia*, arXiv:2002.02194.

KEY TERMS AND DEFINITIONS

Deep Learning: A subset of a broader family of machine learning methods that makes use of multiple layers to extract data from raw input in order to learn its features.

Downsampling: The process of reducing the rate at which a digital signal is processed. It is the opposite of upsampling.

Instance Normalization: A mathematical technique employed to scale numeric values in data used for training a model.

Neural Network: An artificial network of nodes, used for predictive modelling. It is generally used to tackle classification problems and AI related applications.

Upsampling: The process of increasing the rate at which a digital signal is processed. It is the opposite of downsampling.

Chapter 16
Deep Convolutional Neural Network for Object Classification:
Under Constrained and Unconstrained Environments

Amira Ahmad Al-Sharkawy
Electronics Research Institute, Egypt

Gehan A. Bahgat
ⓘD https://orcid.org/0000-0002-4840-2231
Electronics Research Institute, Egypt

Elsayed E. Hemayed
Zewail City of Science and Technology, Egypt

Samia Abdel-Razik Mashali
Electronics Research Institute, Egypt

ABSTRACT

Object classification problem is essential in many applications nowadays. Human can easily classify objects in unconstrained environments easily. Classical classification techniques were far away from human performance. Thus, researchers try to mimic the human visual system till they reached the deep neural networks. This chapter gives a review and analysis in the field of the deep convolutional neural network usage in object classification under constrained and unconstrained environment. The chapter gives a brief review on the classical techniques of object classification and the development of bio-inspired computational models from neuroscience till the creation of deep neural networks. A review is given on the constrained environment issues: the hardware computing resources and memory, the object appearance and background, and the training and processing time. Datasets that are used to test the performance are analyzed according to the images environmental conditions, besides the dataset biasing is discussed.

DOI: 10.4018/978-1-7998-6690-9.ch016

INTRODUCTION

Object classification is an increasingly important topic in computer vision. It is defined as the classification of an object existing lonely in an image. For multiple objects images, object localization or detection is required first. The objects to be classified in an image can be in a constrained environment or unconstrained environment. Constrains of the environment could be the background; plain or real, hardware resources required for computation, processing time in real time applications and object appearance. Object classification is used in wide range of applications; such, mobile applications (Xiong, Kim, & Hedau, 2019), tablets and other smart appliances, sorting and quality control in food industry (Naranjo-Torres, et al., 2020).

Classical machine learning techniques were popular, for many decades, for object classification. The popular technique was to extract features from the input images, to form a feature vector, which is used in learning the patterns from the input images, and training a model. Along with being time-consuming, feature extraction depends on the image type. Thus, the accuracy of the system depends on designing the right set of features, which may need an expert for some types of tasks. Humans can identify thousands of object categories in strewn scenes, despite the variations in the object posture, changes in its illumination and occlusions.

Visual cortex models appeared as a solution for bridging the gap between the performance of the human vision and the computational models. Cortical models are bio-inspired systems based on the available neuroscience research to imitate the human visual performance. Neuroscience experiments provide sufficient information to understand how the visual cortex works. Many frameworks appeared as a result of advances and cooperation between several fields like brain science, cognitive science, and computer vision.

Deep learning techniques, especially deep convolutional neural networks (DCNN), are also bio-inspired from the hierarchical way of the visual cortex to approach the performance of the human visual system. DCNN is powerful in extracting features from the input data directly. Identifying the object using the extracted features in unconstrained environment is done by the convolution and pooling layers (Haq, et al., 2020). Some developing applications begin with constrains such as the image background like in the case of LeafSnap mobile application (Kang & Oh, 2018) that classifies the types of the trees from their leaves. The old version of the application requires that the leaf to be pictured on a white paper, then the application is developed now to picture in unconstrained environment. The availability of different software platforms for building DCNNs such as: Caffe, Theano and TensorFlow facilities the use of deep neural network (DNN) in many applications.

The issue of discussing the object classification using DCNN in constrained and unconstrained environment on general is not discussed explicitly in the published papers. This issue is discussed on specific object type such as fish species classification (Khalifa, Taha, & Hassanien, 2018), and gender classification (Huang et al., 2017).

The objective of this chapter is to highlight the superiority of the DCNN over classical techniques in object classification that came from mimicking the human visual system, analysis of the different architectures, challenges present of constrains of the object classification using DCNN and their presented solutions. Constrains include the computing and storage resources, object appearance, object background, and training and processing time. Also, the datasets types and their biasing effect are discussed. Finally, the future trends in this area are given.

BACKGROUND

Classical Techniques of Classification and its Limitations

For decades, a hand-designed feature extractor is used to gather the related information from the input image. Subsequently, a trained classifier categorizes the feature vectors into the corresponding classes. The classifiers can be like SVM (Support Vector Machine). The power of the classic techniques depends on its feature extractor. A study of large-scale object classification, how it helps to move forward closer to the human performance, is available in (Deng, et al., 2010) for more reliability and better generalization. Examples of classical techniques are the winners of the competition ILSVRC (ImageNet Large Scale Visual Recognition Competition) 2010 and 2011 that applied object classification (Russakovsky, et al., 2015). The dataset used is composed of real life images. NEC team (Lin, et al., 2011) uses SIFT (Scale-Invariant Feature Transform) (Lowe, 2004) and LBP (Local Binary Pattern) (Ahonen, Hadid, & Pietikainen, 2006) features with two nonlinear coding representation and classifies using a stochastic SVM (Support Vector Machine). They achieve an average error rate 28.2%. The classifier SVM (Cortes, & Vapnik, 1995) is very powerful. The winner in 2011 XRCE (Xerox Research Centre Europe) team (Perronnin, Sánchez, & Mensink, 2010, September) uses improved Fisher vector presentation based on multi-scale SIFT descriptors followed by compression using product quantization (Sánchez, & Perronnin, 2011, June), then the one-versus-all linear SVM classifier is applied. They achieve average error rate 25.8%. Starting from 2012, DCNN are the winners. There are limitations of the classic techniques as shown in Table 1 that emphasizes the superiority of DCNNs in learning features, invariant to object position, scale and distortion, and equate human performance.

Table 1. Difference between the classical and DCNN models

Point of comparison	Classical models	DCNN models
Input images	Not applied directly to the classifier input.	Applied directly
Feature extractor perspective	Generating handcrafted features is a difficult task and need an expert, and for better accuracy, the feature vector length is long.	No Feature vector, automatically learn features.
Classifier hardware required resources	Uni-processor and moderate memory size	Multi-core processor and large memory.
Training dataset size	Large training instances to be invariant to shift, scale and distortion	Automatically invariant
Performance with respect to human	A large gap.	Dramatically reduced until surpassing the human performance on ImageNet dataset.

Neuroscience and Cortical Models

Neuroscientists made many efforts to understand how the human visual work. The visual cortex area is a part of the brain which is responsible for the visual information processing. Goodale and Milner (1992) provide two streams hypothesis, based on neuropsychological and electrophysiological studies, and suggest that the neural substrates have two discrete pathways:

1. The ventral stream pathway is responsible for the object recognition and identification.
2. The dorsal stream is responsible for the spatial localization of the object, motion and controlling the eyes and arms.

Deep Convolutional Neural Networks

Deep learning models are like the primate visual system in how the complex concept such as an object, is defined by combining the simpler concepts in hierarchical representation; such that object parts, defined by corners and contours, that are defined by edges (Goodfellow, Bengio, & Courville, 2016). Cadieu et al. (2014) research demonstrated that DCNNs; AlexNet and ZFNet which surpassed the-state-of-the-art techniques on ImageNet dataset, outperform the models for the visual cortex (Pinto, Cox, & DiCarlo, 2008), (Freeman, & Simoncelli, 2011).

Deep learning is an advanced type of representation learning. It has various techniques such as stacked auto encoders, deep Boltzmann machines, deep belief networks, convolutional neural networks (CNN), and recurrent neural networks (RNN). The best choice for object classification is the DCNN according to the results of ILSVRC as shown in Figure 1. It is based on convolution-based layers. The participants in 2010 and 2011 used classical techniques (Russakovsky, et al., 2015). In 2012, there was a breakthrough in the large-scale object recognition field when Krizhevsky, Sutskever, & Hinton (2012) proposed AlexNet to win the ILSVRC. They reduced the top-5 error rate of the state-of-the-art from 26.1% to 15.32% in classification (Russakovsky, et al., 2015). After that, many researchers followed the

Figure 1. Best object classification error rate in ILSVRC competitions (Russakovsky, et al., 2015; ILS-VRC, 2016; ILSVRC, 2017)

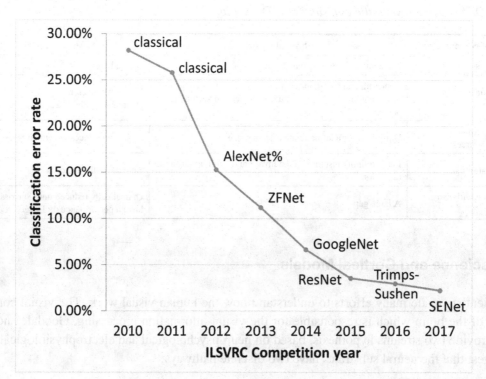

success and made larger and deeper neural networks. In 2013, Clarifai team presented ZFNet with error rate 11.2% (Zeiler, & Fergus, 2014, September). In ILSVRC-2014, GoogLeNet team achieves 6.67% error rate (Szegedy, et al., 2015). In 2015, MSRA (Microsoft Research Asia) team uses ResNet with 3.57% error rate (He, et al., 2016). In 2016, Trimps-Sushen team won with 2.99% error rate (ILSVRC, 2016), and in 2017, the classification error rate reached 2.251% (ILSVRC, 2017) using SENeT (Squeeze and Excitation network) (Hu, Shen & Sun, 2018). By 2010, the annotated very large-scale datasets, with high-resolution natural images, appeared and instigated a massive development in the machine-learning field. Also, GPUs (Graphic Processing Units) architectures and their storage have been developed and became powerful enough to implement DNNs on them.

DCNN Architecture

The core of DCNN is the convolutional layer (CL) that corresponds to the simple cells in the mammals' visual cortex. Its role is to apply filters, known as kernels or receptive fields, to the input and produce feature maps (FMs) that is also called activation map. Each filter operates on a small spatial dimension of the output of the previous layer to capture the local features. The size of the filter depends on the application of DCNN, but it affects the power consumption, latency and accuracy (Hochreiter, 1998). The convolution filters can be in a 3D form where they are spatially small along the height and width, but the depth is the same as the depth of the input that controls the number of neurons. There are hyperparameters of CL; the stride, which is the distance between two adjacent receptive fields, and the zero-padding on the border of the output. The lower used stride; the more overlapped receptive fields, and the larger output volume. Another parameter is the learning rate, which has small value; 0 to 1. It controls the percentage of the estimated weight error update after each batch. The neurons that generate the entries of the same FM share the same parameters because they apply the same filters used. This is called parameter sharing. Its role is to detect features regardless of their locations and reduce pruning to the overfitting problem and saving memory. The overfitting problem arises when the network fits well to a training set and fails to operate on other dataset. A pixel in the feature map l of a CL is given by (Indolia et al, 2018):

$$FM_{ij}^{l} = \sigma \left(W^{l} * X_{ij} + b^{l} \right).$$

$$(1)$$

where σ is the activation function, W^{l} is the weight of size $k \times k$. X_{ij} is the part of the input, and b^{l} is the bias. This operation computes linear regularities in the input. The nonlinear features are learned using the activation function such as tanh, sigmoid and ReLU (Rectified Linear Units). The RELU is non-saturated nonlinear functions, defined as:

$$f(x) = \max(0, x).$$

$$(2)$$

It is more effective because it speeds up the training of the network, and reduces the vanishing gradient problem which arises while training the network and the error between the output of the network and the target could vanish while it flows back to the input layer.

Subsampling or pooling layers correspond to the complex cells in the visual cortex that pool simple cells activities (Hubel, & Wiesel, 1962). They are used to reduce the dimension of the FMs, which in turn reduces the number of parameters, computation cost, and training time in the successive layers and reduces the overfitting problem. The filters are better to be of size 2×2 and stride S=2, using larger size makes the pooling too aggressive and worsens the performance. Common operations are max pooling (Krizhevsky, Sutskever, & Hinton, 2012), average pooling (He, et al., 2016), and stochastic pooling (Zeiler, & Fergus, 2013. Max Pooling is the most popular for its simplicity. Stochastic Pooling activation is randomly chosen from each region by a multinomial distribution, to guarantee that not only the strongest activation is picked, but also give a chance for other activations. Pooling layer has hyperparameters: stride (S) and receptive field (F). Pooling regions can be overlapped or be non-overlapped (Sermanet et al, 2013). The sub-sampling reduces the sensitivity to shifting and distortion (Shen et al., 2019). Researchers proposed a method called Fractional Max-Pooling, where the pooling filter size is ($\alpha \times \alpha$) and $1 < \alpha < 2$. This is achieved by choosing pooling region randomly, or pseudo-randomly, or can be overlapped or disjoint (Graham, 2014).

Fully connected layer is a layer where its neurons are connected to all neurons in the previous layer. This full connection enables to express complex functions. The equation of the output of this layer is given by:

$$x_j^l = \sigma \left(\sum_i w_{ij}^l x_i^{l-1} + b^l \right).$$

(3)

where x_{ij}^{l-1} .is the output of the previous layer at point (i, j). $w_{i,j}$ .is the weight of layer l. Fully connected layer: consumes most memory of the network, and affects considerably the latency. Thus it is recommended to choose the minimum number of layers and layer size.

Network training is based on error minimization methods such as backpropagation which consumes twice the time of forward process. It is optimized by gradient descent that adjusts the weights; Stochastic Gradient Descent is used in AlexNet, patch stochastic gradient descent in VGGNet, asynchronous stochastic gradient descent (Dean, et al., 2012).

The loss layer is the last layer of DCNN that calculates the variation between the actual output and the predicted output during training. The loss functions used is like Softmax, SVM, Euclidean, and Sigmoid cross-entropy.

Normalization is applied in order to force the data dimensions to be at the same scale. It improves the performance by decreasing the error rates and providing better generalization. Normalizing guarantee a fixed distribution for features and eliminate the covariate shift problem, which is the change in the distribution between the training and testing data. There are types of normalization methods; certain kinds are inspired by the inhibition schemes of the biological brain's neurons such as the brightness normalization used in AlexNet. The most common type is batch normalization (BN) that normalizes for each mini batch in training. It facilitates the data to flow easily through layers, which speed up the training time and allow higher learning rates.

Popular DCNN

LeNet

LeNet (LeCun, Bottou, Bengio, & Haffner, 1998) is the first practical DCNN. Its training was on MNIST (Modified NIST) dataset, which is a handwritten digits on uniform background. LeNet-5 performance was 0.8% error rate. Furthermore, LeNet is used for certain object classification in natural scenes (LeCun, Huang, & Bottou, 2004). It is trained on objects with different pose, lightening and surrounding clutter from NORB and jittered dataset. But, LeNet fail to classify images in (Brandenburg, et al., 2019). LeNet benefits from the parameter sharing concept in reducing the number of parameters; whereas LeNet contains 340,908 connections, the trained parameters are 60,000.

AlexNet

AlexNet (Krizhevsky, Sutskever, & Hinton, 2012) was a breakthrough in the deep learning and computer vision. It was the first model to perform properly on ImageNet. Its basic architecture is like LeNet but deeper and larger. AlexNet contains a softmax layer, which is responsible for the label distribution over 1000 classes. AlexNet is invariant to changes in the illuminations, color and intensity. The whole network consists of 650,000 neurons and 60,000,000 parameters. The authors pre-trained their model on the entire ImageNet dataset that contained 15 million images with 22,000 categories.

ZFNet

ZFNet is proposed by Zeiler and Fergus (2014) who proposed also a novel technique called 'DeconvNet' that helps in visualization how DCNN works (Zeiler, Taylor, & Fergus, 2011). The technique is a reverse of the convolution operations where it maps the output features to the input pixels. The result of visualizing DCNN features shows similarity to the primate visual cortex;

- First layer filters learns directed edges in different orientations and frequencies.
- Second layer represents curves, circles, and parallel lines.
- Third layer learns more complex features like object parts.
- Fourth layer learns specific object parts such as faces of dogs and humans.
- Fifth layer learns the entire objects with different poses.

ZFNet was trained using only 1.3 million images from ImageNet, yet it outperforms AlexNet.

VGGNet

VGGNet is provided by Simonyan, & Zisserman (2014) provided two very-deep models called VGGNet with 16 and 19 weighted layers. They generalize well on other datasets; Pascal VOC 2007, Pascal VOC 2012, Caltech-101, and Caltech-256, better than the generalization of ZFNet. They used dropout to avoid overfitting and data augmentation.

NIN

Network In Network (NIN) architecture (Lin, Chen, & Yan, 2013) was the first inspiration for module based DCNNs that provide a high performance based on:

1. Replacing the simple CL in conventional DCNNs with MLPconv (Multi-layer Perception convolution) module. It consists of CL and two MLP layers with ReLU activation functions. Each module is followed by max-pooling layer.
2. Replacing the FC layers with a global average pooling to reduce the number of parameters.
3. For preventing overfitting, NIN uses dropout, and data augmentation. Recently, a modified NIN architecture is proposed with the replace of ReLU by linear exponential unit (eLU) to reduce the learning time and solve the vanishing gradient problem (Alaeddine, and Jihene, 2020). The depth is increased, but the filter size is decreased to reduce the number of parameters. The network was tested on cifar-10 dataset.

GoogleNet

GoogLeNet (Szegedy, et al., 2015) is based on inception module (Figure 2), thus GoogleNet is called Inception-v1 network. The operations in the network occur in consecutive order and parallel inside the inception module. The last FC layers are replaced by an average pooling layer and one FC layer to get rid of the abundance of parameters and consequently reduce the needed computational resources. The number of parameters is reduced to 4 million parameters compared to 60 million parameters in AlexNet.

Figure 2. Inception module

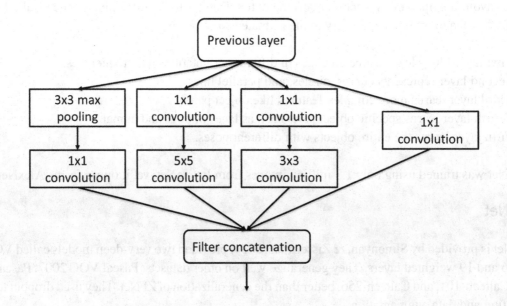

ResNet

ResNet allows CNNs to have a large number of layers with increased performance, while the performance of the plain network is decreased after a certain number of layers (He, et al., 2016). They provided three versions of ResNet: ResNet-50, ResNet-101, and ResNet-152, which have 50 layers, 101 layers and 152 layers, respectively. The building block of ResNet is the residual block. It consists of stacked convolution layers but shortened with identity function as shown in Figure 3, where for the weights W1 and W2 of the CL, $F(X)$ is given by:

$$F(X) = W_2 . ReLU . (W_1 . X).$$

ResNet is trained on a machine of 8 GPUs which took from two to three weeks.

Figure 3. The residual module

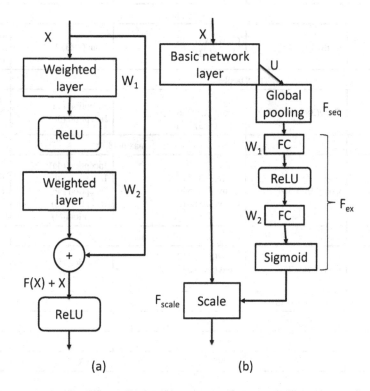

(a) (b)

BN-Inception (Inception v2)

In 2015, Ioffe & Szegedy (2015) provided Inception-v2 by improving the inception structure using a novel method called Batch Normalization. Adding batch-norm layers to the network substantially speeded up training, and achieved high accuracy. Moreover, it eliminates some problems used to associate with training process such as increasing the learning rate, accelerating its decay, and covariate shift, which is changing the distribution of layer features through training. Since BN has a regularization effect, dropout is removed and the local response normalization (LRN) layer.

Table 2 shows a comparison between different DCNN architectures. There is a general architecture of DCNN can be deduced, which consists of 5 stages of: 1) Grouped Convolution block (GCB), 2) Max pooling, 3) FC stage, 4) Softmax. In case of AlexNet and ZFNet, GCB is single CL and the max pooling is absent after the third and fourth CL. In VGGNet, GCB contains 2 to 3 consecutive CL. In GoogleNet, the third to fifth GCB contains 2 to 5 inception modules, their internal details are given in (Szegedy, et al., 2015). In ResNet-50, the second to fifth GCB contains repeated residual modules and the max pooling is absent due to the use of 1x1 CL.

Table 2. Comparison between different DCNN architectures. CL is denoted by 'Conv', the equivalent filter dimensions are written as 'width x height, depth' and max pooling layer is denoted by 'max pool'.

AlexNet	ZFNet	VGGNet-19	GoogleNet	ResNet-50
Conv11×11),48	Conv(7×7),96	Conv(3x3),64 Conv(3x3),64	Conv(7×7),64	Conv(7×7),64
max pool				
Conv(5×5),128	Conv(5×5),256	Conv(3x3),128 Conv(3x3),128	Conv(3×3),192	[conv1×1,64 conv3×3,64 conv1×1,256]x3
max pool				
Conv(3×3),192	Conv(3×3),384	Conv(3x3),256 Conv(3x3),256 Conv(3x3),256	Inception (3a) Inception (3b)	[conv1×1,128 conv3×3,128 conv1×1,512]x4
-	-	max pool		
Conv(3×3),192	Conv(3×3),384	Conv(3x3),512 Conv(3x3),512 Conv(3x3),512	Inception (4a) Inception (4b) Inception (4c) Inception(4d) Inception(4e)	[conv1×1,256 conv3×3,265 conv1×1,1024]x6
-	-	max pool		
Conv(3×3),128	Conv(3×3),256	Conv(3x3),512 Conv(3x3),512 Conv(3x3),512	Inception (5a) Inception (5b)	[conv1×1,512 conv3×3,512 conv1×1,2048]x3
max pool			Average pool	
FC-4096			-	-
FC-4096			-	-
-		FC-1000		
Soft-max				

SENet

In ILSVRC-2017, WMW team (Hu, Shen, and Sun 2018) has won the competition using the model: SENet (Squeeze-and-Excitation Network). SENet surpassed the state-of-the-art by 25% with achieving 2.251 top-5 testing error, 18.68% top-1 validation error, and 4.47% top-5 validation error.

SE network consists of stacked SE blocks. Its basic idea is to provide a dynamic recalibration of features. The objective of the side path to weight the output of each feature map in the CL. At the beginning, the weights are equal, and then the network adjusts these weights proportional to how it is more relevant. They used average pooling layer to squeeze the output feature maps into a single value. ReLU layer is used to provide the needed non-linearity. A reduction ratio is used to reduce the dimensionality provided by the FC layers. SE blocks can be integrated with any of the former networks such as Alexnet, VGGNet, Inception, and ResNet. Adding SE blocks for these networks provide a better performance that approach and sometimes outperform deeper networks of the original networks with much lower overhead.

Mobile Based Networks

There are networks developed recently that is designed to implement DCNN on mobile devices with its hardware and costs constrain, such as MobileNet, MobileNetV1 (version 1), MobileNetV2 (version 2), (Sandler et al., 2018) and ANTNet (Attention NesTed Network) (Xiong, Kim, & Hedau, 2019). The issue of design depends on the number of computation required. The recent version MobileNetV2 is composed mainly of blocks that are called residual bottleneck. While the ANTNet is composed mainly from ANT blocks.

Constrained and Unconstrained Environment

The issue of using DCNN to classify objects is discussed separately depending on the object type. This issue is considered in different applications other than object classification such as face recognition; in (Fredj, Bouguezzi, & Souani, 2020), face recognition in unconstrained environment using aggressive data augmentation with massive noisy and occluded faces is considered. In (Chaudhry & Chandra, 2017), face recognition in unconstrained environment is applied using visual mobile assistive system that is subject to blurring and noise due to camera shaking, it succeeded in daylight and artificial lightening. Human detection in surveillance system in occluded and noisy environment is presented (Haq, et al., 2020). In (Xie, Hu, & Wu, 2019), constrained face dataset, and unconstrained datasets is composed of faces taken from movies with different pose, real world illumination and age, facial expressions, occlusions, varied focus, and different resolution. In (Jana, Bhaumik, & Mohanta, 2019), the case of unconstrained videos taken by inexperienced amateurs suffering from quality aspects such as weak illumination, fluctuating of camera motion, real or chaotic background is considered.

Data Sets

The trend of increasing the size of the datasets comes along with the growth of the world digitization. The labeled datasets have grown considerably in the last few years, as shown in Figure 4. The examples given in figure are; Caltech-101 (Fei-Fei, Fergus, & Perona, 2006), Pascal VOC07 (Visual Object Classes) (Everingham, Van Gool, Williams, Winn, & Zisserman, 2010), Cifar-10 (Canadian Institute for Advanced Research) (Krizhevsky, & Hinton, 2009), ILSRVC 2012 (Russakovsky, et al., 2015), and ImageNet (Russakovsky, et al., 2015). Noting that there can be more than one object in the image, but it is located by a boundary box.

Figure 4. Object classification datasets emerged over time (Fei-Fei, Fergus, & Perona, 2006; Everingham, Van Gool, Williams, Winn, & Zisserman, 2010;Krizhevsky, & Hinton, 2009; Russakovsky, et al., 2015)

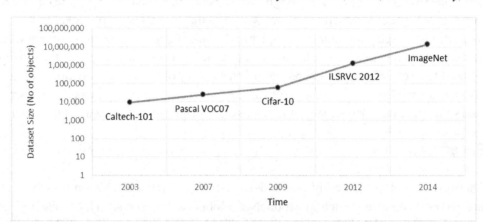

The datasets can contain objects with constrained and unconstrained environmental conditions. In this chapter, the images under constrained environment are defined as images containing object with uniform background, while images under unconstrained environment are the images containing object with real-world background.

Datasets are classified according to size. Small datasets contain tens of thousands of labeled images. They have good performance with small recognition tasks. Large dataset contains from hundreds of thousands to tens of millions of labeled images. Small datasets such as NORB (New York University Object Recognition Benchmark) dataset (LeCun, Huang, & Bottou, 2004, June), Caltech-101, Caltech-256 dataset (Griffin, Holub, & Perona, 2007), CIFAR-10 (Canadian Institute For Advanced Research), CIFAR-100 (Krizhevsky, & Hinton, 2009), LabelMe Dataset (Russell, Torralba, Murphy, & Freeman, 2008), Pascal VOC07, Pascal VOC12 (Everingham, & Winn, 2012), and SUN (Xiao, Hays, Ehinger, Oliva, & Torralba, 2010, June). Very large-scale datasets are such as Tiny images (Torralba, Fergus, & Freeman, 2008), and ImagNet that are used in the ILSVRC competition. One of the reasons that help the appearance of the very large-scale datasets was the availability of online annotation tools such as Amazon Mechanical Turk and LabelMe websites. Table 3 shows a comparison between different datasets. Most of the datasets are of unconstrained environmental condition. The most reliable dataset is the largest, with real-life images and large number of images per category. These conditions are satisfied in Tiny images and ImageNet datasets. Thus, ImageNet is used in the ILSVRC competitions.

Table 3. A comparison between different datasets

Dataset	Number of images	Number of categories	Number of images /Category	Resolution (in pixels)	Source	Environmental conditions
NORB	194,400	5	10	640×480	Taken with two cameras for objects in various conditions of lightening, elevation, and azimuths.	Constrained and unconstrained
Caltech-256	*30,607*	256	At least 80	*300×200*	Collected from Google with improvements.	Constrained and unconstrained
CIFAR-100	60,000	100	600	32×32	Subset from Tiny Images.	Unconstrained
LabelMe	30,369	183	At least 30	High resolution	Outdoor pictures in different cities of Spain	Unconstrained
Pascal VOC2012	11,530 images (27,450 annotated objects)	20	-	469×387	Downloaded from Flickr website.	Unconstrained
SUN	131,067 images (313,884 segmented objects)	908 scene categories (4,479 object categories)	22 to 2,360	200×200 or larger	Collected from online image search engines based on WordNet & other categories.	Unconstrained
Tiny Images	79,302,017	75,062 words	1,056 images per word	32 ×32	Collected from 7 search engines (Google, Flickr, Ask, Altavista, Picsearch, Cydral, and Webshots) based on WordNet.	Unconstrained
ImageNet	14,197,122 (1,034,908 annotated)	27 High level Categories, each have 51 to 3,822 synsets (low level category)	Synset contains 453 to 1,207	High resolution	Collected from the internet based on WordNet.	Unconstrained

CHALLENGES OF DCNN IN OBJECT CLASSIFICATION IN CONSTRAINED ENVIROMENT

Despite the DCNNs huge advantages, they still have weaknesses: computation time and overfitting problem. Constrains of the environment that faces the usage of object classification using DCNN are several; the hardware resources that compromises the processing unit and the memory size, the equivalent power consumption, training and processing time, object background, object properties, accuracy, and training dataset.

Hardware Resources:

GPUs architectures and their storage have been developed and became powerful enough to implement DNNs on them. For training AlexNet, two GPUs of type GTX 580 with 3GB memory for each are used (Krizhevsky, Sutskever, & Hinton, 2012). They provided a parallelization scheme for communication between GPUs by putting half of the neurons in each GPU. For minimizing the communication overhead, they make the communication between two GPUs in certain layers.

GPU is unconstrained platform, which are not power and resource utilization effective such as mobile, automotive, IOT (Internet of Things) devices, and portable medical devices. Constrained accelerated platforms are such as FPGA (Field Programmable Gate Array) and SOC (System on Chip) that compromises processor and FPGA for hardware/software codesign. Optimization is required in choosing the suitable platform to achieve high accuracy. Constrains are the power consumption, needed resources and execution time (latency). In (Laguduva et al., 2020), each layer of the DCNN is studied with respect to these parameters. This study is applied on four DCNNs; LeNet, AlexNet, VGG11 and VGG 16. Their implementation is optimized on low power consuming platform (constrained environment). They are evaluated using MNIST and CIFAR-10 datasets. The DCNN parts that are optimized are filter size, number of fully connected layers. They achieved 11x reduction in power consumption on small low power heterogeneous platform that can be used in constrained IOT device called PYNQ-Z1 and 96x reduction on FPGA with more resources, while keeping the same accuracy. DCNN require high computation and intensive resources for their large number of trainable parameters in the range of tens to hundreds of millions. SOC and FPGA support less execution time. Mapping software implementation into hardware using high level synthesis tool is a challenge that needs a programmer aid. PYNQ-Z1 board is an embedded system hardware platform programmed by the open-source package and libraries called PYNQ designed by Xilinx. The board compromises Zynq-7000 SoC that consists of Dual ARM Cortex A9 and FPGA. The language of PYNQ is Python. Subsampling techniques are used to reduce the dimensionality of the features. ASIC advantage is high performance, lower area and lower power consumption but disadvantage is the unreconfigurability and the complexity of the design cycle. Thus reconfigurable devices are more preferable. Power consumed by FPGA is measured using kill-a-watt meter that is commonly used to measure power consumption of network on FPGA (Hochreiter, 1998).

Mobiles, tablets and any other smart appliances that has embedded vision applications are characterized by limited hardware resources and power consumption, thus, DCNN networks used to classify objects are reconstructed in a way to reduce the number of parameters of the network by considering grouped convolution blocks instead of large size CLs (Xiong, Kim, & Hedau, 2019). Examples of these networks are MobileNetV1, MobileNetV2, ANTNet (Attention NesTed Network) (Xiong, Kim, & Hedau, 2019), ResNet, Inception and Xception networks. In the grouped convolution, each output channel is connected to different group of input channels. The advantage of this topology is the reduction of the number of the network parameters, thus there is a reduction in the training and processing time, and the power consumption.

Training and Processing Time

The DCNN training time is huge relative to the classical techniques, and this due to the large number of the network parameters in the range of millions that needs to be optimized and performs more than 1 Billion high precision operations (Luan et al, 2018). The solution for that is the use of Gabor filters, and the pre-trained models. Gabor based DCNN uses Gabor kernels with different orientations, and scales to extract texture features of the object under uncertain detector orientation (Luan et al., 2018). In (Zhou, & Wichman, 2020), they used gabor kernels with different frequencies. The usage of Gabor kernels reduces the DCNN parameters and thus, reduces the training time. DCNN may take several days to be trained depending on its architecture, the training data size, and the GPU used in training. A solution to reduce the training time is using a pretrained networks on large dataset, then by transfer learning and retraining, the network can learn in a reduced time. An example is the tree classification from its leaves in the application that is called LeafSnap (Kang & Oh, 2018). The network is pretrained on ImageNet dataset then retrained on the leaves dataset; MOIP.

In the food industry, food classification, and food quality inspection (Naranjo-Torres, Mora, & Hernández-García,2020) is considered as real-time problem, in order to classify the food while the assembly lines move with a certain velocity. In (LeCun, Huang, & Bottou, 2004, June), the LeNet used to detect and classify certain object in natural scenes using real-time system with rate 30 frames per second.

Table 4 shows a comparison between DCNNs according to the hardware platform, training time, number of weighted layers of each DCNN and the main contribution presented by each. The training time with respect to the used GPU number and type are approximately linear, using 2 GPUs reduces the training time of Alexnet with respect to ZFNet. No details are given for the type of GPU used by GoogleNet and ResNet-152. The SENet training time is given in epochs, and the single path forward and backwards is 203 ms (Hu, et al, 2018), thus the estimated training time is 24 minutes. As for the networks designed to operate on mobiles, the time is given by latency, which is the time of classifying an object. The number of weighted layers increases year by year where VGGNet and GoogleNet appeared in the same year. The network based on residual blocks facilities the increase of the number of the network layers.

Table 4. Comparison between GPU, training time, number of weighted layers and main contribution of different CNNs

CNN model	GPU	Training Time/ latency	No of weighted Layers	Main Contribution
AlexNet	2 GTX580	Training: 5-6 days	8	Providing the first CNN architecture for object classification
ZFNet	GTX580	Training: 12 days	8	Visualisation technique
GoogLeNet	Few high end GPU	Training: Week	22	Very deep architecture with reduced parameters and resources
VGGNet	4 NVIDIA Titan-Black	Training: 2-3 weeks	16, 19	Very deep and straightforward architecture
ResNet-152	8 GPUs machine	Training: 2-3 weeks	152	Ultra deep networks based on residual blocks
SENet	8 NVIDIA Titan X GPUs	Training: 400 epochs,	154	Present SE blocks
MobileNetV2	Dual core Cyclone+M7 coprocessor	Latency: 197.2 ms	53	Networks for mobiles
ANTNet	Dual core Cyclone+M7 coprocessor	Latency: 157.7 ms	45	Networks for mobiles

Object Background:

There are two schemes of image acquisition for object classification depending on its background: A constraint on the background to be uniform such as capturing the image of leaf of the trees on white paper to identify the type of the tree using a mobile application called LeafSnap (Kang & Oh, 2018). Classical classifier is used. This scheme is not convenient for the user. The other scheme is less stringent, the unconstraint background, focusing on the leaf present on the tree or on a branch of the tree, or soil or the sky. This scheme is convenient for the user, but on the expense of recognition performance. The automatic feature learning the DNN is used. This software is developed to classify flowers and fruit.

Object Appearance:

There are problems arise from the object classification in an unconstrained environment of the image, there are problems arise that reduce the recognition performance, such as the variations of the object view due to difference in the illumination and real-world illumination, different pose (facing direction of object), and occlusion (whole or partly appearance of the object, resolution of picture, noise in case of surveillance cameras and varied focus and different resolution depending on the camera (Zhang, Shang, & Wu, 2019) (Xie, Hu, & Wu, 2019). Figure 5 shows the possible variations of an object.

Figure 5. Possible variations of the object;(a) and (b)illumination difference, (c) and (d) object and different pose, (e)occlusion, (f) low resolution look and (g) added noise

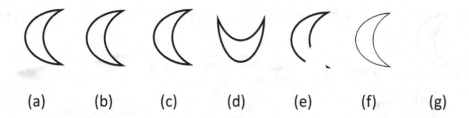

(a)   (b)   (c)   (d)   (e)   (f)   (g)

In (Khalifa, Taha, & Hassanien, 2018), the challenges faced fish classification is the classification of underwater fish species due to the similarity in color, shape and texture. Also, the challenges are changes of light intensity, fish orientation changeable background, similarity in patterns of different species (Salman et al, 2018). In vehicle detection, License plate recognition, the unconstrained challenges are the dirty obscured plate, night illumination, logo, and bad weather. Vehicle logo recognition facilities in vehicle recognition, while, small logo is a problem (Liu, et al., 2019).

Gender classification using Siamese DCNN classifies under constrained and unconstrained conditions. It is based on the human face. The importance of gender classification is in the verification of payment, visual surveillance, and human machine interaction.

There are 3 categories of occlusion: occlusion caused by illumination changes, disguise, and self-occlusion done by pose variation. Occlusion causes feature missing, alignment error. It is required to weaken or eliminate the occlusion for robust classification. The solution is from the view of subspace regression: collaborative representation, occlusion coding, (Li, & Liang, 2018). Another problem is the case of overlapped objects.

Unconstrained images taken by inexperienced amateurs suffer from quality aspects such as weak illumination, fluctuating of camera motion, real or chaotic background (Jana, Bhaumik, & Mohanta, 2019). In security, such as the object classification of X-ray baggage images (Akcay, Kundegorski, Willcocks, & Breckon, 2018), overlapped objects in a bag failed to be classified correctly. The solution is using object detection or localization DCNNs such as Sliding Window Based CNN, Faster RCNN (F-RCNN), R-FCN, YOLOv2.

Altering the RGB intensities of the training images by implementing Principle Component Analysis (PCA) on the RGB values helps the network to become invariant to changes in the illuminations, color and intensity when identifying objects, besides, reducing the top-1 error rate by 1% (Krizhevsky, Sutskever, & Hinton, 2012). Due to the local receptive field concept, when the input of a convolution layer is shifted, its output FM is also shifted by the same amount, which makes CNN more robust to changes in position and distortion.

Dataset:

Unconstrained conditions in the dataset are: real-world photos; faces with natural expressions, uncertain shooting angle, in unconstrained environment where there are occlusion and blurs. Learning algorithms aim is to increase the distance between negative pairs and decrease the distance between positive pairs. The linear transformation learning such as Large-Margin Nearest Neighbors (LMNN) does not fit with unconstrained conditions, but using DCNN solves this problem due to the presence of nonlinear activation functions, such as Discriminative Deep Metric Learning.

Some applications suffers from small dataset which causes overfitting problem; Overfitting means that the network is more accurate in the classification of known data, which is relevant to the training data; however, inaccurate in generalization, that is the classification of new data. Other applications, despite using very large-scale datasets like ImageNet, CNNs still prone to overfitting problem due to: the size of CNNs with many layers and millions of parameters, and the bias of the dataset. There are methods avoid this problem as shown in Figure 6, such as limiting the network size, using parameter sharing concept, using pooling layer to down sample the network parameters, and using normalization layer. Recently, many regularization techniques are presented, where DCNNs may employ more than one regularization technique. Data augmentation is the easiest regularization technique that works on the input nodes. It increases the size of the training data by for example, randomly cropping the input images generating smaller patches and their horizontal reflections, using rotation transformation. Another form is by changing the intensities of the RGB channels of the training data (Krizhevsky, Sutskever, & Hinton, 2012).

Other techniques are available when dataset solutions are not enough. Dropout is the most recent popular regularization technique that works on the hidden nodes where the output of some randomly-chosen hidden units, with their connections, are discarded in both forward and backwards passes during the training process. Therefore, the network architecture is changed whenever an input is presented but with shared weights. Dropout breaks the dependencies between the neurons, prevents the co-adaptation on the training data, and enforces learning of more powerful features by the neurons. Although the dropout is the best in reducing overfitting and improving generalization, it increases the training time 2-3 times longer (Srivastava, Hinton, Krizhevsky, Sutskever, & Salakhutdinov, 2014). Global Average Pooling technique replaces the FC with a global average pooling layer. NIN (Network in Network) experiments (Lin, Chen, & Yan, 2013) proved it is better than FC layers in reducing the test error by 1%. Afterwards it is used by GoogleNet (Szegedy, et al., 2015), and ResNet (He, Zhang, Ren, & Sun, 2016), and Inception-ResNet (Szegedy, Ioffe, Vanhoucke, & Alemi, 2017, February). DropConnect is a regularization technique that works on the weights. It is a generalization of dropout but with weights rather than hidden units. It is used for regularization of the FC layers by updating only some randomly-chosen set of weights and discarding the others by setting them to zero (Wan, Zeiler, Zhang, Le Cun, & Fergus, 2013). DisturbLabel is a regularization technique that works on the loss layer. It is about generating incorrect data labels and replacing some randomly chosen set of the training data-labels with the incorrect ones in each iteration. This technique cooperating with the dropout, produce better results (Xie, Wang, Wei, Wang, & Tian, 2016).

Figure 6. The solutions of overfitting problem

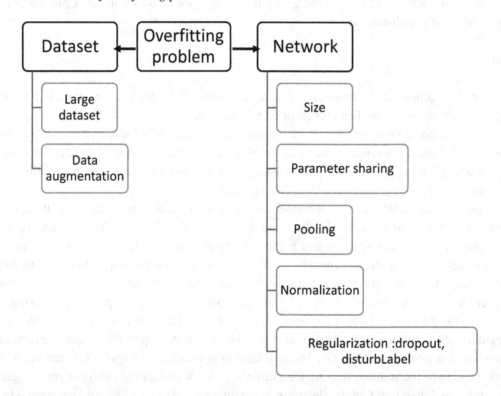

Challenges of Datasets

Pinto, Cox, & DiCarlo, (2008) demonstrated that the small datasets could not cover the dimensionality of the real domain of the problem, and one of the approaches to improve the object recognition is to build a very large-scale dataset of annotated natural images that are captured in an unbiased way with different sources of variation in pose, size, lighting, orientation. Ponce et al. (2006) added that the datasets should have a broad range of labeled objects and different stages of difficulty such as variation in viewpoint, occlusion, and intra-class variability.

Dataset Bias

The real visual world is a bias-free, unlike the datasets. The dataset bias is an important issue in computer vision field because the more unbiased the dataset, the better generalized the computer vision model. However, it is difficult to cover the dimensionality and variance of the real world in a dataset. Computer vision scientists compensate this deficiency by using very large scale datasets (Pinto, Cox, & Dicarlo, 2008; Ponce et al., 2006). Torralba & Efros (2011, June) set some standard checks to measure how good datasets are: 1) Cross-dataset generalization bias is based on training on a dataset while testing on another one. They found that the performance of the test set is decreased if the training set is from a different dataset, on the opposite, it increased if the training and testing sets are from the same dataset. In this test, the ImageNet dataset generalizes the best. 2) Negative set bias is based on the datasets defining the objects with positive and negative instances. The positive instances are the objects included in the datasets, and the negative instances are the objects that exist in the combined datasets. It is an indicator of how the dataset covers the real visual world objects. In this check, SUN 09 shows a drop in performance, but ImageNet does not. The two checks are tested on popular datasets; Caltech-101, MSRC (Microsoft Research in Cambridge), LabelMe, ImageNet, PASCAL VOC, and SUN-09. They mentioned that the datasets has strong built-in bias due to; 1) the orientation of the background of images towards either urban environment or landscapes, 2) the quality of images either from professional photos or quick snapshots, 3) focusing on the object or an entire scene. ImageNet dataset is the best among all.

Solutions

(Khosla, Zhou, Malisiewicz, Efros, & Torralba, 2012) proposed a framework to compensate the damage results from the data bias and learn objects of the visual world. They assert the cross dataset generalization conception that inspired from (Torralba & Efros, 2011). The idea of their algorithm to model the bias of each dataset in a feature vector using multiple feature extractors such as SIFT, HOG, and bag of words. They claimed that the idea is applicable for any number of datasets. The experiments were on a five common object classes: bird, car, chair, dog, and person from the object datasets: Pascal07, SUN, Caltech101, and LabelMe. The results demonstrated that the framework learned different types of biases and reduced their effect. Their framework outperformed the baseline SVM results by overall 2.8 mAP (mean Average Precision).

(Zhang, Wang, & Zhu, 2018) proposed a study to find the faults of DCNNs results and to be used as a guide for collecting new datasets. The idea to analyze pre-trained models, and use the training set samples to find out the failure modes of DCNN. The experiments were performed on SUN and Celeb-Faces datasets. They proposed a visualization method to discover the hidden layers patterns without the need of testing images that outperforms the literature methods. The experiments demonstrated that that the flaw in representation result from dataset bias cause overfitting and lessen generalization.

(Li & Vasconcelos, 2019) proposed an algorithm to remove representation bias from datasets called REPAIR (Removing Representation Bias by Dataset Resampling). The main idea is to resample new images from the original dataset where the algorithm learns to reduce the bias during reweighting. They used multiple datasets like Colored MNIST. Their experiments demonstrated that the computer vision models that are trained on REPAIR datasets generalize better in cross dataset generalization. In the other hand, (Barbu et al., 2019) tried to collect a bias-free testing set for object recognition called ObjectNet. It is without training set to test the generalization of object classifiers and detectors. ObjectNet consists of

50,000 images and 313 object categories; the same number of images as ImageNet test set. The special about this test set that it approaches the visual world with random capturing viewpoint, background, and rotation. Their experiments demonstrated a drop in performance (40-45%) of object detectors when compared to the state-of-the-art benchmarks.

In ImageNet benchmark, the standard methodology used for testing the DCNN is calculating top-1 error and top-5 error, which are the error when considering the first class and the top 5 classes chosen, respectively. Table 5 shows a comparison between the three errors for different DCNNs appeared from 2012 till 2019. The Validation is used as guidance for hyper-parameter selection. The difference between the validation and the testing error is small except for the ZFNet in case of no external data used. The use of external data reduces the data biasing. The small difference between the accuracy without external test data and with shows the reliability of the networks. The classification error decreases year by year, and the last two networks are for mobile applications, thus, their accuracies are less because of the hardware constrain.

Table 5. Comparison between validation and testing classification errors of different DCNNs

CNN model	Year	Top-1 Val. error	Top5 Val. Error	Top-5 Test error	External data for test
AlexNet	2012	38.1%	16.4%	16.4%	No
AlexNet	2012	36.7%	15.4%	15.3%	yes
ZFNet	2013	36%	11.74%	14.8%	No
ZFNet	2013	--	--	11.2%	yes
GoogLeNet	2014	--	6.67%	6.67%	No
VGGNet ILRVC-submission	2014	24.7%	7.5%	7.32%	No
VGGNet after-submission	2014	23.7%	6.8%	6.8%	No
BN-Inception	2015	--	4.9	4.82	No
ResNet	2015	19.38%	4.94%	3.57%	No
Trimps-Sushen	2016	--	2.92%	2.99%	No
Trimps-Sushen	2016	--		2.99%	Yes
SENet	2017	--	2.3%	2.25%	yes
MobileNetV2	2018		--	7.5%	--
ANTNet	2019	--	--	7.7%	--

Other Factors:

The problem of vanishing gradient problem arises while training the network and the error between the output of the network and the target flows back to the input layer. In case of DCNN, the number of layers is increased that can cause the gradient could vanish. (Hochreiter, 1998)

FUTURE RESEARCH DIRECTIONS

The development in this field reaches the idea of autonomous creation of DCNN based on the object classification problem (Ma, et al., 2020), where the number of layers are optimized using the genetic algorithm. The healthcare application is an open field for DCNN in classifying disease types in human organs, helping blind people in classifying objects around them that can be pictured by portable device such as mobile, or even a watch. On the other hand, researchers are heading towards analyzing the DCNN with respect to efficient architecture modules, learning methodologies, The use of DCNN in portable devices such as IOT, mobile, tablets, medical portable devices will be more common by developing DCNNs models suitable for the hardware constrain of these devices.

CONCLUSION

In this chapter, the object classification problem is introduced using DCNN in constrained environment. The superiority of the DCNN over the classical techniques and the conventional neural networks are presented. How the DCNN that is bio-inspired approached the human visual performance and the accuracy of such models is continuously improving. The popular DCNN models are presented. The challenges of using the DCNN in constrained environment and the equivalent solutions are presented. The main factors of this constrain are the available hardware resources, the long training time and the limitations of real time, object background and object illumination, pose, difference in scale and color, and the dataset. We can conclude that most of these challenges are being solved with an acceptable degree and the development in this field is in its way to achieve better performance.

REFERENCES

Ahonen, T., Hadid, A., & Pietikainen, M. (2006). Face description with local binary patterns: Application to face recognition. *IEEE Transactions on Pattern Analysis and Machine Intelligence*, 28(12), 2037–2041. doi:10.1109/TPAMI.2006.244

Akcay, S., Kundegorski, M. E., Willcocks, C. G., & Breckon, T. P. (2018). Using deep convolutional neural network architectures for object classification and detection within x-ray baggage security imagery. *IEEE Transactions on Information Forensics and Security*, 13(9), 2203–2215. doi:10.1109/TIFS.2018.2812196

Alaeddine, H., & Jihene, M. (2020). Deep network in network. *Neural Computing & Applications*, 1–13.

Barbu, A., Mayo, D., Alverio, J., Luo, W., Wang, C., & Gutfreund, D. ... Katz, B. (2019). ObjectNet: A large-scale bias-controlled dataset for pushing the limits of object recognition models. *Advances in Neural Information Processing Systems, (NeurIPS)*, 1–11. Retrieved from https://objectnet.dev

Brandenburg, S., Machado, P., Shinde, P., Ferreira, J. F., & McGinnity, T. M. (2019, November). Object Classification for Robotic Platforms. In *Iberian Robotics conference* (pp. 199–210). Cham: Springer.

Cadieu, C. F., Hong, H., Yamins, D. L., Pinto, N., Ardila, D., Solomon, E. A., ... DiCarlo, J. J. (2014). Deep neural networks rival the representation of primate IT cortex for core visual object recognition. *PLoS Computational Biology, 10*(12), e1003963. doi:10.1371/journal.pcbi.1003963

Chaudhry, S., & Chandra, R. (2017). Face detection and recognition in an unconstrained environment for mobile visual assistive system. *Applied Soft Computing, 53*, 168–180. doi:10.1016/j.asoc.2016.12.035

Cortes, C., & Vapnik, V. (1995). Support-vector networks. *Machine Learning, 20*(3), 273–297. doi:10.1007/BF00994018

Dean, J., Corrado, G., Monga, R., Chen, K., Devin, M., Mao, M., . . . Le, Q. V. (2012). Large scale distributed deep networks. In Advances in neural information processing systems (pp. 1223-1231). Academic Press.

Deng, J., Berg, A. C., Li, K., & Fei-Fei, L. (2010, September). What does classifying more than 10,000 image categories tell us? In *European conference on computer vision* (pp. 71-84). Springer. 10.1007/978-3-642-15555-0_6

Everingham, M., Van Gool, L., Williams, C. K., Winn, J., & Zisserman, A. (2010). The Pascal visual object classes (voc) challenge. *International Journal of Computer Vision, 88*(2), 303–338. doi:10.100711263-009-0275-4

Everingham, M., & Winn, J. (2012). The PASCAL visual object classes challenge 2012 (VOC2012) development kit. *Pattern Analysis, Statistical Modelling and Computational Learning*. Technical Report. Retrieved from http://host.robots.ox.ac.uk/pascal/VOC/voc2012/devkit_doc.pdf

Fei-Fei, L., Fergus, R., & Perona, P. (2006). One-shot learning of object categories. *IEEE Transactions on Pattern Analysis and Machine Intelligence, 28*(4), 594–611. doi:10.1109/TPAMI.2006.79

Fredj, H. B., Bouguezzi, S., & Souani, C. (2020). Face recognition in unconstrained environment with CNN. *The Visual Computer*, 1–10.

Freeman, J., & Simoncelli, E. P. (2011). Metamers of the ventral stream. *Nature Neuroscience, 14*(9), 1195–1201. doi:10.1038/nn.2889

Goodale, M. A., & Milner, A. D. (1992). Separate visual pathways for perception and action. In A. W. Ellis & A. W. Young (Eds.), *Human Cognitive Neuropsychology: A Textbook With Readings* (pp. 20–25). Psychology Press.

Goodfellow, I., Bengio, Y., & Courville, A. (2016). *Deep learning* (pp. 428–468). MIT press.

Graham, B. (2014). *Fractional max-pooling.* arXiv preprint arXiv:1412.6071

Griffin, G., Holub, A., & Perona, P. (2007). *Caltech-256 object category dataset.* Retrieved from https://authors.library.caltech.edu/7694/1/CNS-TR-2007-001.pdf

Haq, E. U., Jianjun, H., Li, K., & Haq, H. U. (2020). Human detection and tracking with deep convolutional neural networks under the constrained of noise and occluded scenes. *Multimedia Tools and Applications*, 1–24.

He, K., Zhang, X., Ren, S., & Sun, J. (2015). Delving deep into rectifiers: Surpassing human-level performance on ImageNet classification. In *Proceedings of the IEEE international conference on computer vision* (pp. 1026-1034). 10.1109/ICCV.2015.123

He, K., Zhang, X., Ren, S., & Sun, J. (2016). Deep residual learning for image recognition. In *Proceedings of the IEEE conference on computer vision and pattern recognition* (pp. 770-778). IEEE.

Hochreiter, S. (1998). The vanishing gradient problem during learning recurrent neural nets and problem solutions. *International Journal of Uncertainty, Fuzziness and Knowledge-based Systems*, *6*(02), 107–116. doi:10.1142/S0218488598000094

Hu, J., Shen, L., & Sun, G. (2018). Squeeze-and-excitation networks. In *Proceedings of the IEEE conference on computer vision and pattern recognition* (pp. 7132-7141). IEEE.

Huang, Y., Liu, S., Hu, J., & Deng, W. (2017, May). Metric-promoted siamese network for gender classification. In *2017 12th IEEE International Conference on Automatic Face & Gesture Recognition (FG 2017)* (pp. 961-966). IEEE. 10.1109/FG.2017.119

Hubel, D. H., & Wiesel, T. N. (1962). Receptive fields, binocular interaction and functional architecture in the cat's visual cortex. *The Journal of Physiology*, *160*(1), 106–154. doi:10.1113/jphysiol.1962.sp006837

ILSVRC. (2016). *ImagNet: Large Scale Visual Recognition Challenge 2016 (ILSVRC2016)*. Retrieved from http://www.image-net.org/challenges/LSVRC/2016/results#team

ILSVRC. (2017) *ImagNet: Large Scale Visual Recognition Challenge 2017 (ILSVRC2017)*. Retrieved from http://image-net.org/challenges/LSVRC/2017/results

Indolia, S., Goswami, A. K., Mishra, S. P., & Asopa, P. (2018). Conceptual understanding of convolutional neural network-a deep learning approach. *Procedia Computer Science*, *132*, 679–688. doi:10.1016/j.procs.2018.05.069

Ioffe, S., & Szegedy, C. (2015). *Batch normalization: Accelerating deep network training by reducing internal covariate shift*. arXiv preprint arXiv:1502.03167

Jana, P., Bhaumik, S., & Mohanta, P. P. (2019, June). Key-frame based event recognition in unconstrained videos using temporal features. In *2019 IEEE Region 10 Symposium (TENSYMP)* (pp. 349-354). IEEE. 10.1109/TENSYMP46218.2019.8971058

Kang, E., & Oh, I. S. (2018, January). Weak constraint leaf image recognition based on convolutional neural network. In *2018 International Conference on Electronics, Information, and Communication (ICEIC)* (pp. 1-4). IEEE. 10.23919/ELINFOCOM.2018.8330637

Khalifa, N. E. M., Taha, M. H. N., & Hassanien, A. E. (2018, September). Aquarium family fish species identification system using deep neural networks. In *International Conference on Advanced Intelligent Systems and Informatics* (pp. 347-356). Springer.

Khosla, A., Zhou, T., Malisiewicz, T., Efros, A. A., & Torralba, A. (2012). Undoing the damage of dataset bias. *Lecture Notes in Computer Science*, *7572*, 158–171. doi:10.1007/978-3-642-33718-5_12

Krizhevsky, A., & Hinton, G. (2009). *Learning multiple layers of features from tiny images*. Retrieved from http://citeseerx.ist.psu.edu/viewdoc/download?doi=10.1.1.222.9220&rep=rep1&type=pdf

Krizhevsky, A., Sutskever, I., & Hinton, G. E. (2012). Imagenet classification with deep convolutional neural networks. In Advances in neural information processing systems (pp. 1097-1105). Academic Press.

Laguduva, V. R., Mahmud, S., Aakur, S. N., Karam, R., & Katkoori, S. (2020, January). Dissecting Convolutional Neural Networks for Efficient Implementation on Constrained Platforms. In *2020 33rd International Conference on VLSI Design and 2020 19th International Conference on Embedded Systems (VLSID)* (pp. 149-154). IEEE.

LeCun, Y., Bottou, L., Bengio, Y., & Haffner, P. (1998). Gradient-based learning applied to document recognition. *Proceedings of the IEEE*, *86*(11), 2278–2324. doi:10.1109/5.726791

LeCun, Y., Huang, F. J., & Bottou, L. (2004, June). Learning methods for generic object recognition with invariance to pose and lighting. In *Proceedings of the 2004 IEEE Computer Society Conference on Computer Vision and Pattern Recognition, 2004. CVPR 2004.* (Vol. 2, pp. 97-104). IEEE. 10.1109/CVPR.2004.1315150

Li, X. X., & Liang, R. H. (2018). A review for face recognition with occlusion: From subspace regression to deep learning. *Chinese Journal of Computers*, *41*(1), 177–207.

Li, Y., & Vasconcelos, N. (2019). Repair: Removing representation bias by dataset resampling. *Proceedings of the IEEE Computer Society Conference on Computer Vision and Pattern Recognition, 2019-June*, 9564–9573. 10.1109/CVPR.2019.00980

Lin, M., Chen, Q., & Yan, S. (2013). *Network in network*. arXiv preprint arXiv:1312.4400

Lin, Y., Lv, F., Zhu, S., Yang, M., Cour, T., Yu, K., ... Huang, T. (2011, June). Large-scale image classification: Fast feature extraction and SVM training. In *Computer Vision and Pattern Recognition Conference (CVPR) 2011* (pp. 1689-1696). IEEE. 10.1109/CVPR.2011.5995477

Liu, R., Han, Q., Min, W., Zhou, L., & Xu, J. (2019). Vehicle logo recognition based on enhanced matching for small objects, constrained region and SSFPD network. *Sensors (Basel)*, *19*(20), 4528. doi:10.339019204528

Lowe, D. G. (2004). Distinctive image features from scale-invariant keypoints. *International Journal of Computer Vision*, *60*(2), 91–110. doi:10.1023/B:VISI.0000029664.99615.94

Luan, S., Chen, C., Zhang, B., Han, J., & Liu, J. (2018). Gabor convolutional networks. *IEEE Transactions on Image Processing*, *27*(9), 4357–4366. doi:10.1109/TIP.2018.2835143

Ma, B., Li, X., Xia, Y., & Zhang, Y. (2020). Autonomous deep learning: A genetic DCNN designer for image classification. *Neurocomputing*, *379*, 152–161. doi:10.1016/j.neucom.2019.10.007

Naranjo-Torres, J., Mora, M., Hernández-García, R., Barrientos, R. J., Fredes, C., & Valenzuela, A. (2020). A Review of Convolutional Neural Network Applied to Fruit Image Processing. *Applied Sciences*, *10*(10), 3443. doi:10.3390/app10103443

Perronnin, F., Sánchez, J., & Mensink, T. (2010, September). Improving the fisher kernel for large-scale image classification. In *European conference on computer vision* (pp. 143-156). Springer. 10.1007/978-3-642-15561-1_11

Pinto, N., Cox, D. D., & DiCarlo, J. J. (2008). Why is real-world visual object recognition hard? *PLoS Computational Biology*, *4*(1), e27. doi:10.1371/journal.pcbi.0040027

Ponce, J., Berg, T. L., Everingham, M., Forsyth, D. A., Hebert, M., Lazebnik, S., & Williams, C. K. (2006). Dataset issues in object recognition. In *Toward category-level object recognition* (pp. 29–48). Berlin: Springer. doi:10.1007/11957959_2

Russakovsky, O., Deng, J., Su, H., Krause, J., Satheesh, S., Ma, S., ... Fei-Fei, L. (2015). ImageNet Large Scale Visual Recognition Challenge. *International Journal of Computer Vision*, *115*(3), 211–252. doi:10.100711263-015-0816-y

Russell, B. C., Torralba, A., Murphy, K. P., & Freeman, W. T. (2008). LabelMe: A database and web-based tool for image annotation. *International Journal of Computer Vision*, *77*(1-3), 157–173. doi:10.100711263-007-0090-8

Salman, A., Jalal, A., Shafait, F., Mian, A., Shortis, M., Seager, J., & Harvey, E. (2016). Fish species classification in unconstrained underwater environments based on deep learning. *Limnology and Oceanography, Methods*, *14*(9), 570–585. doi:10.1002/lom3.10113

Sánchez, J., & Perronnin, F. (2011, June). High-dimensional signature compression for large-scale image classification. In *Computer Vision and Pattern Recognition CVPR 2011* (pp. 1665–1672). IEEE. doi:10.1109/CVPR.2011.5995504

Sandler, M., Howard, A., Zhu, M., Zhmoginov, A., & Chen, L. C. (2018). Mobilenetv2: Inverted residuals and linear bottlenecks. In *Proceedings of the IEEE conference on computer vision and pattern recognition* (pp. 4510-4520). IEEE.

Sermanet, P., Eigen, D., Zhang, X., Mathieu, M., Fergus, R., & LeCun, Y. (2013). *Overfeat: Integrated recognition, localization and detection using convolutional networks.* arXiv preprint arXiv:1312.6229

Shen, X., Tian, X., He, A., Sun, S., & Tao, D. (2016, October). Transform-invariant convolutional neural networks for image classification and search. In *Proceedings of the 24th ACM international conference on Multimedia* (pp. 1345-1354). 10.1145/2964284.2964316

Simonyan, K., & Zisserman, A. (2014). *Very deep convolutional networks for large-scale image recognition.* arXiv preprint arXiv:1409.1556

Srivastava, N., Hinton, G., Krizhevsky, A., Sutskever, I., & Salakhutdinov, R. (2014). Dropout: A simple way to prevent neural networks from overfitting. *Journal of Machine Learning Research*, *15*(1), 1929–1958.

Szegedy, C., Ioffe, S., Vanhoucke, V., & Alemi, A. A. (2017, February). Inception-v4, inception-resnet and the impact of residual connections on learning. *Thirty-first AAAI conference on artificial intelligence*.

Szegedy, C., Liu, W., Jia, Y., Sermanet, P., Reed, S., Anguelov, D., ... Rabinovich, A. (2015). Going deeper with convolutions. In *Proceedings of the IEEE Conference on Computer Vision and Pattern Recognition* (pp. 1-9). IEEE.

Torralba, A., & Efros, A. A. (2011, June). Unbiased look at dataset bias. In *Computer Vision and Pattern Recognition Conference CVPR 2011* (pp. 1521–1528). IEEE.

Torralba, A., Fergus, R., & Freeman, W. T. (2008). 80 million tiny images: A large data set for nonparametric object and scene recognition. *IEEE Transactions on Pattern Analysis and Machine Intelligence*, *30*(11), 1958–1970. doi:10.1109/TPAMI.2008.128

Wan, L., Zeiler, M., Zhang, S., Le Cun, Y., & Fergus, R. (2013, February). Regularization of neural networks using dropconnect. In *International conference on machine learning* (pp. 1058-1066). Academic Press.

Xiao, J., Hays, J., Ehinger, K. A., Oliva, A., & Torralba, A. (2010, June). Sun database: Large-scale scene recognition from abbey to zoo. In *2010 IEEE Computer Society Conference on Computer Vision and Pattern Recognition* (pp. 3485-3492). IEEE. 10.1109/CVPR.2010.5539970

Xie, L., Wang, J., Wei, Z., Wang, M., & Tian, Q. (2016). Disturblabel: Regularizing cnn on the loss layer. In *Proceedings of the IEEE Conference on Computer Vision and Pattern Recognition* (pp. 4753-4762). 10.1109/CVPR.2016.514

Xie, S., Hu, H., & Wu, Y. (2019). Deep multi-path convolutional neural network joint with salient region attention for facial expression recognition. *Pattern Recognition*, *92*, 177–191. doi:10.1016/j.patcog.2019.03.019

Xiong, Y., Kim, H. J., & Hedau, V. (2019). *Antnets: Mobile convolutional neural networks for resource efficient image classification.* arXiv preprint arXiv:1904.03775

Zeiler, M. D., & Fergus, R. (2013, January). Stochastic pooling for regularization of deep convolutional neural networks. *1st International Conference on Learning Representations, ICLR 2013*.

Zeiler, M. D., & Fergus, R. (2014, September). Visualizing and understanding convolutional networks. In *European conference on computer vision* (pp. 818-833). Springer.

Zeiler, M. D., Taylor, G. W., & Fergus, R. (2011, November). Adaptive deconvolutional networks for mid and high level feature learning. In *2011 International Conference on Computer Vision* (pp. 2018-2025). IEEE. 10.1109/ICCV.2011.6126474

Zhang, M. M., Shang, K., & Wu, H. (2019). Deep compact discriminative representation for unconstrained face recognition. *Signal Processing Image Communication*, *75*, 118–127. doi:10.1016/j.image.2019.03.015

Zhang, Q., Wang, W., & Zhu, S. C. (2018). Examining CNN representations with respect to dataset bias. *32nd AAAI Conference on Artificial Intelligence, AAAI 2018*, 4464–4473.

Zhou, B., & Wichman, R. (2020). Visible light-based robust positioning under detector orientation uncertainty: A Gabor convolutional network-based approach extracting stable texture features. In *Proceedings of 2020 IEEE International Workshop on Machine Learning for Signal Processing, SEPT.* (pp. 21–24). Espoo, Finland: IEEE.

ADDITIONAL READING

Bengio, Y., Courville, A., & Vincent, P. (2013). Representation learning: A review and new perspectives. *IEEE Transactions on Pattern Analysis and Machine Intelligence*, *35*(8), 1798–1828. doi:10.1109/TPAMI.2013.50

Bianco, S., Cadene, R., Celona, L., & Napoletano, P. (2018). Benchmark analysis of representative deep neural network architectures. *IEEE Access : Practical Innovations, Open Solutions*, *6*, 64270–64277. doi:10.1109/ACCESS.2018.2877890

Fukushima, K. (1980). Neocognitron: A self-organizing neural network model for a mechanism of pattern recognition unaffected by shift in position. *Biological Cybernetics*, *36*(4), 193–202. doi:10.1007/BF00344251

Goodfellow, I., Bengio, Y., & Courville, A. (2016). *Deep learning*. MIT press.

Mutch, J., Knoblich, U., & Poggio, T. (2010). *CNS: a GPU-based framework for simulating cortically-organized networks*. Massachusetts Institute of Technology, Cambridge, MA, Technical Report MIT-CSAIL-TR-2010-013/CBCL-286.

Premebida, C., Melotti, G., & Asvadi, A. (2019). RGB-D Object Classification for Autonomous Driving Perception. In *RGB-D Image Analysis and Processing* (pp. 377–395). Cham: Springer. doi:10.1007/978-3-030-28603-3_17

Rawat, W., & Wang, Z. (2017). Deep convolutional neural networks for image classification: A comprehensive review. *Neural Computation*, *29*(9), 2352–2449. doi:10.1162/neco_a_00990

Serre, T. (2016). Models of visual categorization. *Wiley Interdisciplinary Reviews: Cognitive Science*, *7*(3), 197–213. doi:10.1002/wcs.1385

KEY TERMS AND DEFINITIONS

Deep Convolutional Neural Network: It is a type of neural network with hidden layers more than one and its neurons operates using convolution operations.

ImageNet Large Scale Visual Recognition Challenge (ILSVRC): It is a competition held yearly from 2010 till 2017 that evaluates the algorithms presented on a large labeled dataset for object recognition including classification and localization.

Overfitting Problem: This problem arises when the network fits well to a training set and fails to operate on other datasets.

Support Vector Machine (SVM): It is supervised learning classifier.

Top-1 and Top-5 Error: Top-1 error means that the output category from DCNN is the correct category, and the top-5 error is the expected category is one of the top five recommended categories.

Vanishing Gradient Problem: This problem arises while training the network, the error between the output of the network and the target could vanish while it flows back to the input layer.

Visual Cortex (V1): It is the part in the brain that is responsible of processing the visual information.

Compilation of References

Abramoff, M. D., Alward, W. L., Greenlee, E. C., Shuba, L., Kim, C. Y., Fingert, J. H., & Kwon, Y. H. (2007). Automated segmentation of the optic disc from stereo color photographs using physiologically plausible features. *Investigative Ophthalmology & Visual Science*, *48*(4), 1665–1673. doi:10.1167/iovs.06-1081 PMID:17389498

Adi, K., Widodo, C. E., Widodo, A. P., Gernowo, R., Pamungkas, A., & Syifa, R. A. (2018). Detection Lung Cancer Using Gray Level Co-Occurrence Matrix (GLCM) and Back Propagation Neural Network Classification. *Journal of Engineering Science & Technology Review*, *11*(2).

Ahonen, T., Hadid, A., & Pietikäinen, M. (2004). Face recognition with local binary patterns. In *European conference on computer vision* (pp. 469-481). Springer.

Ahonen, T., Hadid, A., & Pietikainen, M. (2006). Face description with local binary patterns: Application to face recognition. *IEEE Transactions on Pattern Analysis and Machine Intelligence*, *28*(12), 2037–2041. doi:10.1109/TPAMI.2006.244

Akcay, S., Kundegorski, M. E., Willcocks, C. G., & Breckon, T. P. (2018). Using deep convolutional neural network architectures for object classification and detection within x-ray baggage security imagery. *IEEE Transactions on Information Forensics and Security*, *13*(9), 2203–2215. doi:10.1109/TIFS.2018.2812196

Alaeddine, H., & Jihene, M. (2020). Deep network in network. *Neural Computing & Applications*, 1–13.

Alaei, Nagabhushan, & Pal. (2011). A benchmark Kannada Handwritten Document Dataset and its Segmentation. *Proceedings of International Conference on Document Analysis and Recognition*, 1520-5363.

Al-Dhabyani, M., Gomaa, M., Khaled, H., & Fahmy, A. (2020). Dataset of Breast Ultrasound Images. *Data in Brief*, *28*, 1–5. doi:10.1016/j.dib.2019.104863 PMID:31867417

Alhindi, T. J., Kalra, S., Hin, N. K., Afrin, A., & Tizhoosh, H. R. (2018). Comparing LBP, HOG and deep features for classification of histopathology images. In *2018 International Joint Conference on Neural Networks (IJCNN)* (pp. 1-7). Rio de Janeiro, Brazil: IEEE. 10.1109/IJCNN.2018.8489329

Alioua, N., Amine, A., Rziza, M., & Aboutajdine, D. (2011, April). Eye state analysis using iris detection based on Circular Hough Transform. In *2011 International Conference on Multimedia Computing and Systems* (pp. 1-5). IEEE. 10.1109/ICMCS.2011.5945576

Almazan, J., Gordo, A., Fornes, A., & Valveny, E. (2014). Word Spotting and Recognition with Embedded Attributes. *IEEE Transactions on Pattern Analysis and Machine Intelligence*, *36*(12), 2552–2566. doi:10.1109/TPAMI.2014.2339814 PMID:26353157

Almutairi, A. (2018). A Comparative Study on Steganography Digital Images: A Case Study of Scalable Vector Graphics (SVG) and Portable Network Graphics (PNG). *Images Formats. Int. J. Adv. Comput. Sci. Appl*, *9*, 170–175.

Alom, M. Z., Sidike, P., Hasan, M., Taha, T. M., & Asari, V. K. (2018). Handwritten Bangla Character Recognition Using the State-of-the-Art Deep Convolutional Neural Networks. *Computational Intelligence and Neuroscience, 2018*, 1–13. doi:10.1155/2018/6747098 PMID:30224913

Amali, D. G. B., & M, D. (2018). A new quantum tunneling particle swarm optimization algorithm for training Feed-forward neural networks. *International Journal of Intelligent Systems and Applications, 10*(11), 64-75. doi:10.5815/ijisa.2018.11.07

Amien, M. B., Abd-elrehman, A., & Ibrahim, W. (2013). An intelligent-model for automatic brain-tumor diagnosis based-on MRI images. *International Journal of Computers and Applications, 72*(23).

Amin, J., Sharif, M., Yasmin, M., & Fernandes, S. L. (2017). A distinctive approach in brain tumor detection and classification using MRI. *Pattern Recognition Letters*. doi:10.1016/j.patrec.2017.10.036

Anbarjafari, G., Rasti, P., Noroozi, F., Gorbova, J., & Haamer, R.E. (2018). *Machine learning for face, emotion, and pain recognition*. SPIE. Doi:10.1117/3.2322572

Andrews, H. C. (1970). *Computer techniques in image processing*. CTIP.

Andrews, H. C., Tescher, A. G., & Kruger, R. P. (1972). Image processing by digital computer. *IEEE Spectrum, 9*(7), 20–32. doi:10.1109/MSPEC.1972.5218964

Armato, S. G. III, McLennan, G., Bidaut, L., McNitt-Gray, M. F., Meyer, C. R., Reeves, A. P., ... Kazerooni, E. A. (2011). The lung image database consortium (LIDC) and image database resource initiative (IDRI): A completed reference database of lung nodules on CT scans. *Medical Physics, 38*(2), 915–931. doi:10.1118/1.3528204 PMID:21452728

Arnold, M. B. (1960). *Emotion and personality*. New York: Columbia University Press.

Arora, S., & Singh, S. (2019). Butterfly optimization algorithm: A novel approach for global optimization. *Soft Computing, 23*(3), 715–734. doi:10.100700500-018-3102-4

Arya, S., & Agrawal, A. (2018). Face Recognition with Partial Face Recognition and Convolutional Neural Network. *International Journal of Advanced Research in Computer Engineering & Technology, 7*(1), 91–94.

Averill, J. R. (1980). A constructivist view of emotion. In R. Plutchik & H. Kellerman (Eds.), *Theories of emotion* (pp. 305–339). New York: Academic Press. doi:10.1016/B978-0-12-558701-3.50018-1

Azad, M. M., & Hasan, M. M. (2017). Color image processing in digital image. *International Journal of New Technology and Research, 3*(3).

Bagchi, C., Amali, D. G. B., & Dinakaran, M. (2019). Accurate Facial Ethnicity Classification Using Artificial Neural Networks Trained with Galactic Swarm Optimization Algorithm. In *Information Systems Design and Intelligent Applications* (pp. 123–132). Singapore: Springer. doi:10.1007/978-981-13-3329-3_12

Balci, K., & Atalay, V. (n.d.). PCA for gender estimation: Which eigenvectors contribute? *Object recognition supported by user interaction for service robots*. doi:10.1109/icpr.2002.1047869

Barbu, A., Mayo, D., Alverio, J., Luo, W., Wang, C., & Gutfreund, D. ... Katz, B. (2019). ObjectNet: A large-scale bias-controlled dataset for pushing the limits of object recognition models. *Advances in Neural Information Processing Systems, (NeurIPS)*, 1–11. Retrieved from https://objectnet.dev

Barros, P., Magg, S., Weber, C., & Wermter, S. (2014). A multichannel convolutional neural network for hand posture recognition. In *International Conference on Artificial Neural Networks*. Springer International Publishing. 10.1007/978-3-319-11179-7_51

Batra, A., & Kaushik, D. G. (2017). SECTUBIM: Automatic Segmentation And Classification of Tumeric Brain MRI Images using FHS (FCM HWT and SVM). *International Journal of Engineering Science and Computing, 7*(6), 13190–13194.

Beiji, Z., Sijian, Z., & Chengzhang, Z. (2015). Automatic positioning and segmentation of color fundus image discs. *Optics and Precision Engineering, 23*(4), 1187–1195. doi:10.3788/OPE.20152304.1187

Beni, G., & Wang, J. (1993). Swarm intelligence in cellular robotic systems. *Robots and Biological Systems: Towards a New Bionics*, 703-712. doi:10.1007/978-3-642-58069-7_38

Bhatkalkar, B., Joshi, A., Prabhu, S., & Bhandary, S. (2020). Automated fundus image quality assessment and segmentation of optic disc using convolutional neural networks. *International Journal of Electrical & Computer Engineering, 10.*

Bhat, S. H., & Kumar, P. (2019). Segmentation of optic disc by localized active contour model in retinal fundus image. In *Smart Innovations in Communication and Computational Sciences* (pp. 35–44). Singapore: Springer. doi:10.1007/978-981-13-2414-7_4

Bhutada, G. G., Anand, R. S., & Saxena, S. C. (2011). Edge preserved image enhancement using adaptive fusion of images denoised by wavelet and curvelet transform. *Digital Signal Processing, 21*(1), 118–130. doi:10.1016/j.dsp.2010.09.002

Bick, J., Zhu, T., Stamoulis, C., Fox, N. A., Zeanah, C., & Nelson, C. A. (2017). Early deprivation, atypical brain development, and internalizing symptoms in late childhood. *Neuroscience, 342*, 140–153. doi:10.1016/j.neuroscience.2015.09.026 PMID:26384960

Bozorgtabara, B., Rada, M. S., Ekenelb, H. K., & Thiran, J. P. (2019). Learn to synthesize and synthesize to learn. *Computer Vision and Image Understanding, 185*, 1–11. doi:10.1016/j.cviu.2019.04.010

Brandenburg, S., Machado, P., Shinde, P., Ferreira, J. F., & McGinnity, T. M. (2019, November). Object Classification for Robotic Platforms. In *Iberian Robotics conference* (pp. 199–210). Cham: Springer.

Byra, M., Jarosik, P., Dobruch-Sobczak, K., Klimonda, Z., Piotrzkowska-Wroblewska, H., Litniewski, J., & Nowicki, A. (2020). *Breast mass segmentation based on ultrasonic entropy maps and attention gated U-Net*. arXiv preprint arXiv:2001.10061

Cadieu, C. F., Hong, H., Yamins, D. L., Pinto, N., Ardila, D., Solomon, E. A., ... DiCarlo, J. J. (2014). Deep neural networks rival the representation of primate IT cortex for core visual object recognition. *PLoS Computational Biology, 10*(12), e1003963. doi:10.1371/journal.pcbi.1003963

Cameron, J. L., Eagleson, K. L., Fox, N. A., Hensch, T. K., & Levitt, P. (2017). Social origins of developmental risk for mental and physical illness. *The Journal of Neuroscience, 37*(45), 10783–10791. doi:10.1523/JNEUROSCI.1822-17.2017 PMID:29118206

Chanda, B., & Dutta Majumder, D. (2002). *Digital Image Processing and Analysis* (1st ed.). Prentice-Hall of India.

Chandrakala, H. T., & Thippeswamy, G. (2016). A Comprehensive Survey on OCR techniques for Kannada Script. *International Journal of Science and Research, 5*(4).

Chandrakala, Thippeswamy, & Sahana. (2018). Enhancement of degraded document images using Retinex and Morphological operations. *International Journal of Computer Science and Information Security, 16*(4).

Chandrakala, H. T., & Thippeswamy, G. (2017). Epigraphic Document image enhancement using Retinex method. *Proceedings of 3rd international symposium of signal processing and intelligent recognition systems, Book chapter in Advanced in signal processing and intelligent recognition systems.*

Chandraprabha, R., & Singh, S. (2016). Artificial Intelligent System For Diagnosis Of Cervical Cancer: A Brief Review And Future Outline. *Journal of Latest Research in Engineering and Technology*, 38-41.

Chang, C. C., & Lin, C. J. (2011). LIBSVM: A library for support vector machines. *ACM Transactions on Intelligent Systems and Technology*, *2*(3), 1–27. doi:10.1145/1961189.1961199

Chang, R. F., Chang-Chien, K. C., Takada, E., Huang, C. S., Chou, Y. H., Kuo, C. M., & Chen, J. H. (2010). Rapid image stitching and computer-aided detection for multipass automated breast ultrasound. *Medical Physics*, *37*(5), 2063–2073. doi:10.1118/1.3377775 PMID:20527539

Chaudhry, S., & Chandra, R. (2017). Face detection and recognition in an unconstrained environment for mobile visual assistive system. *Applied Soft Computing*, *53*, 168–180. doi:10.1016/j.asoc.2016.12.035

Chen, J., Zhang, L., & Lu, L. (2020). A novel medical image fusion method based on Rolling Guidance Filtering. *Internet of Things.* . doi:10.1016/j.iot.2020.100172

Chen, B., Wang, Y., Sun, X., Guo, W., Zhao, M., Cui, G., ... Yu, J. (2012). Analysis of patient dose in full field digital mammography. *European Journal of Radiology*, *81*(5), 868–872. doi:10.1016/j.ejrad.2011.02.027 PMID:21397423

Chen, C. M., Chou, Y. H., Han, K. C., Hung, G. S., Tiu, C. M., Chiou, H. J., & Chiou, S. Y. (2003). Breast lesions on sonograms: Computer-aided diagnosis with nearly setting- independent features and artificial neural networks. *Radiology*, *226*(2), 504–514. doi:10.1148/radiol.2262011843 PMID:12563146

Chen, D. R., Chang, R. F., Kuo, W. J., Chen, M. C., & Huang, Y. L. (2002). Diagnosis of breast tumors with sonographic texture analysis using wavelet transform and neural networks. *Ultrasound in Medicine & Biology*, *28*(10), 1301–1310. doi:10.1016/S0301-5629(02)00620-8 PMID:12467857

Chen, D., Ren, S., Wei, Y., Cao, X., & Sun, J. (2014). Joint cascade face detection and alignment. In *European Conference on Computer Vision* (pp. 109-122). Springer.

Cheng, Shana, Ju, Guo, & Zhang. (2010). Automated breast cancer detection and classification using ultrasound images: A survey. *Pattern Recognition, 43*, 299 – 317.

Cheng, H., Shi, X., Min, R., Hu, L., Cai, X., & Du, H. (2006). Approaches for automated detection and classification of masses in mammograms. *Pattern Recognition*, *39*(4), 646–668. doi:10.1016/j.patcog.2005.07.006

Cheng, X., Zhang, Y., Chen, Y., Wu, Y., & Yue, Y. (2017). Pest identification via deep residual learning in complex background. *Computers and Electronics in Agriculture*, *141*, 351–356. doi:10.1016/j.compag.2017.08.005

Chen, H., Tsai, S. S., Schroth, G., Chen, D. M., Grzeszczuk, R., & Girod, B. (2011). Robust Text Detection in Natural Images with Edge-Enhanced Maximally Stable Extremal Regions. *18th IEEE International Conference on Image Processing.* 10.1109/ICIP.2011.6116200

Chen, H., Zhang, J., Xu, Y., Chen, B., & Zhang, K. (2012). Performance comparison of artificial neural network and logistic regression model for differentiating lung nodules on CT scans. *Expert Systems with Applications*, *39*(13), 11503–11509. doi:10.1016/j.eswa.2012.04.001

Chen, M., Hao, Y., Hwang, K., Wang, L., & Wang, L. (2017). Disease Prediction by Machine Learning over Big Data from Healthcare Communities. *IEEE Access: Practical Innovations, Open Solutions*, *5*(c), 8869–8879. doi:10.1109/ACCESS.2017.2694446

Chew, Tan, Cao, Shen, Chee, & Chang. (2000). Text extraction from historical handwritten documents by edge detection. *6th International Conference on Control, Automation, Robotics and Vision, ICARCV2000.*

Chhabra, T., Dua, G., & Malhotra, T. (2013). Comparative analysis of denoising methods in CT images. *International Journal of Emerging Trends in Electrical and Electronics*, *3*(2).

Chiang, T. C., Huang, Y. S., Chen, R. T., Huang, C. S., & Chang, R. F. (2019). Tumor detection in automated breast ultrasound using 3-D CNN and prioritized candidate aggregation. *IEEE Transactions on Medical Imaging*, *38*(1), 240–249. doi:10.1109/TMI.2018.2860257 PMID:30059297

Chiovetto, E., Curio, C., Endres, D., & Giese, M. (2018). Perceptual integration of kinematic components in the recognition of emotional facial expressions. *Journal of Vision (Charlottesville, Va.)*, *18*(4), 13. doi:10.1167/18.4.13 PMID:29710303

Chithambaram, T., & Perumal, K. (2017, September). Brain tumor segmentation using genetic algorithm and ANN techniques. In *2017 IEEE International Conference on Power, Control, Signals and Instrumentation Engineering (ICPCSI)* (pp. 970-982). IEEE. 10.1109/ICPCSI.2017.8391855

Choi, Y., Choi, M., Kim, M., Kim, J. H. S., & Choo, J. (2018). *StarGAN: Unified Generative Adversarial Networks for Multi-Domain Image-to-Image Translation*. ArXiv.

Cohen, Afshar, Tapson, & van Schaik. (2017). EMNIST: an extension of MNIST to handwritten letters. *Computer Vision and Pattern Recognition*.

Cortes, C., & Vapnik, V. (1995). Support-vector networks. *Machine Learning*, *20*(3), 273–297. doi:10.1007/BF00994018

Coulibaly, S., Kamsu-Foguem, B., Kamissoko, D., & Traore, D. (2019). Deep neural networks with transfer learning in millet crop images. *Computers in Industry*, *108*, 115–120. doi:10.1016/j.compind.2019.02.003

Criollo, Mestizo, Mulato, LatiNegro, Indigena, White, or Black? The US Hispanic/Latino population and multiple responses in the 2000 census. (2000). *American Journal of Public Health*, *90*(11). doi:10.2105/ajph.90.11.1724 PMID:11076239

Cutter, M. P., & Manduchi, R. (2015). Towards Mobile OCR: How to Take a Good Picture of a Document Without Sight. *Proceedings of the 2015 ACM Symposium on Document Engineering*. 10.1145/2682571.2797066

Dai, B., Chen, R., Zhu, S., & Zhang, W. (2018). Using Random Forest Algorithm for Breast Cancer Diagnosis. *International Symposium on Computer, Consumer and Control (IS3C)*, 449-452. 10.1109/IS3C.2018.00119

Dai, B., Wu, X., & Bu, W. (2017). Optic disc segmentation based on variational model with multiple energies. *Pattern Recognition*, *64*, 226–235. doi:10.1016/j.patcog.2016.11.017

Dandıl, E., Çakıroğlu, M., & Ekşi, Z. (2014, September). Computer-aided diagnosis of malign and benign brain tumors on MR images. In *International Conference on ICT Innovations* (pp. 157-166). Springer.

Daneshvar, S., & Ghassemian, H. (2010). MRI and PET image fusion by combining IHS and retina inspired models. *Information Fusion*, *11*(2), 114–123. doi:10.1016/j.inffus.2009.05.003

de Pinho Pinheiro, C. A., Nedjah, N., & de Macedo Mourelle, L. (2020). Detection and classification of pulmonary nodules using deep learning and swarm intelligence. *Multimedia Tools and Applications*, *79*(21), 15437–15465. doi:10.100711042-019-7473-z

Dean, J., Corrado, G., Monga, R., Chen, K., Devin, M., Mao, M., . . . Le, Q. V. (2012). Large scale distributed deep networks. In Advances in neural information processing systems (pp. 1223-1231). Academic Press.

del Carmen, M. G., Halpern, E. F., Kopans, D. B., Moy, B., Moore, R. H., Goss, P. E., & Hughes, K. S. (2007). Mammographic breast density and race. *AJR. American Journal of Roentgenology*, *188*(4), 1147–1150. doi:10.2214/AJR.06.0619 PMID:17377060

Deng, J., Berg, A. C., Li, K., & Fei-Fei, L. (2010, September). What does classifying more than 10,000 image categories tell us? In *European conference on computer vision* (pp. 71-84). Springer. 10.1007/978-3-642-15555-0_6

Deng, Z., Peng, X., Li, Z., & Qiao, Y. (2019). Mutual component convolutional neural networks for heterogeneous face recognition. *IEEE Transactions on Image Processing, 28*(6), 3102–3114. doi:10.1109/TIP.2019.2894272 PMID:30676957

Devasena, C. L., & Hemalatha, M. (2013). Efficient computer aided diagnosis of abnormal parts detection in magnetic resonance images using hybrid abnormality detection algorithm. *Open Computer Science, 3*(3), 117–128.

Diciotti, S., Lombardo, S., Falchini, M., Picozzi, G., & Mascalchi, M. (2011). Automated segmentation refinement of small lung nodules in CT scans by local shape analysis. *IEEE Transactions on Biomedical Engineering, 58*(12), 3418–3428. doi:10.1109/TBME.2011.2167621 PMID:21914567

Ding, C., Xu, C., & Tao, D. (2015). Multi-Task Pose-Invariant Face Recognition. *IEEE Transactions on Image Processing, 24*(3), 980–993. doi:10.1109/TIP.2015.2390959 PMID:25594967

Ding, S. F., Qi, B. J., & Tan, H. Y. (2011). An overview on theory and algorithm of support vector machines. *Journal of University of Electronic Science and Technology of China, 40*(1), 2–10.

Dong, X., Shen, J., Shao, L., & Van Gool, L. (2015). Sub-Markov random walk for image segmentation. *IEEE Transactions on Image Processing, 25*(2), 516–527. doi:10.1109/TIP.2015.2505184 PMID:26661298

Dougherty, G. (2010). Digital Image Processing for Medical Applications. Cambridge University Press.

Dubey, Y. K., & Mushrif, M. M. (2016). FCM Clustering Algorithms for Segmentation of Brain MR Images. *Advances in Fuzzy Systems, 2016*, 1–14. doi:10.1155/2016/3406406

Ekman, P., & Friesen, W. V. (1978). *Facial action coding system: A technique for the measurement of facial movement.* Palo Alto, CA: Consulting Psychologists Press.

El Khiyari, H., & Wechsler, H. (2017). Age Invariant Face Recognition Using Convolutional Neural Networks and Set Distances. *Journal of Information Security, 8*(3), 174–185. doi:10.4236/jis.2017.83012

Elbalaoui, A., Ouadid, Y., & Fakir, M. (2018, March). Segmentation of optic disc from fundus images. In *2018 International Conference on Computing Sciences and Engineering (ICCSE)* (pp. 1-7). IEEE. 10.1109/ICCSE1.2018.8374223

Elmahmudi, A., & Ugail, H. (2019). Deep Face recognition using imperfect facial data. *Future Generation Computer Systems, 99*, 213–225. doi:10.1016/j.future.2019.04.025

Eslami, A., Karamalis, A., Katouzian, A., & Navab, N. (2013). Segmentation by retrieval with guided random walks: Application to left ventricle segmentation in MRI. *Medical Image Analysis, 17*(2), 236–253. doi:10.1016/j.media.2012.10.005 PMID:23313331

Everingham, M., & Winn, J. (2012). The PASCAL visual object classes challenge 2012 (VOC2012) development kit. *Pattern Analysis, Statistical Modelling and Computational Learning.* Technical Report. Retrieved from http://host.robots.ox.ac.uk/pascal/VOC/voc2012/devkit_doc.pdf

Everingham, M., Van Gool, L., Williams, C. K., Winn, J., & Zisserman, A. (2010). The Pascal visual object classes (voc) challenge. *International Journal of Computer Vision, 88*(2), 303–338. doi:10.100711263-009-0275-4

Fei-Fei, L., Fergus, R., & Perona, P. (2006). One-shot learning of object categories. *IEEE Transactions on Pattern Analysis and Machine Intelligence, 28*(4), 594–611. doi:10.1109/TPAMI.2006.79

Feijoo, J. G., de la Casa, J. M. M., Servet, H. M., Zamorano, M. R., Mayoral, M. B., & Suárez, E. J. C. (2014). *DRIONS-DB: digital retinal images for optic nerve segmentation database.* Academic Press.

Field, D. J. (1987). Relations between the statistics of natural images and the response properties of cortical cells. *Journal of the Optical Society of America. A, Optics and Image Science*, *4*(12), 2379–2394. doi:10.1364/JOSAA.4.002379 PMID:3430225

Filali, H., Riffi, J., Mahraz, A. M., & Tairi, H. (2018). *Multiple face detection based on machine learning*. Paper presented at the Conference on Intelligent Systems and Computer Vision(ISCV), Fez, Morocco. 10.1109/ISACV.2018.8354058

Flusser, J., & Suk, T. (2006). Rotation moment invariants for recognition of symmetric objects. *IEEE Transactions on Image Processing*, *15*(12), 3784–3790. doi:10.1109/TIP.2006.884913 PMID:17153951

Fölster, M., Hess, U., Hühnel, I., & Werheid, K. (2015). Age-related response bias in the decoding of sad facial expressions. *Behavioral Science*, *5*(4), 443–460. doi:10.3390/bs5040443 PMID:26516920

Fondon, I., van Grinsven, M. J., Sanchez, C. I., & Saez, A. (2013, June). Perceptually adapted method for optic disc detection on retinal fundus images. In *Proceedings of the 26th IEEE International Symposium on Computer-Based Medical Systems* (pp. 279-284). IEEE. 10.1109/CBMS.2013.6627802

Fredj, H. B., Bouguezzi, S., & Souani, C. (2020). Face recognition in unconstrained environment with CNN. *The Visual Computer*, 1–10.

Freeman, J., & Simoncelli, E. P. (2011). Metamers of the ventral stream. *Nature Neuroscience*, *14*(9), 1195–1201. doi:10.1038/nn.2889

Friedman, B. H. (2010). Feelings and the body: The Jamesian perspective on autonomic specificity of emotion. *Biological Psychology*, *84*(3), 383–393. doi:10.1016/j.biopsycho.2009.10.006 PMID:19879320

Froba, B., & Ernst, A. (2004). Face detection with the modified census transform. In *Automatic Face and Gesture Recognition, 2004. Proceedings. Sixth IEEE International Conference on* (pp. 91-96). IEEE. 10.1109/AFGR.2004.1301514

Fujiwara, T., Mizuki, R., Miki, T., & Chemtob, C. (2015). Association between facial expression and PTSD symptoms among young children exposed to the Great East Japan Earthquake: A pilot study. *Frontiers in Psychology*, *6*, 1534. doi:10.3389/fpsyg.2015.01534 PMID:26528206

Fu, S., He, H., & Hou, Z. (2014). Learning race from face: A survey. *IEEE Transactions on Pattern Analysis and Machine Intelligence*, *36*(12), 2483–2509. doi:10.1109/TPAMI.2014.2321570 PMID:26353153

G, S., & V, H. D. (2019). Facial Expression Recognition Complications with the Stages of Face Detection and Recognition. *International Journal of Recent Technology And Engineering*, *8*(2), 2728-2740.

Gadea, M., Aliño, M., Espert, R., & Salvador, A. (2015). Deceit and facial expression in children: The enabling role of the "poker face" child and the dependent personality of the detector. *Frontiers in Psychology*, *6*, 1089. doi:10.3389/fpsyg.2015.01089 PMID:26284012

Gao, W., & Ai, H. (2009). Face gender classification on consumer images in a multiethnic environment. *Advances in Biometrics*, 169-178. doi:10.1007/978-3-642-01793-3_18

Gao, W., Zhang, X., Yang, L., & Liu, H. (2010). An Improved Sobel Edge Detection. *3rd International Conference on Computer Science and Information Technology*.

Gatys, L. A., Ecker, A. S., & Bethge, M. (2016). Image style transfer using convolutional neural networks. *Proceedings of the IEEE Conference on Computer Vision and Pattern Recognition*, 2414-2423. 10.1109/CVPR.2016.265

Giachetti, A., Ballerini, L., & Trucco, E. (2014). Accurate and reliable segmentation of the optic disc in digital fundus images. *Journal of Medical Imaging (Bellingham, Wash.)*, *1*(2), 024001. doi:10.1117/1.JMI.1.2.024001 PMID:26158034

Gibson, A., & Patterson, J. (2017). Deep Learning. O'Reilly Media, Inc.

Gomez Flores, W., & Ruiz Ortega, B. A. (2016). New Fully Automated Method for Segmentation of Breast Lesions on Ultrasound Based on Texture Analysis. *Ultrasound in Medicine & Biology, 42*(7), 1637–1650. doi:10.1016/j.ultrasmedbio.2016.02.016 PMID:27095150

Gomez, W., Pereira, W. C. A., & Infantosi, A. F. C. (2012). Analysis of co-occurrence texture statistics as a function of gray-level quantization for classifying breast ultrasound. *IEEE Transactions on Medical Imaging, 31*(10), 1889–1899. doi:10.1109/TMI.2012.2206398 PMID:22759441

Gonzalez & Woods. (2008). Digital Image Processing. Pearson Education, Inc.

Gonzalez, R. C., & Woods, R. E. (2008). Digital image processing (3rd ed.). Academic Press.

Gonzalez, R. C., & Woods, R. E. (2002). *Digital Image Processing* (2nd ed.). Prentice Hall.

Gonzalez, R. C., Woods, R. E., & Eddins, S. L. (2004). *Digital image processing using MATLAB. Pearson Education India.*.

Goodale, M. A., & Milner, A. D. (1992). Separate visual pathways for perception and action. In A. W. Ellis & A. W. Young (Eds.), *Human Cognitive Neuropsychology: A Textbook With Readings* (pp. 20–25). Psychology Press.

Goodfellow, I., Bengio, Y., & Courville, A. (2016). *Deep learning* (pp. 428–468). MIT press.

Grady, L. (2006). Random walks for image segmentation. *IEEE Transactions on Pattern Analysis and Machine Intelligence, 28*(11), 1768–1783. doi:10.1109/TPAMI.2006.233 PMID:17063682

Graham, B. (2014). *Fractional max-pooling.* arXiv preprint arXiv:1412.6071

Griffin, G., Holub, A., & Perona, P. (2007). *Caltech-256 object category dataset.* Retrieved from https://authors.library.caltech.edu/7694/1/CNS-TR-2007-001.pdf

Gu, G., Kim, S. T., Kim, K., Baddar, W. J., & Ro, Y. M. (2017). *Differential Generative Adversarial Networks: Synthesizing Non-linear Facial Variations with Limited Number of Training Data.* ArXiv.

Gu, J., Wang, Z., Kuen, J., Ma, L., Shahroudy, A., Shuai, B., ... Chen, T. (2018). Recent advances in convolutional neural networks. *Pattern Recognition, 77*, 354–377. doi:10.1016/j.patcog.2017.10.013

Guo, Y., Cheng, H. D., Huang, J., Tian, J., Zhao, W., Sun, L., & Su, Y. (2006). Breast ultrasound image enhancement using fuzzy logic. *Ultrasound in Medicine & Biology, 32*(2), 237–247. doi:10.1016/j.ultrasmedbio.2005.10.007 PMID:16464669

Gupta & Mazumdar. (2013). Sobel Edge Detection Algorithm. *International Journal of Computer Science and Management Research, 2*(2).

Gutta, S., Wechsler, H., & Phillips, P. (n.d.). Gender and ethnic classification of face images. *Proceedings Third IEEE International Conference on Automatic Face and Gesture Recognition.* doi:10.1109/afgr.1998.670948

Hall, E. L. (1974). Almost uniform distributions for computer image enhancement. *IEEE Transactions on Computers, 100*(2), 207–208. doi:10.1109/T-C.1974.223892

Han, F., Wang, H., Zhang, G., Han, H., Song, B., Li, L., ... Liang, Z. (2015). Texture feature analysis for computer-aided diagnosis on pulmonary nodules. *Journal of Digital Imaging, 28*(1), 99–115. doi:10.100710278-014-9718-8 PMID:25117512

Han, J., Pei, J., & Kamber, M. (2011). *Data mining: concepts and techniques.* Elsevier.

Haq, E. U., Jianjun, H., Li, K., & Haq, H. U. (2020). Human detection and tracking with deep convolutional neural networks under the constrained of noise and occluded scenes. *Multimedia Tools and Applications*, 1–24.

Harré, R. (1989). *The Social Construction of Emotions*. Oxford, UK: Blackwell Pub.

He, K., Zhang, X., Ren, S., & Sun, J. (2015). Delving deep into rectifiers: surpassing human-level performance on ImageNet classification. *Proceedings of the IEEE international conference on computer vision*, 1026–34. 10.1109/ICCV.2015.123

He, K., Zhang, X., Ren, S., & Sun, J. (2016). Deep residual learning for image recognition. In *Proceedings of the IEEE conference on computer vision and pattern recognition* (pp. 770-778). IEEE.

He, K., Zhang, X., Ren, S., & Sun, J. (2016). Identity mappings in deep residual networks. *European conference on computer vision*. 630–45.

Hemalatha, Thamizhvani, Dhivya, Joseph, Babu, & Chandrasekaran. (2018). Active Contour Based Segmentation Techniques for Medical Image Analysis. *Medical and Biological Image Analysis*, 17-34.

Heng, Z., Dipu, M., & Yap, K. (2018). Hybrid supervised deep learning for ethnicity classification using face images. *2018 IEEE International Symposium on Circuits and Systems (ISCAS)*. 10.1109/ISCAS.2018.8351370

Hess, U., Adams, R. B. J. Jr, Simard, A., Stevenson, M. T., & Kleck, R. E. (2012). Smiling and sad wrinkles: Age-related changes in the face and the perception of emotions and intentions. *Journal of Experimental Social Psychology*, *48*(6), 1377–1380. doi:10.1016/j.jesp.2012.05.018 PMID:23144501

He, T., Zhang, Z., Zhang, H., Zhang, Z., Xie, J., & Li, M. (2019). Bag of tricks for image classification with convolutional neural networks. In *Proceedings of the IEEE Conference on Computer Vision and Pattern Recognition* (pp. 558-567). 10.1109/CVPR.2019.00065

He, Z., Lv, W., & Hu, J. (2020). A Simple Method to Train the AI Diagnosis Model of Pulmonary Nodules. *Computational and Mathematical Methods in Medicine*. PMID:32802147

Hiremath & Rani. (2020). A Concise Report on Image Types, Image File Format and Noise Model for Image Preprocessing. International Research Journal of Engineering and Technology, 7(8).

Hiremath, Akshay, Aditya, Chetan Murthy, & Niranjan. (2017). *Skin Disease Detection using Image Processing*. Academic Press.

Hiremath, Bhavya, Singh, & Biradar. (2018). Digital Image Forgery Detection Using Zernike Moment and Discrete Cosine Transform: A Comparison. *International Research Journal of Engineering and Technology, 5*(5).

Hochreiter, S. (1998). The vanishing gradient problem during learning recurrent neural nets and problem solutions. *International Journal of Uncertainty, Fuzziness and Knowledge-based Systems*, *6*(02), 107–116. doi:10.1142/S0218488598000094

Hochreiter, S., & Schmidhuber, J. (1997). Long short-term memory. *Neural Computation*, *9*(8), 1735–1780. doi:10.1162/neco.1997.9.8.1735 PMID:9377276

Hoover, A., & Goldbaum, M. (2003). Locating the optic nerve in a retinal image using the fuzzy convergence of the blood vessels. *IEEE Transactions on Medical Imaging*, *22*(8), 951–958. doi:10.1109/TMI.2003.815900 PMID:12906249

Horsch, Giger, Venta, & Vyborny. (2001). Automatic segmentation of breast lesions on ultrasound. *Medical Physics*, *28*(8), 1652–1659.

Hosseini, H., & Marvasti, F. (2013). Fast restoration of natural images corrupted by high-density impulse noise. *EURASIP Journal on Image and Video Processing*, *2013*(1), 15. doi:10.1186/1687-5281-2013-15

Hough, P. V. (1962). *U.S. Patent No. 3,069,654*. Washington, DC: U.S. Patent and Trademark Office.

HP Labs India Indic Handwriting Datasets IWFHR. (2006). http://lipitk.sourceforge.net/hpl-datasets.htm

Hsu, C. Y., Chou, Y. H., & Chen, C. M. (2014, March). A Tumor Detection Algorithm for Whole Breast Ultrasound Images Incorporating Breast Anatomy Information. In *2014 International Conference on Computational Science and Computational Intelligence* (Vol. 2, pp. 241-244). IEEE. 10.1109/CSCI.2014.128

Htay, M. M., & Win, Z. M. (2019). Survey on Emotion Recognition Using Facial Expression. *International Journal of Computer*, *33*(2), 1–10.

Hu, B., Lu, Z., Li, H., & Chen, Q. (2014). Convolutional neural network architectures for matching natural language sentences. Advances in Neural Information Processing Systems, 2042-2050.

Huang, Chen, & Chang. (2012). *Whole Breast Lesion Detection Using Naive Bayes Classifier for Portable Ultrasound*. Academic Press.

Huang, X., & Serge Belongie. (2017). Arbitrary Style Transfer in Real-Time With Adaptive Instance Normalization. *The IEEE International Conference on Computer Vision (ICCV)*, 1501-1510. 10.1109/ICCV.2017.167

Huang, Y., Liu, S., Hu, J., & Deng, W. (2017, May). Metric-promoted siamese network for gender classification. In *2017 12th IEEE International Conference on Automatic Face & Gesture Recognition (FG 2017)* (pp. 961-966). IEEE. 10.1109/FG.2017.119

Huang, Z., & Leng, J. (2010, April). Analysis of Hu's moment invariants on image scaling and rotation. In *2010 2nd International Conference on Computer Engineering and Technology* (Vol. 7, pp. V7-476). IEEE.

Huang, H., Meng, F., Zhou, S., Jiang, F., & Manogaran, G. (2019). Brain Image Segmentation Based on FCM Clustering Algorithm and Rough Set. *IEEE Access : Practical Innovations, Open Solutions*, *7*, 12386–12396. doi:10.1109/ACCESS.2019.2893063

Huang, Q., Zhang, F., & Li, X. (2018). Machine Learning in Ultrasound Computer-Aided Diagnostic Systems: A Survey. *BioMed Research International*, *2018*, 1–10. PMID:29687000

Huang, Y., Chen, F., Lv, S., & Wang, X. (2019). Facial expression recognition: A survey. *Symmetry*, *11*(10), 1189. doi:10.3390ym11101189

Huang, Y., Wang, L., & Li, C. (2008). Texture Analysis of Ultrasonic Liver Image Based on Wavelet Transform and Probabilistic Neural Network, *IEEE International Conference on Biomedical Engineering and Informatics*, 248-252. 10.1109/BMEI.2008.156

Hubel, D. H., & Wiesel, T. N. (1962). Receptive fields, binocular interaction and functional architecture in the cat's visual cortex. *The Journal of Physiology*, *160*(1), 106–154. doi:10.1113/jphysiol.1962.sp006837

Hu, H., Cai, Z., Hu, S., Cai, Y., Chen, J., & Huang, S. (2018). Improving monarch butterfly optimization algorithm with self-adaptive population. *Algorithms*, *11*(5), 1–19. doi:10.3390/a11050071

Hu, J., & Li, S. (2012). The multiscale directional bilateral filter and its application for multisensory image fusion. *Information Fusion*, *13*(3), 196–206. doi:10.1016/j.inffus.2011.01.002

Hu, J., Shen, L., & Sun, G. (2018). Squeeze-and-excitation networks. In *Proceedings of the IEEE conference on computer vision and pattern recognition* (pp. 7132-7141). IEEE.

Ibrahim, A. M., & Tawhid, M. A. (2019). A hybridization of differential evolution and monarch butterfly optimization for solving systems of nonlinear equations. *Journal of Computational Design and Engineering*, *6*(3), 354–367. doi:10.1016/j.jcde.2018.10.006

Ikedo, Y., Fukuoka, D., Hara, T., Fujita, H., Takada, E., Endo, T., & Morita, T. (2007). Development of a fully automatic scheme for detection of masses in whole breast ultrasound images. *Medical Physics*, *34*(11), 4378–4388. doi:10.1118/1.2795825 PMID:18072503

ILSVRC. (2016). *ImagNet: Large Scale Visual Recognition Challenge 2016 (ILSVRC2016)*. Retrieved from http://www.image-net.org/challenges/LSVRC/2016/results#team

ILSVRC. (2017) *ImagNet: Large Scale Visual Recognition Challenge 2017 (ILSVRC2017)*. Retrieved from http://image-net.org/challenges/LSVRC/2017/results

Indolia, S., Goswami, A. K., Mishra, S. P., & Asopa, P. (2018). Conceptual understanding of convolutional neural network-a deep learning approach. *Procedia Computer Science*, *132*, 679–688. doi:10.1016/j.procs.2018.05.069

Ioffe, S., & Szegedy, C. (2015). *Batch normalization: Accelerating deep network training by reducing internal covariate shift*. arXiv preprint arXiv:1502.03167

Izard, C. E. (1977). Theories of emotion and emotion-behavior relationships. In *Human Emotions. Emotions, Personality, and Psychotherapy* (pp. 19–42). Boston, MA: Springer. doi:10.1007/978-1-4899-2209-0_2

Jacobs, D., Swyngedouw, M., & Hanquinet, L. (2009). Int. *Migraciones Internacionales*, *10*, 67. doi:10.100712134-009-0091-2

Jain, A. K. (1981). Image data compression: A review. *Proceedings of the IEEE*, *69*(3), 349–389. doi:10.1109/PROC.1981.11971

Jana, P., Bhaumik, S., & Mohanta, P. P. (2019, June). Key-frame based event recognition in unconstrained videos using temporal features. In *2019 IEEE Region 10 Symposium (TENSYMP)* (pp. 349-354). IEEE. 10.1109/TENSYMP46218.2019.8971058

Janani, V., & Meena, P. (2013). Image segmentation for tumor detection using fuzzy inference system. *Int J Comput Sci Mobile Comput*, *2*(5), 244–248.

Jayaraman, S. (2009). Digital Image Processing. New Delhi: Tata McGraw-Hill Education Private Limited.

Jiajun, Q. (2017). *Research on the positioning and segmentation method of the optic disc in the fundus image* (Master's thesis). Shenyang University of Technology.

Jiang, P., Chen, Y., Liu, B., He, D., & Liang, C. (2019). Real-Time Detection of Apple Leaf Diseases Using Deep Learning Approach Based on Improved Convolutional Neural Networks. *IEEE Access: Practical Innovations, Open Solutions*, *7*, 59069–59080. doi:10.1109/ACCESS.2019.2914929

Jiao, L., Zhang, S., Li, L., Liu, F., & Ma, W. (2018). A modified convolutional neural network for face sketch synthesis. *Pattern Recognition*, *76*, 125–136. doi:10.1016/j.patcog.2017.10.025

Jilani, S. K., Ugail, H., Bukar, A. M., Logan, A., & Munshi, T. (2017). A machine learning approach for ethnic classification: The British Pakistani face. *2017 International Conference on Cyberworlds (CW)*. 10.1109/CW.2017.27

Jitkongchuen, D., Phaidang, P., & Pongtawevirat, P. (2016). Grey wolf optimization algorithm with invasion-based migration operation. *2016 IEEE/ACIS 15th International Conference on Computer and Information Science (ICIS)*. doi:10.1109/icis.2016.7550769

Josey, J. D., & Acharya, S. A. (2018). A methodology for automated facial expression recognition using facial landmarks. *Proceedings of 2018 ASEE Annual Conference & Exposition*. https://peer.asee.org/29696

Jothimani, A., Prasanth, P., Anil, S., & Nehru, J. A. (2019). Facial Expression for Emotion Detection using Deep Neural Networks. *International Journal of Recent Technology and Engineering*, 8, 242–248.

Jumaat, A. K., Wan, E. Z. W. A. R., Ibrahim, A., & Mahmud, R. (2010). Segmentation of Masses from Breast Ultrasound Images using Parametric Active Contour Algorithm. *Procedia: Social and Behavioral Sciences*, 8, 640–647. doi:10.1016/j.sbspro.2010.12.089

Jun, B., Choi, I., & Kim, D. (2013). Local transform features and hybridization for accurate face and human detection. *IEEE Transactions on Pattern Analysis and Machine Intelligence*, 35(6), 1423–1436. doi:10.1109/TPAMI.2012.219 PMID:23599056

Ju, W., Xiang, D., Zhang, B., Wang, L., Kopriva, I., & Chen, X. (2015). Random walk and graph cut for co-segmentation of lung tumor on PET-CT images. *IEEE Transactions on Image Processing*, 24(12), 5854–5867. doi:10.1109/TIP.2015.2488902 PMID:26462198

Kang, E., & Oh, I. S. (2018, January). Weak constraint leaf image recognition based on convolutional neural network. In *2018 International Conference on Electronics, Information, and Communication (ICEIC)* (pp. 1-4). IEEE. 10.23919/ELINFOCOM.2018.8330637

Karaboga, D., & Basturk, B. (2007). A powerful and efficient algorithm for numerical function optimization: Artificial bee colony (ABC) algorithm. *Journal of Global Optimization*, 39(3), 459–471. doi:10.100710898-007-9149-x

Kasim, N. A. B. M., Rahman, N. H. B. A., Ibrahim, Z., & Mangshor, N. N. A. (2018). Celebrity Face Recognition using Deep Learning. *Indonesian Journal of Electrical Engineering and Computer Science*, 12(2), 476–481. doi:10.11591/ijeecs.v12.i2.pp476-481

Kaur, N., & Sharma, M. (2017, August). Brain tumor detection using self-adaptive K-means clustering. In *2017 International Conference on Energy, Communication, Data Analytics and Soft Computing (ICECDS)* (pp. 1861-1865). IEEE. 10.1109/ICECDS.2017.8389771

Kaya, A., Keceli, A. S., Catal, C., Yalic, H. Y., Temucin, H., & Tekinerdogan, B. (2019). Analysis of transfer learning for deep neural network based plant classification models. *Computers and Electronics in Agriculture*, 158(January), 20–29. doi:10.1016/j.compag.2019.01.041

Kaya, E., Uymaz, S. A., & Kocer, B. (2018). Boosting galactic swarm optimization with ABC. *International Journal of Machine Learning and Cybernetics*, 10(9), 2401–2419. doi:10.100713042-018-0878-6

Kennedy, J., & Eberhart, R. (1994). Particle swarm optimization. *Proceedings of ICNN'95 - International Conference on Neural Networks*. doi:10.1109/icnn.1995.488968

Ketenci, S., & Gangal, A. (2017). Automatic reduction of periodic noise in images using adaptive Gaussian star filter. *Turkish Journal of Electrical Engineering and Computer Sciences*, 25(3).

Khalifa, N. E. M., Taha, M. H. N., & Hassanien, A. E. (2018, September). Aquarium family fish species identification system using deep neural networks. In *International Conference on Advanced Intelligent Systems and Informatics* (pp. 347-356). Springer.

Khan, N. H., & Adnan, A. (2018). Urdu Optical Character Recognition Systems: Present Contributions and Future Directions. *IEEE Access : Practical Innovations, Open Solutions*, 6, 46019–46046. doi:10.1109/ACCESS.2018.2865532

Khosla, A., Zhou, T., Malisiewicz, T., Efros, A. A., & Torralba, A. (2012). Undoing the damage of dataset bias. *Lecture Notes in Computer Science, 7572*, 158–171. doi:10.1007/978-3-642-33718-5_12

Khotanzad, A., & Hong, Y. H. (1990). Invariant image recognition by Zernike moments. Pattern Analysis and Machine Intelligence. *IEEE Transactions on, 12*(5), 489–497.

Kim, J. H., Cha, J. H., Kim, N., Chang, Y., Ko, M. S., Choi, Y. W., & Kim, H. H. (2014). Computer-aided detection system for masses in automated whole breast ultrasonography: Development and evaluation of the effectiveness. *Ultrasonography (Seoul, Korea), 33*(2), 105–115. doi:10.14366/usg.13023 PMID:24936503

Kitsch, R. (1971). Computer detection of the constituent structure of biological image, Compute. *Biomod.*

Ko, B. C. (2018). A brief review of facial emotion recognition based on visual information. *Sensors (Basel), 18*(2), 401. doi:10.339018020401 PMID:29385749

Koli, M., & Balaji, S. (2013). Literature survey on impulse noise reduction. *Signal and Image Processing: an International Journal, 4*(5), 75–95. doi:10.5121ipij.2013.4506

Konar, A., & Chakraborty, A. (2015). *Emotion recognition: A pattern analysis approach*. John Wiley & Sons, Inc.; doi:10.1002/9781118910566

Kozegar, E., Soryani, M., Behnam, H., Salamati, M., & Tan, T. (2019). Computer aided detection in automated 3-D breast ultrasound images: A survey. *Artificial Intelligence Review*, 1–23.

Krizhevsky, A., Sutskever, I., & Hinton, G. E. (2012). Imagenet classification with deep convolutional neural networks. Advances in neural information processing systems, 1097-1105.

Krizhevsky, A., Sutskever, I., & Hinton, G. E. (2012). Imagenet classification with deep convolutional neural networks. In Advances in neural information processing systems (pp. 1097-1105). Academic Press.

Krizhevsky, A., & Hinton, G. (2009). *Learning multiple layers of features from tiny images*. Retrieved from http://citeseerx.ist.psu.edu/viewdoc/download?doi=10.1.1.222.9220&rep=rep1&type=pdf

Krizhevsky, A., Sutskever, I., & Hinton, G. E. (2017). ImageNet classification with deep convolutional neural networks. *Communications of the ACM, 60*(6), 84–90. doi:10.1145/3065386

Kukharev, G. A., Kamenskaya, E. I., Matveev, Y. N., & Shchegoleva, N. L. (2013). *Methods of facial images processing and recognition in biometrics*. St. Petersburg: Politechnika.

Kumar, S., Jaiswal, S., Kumar, R., & Kumar Singh, S. (2016). Emotion recognition using facial expression. In P. Rajarshi P (Ed.), Innovative research in attention modeling and computer vision applications (pp. 327-345). IGI Publication. doi:10.4018/978-1-4666-8723-3.ch013

Kumar, A., Kaur, A., & Kumar, M. (2018). Face Detection Techniques: A Review. *Artificial Intelligence Review, 52*(2), 927–948. doi:10.100710462-018-9650-2

Kumari, J., Rajesh, R., & Pooja, K. (2015). Facial Expression Recognition: A Survey. *Procedia Computer Science, 58*, 486–491. doi:10.1016/j.procs.2015.08.011

Kumar, M. V. (2020, July). Detection of Lung Nodules using Convolution Neural Network: A Review. In *2020 Second International Conference on Inventive Research in Computing Applications (ICIRCA)* (pp. 590-594). IEEE. 10.1109/ICIRCA48905.2020.9183183

Kumin, L. (2003). *Early communication skills for children with Down syndrome. A Guide for Parents and Professionals*. Woodbine House.

Kumuda, T., & Basavaraj, L. (2015). Detection and localization of text from natural scene images using texture features. *2015 IEEE International Conference on Computational Intelligence and Computing Research (ICCIC)*, 1-4. 10.1109/ICCIC.2015.7435688

Kwong, J. C. T., Garcia, F. C., Abu, P. A., & Reyes, R. S. J. (2018). Emotion recognition via facial expression: Utilization of numerous feature descriptors in different machine learning algorithms. *Proceedings of TENCON 2018 - 2018 IEEE Region 10 Conference*. 10.1109/TENCON.2018.8650192

Laguduva, V. R., Mahmud, S., Aakur, S. N., Karam, R., & Katkoori, S. (2020, January). Dissecting Convolutional Neural Networks for Efficient Implementation on Constrained Platforms. In *2020 33rd International Conference on VLSI Design and 2020 19th International Conference on Embedded Systems (VLSID)* (pp. 149-154). IEEE.

Lai, Y. H., & Lai, S. H. (2018). Emotion-preserving representation learning via generative adversarial network for multi-view facial expression recognition. In *Proceedings of the 13th IEEE International Conference on Automatic Face & Gesture Recognition (FG 2018)* (pp. 263–270). Xi'an, China: IEEE. 10.1109/FG.2018.00046

Lange, C. (1885/1912). The mechanisms of the emotions. In B. Rand (Ed.), *The Classical Psychologists* (pp. 672–684). Houghton.

Lapedriza, A., Masip, D., & Vitria, J. (n.d.). Are external face features useful for automatic face classification? *2005 IEEE Computer Society Conference on Computer Vision and Pattern Recognition (CVPR'05) - Workshops*. doi:10.1109/cvpr.2005.569

Lavanyadevi, R., Machakowsalya, M., Nivethitha, J., & Kumar, A. N. (2017, April). Brain tumor classification and segmentation in MRI images using PNN. In *2017 IEEE International Conference on Electrical, Instrumentation and Communication Engineering (ICEICE)* (pp. 1-6). IEEE. 10.1109/ICEICE.2017.8191888

Laws, K. I. (1980, Jan). *Textured image segmentation* (No. USCIPI-940). University of Southern California Los Angeles Image Processing INST.

LeCun, Y., Bengio, Y., & Hinton, G. (2015). Deep learning. *Nature*, *521*(7553), 436–444. doi:10.1038/nature14539 PMID:26017442

LeCun, Y., Bottou, L., Bengio, Y., & Haffner, P. (1998). Gradient-based learning applied to document recognition. *Proceedings of the IEEE*, *86*(11), 2278–2324. doi:10.1109/5.726791

LeCun, Y., Huang, F. J., & Bottou, L. (2004, June). Learning methods for generic object recognition with invariance to pose and lighting. In *Proceedings of the 2004 IEEE Computer Society Conference on Computer Vision and Pattern Recognition, 2004. CVPR 2004.* (Vol. 2, pp. 97-104). IEEE. 10.1109/CVPR.2004.1315150

Lee, H., Park, J., & Hwang, J. Y. (2020). Channel Attention Module with Multi-scale Grid Average Pooling for Breast Cancer Segmentation in an Ultrasound Image. *IEEE Transactions on Ultrasonics, Ferroelectrics, and Frequency Control*, 1. doi:10.1109/TUFFC.2020.2972573

Lee, H., Wu, C., & Lin, T. (2013). Facial Expression Recognition Using Image Processing Techniques and Neural Networks. *Advances in Intelligent Systems and Applications*, *2*, 259–267.

Lei, B., Huang, S., Li, R., Bian, C., Li, H., Chou, Y. H., & Cheng, J. Z. (2018). Segmentation of breast anatomy for automated whole breast ultrasound images with boundary regularized convolutional encoder–decoder network. *Neurocomputing*, *321*, 178–186. doi:10.1016/j.neucom.2018.09.043

Le, T. H. (2011). Applying Artificial Neural Networks for Face Recognition. *Advances in Artificial Neural Systems*, *2011*, 1–16. doi:10.1155/2011/673016

Le, T. H. N., Duong, C. N., Han, L., Luu, K., Quach, K. G., & Savvides, M. (2018). Deep contextual recurrent residual networks for scene labeling. *Pattern Recognition*, *80*, 32–41. doi:10.1016/j.patcog.2018.01.005

Lewinski, P., den Uyl, T. M., & Butler, C. (2014). Automated facial coding: Validation of basic emotions and FACS AUs in FaceReader. *Journal of Neuroscience, Psychology, and Economics*, *7*(4), 227–236. doi:10.1037/npe0000028

Lewis, J. J., O'Callaghan, R. J., Nikolov, S. G., Bull, D. R., & Canagarajah, C. N. (2004). Region-based image fusion using complex wavelets. *Proceedings of the 7th International Conference on Information Fusion (FUSION '04)*, 555-562.

Li, Tang, Guo, Lei, & Zhang. (2017). Deep neural network with attention model for scene text recognition. *IET Computer Vision*, *11*(7), 605-612.

Li, X., Yang, Y., Xiong, H., Song, S., & Jia, H. (2017, May). Pulmonary nodules detection algorithm based on robust cascade classifier for CT images. In *2017 29th Chinese Control And Decision Conference (CCDC)* (pp. 231-235). IEEE. 10.1109/CCDC.2017.7978097

Liao, Liang, & Wu. (2015). An Integrated Approach for Multilingual Scene Text Detection. *Seventh International Conference of Soft Computing and Pattern Recognition*.

Li, H., Lin, Z., Shen, X., Brandt, J., & Hua, G. (2015). A convolutional neural network cascade for face detection. In *Proceedings of the IEEE Conference on Computer Vision and Pattern Recognition* (pp. 5325-5334). 10.1109/CVPR.2015.7299170

Li, H., Wu, X.-J., & Kittler, J. (2018). Infrared and Visible Image Fusion using a Deep Learning Framework. *Conference Paper*. 10.1109/ICPR.2018.8546006

Li, L., Yu, S., Zhong, L., & Li, X. (2015). Multilingual Text Detection with Nonlinear Neural Network. *Mathematical Problems in Engineering*, *2015*. doi:10.1155/2015/431608

Lin, M., Chen, Q., & Yan, S. (2013). *Network in network*. arXiv preprint arXiv:1312.4400

Lindsley, D. B. (1951). Emotion. In S. S. Stevens (Ed.), *Handbook of experimental psychology*. New York: Wiley.

Lindsley, D. B. (1982). Neural mechanisms of arousal, attention, and information processing. In J. Orbach (Ed.), *Neuropsychology after Lashley*. Erlbaum.

Lin, X., Wang, J., Han, F., Fu, J., & Li, A. (2012). Analysis of eighty-one cases with breast lesions using automated breast volume scanner and comparison with handheld ultrasound. *European Journal of Radiology*, *81*(5), 873–878. doi:10.1016/j.ejrad.2011.02.038 PMID:21420814

Lin, Y., Lv, F., Zhu, S., Yang, M., Cour, T., Yu, K., ... Huang, T. (2011, June). Large-scale image classification: Fast feature extraction and SVM training. In *Computer Vision and Pattern Recognition Conference (CVPR) 2011* (pp. 1689-1696). IEEE. 10.1109/CVPR.2011.5995477

Li, S., & Deng, W. (2018). Deep Facial Expression Recognition: A survey. In *Proceedings of EEE Transactions on Affective Computing* (pp. 99). DOI: 10.1109/TAFFC.2020.2981446

Li, S., Kang, X., & Hu, J. (2013, July). Image Fusion with Guided Filtering. *IEEE Transactions on Image Processing*, *22*(7), 2864–2875. doi:10.1109/TIP.2013.2244222 PMID:23372084

Liu, B., Cheng, H. D., Huang, J., Tian, J., Liu, J., & Tang, X. (2009). Automated Segmentation of Ultrasonic Breast Lesions Using Statistical Texture Classification and Active Contour Based on Probability Distance. *Ultrasound in Medicine & Biology*, *35*(8), 1309–1324. doi:10.1016/j.ultrasmedbio.2008.12.007 PMID:19481332

Liu, B., Zhang, Y., He, D. J., & Li, Y. (2018). Identification of apple leaf diseases based on deep convolutional neural networks. *Symmetry*, *10*(1), 11. doi:10.3390ym10010011

Liu, J. W., & Guo, L. (2015, July). Selection of initial parameters of K-means clustering algorithm for MRI brain image segmentation. In *2015 International Conference on Machine Learning and Cybernetics (ICMLC)* (Vol. 1, pp. 123-127). IEEE. 10.1109/ICMLC.2015.7340909

Liu, J., Wang, S., Linguraru, M. G., Yao, J., & Summers, R. M. (2015). Computer-aided detection of exophytic renal lesions on non-contrast CT images. *Medical Image Analysis*, *19*(1), 15–29. doi:10.1016/j.media.2014.07.005 PMID:25189363

Liu, M., Breuel, T., & Kautz, J. (2017). Unsupervised Image-to-Image Translation Networks. *Conference on Neural Information Processing Systems (NIPS)*. 10.1007/978-3-319-70139-4

Liu, P., Li, X., Cui, H., Li, S., & Yuan, Y. (2019). *Hand Gesture Recognition Based on Single-Shot Multibox Detector Deep Learning*. Mobile Information Systems. doi:10.1155/2019/3410348

Liu, R., Han, Q., Min, W., Zhou, L., & Xu, J. (2019). Vehicle logo recognition based on enhanced matching for small objects, constrained region and SSFPD network. *Sensors (Basel)*, *19*(20), 4528. doi:10.339019204528

Liu, Y., Chen, X., Peng, H., & Wang, Z. (2017). Multi-focus image fusion with a deep convolutional neural network. *Information Fusion*, *36*, 191–207. doi:10.1016/j.inffus.2016.12.001

Liu, Y., Chen, X., Ward, R. K., & Jane Wang, Z. (2016). Image fusion with convolutional sparse representation. *IEEE Signal Processing Letters*, *23*(12), 1882–1886. doi:10.1109/LSP.2016.2618776

Li, X. X., & Liang, R. H. (2018). A review for face recognition with occlusion: From subspace regression to deep learning. *Chinese Journal of Computers*, *41*(1), 177–207.

Li, X. X., Li, B., Tian, L. F., & Zhang, L. (2018). Automatic benign and malignant classification of pulmonary nodules in thoracic computed tomography based on RF algorithm. *IET Image Processing*, *12*(7), 1253–1264. doi:10.1049/iet-ipr.2016.1014

Li, Y., & Vasconcelos, N. (2019). Repair: Removing representation bias by dataset resampling. *Proceedings of the IEEE Computer Society Conference on Computer Vision and Pattern Recognition*, *2019-June*, 9564–9573. 10.1109/CVPR.2019.00980

Li, Y., Wang, Sh., Zhao, Y., & Ji, Q. (2013). Simultaneous facial feature tracking and facial expression recognition. *IEEE Transactions on Image Processing*, *22*(7), 2559–2573. doi:10.1109/TIP.2013.2253477 PMID:23529088

Lo, C. M., Chen, R. T., Chang, Y. C., Yang, Y. W., Hung, M. J., Huang, C. S., & Chang, R. F. (2014). Multi-dimensional tumor detection in automated whole breast ultrasound using topographic watershed. *IEEE Transactions on Medical Imaging*, *33*(7), 1503–1511. doi:10.1109/TMI.2014.2315206 PMID:24718570

Long, J., Shelhamer, E., & Darrell, T. (2015). Fully convolutional networks for semantic segmentation. *Proceedings of the IEEE Conference on Computer Vision and Pattern Recognition*, 3431–3440.

Long, J., Shelhamer, E., & Darrell, T. (2015). Fully convolutional networks for semantic segmentation. *Proceedings of the IEEE Conference on Computer Vision and Pattern Recognition*.

Long, W., & Xu, S. (2016). A novel grey wolf optimizer for global optimization problems. *2016 IEEE Advanced Information Management, Communicates, Electronic and Automation Control Conference (IMCEC)*. doi:10.1109/imcec.2016.7867415

Lowe, D. G. (2004). Distinctive image features from scale-invariant keypoints. *International Journal of Computer Vision*, *60*(2), 91–110. doi:10.1023/B:VISI.0000029664.99615.94

Lu, X., Chen, H., & Jain, A. K. (2005). Multimodal facial gender and ethnicity identification. *Advances in Biometrics*, 554-561. doi:10.1007/11608288_74

Luan, S., Chen, C., Zhang, B., Han, J., & Liu, J. (2018). Gabor convolutional networks. *IEEE Transactions on Image Processing*, *27*(9), 4357–4366. doi:10.1109/TIP.2018.2835143

Lundgren, A., Castro, D., Lima, E., & Bezerra, B. (2019). OctShuffleMLT: A Compact Octave Based Neural Network for End-to-End Multilingual Text Detection and Recognition. *International Conference on Document Analysis and Recognition Workshops*. 10.1109/ICDARW.2019.30062

Lundqvist, D., Flykt, A., & Öhman, A. (1998). *The Karolinska Directed Emotional Faces -KDEF, CD ROM from Department of Clinical Neuroscience, Psychology section*. Karolinska Institutet.

Lu, S. (2011). Accurate and efficient optic disc detection and segmentation by a circular transformation. *IEEE Transactions on Medical Imaging*, *30*(12), 2126–2133. doi:10.1109/TMI.2011.2164261 PMID:21843983

Lu, X., & Jain, A. K. (2004). *Ethnicity identification from face images*. Biometric Technology for Human Identification. doi:10.1117/12.542847

Lyakso, E. E., & Nozdrachev, A. D. (2012). *Psychophysiology. Textbook for students of institutions of higher professional education*. Moscow: Publishing Center "Academy".

Lyakso, E. E., Frolova, O. V., Grigor'ev, A. S., Sokolova, V. D., & Yarotskaya, K. A. (2017). Recognition by adults of Emotional State in Typically Developing Children and Children with Autism Spectrum Disorders. *Neuroscience and Behavioral Physiology*, *47*(9), 1051–1059. doi:10.100711055-017-0511-2

Lyakso, E., Frolova, O., Grigorev, A., Gorodnyi, V., & Nikolaev, A. (2019). Strategies of speech interaction between adults and preschool children with typical and atypical development. *Behavioral Science*, *9*(12), 159. doi:10.3390/bs9120159 PMID:31888116

Ma, B., Li, X., Xia, Y., & Zhang, Y. (2020). Autonomous deep learning: A genetic DCNN designer for image classification. *Neurocomputing*, *379*, 152–161. doi:10.1016/j.neucom.2019.10.007

Mahesh, V. G., & Raj, A. N. J. (2015). Invariant face recognition using Zernike moments combined with feed forward neural network. *International Journal of Biometrics*, *7*(3), 286–307. doi:10.1504/IJBM.2015.071950

Mahesh, V. G., Raj, A. N. J., & Fan, Z. (2017). Invariant moments based convolutional neural networks for image analysis. *International Journal of Computational Intelligence Systems*, *10*(1), 936–950. doi:10.2991/ijcis.2017.10.1.62

Manjunath Aradhya, V. N., Pavithra, M. S., & Naveena, C. (2011). *A Robust Multilingual Text Detection Approach Based on Transforms and Wavelet Entropy. Procedia Technology, 4(2012)*, 232 – 237.

Manzak, D., Cetinel, G., & Manzak, A. (2019). Automated Classification of Alzheimer's Disease using Deep Neural Network (DNN) by Random Forest Feature Elimination. *14th International Conference on Computer Science and Education, ICCSE 2019, Iccse*, 1050–1053. 10.1109/ICCSE.2019.8845325

Marín, D., Aquino, A., Gegúndez-Arias, M. E., & Bravo, J. M. (2010). A new supervised method for blood vessel segmentation in retinal images by using gray-level and moment invariants-based features. *IEEE Transactions on Medical Imaging*, *30*(1), 146–158. doi:10.1109/TMI.2010.2064333 PMID:20699207

Mariotti, A., & Pascolini, D. (2012). Global estimates of visual impairment. *The British Journal of Ophthalmology*, *96*(5), 614–618. doi:10.1136/bjophthalmol-2011-300539 PMID:22133988

Markaki, M., & Stylianou, Y. (2011). Voice pathology detection and discrimination based on modulation spectral features. *IEEE Transactions on Audio, Speech, and Language Processing, 19*(7), 1938–1948. doi:10.1109/TASL.2010.2104141

Martinez & Benavente. (1998). *The AR Face Database.* CVC Technical Report #24.

Martinez, A. M. (2017). Visual perception of facial expressions of emotion. *Current Opinion in Psychology, 17,* 27–33. doi:10.1016/j.copsyc.2017.06.009 PMID:28950969

Masood, S., Gupta, S., Wajid, A., Gupta, S., & Ahmed, M. (2017). Prediction of human ethnicity from facial images using neural networks. *Advances in Intelligent Systems and Computing,* 217-226. doi:10.1007/978-981-10-3223-3_200

Mathias, M., Benenson, R., Pedersoli, M., & Van Gool, L. (2014, September). Face detection without bells and whistles. In *European conference on computer vision* (pp. 720-735). Springer.

MathWorks, Inc. (2005). *MATLAB: the language of technical computing. Desktop tools and development environment, version 7* (Vol. 9). MathWorks.

Mercer, C. E., Szczepura, K., Kelly, J., Millington, S. R., Denton, E. R., Borgen, R., ... Hogg, P. (2015). A 6-year study of mammographic compression force: Practitioner variability within and between screening sites. *Radiography, 21*(1), 68–73. doi:10.1016/j.radi.2014.07.004

Mirjalili, S., Mirjalili, S. M., & Lewis, A. (2014). Grey wolf optimizer. *Advances in Engineering Software, 69,* 46–61. doi:10.1016/j.advengsoft.2013.12.007

Mita, T., Kaneko, T., & Hori, O. (2005). Joint haar-like features for face detection. In *Computer Vision, 2005. ICCV 2005. Tenth IEEE International Conference on* (Vol. 2, pp. 1619-1626). IEEE. 10.1109/ICCV.2005.129

Mitchell, H. B. (2010). *Image Fusion-Theories, Techniques and Applications.* Berlin: Springer-Verlag.

Mohanty, S. P., Hughes, D. P., & Salathé, M. (2016). Using deep learning for image-based plant disease detection. *Frontiers in Plant Science, 7*(September), 1–10. doi:10.3389/fpls.2016.01419 PMID:27713752

Monkam, P., Qi, S., Ma, H., Gao, W., Yao, Y., & Qian, W. (2019). Detection and classification of pulmonary nodules using convolutional neural networks: A survey. *IEEE Access: Practical Innovations, Open Solutions, 7,* 78075–78091. doi:10.1109/ACCESS.2019.2920980

Moon, W. K., Lo, C. M., Chen, R. T., Shen, Y. W., Chang, J. M., Huang, C. S., ... Chang, R. F. (2014). Tumor detection in automated breast ultrasound images using quantitative tissue clustering. *Medical Physics, 41*(4), 042901. doi:10.1118/1.4869264 PMID:24694157

Moon, W. K., Shen, Y. W., Bae, M. S., Huang, C. S., Chen, J. H., & Chang, R. F. (2013). Computer-aided tumor detection based on multi-scale blob detection algorithm in automated breast ultrasound images. *IEEE Transactions on Medical Imaging, 32*(7), 1191–1200. doi:10.1109/TMI.2012.2230403 PMID:23232413

Morales, S., Naranjo, V., Angulo, J., & Alcañiz, M. (2013). Automatic detection of optic disc based on PCA and mathematical morphology. *IEEE Transactions on Medical Imaging, 32*(4), 786–796. doi:10.1109/TMI.2013.2238244 PMID:23314772

Mukhopadhyay, P., & Chaudhuri, B. B. (2015). A survey of Hough Transform. *Pattern Recognition, 48*(3), 993–1010. doi:10.1016/j.patcog.2014.08.027

Munteanu, C., & Rosa, A. (2004). Gray-Scale Image Enhancement as an Automatic Process Driven by Evolution. *IEEE Transactions on Systems, Man, and Cybernetics. Part B, Cybernetics, 34*(2), 1292–1298. doi:10.1109/TSMCB.2003.818533 PMID:15376874

Muramatsu, C., Hiramatsu, Y., Fujita, H., & Kobayashi, H. (2018, January). Mass detection on automated breast ultrasound volume scans using convolutional neural network. In *2018 International Workshop on Advanced Image Technology (IWAIT)* (pp. 1-2). IEEE. 10.1109/IWAIT.2018.8369795

Muthiah-Nakarajan, V., & Noel, M. M. (2016). Galactic swarm optimization: A new global optimization metaheuristic inspired by galactic motion. *Applied Soft Computing*, *38*, 771–787. doi:10.1016/j.asoc.2015.10.034

Muthuselvi, S., & Prabhu, P. (2016). Digital image processing technique-A survey. International Multidisciplinary Research Journal Golden Research Thoughts, 5(11).

Nabizadeh, N., John, N., & Wright, C. (2014). Histogram-based gravitational optimization algorithm on single MR modality for automatic brain lesion detection and segmentation. *Expert Systems with Applications*, *41*(17), 7820–7836. doi:10.1016/j.eswa.2014.06.043

Nachtigall, L. G., Araujo, R. M., & Nachtigall, G. R. (2017). Classification of apple tree disorders using convolutional neural networks. *Proceedings - 2016 IEEE 28th International Conference on Tools with Artificial Intelligence, ICTAI 2016*, 472–476. 10.1109/ICTAI.2016.75

Naranjo-Torres, J., Mora, M., Hernández-García, R., Barrientos, R. J., Fredes, C., & Valenzuela, A. (2020). A Review of Convolutional Neural Network Applied to Fruit Image Processing. *Applied Sciences*, *10*(10), 3443. doi:10.3390/app10103443

Nassif, A. B., Shahin, I., Attili, I., Azzeh, M., & Shaalan, K. (2019). Speech recognition using deep neural networks: A systematic review. *IEEE Access: Practical Innovations, Open Solutions*, *7*, 19143–19165. doi:10.1109/ACCESS.2019.2896880

Negi, A., Raj, A. N. J., Nersisson, R., Zhuang, Z., & Murugappan, M. (2020). RDA-UNET-WGAN: An Accurate Breast Ultrasound Lesion Segmentation Using Wasserstein Generative Adversarial Networks. *Arabian Journal for Science and Engineering*, *45*(8), 6399–6410. doi:10.100713369-020-04480-z

Ng, H. W., Nguyen, V. D., Vonikakis, V., & Winkler, S. (2015). Deep Learning for Emotion Recognition on Small Datasets Using Transfer Learning. *ACM International Conference on Multimodal Interaction (ICMI)*. 10.1145/2818346.2830593

Nguyen, C., Wang, Y., & Nguyen, H. (2013). Random forest classifier combined with feature selection for breast cancer diagnosis and prognostic. *Journal of Biomedical Science and Engineering*, *6*(05), 551–560. doi:10.4236/jbise.2013.65070

Nielsen. (2015). *Neural Networks and Deep Learning*. Determination Press.

Noldus Information Technology. (2019). *FaceReader 7.1*. Technical Specification.

Ojala, T., Pietikainen, M., & Maenpaa, T. (2002). Multiresolution gray-scale and rotation invariant texture classification with local binary patterns. *IEEE Transactions on Pattern Analysis and Machine Intelligence*, *24*(7), 971–987. doi:10.1109/TPAMI.2002.1017623

Oquab, M., Bottou, L., Laptev, I., & Sivic, J. (2014). Learning and Transferring Mid-Level Image Representations using Convolutional Neural Networks. *The IEEE Conference on Computer Vision and Pattern Recognition (CVPR)*, 1717-1724. 10.1109/CVPR.2014.222

Pace-Schott, E. F., Amole, M. C., Aue, T., Balconi, M., Bysma, L. M., Critchley, H., ... Kotynski, A. (2019). Physiological feelings. *Neuroscience and Biobehavioral Reviews*, *103*, 267–304. doi:10.1016/j.neubiorev.2019.05.002 PMID:31125635

Pal, S. K., & Majumder, D. K. D. (1986). *Fuzzy mathematical approach to pattern recognition*. New York, NY: Wiley.

Park, D., Ramanan, D., & Fowlkes, C. (2010). Multiresolution models for object detection. *European conference*.

Parke, F. I. (1974). *A parametric model for human faces* (PhD thesis). The University of Utah.

Park, K., Hong, Y., Kim, G., & Lee, J. (2018). Classification of apple leaf conditions in hyper-spectral images for diagnosis of Marssonina blotch using mRMR and deep neural network. *Computers and Electronics in Agriculture, 148*(February), 179–187. doi:10.1016/j.compag.2018.02.025

Parrot, W. G. (2019). The Social Construction of Emotions. In B. Christensen (Ed.), *The Second Cognitive Revolution. Theory and History in the Human and Social Sciences* (pp. 131–139). Cham: Springer. doi:10.1007/978-3-030-26680-6_14

Patel, M. B., & Agrawal, D. L. (2016). A Survey Paper on Facial Expression Recognition System. *Journal of Emerging Technologies and Innovative Research, 3*(2), 44–46.

Pellegretti, P., Vicari, M., Zani, M., Weigel, M., Borup, D., Wiskin, J., ... Langer, M. (2011, October). A clinical experience of a prototype automated breast ultrasound system combining transmission and reflection 3D imaging. In *2011 IEEE International Ultrasonics Symposium* (pp. 1407-1410). IEEE. 10.1109/ULTSYM.2011.0348

Peng, Y., & Yin, H. (2019). ApprGAN: Appearance-Based Generative Adversarial Network for Facial Expression Synthesis. *IET Image Processing, 13*(14), 2706–2715. doi:10.1049/iet-ipr.2018.6576

Perez, L., & Wang, J. (2017, December 13). *The effectiveness of data augmentation in image classification using deep learning.* Retrieved from https://arxiv.org/abs/1712.04621

Perronnin, F., Sánchez, J., & Mensink, T. (2010, September). Improving the fisher kernel for large-scale image classification. In *European conference on computer vision* (pp. 143-156). Springer. 10.1007/978-3-642-15561-1_11

Phung, S. L., & Bouzerdoum, A. (2009). *MATLAB library for convolutional neural networks.* University of Wollongong, Tech. Rep. http://www. elec. uow. edu.au/staff/sphung

Pietik¨ainen, M., & Okun, O. (2001). Edge-Based Method for Text Detection from Complex Document Images. *Proceedings of Sixth International Conference on Document Analysis and Recognition.* 10.1109/ICDAR.2001.953800

Ping, J. (2018). *Research on segmentation method of fundus image* (Master's thesis). Jilin University of China.

Pinto, N., Cox, D. D., & DiCarlo, J. J. (2008). Why is real-world visual object recognition hard? *PLoS Computational Biology, 4*(1), e27. doi:10.1371/journal.pcbi.0040027

Polly, F. P., Shil, S. K., Hossain, M. A., Ayman, A., & Jang, Y. M. (2018, January). Detection and classification of HGG and LGG brain tumor using machine learning. In *2018 International Conference on Information Networking (ICOIN)* (pp. 813-817). IEEE. 10.1109/ICOIN.2018.8343231

Ponce, J., Berg, T. L., Everingham, M., Forsyth, D. A., Hebert, M., Lazebnik, S., & Williams, C. K. (2006). Dataset issues in object recognition. In *Toward category-level object recognition* (pp. 29–48). Berlin: Springer. doi:10.1007/11957959_2

Prabhakar, T., & Poonguzhali, S. (2017, August). Automatic detection and classification of benign and malignant lesions in breast ultrasound images using texture morphological and fractal features. In *2017 10th Biomedical Engineering International Conference (BMEiCON)* (pp. 1-5). IEEE. 10.1109/BMEiCON.2017.8229114

Prabhakar, T., & Poonguzhali, S. (2016). Denoising and automatic detection of breast tumor in ultrasound images. *Asian Journal Information Technology, 15*(18), 3506–3512.

Prabusankarlal, K. M., Thirumoorthy, P., & Manavalan, R. (2015). Assessment of combined textural and morphological features for diagnosis of breast masses in ultrasound. *Human-centric Computing and Information Sciences, 5*(1), 1–17. doi:10.118613673-015-0029-y

Prasad, K., Sajith, P. S., Neema, M., Madhu, L., & Priya, P. N. (2019). Multiple eye disease detection using Deep Neural Network. *IEEE Region 10 Annual International Conference, Proceedings/TENCON, 2019-Octob*, 2148–2153. 10.1109/TENCON.2019.8929666

Prochazka, A., Gulati, S., Holinka, S., & Smutek, D. (2019). Classification of Thyroid Nodules in Ultrasound Images Using Direction- Independent Features Extracted by Two-Threshold Binary Decomposition. *Technology in Cancer Research & Treatment*, *18*, 1–8. doi:10.1177/1533033819830748 PMID:30774015

Qian & Weng. (2016). Medical image segmentation based on FCM and Level Set algorithm. *7th IEEE International Conference on Software Engineering and Service Science (ICSESS)*, 225-228.

Qu, Y.-D., Cui, C.-S., Chen, S.-B., & Li, J.-Q. (2005). A fast subpixel edge detection method using Sobel–Zernike moments operator. *Image and Vision Computing*, *23*(1), 11–17. doi:10.1016/j.imavis.2004.07.003

Radewan, C. H. (1975, March). Digital image processing with pseudo-color. In *Acquisition and Analysis of Pictorial Data* (Vol. 48, pp. 50–56). International Society for Optics and Photonics. doi:10.1117/12.954071

Rahul, B., Amudha, & Gupta. (2018). Multilingual Text Detection and Identification from Indian Signage Boards. *International Conference on Advances in Computing, Communications and Informatics*.

Ramakrishnan, A., Urala, B., Sundaram, S., & Harshitha, P. (2014). *Development of OHWR System for Tamil*. Academic Press.

Ramaswamy Reddy, A., Prasad, E. V., & Reddy, L. S. S. (2013). Comparative analysis of brain tumor detection using different segmentation techniques. *International Journal of Computer Applications, 82*(14).

Rastghalam, R., & Pourghassem, H. (2016). Breast cancer detection using MRF-based probable texture feature and decision-level fusion-based classification using HMM on thermography images. *Pattern Recognition*, *51*, 176–186. doi:10.1016/j.patcog.2015.09.009

Rasti, R., Teshnehlab, M., & Phung, S. L. (2017). Breast cancer diagnosis in DCE-MRI using mixture ensemble of convolutional neural networks. *Pattern Recognition*, *72*, 381–390. doi:10.1016/j.patcog.2017.08.004

Ravindraiah, R., & Tejaswini, K. (2013). A survey of image segmentation algorithms Based on fuzzy clustering. *International Journal of Computer Science and Mobile Computing*, *2*(7), 200–206.

Reader, C., & Hubble, L. (1981). Trends in image display systems. *Proceedings of the IEEE*, *69*(5), 606–614. doi:10.1109/PROC.1981.12028

Reisenzein, R. (2019). Cognition and emotion: A plea for theory. *Cognition and Emotion*, *33*(1), 109–118. doi:10.1080/02699931.2019.1568968 PMID:30654695

Ren, X., Zhou, Y., He, J., Chen, K., Yang, X., & Sun, J. (2017). A Convolutional Neural Network-Based Chinese Text Detection Algorithm via Text Structure Modeling. *IEEE Transactions on Multimedia*, *19*(3), 506–518. doi:10.1109/TMM.2016.2625259

Ren, X., Zhou, Y., Huang, Z., Sun, J., Yang, X., & Chen, K. (2017). A Novel Text Structure Feature Extractor for Chinese Scene Text Detection and Recognition. *IEEE Access : Practical Innovations, Open Solutions*, *5*, 3193–3204. doi:10.1109/ACCESS.2017.2676158

Revathi, P., & Hemalatha, M. (2012). Classification of Cotton Leaf Spot Diseases Using Image Processing Edge Detection Techniques. *International Conference on Emerging Trends in Science, Engineering and Technology*. 10.1109/INCOSET.2012.6513900

Revina, I., & Emmanuel, W. (2018). A Survey on Human Face Expression Recognition Techniques. *Journal Of King Saud University - Computer And. Information Sciences*.

Ronneberger, O., Fischer, P., & Brox, T. (2015, October). U-net: Convolutional networks for biomedical image segmentation. In *International Conference on Medical image computing and computer-assisted intervention* (pp. 234-241). Springer. 10.1007/978-3-319-24574-4_28

Rosenblatt, F. (1961). *Principles of neurodynamics: Perceptions and the theory of brain mechanism*. Washington, DC: Spartan Books. doi:10.21236/AD0256582

Rowley, H. A., Baluja, S., & Kanade, T. (1998). Neural network-based face detection. *IEEE Transactions on Pattern Analysis and Machine Intelligence*, *20*(1), 23–38. doi:10.1109/34.655647

Rowley, H., Baluja, S., & Kanade, T. (1998). Rotation invariant neural network-based face detection. In *Proceedings of IEEE Conference on Computer Vision and Pattern Recognition* (p. 38). IEEE.

Ruffman, T., Henry, J. D., Livingstone, V., & Phillips, L. H. (2008). A meta-analytic review of emotion recognition and aging: Implications for neuropsychological models of aging. *Neuroscience and Biobehavioral Reviews*, *32*(4), 863–881. doi:10.1016/j.neubiorev.2008.01.001 PMID:18276008

Russakovsky, O., Deng, J., Su, H., Krause, J., Satheesh, S., Ma, S., ... Fei-Fei, L. (2015). ImageNet Large Scale Visual Recognition Challenge. *International Journal of Computer Vision*, *115*(3), 211–252. doi:10.100711263-015-0816-y

Russell, B. C., Torralba, A., Murphy, K. P., & Freeman, W. T. (2008). LabelMe: A database and web-based tool for image annotation. *International Journal of Computer Vision*, *77*(1-3), 157–173. doi:10.100711263-007-0090-8

Salman, A., Jalal, A., Shafait, F., Mian, A., Shortis, M., Seager, J., & Harvey, E. (2016). Fish species classification in unconstrained underwater environments based on deep learning. *Limnology and Oceanography, Methods*, *14*(9), 570–585. doi:10.1002/lom3.10113

Samadiani, N., Huang, G., Cai, B., Luo, W., Chi, C. H., Xiang, Y., & He, J. (2019). A review on automatic facial expression recognition systems assisted by multimodal sensor data. *Sensors (Basel)*, *19*(8), E1863. doi:10.339019081863 PMID:31003522

Sánchez, J., & Perronnin, F. (2011, June). High-dimensional signature compression for large-scale image classification. In *Computer Vision and Pattern Recognition CVPR 2011* (pp. 1665–1672). IEEE. doi:10.1109/CVPR.2011.5995504

Sandler, M., Howard, A., Zhu, M., Zhmoginov, A., & Chen, L. C. (2018). Mobilenetv2: Inverted residuals and linear bottlenecks. In *Proceedings of the IEEE conference on computer vision and pattern recognition* (pp. 4510-4520). IEEE.

Sato, W., Hyniewska, S., Minemoto, K., & Yoshikawa, S. (2019). Facial expressions of basic emotions in Japanese laypeople. *Frontiers in Psychology*, *10*, 259. doi:10.3389/fpsyg.2019.00259 PMID:30809180

Senthil Kumar, S., & Muttan, S. (2006). PCA based image fusion. *Proceedings of SPIE*, *6233*.

Sermanet, P., Eigen, D., Zhang, X., Mathieu, M., Fergus, R., & LeCun, Y. (2013). *Overfeat: Integrated recognition, localization and detection using convolutional networks*. arXiv preprint arXiv:1312.6229

Setty, S., Husain, M., Beham, P., Gudavalli, J., Kandasamy, M., Vaddi, R., . . . Kumar, V. (2013, December). Indian movie face database: a benchmark for face recognition under wide variations. In *2013 fourth national conference on computer vision, pattern recognition, image processing and graphics (NCVPRIPG)* (pp. 1-5). IEEE. 10.1109/NCVPRIPG.2013.6776225

Sha, Y., Shi, P., You, J., Bao, X., Fu, S., & Zeng, G. (2017). Chinese And English Bilingual Scene Text Detection. *IEEE 3rd Information Technology and Mechatronics Engineering Conference.*

Shakhnarovich, G., Viola, P., & Moghaddam, B. (n.d.). A unified learning framework for real time face detection and classification. *Proceedings of Fifth IEEE International Conference on Automatic Face Gesture Recognition.* doi:10.1109/afgr.2002.1004124

Shan, J., (2011). *A fully automatic segmentation method for breast ultrasound images.* Academic Press.

Shaohua, Z., Jian, C., Lin, P., Jian, G., & Lun, Y. (2014). New method for automatic detection of macular center and optic disc in fundus images. *Dianzi Yu Xinxi Xuebao, 36*(11), 2586–2592.

Sharma, M. J. A., Manne, H. K., & Kashyap, G. S. C. (2017). Facial detection using deep learning. *IOP Conference Series. Materials Science and Engineering, 263.*

Shen, W., Zhou, M., Yang, F., Yu, D., Dong, D., Yang, C., ... Tian, J. (2017). Multi-crop convolutional neural networks for lung nodule malignancy suspiciousness classification. *Pattern Recognition, 61,* 663–673. doi:10.1016/j.patcog.2016.05.029

Shen, X., Tian, X., He, A., Sun, S., & Tao, D. (2016, October). Transform-invariant convolutional neural networks for image classification and search. In *Proceedings of the 24th ACM international conference on Multimedia* (pp. 1345-1354). 10.1145/2964284.2964316

Shmueli, B. (2019b, Jul 2). *Multi-Class Metrics Made Simple, Part I: Precision and Recall.* Retrieved from https://towardsdatascience.com/the-best-classification-metric-youve-never-heard-of-the-matthews-correlation-coefficient-3bf50a2f3e9a

Shmulei, B. (2019a, Nov 22). *Matthews Correlation Coefficient Is the Best Classification Metric You've Never Heard Of.* Retrieved from https://towardsdatascience.com/the-best-classification-metric-youve-never-heard-of-the-matthews-correlation-coefficient-3bf50a2f3e9a

Shukla, R. K., & Tiwari, A. K. (2019). Machine Learning approaches for Face Identification Feed Forward Algorithms. *Proceedings of 2nd International Conference on Advanced Computing and Software Engineering.* 10.2139srn.3350264

Simonyan, K., & Zisserman, A. (2014). *Very deep convolutional networks for large-scale image recognition.* arXiv preprint arXiv:1409.1556

Simonyan, K., & Zisserman, A. (2015). *Very deep convolutional networks for largescale image Recognition.* arXiv preprint arXiv:1409.1556

Simonyan, K., & Zisserman, A. (2015, April 10). *Very deep Convolutional networks for large-scale image recognition.* Retrieved from https://arxiv.org/abs/1409.1556

Sinelnikov, R. D. (2009). The doctrine of bones, the connection of bones, and muscles. Atlas of human anatomy (7th ed., vol. 1). Moscow: New wave.

Singh, D. V. (2013). *Digital Image Processing with MATLAB and Lab VIEW.* Reed Elsevier India Private Limited.

Skiendziel, T., Rosch, A. G., & Schultheiss, O. C. (2019). Assessing the convergent validity between the automated emotion recognition software Noldus FaceReader 7 and Facial Action Coding System Scoring. *PLoS One, 14*(10), e0223905. doi:10.1371/journal.pone.0223905 PMID:31622426

Springenberg, J. T., Dosovitskiy, A., Brox, T., & Riedmiller, M. (2015, April 13). *Striving for simplicity: The all Convolutional net.* Retrieved from https://arxiv.org/abs/1412.6806

Sricharan, H. D. K., & Chellappa, R. (2017). ExprGAN: Facial Expression Editing with Controllable Expression Intensity. *The Thirty-Second AAAI Conference on Artificial Intelligence.*

Srivastava, N., Hinton, G., Krizhevsky, A., Sutskever, I., & Salakhutdinov, R. (2014). Dropout: A simple way to prevent neural networks from overfitting. *Journal of Machine Learning Research, 15*(1), 1929–1958.

Suero, A., Marin, D., Gegúndez-Arias, M. E., & Bravo, J. M. (2013, March). Locating the Optic Disc in Retinal Images Using Morphological Techniques. In IWBBIO (pp. 593-600). Academic Press.

Sun, A., Li, Y., Huang, Y., Li, Q., & Lu, G. (2018). Facial expression recognition using optimized active regions. *Human-centric Computing and Information Sciences, 8*(1).

Szegedy, C., Ioffe, S., Vanhoucke, V., & Alemi, A. A. (2017, February). Inception-v4, inception-resnet and the impact of residual connections on learning. *Thirty-first AAAI conference on artificial intelligence.*

Szegedy, C., Liu, W., Jia, Y., Sermanet, P., Reed, S., Anguelov, D., ... Rabinovich, A. (2015). Going deeper with convolutions. In *Proceedings of the IEEE Conference on Computer Vision and Pattern Recognition* (pp. 1-9). IEEE.

Szegedy, C., Liu, W., Jia, Y., Sermanet, P., Reed, S., Anguelov, D., ... Rabinovich, A. (2105). Going deeper with convolutions. *Proceedings of the IEEE conference on computer vision and pattern recognition,* 1–9.

Tahmasbi, A., Saki, F., & Shokouhi, S. B. (2011). Classification of benign and malignant masses based on Zernike moments. *Computers in Biology and Medicine, 41*(8), 726–735. doi:10.1016/j.compbiomed.2011.06.009 PMID:21722886

Tahmooresi, M., Afshar, A., Bashari, R., Babak, B. N., & Bamiah, K. M. (2018). Early Detection of Breast Cancer Using Machine Learning Techniques. Journal of Telecommunication. *Electronic and Computer Engineering., 10,* 21–27.

Terzis, V., Moridis, C. N., & Economides, A. A. (2010). Measuring instant emotions during a self-assessment test: The use of FaceReader. In *Proceedings of the 7ᵗʰ International Conference on Methods and Techniques in Behavioral Research* (pp. 192-195). 10.1145/1931344.1931362

Tian, Y. I., Kanade, T., & Cohn, J. F. (2001). Recognizing action units for facial expression analysis. *IEEE Transactions on Pattern Analysis and Machine Intelligence, 23*(2), 97–115. doi:10.1109/34.908962 PMID:25210210

Torralba, A., & Efros, A. A. (2011, June). Unbiased look at dataset bias. In *Computer Vision and Pattern Recognition Conference CVPR 2011* (pp. 1521–1528). IEEE.

Torralba, A., Fergus, R., & Freeman, W. T. (2008). 80 million tiny images: A large data set for nonparametric object and scene recognition. *IEEE Transactions on Pattern Analysis and Machine Intelligence, 30*(11), 1958–1970. doi:10.1109/TPAMI.2008.128

Trivedi, A., & Geraldine Bessie Amali, D. (2017). A comparative study of machine learning models for ethnicity classification. *IOP Conference Series. Materials Science and Engineering, 263,* 042091. doi:10.1088/1757-899X/263/4/042091

Tsai, Y., Lin, H., & Yang, F. (2017). Facial Expression Synthesis Based on Imitation. *International Journal of Advanced Robotic Systems, 9*(4), 148. doi:10.5772/51906

Vaillant, R., Monrocq, C., & Le Cun, Y. (1994). Original approach for the localisation of objects in images. *IEE Proceedings. Vision Image and Signal Processing, 141*(4), 245–250. doi:10.1049/ip-vis:19941301

Vakanski, A., Xian, M., & Freer, P. E. (2020). Attention-Enriched Deep Learning Model for Breast Tumor Segmentation in Ultrasound Images. *Ultrasound in Medicine & Biology, 46*(10), 2819–2833. doi:10.1016/j.ultrasmedbio.2020.06.015 PMID:32709519

Vapnik, V. N. (1999). An overview of statistical learning theory. *IEEE Transactions on Neural Networks, 10*(5), 988–999. doi:10.1109/72.788640 PMID:18252602

Vijayarajan, R., & Muttan, S. (2014). Fuzzy C-Means clustering based principal component averaging fusion. *International Journal of Fuzzy Systems*, *16*(2), 153–159.

Vijayarajan, R., & Muttan, S. (2014). Local principal component averaging image fusion. *International Journal of Imaging and Robotics*, *13*(2), 94–103.

Viola, P., & Jones, M. (2001). Rapid object detection using a boosted cascade of simple features. In *Computer Vision and Pattern Recognition, 2001. CVPR 2001. Proceedings of the 2001 IEEE Computer Society Conference on* (Vol. 1, pp. I-I). IEEE. 10.1109/CVPR.2001.990517

Völkle, M. C., Ebner, N. C., Lindenberger, U., & Riediger, M. (2012). Let me guess how old you are: Effects of age, gender, and facial expression on perceptions of age. *Psychology and Aging*, *27*(2), 265–277. doi:10.1037/a0025065 PMID:21895379

Waade, G. G., Moshina, N., Sebuødegård, S., Hogg, P., & Hofvind, S. (2017). Compression forces used in the Norwegian breast cancer screening program. *The British Journal of Radiology*, *90*(1071), 20160770. doi:10.1259/bjr.20160770 PMID:28102696

Wan, L., Zeiler, M., Zhang, S., Le Cun, Y., & Fergus, R. (2013, February). Regularization of neural networks using dropconnect. In *International conference on machine learning* (pp. 1058-1066). Academic Press.

Wang, W., He, F., & Zhao, Q. (2016). Facial ethnicity classification with deep Convolutional neural networks. *Biometric Recognition*, 176-185. doi:10.1007/978-3-319-46654-5_20

Wang, X. Y., & Xu, J. G. (2009). Fundus Oculi Images Enhancement Based on Histograms Equalization and Its Simulation with MATLAB. *Journal of Hebei North University (Natural Science Edition), 4*.

Wang, G. G., Deb, S., & Cui, Z. (2019). Monarch butterfly optimization. *Neural Computing & Applications*, *31*(7), 1995–2014. doi:10.100700521-015-1923-y

Wang, G. G., & Tan, Y. (2019). Improving Metaheuristic Algorithms With Information Feedback Models. *IEEE Transactions on Cybernetics*, *49*(2), 542–555. doi:10.1109/TCYB.2017.2780274 PMID:29990274

Wang, Z., Bovik, A. C., Sheikh, H. R., & Simoncelli, E. P. (2004). Image quality assessment: From error visibility to structural similarity. *IEEE Transactions on Image Processing*, *13*(4), 600–612. doi:10.1109/TIP.2003.819861 PMID:15376593

Wang, Z., Cuia, Z., & Zhu, Y. (2020). Multi-modal medical image fusion by Laplacian pyramid and adaptive sparse representation. *Computers in Biology and Medicine*, *123*, 103823. doi:10.1016/j.compbiomed.2020.103823 PMID:32658780

Wassmann, C. (2014). "Picturesque incisiveness": Explaining the celebrity of James's Theory of Emotion. *Journal of the History of the Behavioral Sciences*, *50*(2), 166–188. doi:10.1002/jhbs.21651 PMID:24615670

Watanabe, T., & Iima, H. (2018). Nonlinear Optimization Method Based on Stochastic Gradient Descent for Fast Convergence. *2018 IEEE International Conference on Systems, Man, and Cybernetics*. 10.1109/SMC.2018.00711

Watermann, D. O., Földi, M., Hanjalic-Beck, A., Hasenburg, A., Lüghausen, A., Prömpeler, H., ... Stickeler, E. (2005). Three-dimensional ultrasound for the assessment of breast lesions. *Ultrasound in Obstetrics and Gynecology: The Official Journal of the International Society of Ultrasound in Obstetrics and Gynecology*, *25*(6), 592–598. doi:10.1002/uog.1909 PMID:15912473

Williams, M. L., Wilson, R. C., & Hancock, E. R. (1999). Deterministic search for relational graph matching. *Pattern Recognition*, *32*(7), 1255–1271. doi:10.1016/S0031-3203(98)00152-6

Wu, B., Haizhou, A. I., Huang, C., & Lao, S. (2004). *Fast rotation invariant multi-view face detection based on real adaboost. In Null* (p. 79). IEEE.

Wu, X., Xu, K., & Hall, P. (2017). A Survey of Image Synthesis and Editing with Generative Adversarial Networks. *Tsinghua Science and Technology, 22*(6), 660–674. doi:10.23919/TST.2017.8195348

Xiaofen, C., & Yuecun, W. (2008). *Color image edge detection* (Doctoral dissertation).

Xiao, J., Hays, J., Ehinger, K. A., Oliva, A., & Torralba, A. (2010, June). Sun database: Large-scale scene recognition from abbey to zoo. In *2010 IEEE Computer Society Conference on Computer Vision and Pattern Recognition* (pp. 3485-3492). IEEE. 10.1109/CVPR.2010.5539970

Xiaomei, X., Xiaobo, L., & Yanli, L. (2017). Video disc automatic segmentation algorithm. *Chinese Science and Technology Papers, 12*(20), 2349–2354.

Xie, L., Wang, J., Wei, Z., Wang, M., & Tian, Q. (2016). Disturblabel: Regularizing cnn on the loss layer. In *Proceedings of the IEEE Conference on Computer Vision and Pattern Recognition* (pp. 4753-4762). 10.1109/CVPR.2016.514

Xie, S., Hu, H., & Wu, Y. (2019). Deep multi-path convolutional neural network joint with salient region attention for facial expression recognition. *Pattern Recognition, 92*, 177–191. doi:10.1016/j.patcog.2019.03.019

Xie, W., Shen, L., & Jiang, J. (2017). A novel transient wrinkle detection algorithm and its application for expression synthesis. *IEEE Transactions on Multimedia, 19*(2), 279–292. doi:10.1109/TMM.2016.2614429

Xiong, Y., Kim, H. J., & Hedau, V. (2019). *Antnets: Mobile convolutional neural networks for resource efficient image classification.* arXiv preprint arXiv:1904.03775

Yamashita, R., Nishio, M., Richard, K. G. D., & Togashi, K. (2018). Convolutional neural networks: An overview and application in radiology. *Insights Into Imaging, 9*(4), 611–629. doi:10.100713244-018-0639-9 PMID:29934920

Yang, Z., & Ai, H. (n.d.). Demographic classification with local binary patterns. *Advances in Biometrics*, 464-473. doi:10.1007/978-3-540-74549-5_49

Yan, J., Zhang, X., Lei, Z., & Li, S. Z. (2014). Face detection by structural models. *Image and Vision Computing, 32*(10), 790–799. doi:10.1016/j.imavis.2013.12.004

Yap, M. H., Pons, G., Martí, J., Ganau, S., Sentís, M., Zwiggelaar, R., ... Martí, R. (2017). Automated breast ultrasound lesions detection using convolutional neural networks. *IEEE Journal of Biomedical and Health Informatics, 22*(4), 1218–1226. doi:10.1109/JBHI.2017.2731873 PMID:28796627

Ye, Q., & Doermann, D. (2015). Text Detection and Recognition in Imagery: A Survey. *IEEE Transactions on Pattern Analysis and Machine Intelligence, 37*(7), 1480–1500. doi:10.1109/TPAMI.2014.2366765 PMID:26352454

Yin, P., Wu, Q., Xu, Y., Min, H., Yang, M., Zhang, Y., & Tan, M. (2019, October). PM-Net: Pyramid Multi-label Network for Joint Optic Disc and Cup Segmentation. In *International Conference on Medical Image Computing and Computer-Assisted Intervention* (pp. 129-137). Springer. 10.1007/978-3-030-32239-7_15

Yin, X., Yin, X., Huang, K., & Hao, H. (2014). Robust Text Detection in Natural Scene Images. *IEEE Transactions on Pattern Analysis and Machine Intelligence, 36*(5), 970–983. doi:10.1109/TPAMI.2013.182 PMID:26353230

Yuan, Z. (2012). *Research on key technologies in fundus retinal vascular segmentation* (Master's thesis). University of Electronic Science and Technology of China.

Yu, H., Garrod, O., & Schyns, P. (2012). Perception-driven facial expression synthesis. *Computers & Graphics, 36*(3), 152–162. doi:10.1016/j.cag.2011.12.002

Zeiler, M. D., & Fergus, R. (2013, January). Stochastic pooling for regularization of deep convolutional neural networks. *1st International Conference on Learning Representations, ICLR 2013*.

Zeiler, M. D., & Fergus, R. (2014, September). Visualizing and understanding convolutional networks. In *European conference on computer vision* (pp. 818-833). Springer.

Zeiler, M. D., Taylor, G. W., & Fergus, R. (2011, November). Adaptive deconvolutional networks for mid and high level feature learning. In *2011 International Conference on Computer Vision* (pp. 2018-2025). IEEE. 10.1109/ICCV.2011.6126474

Zeno, B., Kalinovskiy, I., & Matveev, Yu. (2019). IP-GAN: Learning identity and pose disentanglement in generative adversarial networks. *Lecture Notes in Computer Science*, *11731*, 535–547. doi:10.1007/978-3-030-30493-5_51

Zhang, W., Zelinsky, G., & Samaras, D. (2007). Real-time accurate object detection using multiple resolutions. In *Computer Vision, 2007. ICCV 2007. IEEE 11th International Conference on* (pp. 1-8). IEEE. 10.1109/ICCV.2007.4409057

Zhang, G., Huang, X., Li, S. Z., Wang, Y., & Wu, X. (2004). Boosting local binary pattern (LBP)-based face recognition. In *Advances in biometric person authentication* (pp. 179–186). Berlin: Springer. doi:10.1007/978-3-540-30548-4_21

Zhang, J.-Y., Yan, C., & Huang, X.-X. (2009). Edge Detection of Images Based on Improved Sobel Operator and Genetic Algorithms. *2009 International Conference on Image Analysis and Signal Processing*. 10.1109/IASP.2009.5054605

Zhang, K., Zhang, Z., Li, Z., & Qiao, Y. (2016). Joint face detection and alignment using multitask cascaded convolutional networks. *IEEE Signal Processing Letters*, *23*(10), 1499–1503. doi:10.1109/LSP.2016.2603342

Zhang, M. M., Shang, K., & Wu, H. (2019). Deep compact discriminative representation for unconstrained face recognition. *Signal Processing Image Communication*, *75*, 118–127. doi:10.1016/j.image.2019.03.015

Zhang, P., Lan, C., Xing, J., Zeng, W., Xue, J., & Zheng, N. (2019). View adaptive neural networks for high performance skeleton-based human action recognition. *IEEE Transactions on Pattern Analysis and Machine Intelligence*, *41*(8), 1963–1978. doi:10.1109/TPAMI.2019.2896631 PMID:30714909

Zhang, Q., Wang, W., & Zhu, S. C. (2018). Examining CNN representations with respect to dataset bias. *32nd AAAI Conference on Artificial Intelligence, AAAI 2018*, 4464–4473.

Zhang, Y., Zhang, Z., Miao, D., & Wang, J. (2019). Three-way enhanced convolutional neural networks for sentence-level sentiment classification. *Information Sciences*, *477*, 55–64. doi:10.1016/j.ins.2018.10.030

Zhao, Y., Yin, Y., & Fu, D. (2008). Decision level fusion of infrared and visible images for face recognition. *Proceedings of the Chinese Control and Decision Conference*, 2411-2414.

Zhihua, Z., & Jue, W. (2007). Machine learning and its application. Tsinghua University Press.

Zhong, Y., & Zhao, M. (2020). Research on deep learning in apple leaf disease recognition. *Computers and Electronics in Agriculture*, *168*, 105146. doi:10.1016/j.compag.2019.105146

Zhou, B., & Wichman, R. (2020). Visible light-based robust positioning under detector orientation uncertainty: A Gabor convolutional network-based approach extracting stable texture features. In *Proceedings of 2020 IEEE International Workshop on Machine Learning for Signal Processing, SEPT.* (pp. 21–24). Espoo, Finland: IEEE.

Zhou, T., Ruan, S., & Canu, S. (2019). A review: Deep learning for medical image segmentation usingmulti-modality fusion. *Array*, *3-4*, 100004. doi:10.1016/j.array.2019.100004

Zhu, X., & Ramanan, D. (2012). Face detection, pose estimation, and landmark localization in the wild. In *Computer Vision and Pattern Recognition (CVPR), 2012 IEEE Conference on* (pp. 2879-2886). IEEE.

Zhuang, Z., Raj, A. N. J., Jain, A., Ruban, N., Chaurasia, S., Li, N., ... Murugappan, M. (2019). Nipple Segmentation and Localization Using Modified U-Net on Breast Ultrasound Images. *Journal of Medical Imaging and Health Informatics*, *9*(9), 1827–1837. doi:10.1166/jmihi.2019.2828

About the Contributors

Vijayalakshmi G. V. Mahesh received the B. E. degree in Electronics and Communication Engineering from Bangalore University, India, in 1999, the M.Tech. degree in Digital Communication and Networking from Visvesvaraya Technological University in 2005 and Ph.D degree from VIT, Vellore, India. Currently she is working as an Associate Professor at BMS Institute of Technology and Management, Bangalore. Her research interests include Machine Learning, Image Processing, Signal Processing, Artificial Intelligence and Pattern Recognition.

* * *

Meenakshi A. is working as Asst Professor in SRM Institute of Science and Technology, Chennai with 20 years of teaching experience for undergraduate and post graduate students inComputer Science department. She has a Doctorate degree in Computer Scienceand Engineering from SRMIST. She' also has completed her Master Degree and Bachelor Degree from university of Madras. She has published her papers over 3 International Journals. She is a member of Indian Science Congress. She has always enjoyed teaching and providing knowledge to the student from different forms of life. Her work experience involved in taking class,begin a counsellor to counsel the students to have a good career. Her research area include Resource Alllocation,Data analytics and Deep learning .

Amira A. Al-Sharkawy is an assistant researcher in Electronic Research Institute. She is an enthusiast in computer vision and deep learning fields. She is a PhD student in computer Engineering, Cairo University. She is holding a master degree from Faculty of Engineering, Cairo University, in title of "Object Recognition using Deep Convolutional Neural Networks".

Nandana B. completed her secondary and higher secondary schooling from Trivandrum, Kerala and is pursuing the final year of B.Tech in Electronics and Computer Engineering from Vellore Institute of Technology, Chennai Campus. Although her area of interest is computer architecture and hardware, she also keeps herself knowledgeable about various Machine Learning and Deep Learning Techniques and is very keen on working on it.

Gehan Bahgat was appointed to the academic staff of the Electronic Research Institute in 2001, Computers and Systems Dept., the digital signal processing group. She received her Bachelor degree, Master of Science and Philosophy of Doctor from Cairo University, faculty of Engineering, Electronics and Electrical Communications dept. She has searching responsibilities in the general area of image processing, pattern recognition and deep convolutional neural network, and in the specialist area of oscillatory neural network, fingerprint recognition and implementation on FPGA. She served two conferences program committees and participated in two projects. She is a reviewer for some IET journals and others.

Chandreyee Basu is an undergraduate student at Vellore Institute of Technology, in Tamil Nadu, India. She is currently pursuing her Bachelor's degree in Electronics and Computer Engineering, and is in her final year. As part of her academic curriculum, she has worked on projects relating to Microcontrollers, IoT, Data Communication Networks and Database Management Systems. She completed an internship relating to Salesforce development and third party integration in cloud environment at the end of her sixth semester. Her primary areas of interest include Cloud Computing, Computer Vision, and Machine Learning.

Geraldine Bessie Amali D received her Ph.D. and M.Tech. degrees in Computer Science and Engineering from Vellore Institute of Technology, Vellore, India. She is working as an Assistant Professor at VIT and has more than 8 years' experience teaching computer science. Her research interests include machine learning and biologically inspired optimization algorithms.

Olga V. Frolova received Ph.D. in Speech Psychophysiology (2008) from St. Petersburg State University. Currently, she is the researcher of the Child Speech Research Group, Biological Faculty, St. Petersburg State University (Russia). The field of scientific interests is child speech development in orphans, mother-child speech interaction, and child speech acoustics. O. Frolova has published more than 30 papers on speech development of typically developing children and orphans with developmental disorders and intellectual disabilities.

Thippeswamy G. received his Master of Engineering from Department of Computer Science and Engineering, Bangalore University and PhD in Computer Science from Mangalore University. His area of research specialization is Computer Vision and Image Processing. He has published more than 40 papers in International conferences, book chapters and peer reviewed journals. He is a reviewer of many International journals. He was Co-Principal Investigator for the DST-FBPR sponsored International Collaborative Research Project, Moscow State University, Russia during 2009-11 and 2017-19. He is a life member of Indian Society for Technical Education (ISTE) and Computer Society of India (CSI). He is a fellow of Institution of Engineers, India (FIE). His present research interests include image processing, data mining and computer vision. He has a teaching experience of 26 years. Currently he is Professor and Dean of Academics in BMS Institute of Technology and Management, Bangalore, India.

Varun P. Gopi (Member, IEEE) received the B.Tech. degree in electronics and communication engineering from the Amal Jyothi College of Engineering, Kanjirappally, India, affiliated to Mahatma Gandhi University, Kottayam, India, in 2007, the M.Tech. degree in signal processing from the College of Engineering Trivandrum, affiliated to Kerala University, Thiruvananthapuram, India, in 2009, and the Ph.D. degree in medical image processing from the Department of Electronics and Communication Engineering, National Institute of Technology at Tiruchirappalli (NIT), Tiruchirappalli, India, in 2014. He is currently an Assistant Professor with the Department of Electronics and Communication Engineering, NIT Tiruchirappalli. His research interests include medical image processing, signal processing, computer vision, and compressed sensing. He was a recipient of the Canadian Commonwealth Scholarship Award under the Graduate Student Exchange Program, Department of Electrical and Computer Engineering, University of Saskatchewan, Saskatoon, SK, Canada, in 2012.

Chandrakala H. T. received Master of Technology with university silver medal from the Department of Computer Science and Engineering, Visveswaraya Technological University, Belgaum, India in 2012. She received Doctorate from the Visveswaraya Technological University, Belgaum, India in 2019. She has published more than 15 papers in International conferences, book chapters and peer reviewed journals. She is a life member of Indian Society for Technical Education (ISTE) and Institution of Engineers, India (MIE). Her present research interests are image enhancement, segmentation and pattern recognition specific to document images. She is currently Assistant Professor in the Department of Computer Science, Government First Grade College Madhugiri, Tumkur University, Tumkur, India.

Elsayed Hemayed is currently working as a Professor at Cairo University and Zewail City of Science and Technology and as a consultant for visual surveillance systems and video analytics in specific and IT systems in general. He got his PhD from University of Louisville, KY in 1999. He got the Graduate Dean's Citation Award in recognition of excellent achievement as a candidate for an advanced degree and the John M. Houchens Prize in recognition of excellent doctoral dissertation. He got his master and his B.Sc. from Cairo University in 1992 and 1989 respectively. From 2007 to 2014, Dr Hemayed was working as an Assistant Professor then an Associate Professor at Cairo University. From 2004 to 2007, Dr. Hemayed was working as an Assistant Professor of software engineering in the UAE University. From 1999 to 2005, Dr Hemayed was working in Trendium Inc, Florida in the area of software engineering and network performance. He occupied different levels in Trendium starting as a senior member of technical staff and finally as a VP of Technical Services and Solution Development and Member of the Corporate Executive Team. He was awarded the year 2005 Trendium Pioneer in recognition of the contribution to the architecture of Trendium Products. He worked also as a Research Scientist Assistant in Cairo University, Egypt and University of Louisville, USA from 1989 to 1994 and from 1994 to 1999 respectively. Dr Hemayed is a senior member of IEEE and a member of ACM and has been a regular reviewer of international conferences and journals. He has published over 80 papers. His research interest includes computer vision, machine learning and data analytic.

Shilpa Hiremath working as Assistant Professor in the,Department of electronics and communication at BMS Institute of Technology and management. The areas of interest are image processing artificial intelligence.

S. Julius Fusic obtained his B.E degree in Electrical and Electronics Engineering from Anna University affiliated college in 2010 and M.E degree in Power Electronics & Drives from Anna university affiliated college in 2014. Currently he is an Assistant Professor in the Department of Mechatronics Engineering at Thiagarajar College of Engineering Madurai. His research interests include Autonomous systems, Electrical Machines, Power electronics, Mechatronics systems. He published research articles and book chapters on autonomous systems, educational active Learning and so on. He was awarded SAP Award for Excellence from IIT Bombay (Top 253 out of 4051) registered participants) and Mentor for IIT Bombay courses like FDP101X and FDP201X.

Judith Justin, Professor and Head of Department of Biomedical Instrumentation Engineering has a teaching experience of 23 years. She graduated with a Bachelor's degree in Instrumentation and Control Engineering from Government College of Technology, Coimbatore. She acquired her Master's degree in Biomedical Engineering from the Indian Institute of Technology, Madras, Chennai. Pursued doctorate in Information and Communication Engineering from Anna University and has more than 40 publications in Journals and Book Chapters. Her areas of interest are Biosignal and Image Processing, Clinical devices and Nanotechnology.

Keerthana K. S. V. is a Software Engineer at Oracle. She has pursued Bachelor of Technology from one of the India's most prestigious institution, VIT, Vellore. During her time as a student, she was inclined towards ML and AI , and so were all of her university projects. Her thesis also belonged to the same field. She aspires to research in the field of image recognition.

Rekha K. V. fond of Communication in her day to day life she recieved her B.E in Electronics and Communication Engineering field from Kingston Engineering College affiliated to Anna University, Chennai and her M.Tech in Communication Engineering from Vellore Institute of Technology, Vellore. Apart from professional, she is a free style dancer and participated in intra schools and college won prizes too. She currently resides at Vellore with her parents.

S. Karthikeyan obtained his UG degree from Anna University affiliated college and currently pursuing Masters in Mechatronics Engineering in Thiagarajar College of Engineering, Madurai. His are of interest in Deep learning and Machine learning based path prediction in Autonomous systems.

Nishanth Krishnaraj received the Bachelor of Technology degree in Electronics and Communication Engineering with a minor in Computer Science and Engineering from the National Institute of Technology Tiruchirappalli in 2019. His research interests include medical image processing, computer vision and deep learning.

Elena E. Lyakso received Ph.D. in neuroscience (1994) and Dr. Sc. degrees in Speech Psychophysiology (2004) from St. Petersburg State University. Currently, she is the head of the Child Speech Research Group and a Professor at the Department of Higher Nervous Activity and Psychophysiology, Biological Faculty, St. Petersburg State University (Russia). E. Lyakso has published 3 books, 4 textbooks and more than 260 scientific papers on physiological and neurological factors influenced on language acquisition, biological and physiological basis of child speech development in ontogenesis and dysontogenesis. She is a member of European Psychology Society, St. Petersburg society of naturalists, Russian Acoustical Society, Russian Physiological society, the head of the Section on Speech Physiology at Russian Physiological Society.

Bhaskar M. completed his B.E. from Bharathiyar University , Coimbatore, India in 1992 and M.E. in Madurai Kamaraj University, Madurai, India in 1995. He completed his PhD in High Speed On-chip Global Interconnect Transceivers from National Institute of Technology, Tiruchirappalli. in 2015. He has co-authored the book titled 'Digital Signal Processors, Architecture, Programming and Applications' published by Tata McGraw Hill. He has many research publications to his credit.

Kethepalli Mallikarjuna has completed his doctoral research in the field of Image processing in 2017 at JNTU, Kakinada. He has twenty five years of academic experience and held various administrative positions in engineering institutions. Currently he is doing research in compressive sensing for image compression, image segmentation and deep learning based image classification.

Samia Mashali head of Digital Signal Processing group, Computers and Systems Department, Electronics Research Institute, Ministry of the higher education and Scientific Research, PhD in Electronics and Communications Engineering, Cairo University 1985. She was awarded a Badge of Honor, first degree, from Mr President Hosny Mubarak, a State Award in Engineering Science 1996. She was a technical consultant at the Ministry of Communications and Information Technology (MCIT) from 2004 till 2012. During this period, she was an education program director, the Deputy of the Egyptian Education Initiative program director, and ICDL program director. She is the Principle Investigator of six projects. She is a reviewer of a number of Electronics and Communication periodicals, a reviewer for the STDF, Academy of Scientific Research. She is the supervisor & examiner of more than 70 PhD. & MSc. Theses. She published more than 70 papers in international journals and conferences. Her main research technology topics are image processing and pattern recognition, speech processing, digital signal processing, neural networks, multimedia, computer visions, medical imaging, bioinformatics, information technology, IOT and augmented reality.

Yuri N. Matveev received Ph.D. (1985) and D.Sc. (1995) degrees in Computer Science from ITMO University, St. Petersburg, Russia. Currently, he is a Chief Scientist at STC-innovations Ltd. and a Professor at ITMO University in Technologies of Man-Machine Interaction area. He is also a Lead Researcher at Child Speech Research Group, St. Petersburg State University (Russia). He is the author of two books, more than 130 articles and 20 national patents. His research interests include voice, speech and face recognition, speech synthesis. He is a member of Institute of Electrical and Electronics Engineers (IEEE) and International Speech Communication Association (ISCA).

A. Mary Mekala was born in Kanyakumari, India in 1984. She has completed her Bachelor of Engineering in Computer Science & Engineering from Anna University, Chennai, India in 2006, Masters in Computer Science & Engineering from Sathyabhama University, Chennai, India in 2008 and PhD from VIT University in 2019. She is having 10+ years of teaching experience in engineering college in India. She currently works as an Academic Faculty member in India's number 1 private university VIT University. Her research areas are Machine Learning, Bio signal Processing, Image Processing.

Sangeetha N. has obtained her Bachelor of Engineering from University of Madras and Masters from Anna University. She has completed her doctoral research in the field of image watermarking from Anna University in the year 2020. Her research interest includes image authentication and image forensics.

Mayuri Patil is a B. Tech final year student, studying Electronics and Computer engineering in VIT University. For her academic projects, she has worked on subjects like Database management systems, Machine learning, Cloud computing, Networks and communication, etc. Her major academic interests are IoT, computer networking and data analytics and she has completed an internship in data analytics domain.

Chandra Prabha R. is working as Assistant Professor in the,Department of electronics and communication at BMS Institute of Technology and management. The areas of interest are image processing artificial intelligence

Karthik R. obtained his Doctoral degree from Vellore Institute of Technology, India and Master's degree from Anna University, India. He is currently serving as Senior Assistant Professor in the Centre for Cyber Physical Systems, Vellore Institute of Technology, Chennai. His research interest includes Deep Learning, Computer Vision, Digital Image Processing, and Medical Image Analysis. He has published around 30 papers in peer reviewed journals and conferences.

Uma R. is working as Associate Professor in the Department of Computer Science and Engineering, Sri Sairam Engineering College, Chennai, India. with 23 years of teaching experience for undergraduate and post graduate students in Computer Science Department. She has a Doctorate degree in Computer Science and Engineering from Anna University Chennai, India .She also completed her Master Degree in Computer Science and Engineering from College of Engineering Guindy, Anna University, India and Bachelor Degree from university of Madras. She has published her papers over 14 International Journals. She is a member of CSI,IACSIT and life member of ISTE. Her current research interest includes Information Retrieval, Data Mining, Deep learning and Machine learning.

J. Anitha Ruth is working as Asst Professor in SRM Institute of Science and Technology, Chennai with 18 years of teaching experience for undergraduate and post graduate students inComputer Science department.She has a Doctorate degree in Computer Science and Engineering from SRMIST. She' also has completed her Master Degree and Bachelor Degree from university of Madras. She has published her papers over 3 International Journals. She is a member of Indian Science Congress. She has always enjoyed teaching and providing knowledge to the student from different forms of life. Her work experience involved in taking class, begin a counsellor to counsel the students to have a good career. Her research area include Deep learning, Neural network and security.

Strivathsav Ashwin Ramamoorthy received the B.Tech degree in Electrical and Electronics Engineering from National Institute of Technology - Tiruchirappali in 2019. His research interests include medical image processing, computer vision and deep learning.

Sheik Masthan Sar is an Assistant Professor, Department of Mechatronics Engineering, Thiagarajar college of Engineering, Madurai.

Balaji Subramanian received Master of Technology from National Institute of Technology, Tiruchirappalli, and Ph.D. in Electrical Engineering from VIT University, Vellore, India. Currently he is working as Associate Professor in the School of Electrical Engineering (SELECT), VIT University, India. He has published more than 25 research papers in the area of wireless communication in reputed Journals and Conferences. His areas of Research include MIMO, OFDM, Wireless Communication with emphasis on Signal Processing, Machine Learning, IoT and Sensor Networks.

Vijayarajan Rajangam has graduated his Master and Bachelor of Engineering degrees from Madurai Kamaraj University and University of Madras in 1998 and 1999 respectively. He has completed his doctoral research in the field of image fusion at Anna University Chennai, India in the year 2015. His research interest includes image cryptography, image forgery detection, recovery, diabetic retinopathy detection, classification and computer vision algorithms. He has published his research findings in high impact journals and conferences. He is currently a faculty member in the Division of Healthcare advancement, innovation and research, Vellore Institute of Technology, Chennai, India.

Wencan Zhong received the B.E. degree in Applied Physics from Nanjing University of Post and Telecommunications, China, in 2017, the M.E. Degree in Electronic and Communication Engineering from Shantou University, China, in 2020. Do researches on medical image processing, face recognition and text recognition projects with Ph.D. of the University of Singapore and Ph.D. of the VIT University in India.

Index

Recommended Reference Books

ISBN: 978-1-5225-5912-2
© 2019; 349 pp.
List Price: $215

ISBN: 978-1-5225-8176-5
© 2019; 2,218 pp.
List Price: $2,950

ISBN: 978-1-5225-7811-6
© 2019; 317 pp.
List Price: $225

ISBN: 978-1-5225-7268-8
© 2019; 316 pp.
List Price: $215

ISBN: 978-1-5225-7455-2
© 2019; 288 pp.
List Price: $205

ISBN: 978-1-5225-8973-0
© 2019; 200 pp.
List Price: $195

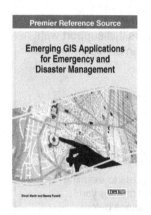
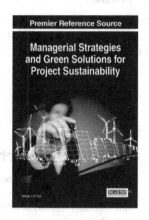

Printed in the United States
By Bookmasters